Database Design

Database Design
Know It All

Stephen Buxton

Lowell Fryman

Ralf Hartmut Güting

Terry Halpin

Jan L. Harrington

William H. Inmon

Sam S. Lightstone

Jim Melton

Tony Morgan

Thomas P. Nadeau

Bonnie O'Neil

Elizabeth O'Neil

Patrick O'Neil

Markus Schneider

Graeme Simsion

Toby J. Teorey

Graham Witt

ELSEVIER

AMSTERDAM • BOSTON • HEIDELBERG • LONDON
NEW YORK • OXFORD • PARIS • SAN DIEGO
SAN FRANCISCO • SINGAPORE • SYDNEY • TOKYO

Morgan Kaufmann is an imprint of Elsevier

MORGAN KAUFMANN PUBLISHERS

Morgan Kaufmann Publishers is an imprint of Elsevier.
30 Corporate Drive, Suite 400
Burlington, MA 01803

This book is printed on acid-free paper. ∞

Library of Congress Cataloging-in-Publication Data
Teorey, Toby J.
    Database design : know it all / Toby Teorey et al.
        p. cm. — (Morgan Kaufmann know it all series)
    Includes index.
    ISBN 978-0-12-374630-6 (alk. paper)
    1. Database design.   I. Title.
QA76.9.D26T42 2008
005.74—dc22   2008040366

For information on all Morgan Kaufmann publications,
visit our Website at *www.mkp.com or www.books.elsevier.com*

Printed and bound by CPI Group (UK) Ltd, Croydon, CR0 4YY
Transferred to Digital Print 2011

Contents

About This Book ix

Contributing Authors xi

CHAPTER 1   **Introduction** 1
- **1.1**   Data and Database Management........................... 1
- **1.2**   The Database Life Cycle 2
- **1.3**   Conceptual Data Modeling 7
- **1.4**   Summary 9
- **1.5**   Literature Summary.. 9

CHAPTER 2   **Entity–Relationship Concepts** 11
- **2.1**   Introduction to ER Concepts............................. 13
- **2.2**   Further Details of ER Modeling 20
- **2.3**   Additional ER Concepts 29
- **2.4**   Case Study.. 32
- **2.5**   Normalization: Preliminaries.............................. 36
- **2.6**   Functional Dependencies 41
- **2.7**   Lossless Decompositions 57
- **2.8**   Normal Forms 65
- **2.9**   Additional Design Considerations....................... 80
- **2.10**   Suggestions for Further Reading........................ 83

CHAPTER 3   **Data Modeling in UML** 85
- **3.1**   Introduction.. 85
- **3.2**   Object Orientation.. 88
- **3.3**   Attributes.. 91
- **3.4**   Associations... 97
- **3.5**   Set-Comparison Constraints............................. 105
- **3.6**   Subtyping 113
- **3.7**   Other Constraints and Derivation Rules............... 118
- **3.8**   Mapping from ORM to UML............................. 132
- **3.9**   Summary 136
- **3.10**   Literature Summary... 138

CHAPTER 4   **Requirements Analysis and Conceptual Data Modeling** **141**
4.1   Introduction 141
4.2   Requirements Analysis 142
4.3   Conceptual Data Modeling 143
4.4   View Integration 152
4.5   Entity Clustering for ER Models 160
4.6   Summary 165
4.7   Literature Summary 167

CHAPTER 5   **Logical Database Design** **169**
5.1   Introduction 169
5.2   Overview of the Transformations Required 170
5.3   Table Specification 172
5.4   Basic Column Definition 181
5.5   Primary Key Specification 187
5.6   Foreign Key Specification 189
5.7   Table and Column Names 200
5.8   Logical Data Model Notations 201
5.9   Summary 203

CHAPTER 6   **Normalization** **205**
6.1   Translating an ER Diagram into Relations 205
6.2   Normal Forms 206
6.3   First Normal Form 207
6.4   Second Normal Form 212
6.5   Third Normal Form 214
6.6   Boyce-Codd Normal Form 216
6.7   Fourth Normal Form 217
6.8   Normalized Relations and Database Performance 219
6.9   Further Reading 224

CHAPTER 7   **Physical Database Design** **225**
7.1   Introduction 225
7.2   Inputs to Database Design 226
7.3   Options Available to the Database Designer 228
7.4   Design Decisions that Do Not Affect Program Logic 229
7.5   Crafting Queries to Run Faster 237
7.6   Logical Schema Decisions 238
7.7   Views 247
7.8   Summary 250

CHAPTER 8   **Denormalization** **251**

   8.1   Basics of Normalization 251

   8.2   Common Types of Denormalization 255

   8.3   Table Denormalization Strategy.................................... 259

   8.4   Example of Denormalization 260

   8.5   Summary 267

   8.6   Further Reading 267

CHAPTER 9   **Business Metadata Infrastructure** **269**

   9.1   Introduction 269

   9.2   Types of Business Metadata... 269

   9.3   The Metadata Warehouse 271

   9.4   Delivery Considerations... 273

   9.5   Integration... 275

   9.6   Administrative Issues 279

   9.7   Metadata Repository: Buy or Build?.............................. 280

   9.8   The Build Considerations... 281

   9.9   The Third Alternative: Use a Preexisting Repository........ 281

   9.10 Summary 282

CHAPTER 10   **Storing: XML and Databases** **283**

   10.1 Introduction 283

   10.2 The Need for Persistence 284

   10.3 SQL/XML's XML Type.. 293

   10.4 Accessing Persistent XML Data..................................... 294

   10.5 XML "On the Fly": Nonpersistent XML Data.................... 295

   10.6 Summary 297

CHAPTER 11   **Modeling and Querying Current Movement**........... **299**

   11.1 Location Management.. 299

   11.2 MOST—A Data Model for Current and
Future Movement... 301

   11.3 FTL—A Query Language Based on Future
Temporal Logic.. 306

   11.4 Location Updates—Balancing Update Cost
and Imprecision 317

   11.5 The Uncertainty of the Trajectory of
a Moving Object 323

   11.6 Practice 333

   11.7 Literature Notes 335

   Index   337

About This Book

All of the elements about database design are here together in a single resource written by the best and brightest experts in the field! Databases are the main repository of a company's historical data—its corporate memory—and they contain the raw material for management's decision support system. The increasing volume of data in modern business calls for the continual refinement of database design methodology. *Database Design: Know It All* expertly combines the finest database design material from the Morgan Kaufmann portfolio into a single book, making it a definitive, one-stop-shopping opportunity so that readers can have the information they need available to quickly retrieve, analyze, transform, and load data—the very processes that more and more organizations use to differentiate themselves. Each chapter is authored by a leading expert in the field; the book consolidates introductory and advanced topics ranging from ER and UML techniques to storing XML and querying moving objects. In this way, what is here is an invaluable resource for anyone working in today's fast-paced, data-centric environment.

Contributing Authors

Stephen Buxton (Chapter 10) is Director of Product Management at Mark Logic Corporation, and a member of the W3C XQuery Working Group and Full-Text Task Force. Until recently, Stephen was Director of Product Management for Text and XML at Oracle Corporation. He is also a coauthor of *Querying XML* published by Elsevier in 2006.

Lowell Fryman (Chapter 9) gained his extensive experience with business metadata during his 14 years as a data warehouse consultant, 25 years in data management, and more than 30 years in IT. He is also a coauthor of *Business Metadata: Capturing Enterprise Knowledge* published by Elsevier in 2008.

Ralf Hartmut Güting (Chapter 11) is a professor of computer science at the University of Hagen in Germany. After a one-year visit to the IBM Almaden Research Center in 1985, extensible and spatial database systems became his major research interests. He is the author of two German textbooks on data structures/algorithms and on compilers and has published about 50 articles on computational geometry and database systems. He is an associate editor of *ACM Transactions on Database Systems.* He is also a coauthor of *Moving Objects Database* published by Elsevier in 2005.

Dr. Terry Halpin (Chapter 3) is a Distinguished Professor in computer science at Neumont University and is recognized as the leading authority on the ORM methodology. He led development efforts in conceptual modeling technology at several companies including Microsoft Corporation, authored more than 150 technical publications, and is a recipient of the DAMA International Achievement Award for Education and the IFIP Outstanding Service Award. He is also a coauthor of *Information Modeling and Relational Databases* published by Elsevier in 2008.

Jan L. Harrington (Chapter 6) is a full-time faculty member in the Department of Computer Science, Information Technology, and Information Systems at Marist College, where she teaches database design and management, object-oriented programming, data communications, and computer architecture. She is also the author of *Relational Database Design Clearly Explained* published by Elsevier in 2003.

William H. Inmon (Chapter 9), considered the father of the data warehouse, is the author of dozens of books, including *Building the Data Warehouse, Building the Operational Data Store,* and *Corporate Information Factory, Second Edition.* His expertise in business metadata derives from practical work advising clients on the use of data warehouses. He created a unique unstructured data solution that applies to many of the problems presented in this book. He is also a coauthor of *Business Metadata: Capturing Enterprise Knowledge* published by Elsevier in 2008.

Sam S. Lightstone (Chapters 1, 4, and 8) is the cofounder and leader of DB2's autonomic computing R&D effort and has been with IBM since 1991. His current research includes automatic physical database design, adaptive self-tuning resources, automatic administration, benchmarking methodologies, and system control. Mr. Lightstone is an IBM Master Inventor. He is also one of the coauthors of *Database Modeling and Design* and *Physical Database Design*, both published by Elsevier in 2006 and 2007, respectively.

Jim Melton (Chapter 10), of Oracle Corporation, is editor of all parts of ISO/IEC 9075 (SQL) and has been active in SCL standardization for two decades. More recently, he has been active in the W3C's XML Query Working Group that defined XQuery, is cochair of that WG, and coedited two of the XQuery specifications. He is also a coauthor of *Querying XML* published by Elsevier in 2006.

Tony Morgan (Chapter 3) is a Distinguished Professor in computer science and vice president of Enterprise Informatics at Neumont University. He has more than 20 years of experience in information system development at various companies, including EDS and Unisys, and is a recognized thought leader in the area of business rules. He is also a coauthor of *Information Modeling and Relational Databases* published by Elsevier in 2008.

Thomas P. Nadeau (Chapters 1, 4, and 8) is a senior technical staff member of Ubiquiti Inc. and works in the area of data and text mining. His technical interests include data warehousing, OLAP, data mining, and machine learning. He is also one of the coauthors of *Database Modeling and Design* and *Physical Database Design*, both published by Elsevier in 2006 and 2007, respectively.

Bonnie O'Neil (Chapter 9) has more than 20 years of experience in data management. She was one of the first data practitioners to pioneer the benefits of business metadata and develop processes for creating and realizing business metadata initiatives. She is also a coauthor of *Business Metadata: Capturing Enterprise Knowledge* published by Elsevier in 2008.

Elizabeth O'Neil (Chapter 2) is a professor of computer science at the University of Massachusetts–Boston. She serves as a consultant to Sybase IQ in Concord, MA, and has worked with a number of corporations, including Microsoft and Bolt, Beranek, and Newman. From 1980 to 1998, she implemented and managed new hardware and software labs in the UMass's computer science department. She is also the coauthor of *Database: Principles, Programming, and Performance, Second Edition,* published by Elsevier in 2001.

Patrick O'Neil (Chapter 2) is a professor of computer science at the University–Boston. He is responsible for a number of important research results in transactional performance and disk access algorithms, and he holds patents for his work in these database areas. He authored the "Database: Principles, Programming, and Performance" and "The Set Query Benchmark" chapters in *The Benchmark Handbook for Database and Transaction Processing Systems* (Morgan Kaufmann, 1993) and is an area editor for *Information Systems*. O'Neil is also an active industry consultant who has worked with a number of prominent companies, including Microsoft, Oracle, Sybase, Informix, Praxis, Price Waterhouse, and Policy Management Systems Corporation. He is also the coauthor of *Database: Principles, Programming, and Performance, Second Edition,* published by Elsevier in 2001.

Markus Schneider (Chapter 11) is an assistant professor of computer science at the University of Florida–Gainesville and holds a Ph.D. in computer science from the University of Hagen in Germany. He is the author of a monograph in the area of spatial databases, a German textbook on implementation concepts for database systems, and has published nearly 40 articles on database systems. He is on the editorial board of *GeoInformatica*. He is also a coauthor of *Moving Objects Database* published by Elsevier in 2005.

Graeme Simsion (Chapters 5 and 7) has more than 25 years of experience in information systems as a DBA, data modeling consultant, business systems designer, manager, and researcher. He is a regular presenter at industry and academic forums and is currently a senior fellow with the Department of Information Systems at the University of Melbourne. He is also the coauthor of *Database Modeling Essentials* published by Elsevier in 2004.

Toby J. Teorey (Chapters 1, 4, and 8) is a professor in the electrical engineering and computer science department at the University of Michigan–Ann Arbor. His current research focuses on database design and performance of computing systems. He is also one of the coauthors of *Database Modeling and Design* and *Physical Database Design*, both published by Elsevier in 2006 and 2007, respectively.

Graham Witt (Chapters 5 and 7) is an independent consultant with more than 30 years of experience in system specification, user-interface design, data modeling, relational database design, data quality, and metadata. During this time he has completed a number of successful projects in these areas for major clients in a variety of industry sectors, including education, health, telecommunications, finance, transportation, and government. He has also developed a reputation as an effective educator in these disciplines and is a frequent presenter at international data management conferences. He is also the coauthor of *Database Modeling Essentials* published by Elsevier in 2004.

Database Design

Introduction

Database technology has evolved rapidly in the three decades since the rise and eventual dominance of relational database systems. While many specialized database systems (object-oriented, spatial, multim, etc.) have found substantial user communities in the science and engineering fields, relational systems remain the dominant database technology for business enterprises.

Relational database design has evolved from an art to a science that has been made partially implementable as a set of software design aids. Many of these design aids have appeared as the database component of computer-aided software engineering (CASE) tools, and many of them offer interactive modeling capability using a simplified data modeling approach. Logical design—that is, the structure of basic data relationships and their definition in a particular database system—is largely the domain of application designers. These designers can work effectively with tools such as ERwin Data Modeler or Rational Rose with UML, as well as with a purely manual approach. Physical design, the creation of efficient data storage and retrieval mechanisms on the computing platform being used, is typically the domain of the database administrator (DBA). Today's DBAs have a variety of vendor-supplied tools available to help them design the most efficient databases. This book is devoted to the *logical* design methodologies and tools most popular for relational databases today. This chapter reviews the basic concepts of database management and introduce the role of data modeling and database design in the database life cycle.

1.1 DATA AND DATABASE MANAGEMENT

The basic component of a file in a file system is a *data item*, which is the smallest named unit of data that has meaning in the real world—for example, last name, first name, street address, ID number, or political party. A group of related data items treated as a single unit by an application is called a *record*. Examples of types of records are order, salesperson, customer, product, and department. A *file* is a collection of records of a single type. Database systems have built upon and expanded these definitions: In a relational database, a data item is called a *column* or *attribute*; a record is called a *row* or *tuple*; and a file is called a *table*.

A *database* is a more complex object. It is a collection of interrelated stored data—that is, interrelated collections of many different types of tables—that serves the needs of multiple users within one or more organizations. The motivations for using databases rather than files include greater availability to a diverse set of users, integration of data for easier access to and updating of complex transactions, and less redundancy of data.

A *database management system* (DBMS) is a generalized software system for manipulating databases. A DBMS supports a logical view (schema, subschema); physical view (access methods, data clustering); data definition language; data manipulation language; and important utilities, such as transaction management and concurrency control, data integrity, crash recovery, and security. Relational database systems, the dominant type of systems for well-formatted business databases, also provide a greater degree of data independence than the earlier hierarchical and network (CODASYL) database management systems. *Data independence* is the ability to make changes in either the logical or physical structure of the database without requiring reprogramming of application programs. It also makes database conversion and reorganization much easier. Relational DBMSs provide a much higher degree of data independence than previous systems; they are the focus of our discussion on data modeling.

1.2 THE DATABASE LIFE CYCLE

The database life cycle incorporates the basic steps involved in designing a global schema of the logical database, allocating data across a computer network, and defining local DBMS-specific schemas. Once the design is completed, the life cycle continues with database implementation and maintenance. This chapter contains an overview of the database life cycle, as shown in Figure 1.1. The result of each step of the life cycle is illustrated with a series of diagrams in Figure 1.2. Each diagram shows a possible form of the output of each step, so the reader can see the progression of the design process from an idea to actual database implementation.

I.   *Requirements analysis.* The database requirements are determined by interviewing both the producers and users of data and using the information to produce a formal requirements specification. That specification includes the data required for processing, the natural data relationships, and the software platform for the database implementation. As an example, Figure 1.2 (step I) shows the concepts of products, customers, salespersons, and orders being formulated in the mind of the end user during the interview process.

II. *Logical design.* The *global schema*, a conceptual data model diagram that shows all the data and their relationships, is developed using techniques such

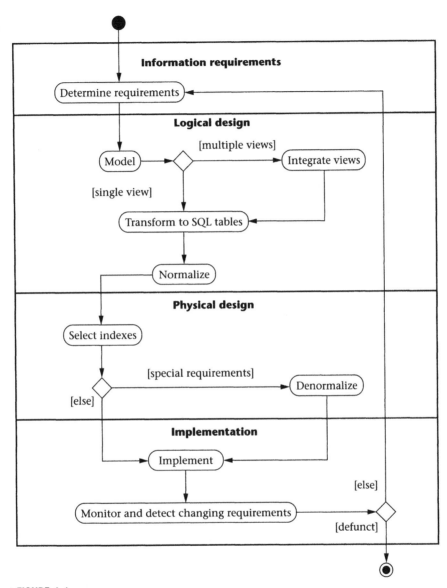

FIGURE 1.1

The database life cycle.

as entity–relationship (ER) or UML. The data model constructs must ultimately be transformed into normalized (global) relations, or tables. The global schema development methodology is the same for either a distributed or centralized database.

a. *Conceptual data modeling.* The data requirements are analyzed and modeled using an ER or UML diagram that includes, for example, semantics

Step I Requirements Analysis (reality)

Step II Logical design

Step II(a) Conceptual data modeling

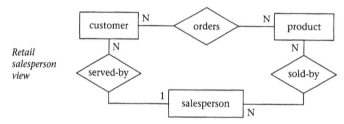

Step II(b) View integration

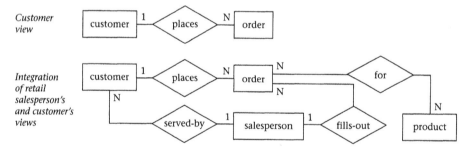

FIGURE 1.2

Life cycle results, step-by-step.

for optional relationships, ternary relationships, supertypes, and subtypes (categories). Processing requirements are typically specified using natural language expressions or SQL commands, along with the frequency of occurrence. Figure 1.2 (step II(a)) shows a possible ER model representation of the product/customer database in the mind of the end user.

b. *View integration.* Usually, when the design is large and more than one person is involved in requirements analysis, multiple views of data and relationships result. To eliminate redundancy and inconsistency from the model, these views eventually must be "rationalized" (resolving inconsistencies due to variance in taxonomy, context, or perception) and then

Step II(c) *Transformation of the conceptual model to SQL tables*

Customer

cust-no	cust-name	. . .

```
create table customer
    (cust_no integer,
    cust_name char(15),
    cust_addr char(30),
    sales_name char(15),
    prod_no integer,
    primary key (cust_no),
    foreign key (sales_name)
        references salesperson
    foreign key (prod_no)
        references product);
```

Product

prod-no	prod-name	qty-in-stock

Salesperson

sales-name	addr	dept	job-level	vacation-days

Order

order-no	sales-name	cust-no

Order-product

order-no	prod-no

Step II(d) *Normalization of SQL tables*

Decomposition of tables and removal of update anomalies

Salesperson

sales-name	addr	dept	job-level

Sales-vacations

job-level	vacation-days

Step III Physical design

Indexing
Clustering
Partitioning
Materialized views
Denormalization

FIGURE 1.2

Continued.

consolidated into a single global view. View integration requires the use of ER semantic tools such as identification of synonyms, aggregation, and generalization. In Figure 1.2 (step II(b)), two possible views of the product/customer database are merged into a single global view based on common data for customer and order. View integration is also important for application integration.

c. *Transformation of the conceptual data model to SQL tables.* Based on a categorization of data modeling constructs and a set of mapping rules, each relationship and its associated entities are transformed into a set of DBMS-specific candidate relational tables. Redundant tables are eliminated as part of this process. In our example, the tables in step II(c) of Figure 1.2 are the result of transformation of the integrated ER model in step II(b).

d. *Normalization of tables.* Functional dependencies (FDs) are derived from the conceptual data model diagram and the semantics of data relationships in the requirements analysis. They represent the dependencies among data elements that are unique identifiers (keys) of entities. Additional FDs that represent the dependencies among key and nonkey attributes within entities can be derived from the requirements specification. Candidate relational tables associated with all derived FDs are normalized (i.e., modified by decomposing or splitting tables into smaller tables) using standard techniques. Finally, redundancies in the data in normalized candidate tables are analyzed further for possible elimination, with the constraint that data integrity must be preserved. An example of normalization of the Sales-person table into the new Salesperson and Sales-vacations tables is shown in Figure 1.2 from step II(c) to step II(d).

We note here that database tool vendors tend to use the term *logical model* to refer to the conceptual data model, and they use the term *physical model* to refer to the DBMS-specific implementation model (e.g., SQL tables). Note also that many conceptual data models are obtained not from scratch, but from the process of *reverse engineering* from an existing DBMS-specific schema (Silberschatz, Korth, & Sudarshan, 2002).

III. *Physical design.* The physical design step involves the selection of indexes (access methods), partitioning, and clustering of data. The logical design methodology in step II simplifies the approach to designing large relational databases by reducing the number of data dependencies that need to be analyzed. This is accomplished by inserting conceptual data modeling and integration steps (II(a) and II(b) of Figure 1.2) into the traditional relational design approach. The objective of these steps is an accurate representation of reality. Data integrity is preserved through normalization of the candidate tables created when the conceptual data model is transformed into a relational model. The purpose of physical design is to optimize performance as closely as possible.

As part of the physical design, the global schema can sometimes be refined in limited ways to reflect processing (query and transaction) requirements if there are obvious, large gains to be made in efficiency. This is called *denormalization*. It consists of selecting dominant processes on the basis of high frequency, high volume, or explicit priority; defining simple extensions to tables that will improve query performance; evaluating total cost for query, update, and storage; and considering the side effects, such as possible loss of integrity. This is particularly important for Online Analytical Processing (OLAP) applications.

IV. ***Database implementation, monitoring, and modification.*** Once the design is completed, the database can be created through implementation of the formal schema using the data definition language (DDL) of a DBMS. Then the data manipulation language (DML) can be used to query and update the database, as well as to set up indexes and establish constraints, such as referential integrity. The language SQL contains both DDL and DML constructs; for example, the *create table* command represents DDL, and the *select* command represents DML.

As the database begins operation, monitoring indicates whether performance requirements are being met. If they are not being satisfied, modifications should be made to improve performance. Other modifications may be necessary when requirements change or when the end users' expectations increase with good performance. Thus, the life cycle continues with monitoring, redesign, and modifications.

1.3 CONCEPTUAL DATA MODELING

Conceptual data modeling is the driving component of logical database design. Let us take a look at how this component came about, and why it is important. Schema diagrams were formalized in the 1960s by Charles Bachman. He used rectangles to denote record types and directed arrows from one record type to another to denote a one-to-many relationship among instances of records of the two types. The ER approach for conceptual data modeling was first presented in 1976 by Peter Chen. The Chen form of the ER model uses rectangles to specify entities, which are somewhat analogous to records. It also uses diamond-shaped objects to represent the various types of relationships, which are differentiated by numbers or letters placed on the lines connecting the diamonds to the rectangles.

The Unified Modeling Language (UML) was introduced in 1997 by Grady Booch and James Rumbaugh and has become a standard graphical language for specifying and documenting large-scale software systems. The data modeling component of UML (now UML 2.0) has a great deal of similarity with the ER model, and will be presented in detail in Chapter 3. We will use both the ER model and UML to illustrate the data modeling and logical database design examples.

In conceptual data modeling, the overriding emphasis is on simplicity and readability. The goal of conceptual schema design, where the ER and UML approaches are most useful, is to capture real-world data requirements in a simple and meaningful way that is understandable by both the database designer and the end user. The end user is the person responsible for accessing the database and executing queries and updates through the use of DBMS software, and therefore has a vested interest in the database design process.

The ER model has two levels of definition—one that is quite simple and another that is considerably more complex. The simple level is the one used by most current design tools. It is quite helpful to the database designer who must communicate with end users about their data requirements. At this level you simply describe, in diagram form, the entities, attributes, and relationships that occur in the system to be conceptualized, using semantics that are definable in a data dictionary. Specialized constructs, such as "weak" entities or mandatory/optional existence notation, are also usually included in the simple form. But very little else is included, to avoid cluttering up the ER diagram while the designer's and end users' understandings of the model are being reconciled.

An example of a simple form of ER model using the Chen notation is shown in Figure 1.3. In this example, we want to keep track of videotapes and customers in a video store. Videos and customers are represented as entities Video and Customer, and the relationship rents shows a many-to-many association between them. Both Video and Customer entities have a few attributes that describe their characteristics, and the relationship rents has an attribute due date that represents the date that a particular video rented by a specific customer must be returned.

From the database practitioner's standpoint, the simple form of the ER model (or UML) is the preferred form for both data modeling and end user verification. It is easy to learn and applicable to a wide variety of design problems that might be encountered in industry and small businesses. As we will demonstrate, the simple form can be easily translated into SQL data definitions, and thus it has an immediate use as an aid for database implementation.

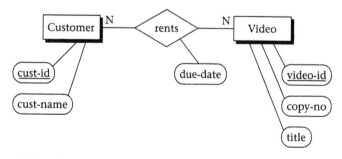

FIGURE 1.3

A simple form of ER model using the Chen notation.

The complex level of ER model definition includes concepts that go well beyond the simple model. It includes concepts from the semantic models of artificial intelligence and from competing conceptual data models. Data modeling at this level helps the database designer capture more semantics without having to resort to narrative explanations. It is also useful to the database application programmer, because certain integrity constraints defined in the ER model relate directly to code—for example, code that checks range limits on data values and null values. However, such detail in very large data model diagrams actually detracts from end user understanding. Therefore, the simple level is recommended as the basic communication tool for database design verification.

1.4 SUMMARY

Knowledge of data modeling and database design techniques is important for database practitioners and application developers. The database life cycle shows the steps needed in a methodical approach to designing a database, from logical design, which is independent of the system environment, to physical design, which is based on the details of the database management system chosen to implement the database. Among the variety of data modeling approaches, the ER and UML data models are arguably the most popular ones in use today, due to their simplicity and readability. A simple form of these models is used in most design tools; it is easy to learn and to apply to a variety of industrial and business applications. It is also a very useful tool for communicating with the end user about the conceptual model and for verifying the assumptions made in the modeling process. A more complex form, a superset of the simple form, is useful for the more experienced designer who wants to capture greater semantic detail in diagram form, while avoiding having to write long and tedious narrative to explain certain requirements and constraints.

1.5 LITERATURE SUMMARY

Much of the early data modeling work was done by Bachman (1969, 1972), Chen (1976), Senko et al. (1973), and others. Database design textbooks that adhere to a significant portion of the relational database life cycle described in this chapter are Teorey and Fry (1982), Muller (1999), Stephens and Plew (2000), Simsion and Witt (2001), and Hernandez and Getz (2003). Temporal (time-varying) databases are defined and discussed in Jensen and Snodgrass (1996) and Snodgrass (2000). Other well-used approaches for conceptual data modeling include IDEF1X (Bruce, 1992; IDEF1X, 2005) and the data modeling component of the Zachmann Framework (Zachmann, 1987; Zachmann Institute for Framework Advancement, 2005). Schema evolution during development, a frequently occurring problem, is addressed in Harriman, Hodgetts, and Leo (2004).

Entity–Relationship Concepts

Until now we have dealt with databases made up of a number of distinct tables, without concerning ourselves very much with how the tables and their constituent columns were originally generated. *Logical database design*, also known simply as *database design* or *database modeling*, studies basic properties and interrelationships among data items, with the aim of providing faithful representations of such items in the basic data structures of a database. Databases with different data models have different structures for representing data; in relational databases the fundamental structures for representing data are what we have been calling *relational tables*. We concentrate on relational databases in this chapter because design for the object-relational model is still in its infancy.

It is the responsibility of the database administrator (DBA) to perform this logical database design, assigning the related data items of the database to columns of tables in a manner that preserves desirable properties. The most important test of logical design is that the tables and attributes faithfully reflect interrelationships among objects in the real world and that this remains true after all likely database updates in the future.

The DBA starts by studying some real-world enterprise, such as a wholesale order business, a company personnel office, or a college registration department, whose operation needs to be supported on a computerized database system. Often working with someone who has great expertise about the details of the enterprise, the DBA comes up with a list of data items and underlying data objects that must be kept track of (in college student registration, this list might include student_names, courses, course_sections, class_rooms, class_periods, etc.), together with a number of rules, or *constraints*, concerning the interrelatedness of these data items. Typical rules for student registration are the following:

- Every registered student has a *unique* student ID number (which we name sid).
- A student can be registered for *at most one* course section for a given class period.

- A classroom can house *at most one* course section for a given class period.
- And so on.

From these data items and constraints, the DBA is expected to perform the logical design of the database. Two common techniques covered in this chapter are used to perform the task of database design. The first is known as the *entity–relationship* approach (or *ER* approach), and the second is the *normalization* approach. The ER approach attempts to provide a taxonomy of data items to allow a DBA to intuitively recognize different types of data classification objects (entities, weak entities, attributes, relationships, etc.) to classify the listed data items and their relationships. After creating an ER diagram that illustrates these objects, a relatively straightforward procedure allows the DBA to translate the design into relational tables and integrity constraints in the database system. The normalization approach seems entirely different, and perhaps less dependent on intuition: all the data items are listed, and then all interrelatedness rules (of a recognized kind, known as *dependencies*) are identified. Design starts with the assumption that all data items are placed in a single huge table and then proceeds to break down the table into smaller tables. In the resulting set of tables, joins are needed to retrieve the original relationships. Both the ER modeling approach and the normalization approach are best applied by a DBA with a developed intuition about data relationships in the real world and about the way those relationships are ultimately modeled as relational tables. The two approaches tend to lead to identical relational table designs and in fact reinforce one another in providing the needed intuition. We will not attempt to discriminate between the two in terms of which is more applicable.

One of the major features of logical database design is the emphasis it places on rules of interrelationships between data items. The naive user often sees a relational table as made up of a set of descriptive columns, one column much like another. But this is far from accurate, because there are rules that limit possible relationships between values in the columns. For example, a `customers` table, conceived as a relation, is a subset of the Cartesian product of four domains, `CP = CID × CNAME × CITY × DISCNT`. However, in any legal `customers` table, two rows with the same customer ID (`cid`) value cannot exist because `cid` is a unique identifier for a `customers` row. Here is a perfect example of the kind of rule we wish to take into account in our logical database design. A faithful table representation enforces such a requirement by specifying that the `cid` column is a *candidate key* or the *primary key* for the `customers` table. A candidate key is a designated set of columns in a table such that two table rows can never be alike in all these column values, and where no smaller subset of the key columns has this property. A primary key is a candidate key that has been chosen by the DBA for external reference from other tables to unique rows in the table.

A faithful representation in a computerized database table of a candidate key or a primary key is provided when the table is created with the SQL Create Table statement (see the syntax given in the declaration in Figure 2.1).

```
create table customers (cid char(4) not null, ssn integer not null unique,
        cname varchar(13), city varchar(20), discnt real, primary key (cid));
```

FIGURE 2.1

SQL declaration of `customers` table with primary key `cid` and candidate key `ssn`.

The fact that the `ssn` column is declared as *not null unique* in a Create Table statement simply means that in any permitted `customers` content, two rows cannot have the same `ssn` value, and thus it is a candidate key. When `cid` is declared as a primary key in the Create Table statement, this is a more far-reaching statement, making `cid` the identifier of `customers` rows that might be used by other tables. Following either of the table definitions of 2.1, a later SQL Insert or Update statement that would duplicate a `cid` value or `ssn` value on two rows of the `customers` table is *illegal* and *has no effect*. Thus, a faithful representation of the table key is maintained by the database system.

Also a number of other clauses of the Create Table statement serve a comparable purpose of limiting possible table content, and we refer to these as *integrity constraints* for a table. The interrelationships between columns in relational tables must be understood at a reasonably deep level in order to properly appreciate some constraints. Although not all concepts of logical design can be faithfully represented in the SQL of today, SQL is moving in the direction of modeling more and more such concepts. In any event, many of the ideas of logical design can be useful as an aid to systematic database definition even in the absence of direct system support.

In the following sections, we first introduce a number of definitions of the ER model. The process of normalization is introduced after some ER intuition has been developed.

2.1 INTRODUCTION TO ER CONCEPTS

The ER approach attempts to define a number of data classification objects; the database designer is then expected to classify data items by intuitive recognition as belonging in some known classification. Three fundamental data classification objects introduced in this section are *entities, attributes,* and *relationships.*

2.1.1 Entities, Attributes, and Simple ER Diagrams

We begin with a definition of the concept of *entity.*

Definition: Entity. An entity is a collection of distinguishable real-world objects with common properties.

For example, in a college registration database we might have the following entities: Students, Instructors, Class_rooms, Courses, Course_sections,

Class_periods, and so on. (Note that entity names are capitalized.) Clearly the set of classrooms in a college fits our definition of an entity: individual classrooms in the entity Class_rooms are distinguishable (by location—i.e., room number) and have other common properties such as seating capacity (not common values, but a common property). Class_periods is a somewhat surprising entity—is "MWF from 2:00 to 3:00 PM" a real-world object? However, the test here is that the registration process deals with these class periods as if they were objects, assigning class periods in student schedules in the same sense that rooms are assigned.

To give examples of entities that we have worked with a good deal in the CAP database, we have Customers, Agents, and Products. (Orders is also an entity, but there is some possibility for confusion in this, and we discuss it a bit later.) There is a foreshadowing here of entities being mapped to relational tables. An entity such as Customers is usually mapped to an actual table, and each row of the table corresponds to one of the distinguishable real-world objects that make up the entity, called an *entity instance*, or sometimes an *entity occurrence*.

Note that we do not yet have a name for the properties by which we tell one entity occurrence from another, the analog to column values to distinguish rows in a relational table. For now we simply refer to entity instances as being distinguishable, in the same sense that we would think of the classrooms in a college as being distinguishable, without needing to understand the room-labeling scheme used. In what follows we always write an entity name with an initial capital letter, but the name becomes all lowercase when the entity is mapped to a relational table in SQL.

We have chosen an unusual notation by assigning plural entity names: Students, Instructors, Class_rooms, and so forth. More standard would be entities named Student, Instructor, and Class_room. Our plural usage is chosen to emphasize the fact that each represents a *set* of real-world objects, usually containing multiple elements, and carries over to our plural table names (also somewhat unusual), which normally contain multiple rows. Entities are represented by rectangles in ER diagrams, as you can see by looking at Figure 2.2.

Note that some other authors use the terminology *entity set* or *entity type* in referring to what we call an *entity*. Then to these authors, an *entity* is what we would refer to as an *entity instance*. We have also noticed occasional ambiguity within a specific author's writing, sometimes referring to an entity set and sometimes to an entity; we assume that the object that is represented by a rectangle in an ER diagram is an entity, a collection of real-world objects, and authors who identify such rectangles in the same way agree with our definition. It is unfortunate that such ambiguity exists, but our notation will be consistent in what follows.

In mathematical discussion, for purposes of definition, we usually represent an entity by a single capital letter, possibly subscripted where several exist (e.g., E, E_1, E_2, etc.). An entity E is made up of a set of real-world objects, which we represent by subscripted lowercase letters: $E = \{e_1, e_2, \ldots, e_n\}$. As mentioned

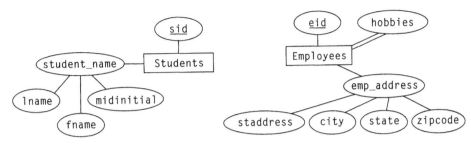

FIGURE 2.2

Example of ER diagrams with entities and attributes.

above, each distinct representative e_i of an entity E is called an entity *instance* or an entity *occurrence*.

Definition: Attribute. An attribute is a data item that describes a property of an entity or a relationship (defined below).

Recall from the definition of *entity* that all entity occurrences belonging to a given entity have common properties. In the ER model, these properties are known as *attributes*. As we will see, there is no confusion in terminology between an attribute in the ER model and an attribute or column name in the relational model, because when the ER design is translated into relational terms, the two correspond. A particular instance of an entity is said to have attribute values for all attributes describing the entity (a null value is possible). The reader should keep in mind that while we list distinct entity occurrences $\{e_1, e_2, \ldots, e_n\}$ of the entity E, we can't actually tell the occurrences apart without reference to attribute values.

Each entity has an *identifier*, an attribute, or set of attributes that takes on unique values for each entity instance; this is the analog of the relational concept of *candidate key*. For example, we define an identifier for the Customers entity to be the customer identifier, cid. There might be more than one identifier for a given entity, and when the DBA identifies a single key attribute to be the universal method of identification for entity occurrences throughout the database, this is called a *primary identifier* for the entity. Other attributes, such as city for Customers, are not identifiers but *descriptive attributes*, known as *descriptors*. Most attributes take on simple values from a domain, as we have seen in the relational model, but a *composite attribute* is a group of simple attributes that together describe a property. For example, the attribute student_names for the Students entity might be composed of the simple attributes lname, fname, and midinitial. Note that an identifier for an entity is allowed to contain an attribute of composite type. Finally, we define a *multivalued attribute* to be one that can take on multiple values for a single entity instance. For example, the Employees entity might have an attached multivalued attribute named hobbies, which takes on multiple values provided by the employee asked to list any hobbies or interests. One employee might have several hobbies, so this is a multivalued attribute.

As mentioned earlier, ER diagrams represent entities as rectangles. Figure 2.2 shows two simple ER diagrams. Simple, single-valued attributes are represented by ovals, attached by a straight line to the entity. A composite attribute is also in an oval attached directly to the entity, while the simple attributes that make up the composite are attached to the composite oval. A multivalued attribute is attached by a double line, rather than a single line, to the entity it describes. The primary identifier attribute is underlined.

2.1.2 Transforming Entities and Attributes to Relations

Our ultimate aim is to transform the ER design into a set of definitions for relational tables in a computerized database, which we do through a set of transformation rules.

Transformation Rule 1. Each entity in an ER diagram is mapped to a single table in a relational database; the table is named after the entity. The table's columns represent all the single-valued simple attributes attached to the entity (possibly through a composite attribute, although a composite attribute itself does not become a column of the table). An identifier for an entity is mapped to a candidate key for the table, as illustrated in Example 2.1, and a primary identifier is mapped to a primary key. Note that the primary identifier of an entity might be a composite attribute, which therefore translates to a set of attributes in the relational table mapping. Entity occurrences are mapped to the table's rows. ∎

EXAMPLE 2.1

Here are the two tables, with one example row filled in, mapped from the Students and Employees entities in the ER diagrams of Figure 2.2. The primary key is underlined.

students

sid	lname	fname	Midinitial
1134	Smith	John	L.
...	...	...	...

employees

eid	staddress	city	state	zipcode
197	7 Beacon St	Boston	MA	02122
...	...	...	...	...

Transformation Rule 2. Given an entity E with primary identifier p, a multivalued attributed attached to E in an ER diagram is mapped to a table of its own; the table is named after the plural multivalued attribute. The columns of this new table are named after p and a (either p or a might consist of several attributes), and rows of the table correspond to (p, a) value pairs, representing all pairings of attribute values of a associated with entity occurrences in E. The primary key attribute for this table is the set of columns in p and a. ■

EXAMPLE 2.2

Here is an example database of two tables reflecting the ER diagram for the Employees entity and the attached multivalued attribute, hobbies, of Figure 2.2.

employees

eid	staddress	city	state	zipcode
197	7 Beacon St	Boston	MA	02102
221	19 Brighton St	Boston	MA	02103
303	153 Mass Ave	Cambridge	MA	02123
...	...	...	...	...

hobbies

eid	hobby
197	chess
197	painting
197	science fiction
221	reading
303	bicycling
303	mysteries
...	...

Definition: Relationship. Given an ordered list of m entities, $E_1, E_2, \ldots, E_m$ (where the same entity may occur more than once in the list), a relationship R defines a rule of correspondence between the instances of these entities. Specifically, R represents a set of m-tuples, a subset of the Cartesian product of entity instances $E_1 \times E_2 \times \ldots \times E_m$.

2.1.3 Relationships among Entities

A particular occurrence of a relationship, corresponding to a tuple of entity occurrences $(e_1, e_2, \ldots, e_n)$, where e_i is an instance of E_i in the ordered list of the definition, is called a *relationship occurrence* or *relationship instance*. The number of entities m in the defining list is called the *degree* of the relationship. A relationship between two entities is known as a *binary relationship*. For example, we define `teaches` to be a binary relationship between `Instructors` and `Course_sections`. We indicate that a relationship instance exists by saying that a particular instructor teaches a specific course section. Another example of a relationship is `works_on`, defined to relate the two entities `Employees` and `Projects` in a large company: `Employees works_on Projects`.

A relationship can also have attached attributes. The relationship `works_on` might have the attribute `percent`, indicating the percent of work time during each week that the employee is assigned to work on each specific project (see Figure 2.3). Note that this `percent` attribute attached to the `works_on` relationship would be multivalued if attached to either entity `Employees` or `Projects`; the `percent` attribute is only meaningful in describing a specific employee-project pair, and it is therefore a natural attribute of the binary relationship `works_on`.

A binary relationship that relates an entity to itself (a subset of $E_1 \times E_1$) is called a *ring*, or sometimes a *recursive relationship*. For example, the `Employees` entity is related to itself through the relationship `manages`, where we say that one employee manages another. Relationships are represented by diamonds in an ER diagram, with connecting lines to the entities they relate. In the case of a ring, the connecting lines are often labeled with the names of the roles played by the entity instances involved. In Figure 2.3 the two named roles are `manager_of` and `reports_to`.

Note that we often leave out attributes in an ER diagram to concentrate on relationships between entities without losing our concentration in excessive detail.

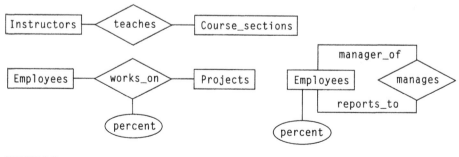

FIGURE 2.3

Examples of ER diagrams with relationships.

EXAMPLE 2.3

The orders Table in CAP Does Not Represent a Relationship

Per the relationship definition, the orders table in the CAP database is not a relationship between Customers, Agents, and Products. This is because (cid, aid, pid) triples in the rows of the orders table do not identify a subset of the Cartesian product, Customers × Agents × Products, as required. Instead, some triples of (cid, aid, pid) values occur more than once, and no doubt clearly the designer's intention, since the same customer can order the same product from the same agent on two different occasions. Instead of a relationship, the orders table represents an entity in its own right, with identifier attribute ordno. This makes a good deal of sense, since we might commonly have reason to look up a row in the orders table for reasons unconnected to relating entity occurrences in Customers, Agents, and Products. For example, on request, we might need to check that a past order has been properly billed and shipped. Thus, the entity Orders occurrences are dealt with individually as objects in their own right.

Although the orders table doesn't correspond directly to a relationship, it is clear that there are any number of possible relationships we could define in terms of the orders table between the Customers, Agents, and Products entities.

EXAMPLE 2.4

Assume that we are performing a study in which we commonly need to know total sales aggregated (summed) from the orders table by customers, agents, and products for the current year. We might do this, for example, to study sales volume relationships between agents and customers, as well as between customers and products, and how those relationships are affected by geographic factors (city values). However, as we begin to plan this application, we decide that it is too inefficient to always perform sums on the orders table to access the basic measures of our study, so we decide to create a new table called yearlies. We define this new table with the following SQL commands:

```
create table yearlies (cid char(4). aid char(3). pid char(3).
   totqty integer, totdoll float);
insert into yearlies
   select cid, aid, pid, sum(qty), sum(dollars) from orders
   group by cid, aid, pid;
```

Once we have the new yearlies table, the totals can be kept up to date by application logic: As each new order is entered, the relevant yearlies row should be updated as well. Now the yearlies table is a relationship, since the (cid, aid, pid) triples in the rows of the table identify a *subset* of the Cartesian product, Customers × Agents × Products; that is to say, there are now no repeated triples in the yearlies table. Since these triples are unique, (cid, aid, pid) forms the primary key for the yearlies table.

A relationship on more than two entities is called an *n-ary relationship*. The yearlies relationship on three distinct entities is also known as a *ternary relationship*. An *n*-ary relationship with $n > 2$ can often be replaced by a number employees

eid	ename	mgrid
e001	Jacqueline	null
e002	Frances	e001
e003	Jose	e001
e004	Deborah	e001
e005	Craig	e002
e006	Mark	e002
e007	Suzanne	e003
e008	Frank	e003
e009	Victor	e004
e010	Chumley	e007

FIGURE 2.4

A table representing an entity, Employees, and a ring (recursive relationship), manages.

of distinct binary relationships in an ER diagram, and this is a good idea if the replacement expresses true binary relationships for the system. Binary relationships are the ones that are familiar to most practitioners and are sufficient for almost all applications. However, in some cases, a ternary relationship cannot be decomposed into expressive binary relationships. The yearlies relationship of Example 2.4 expresses customer-agent-product ordering patterns over a year, a ternary relationship that cannot be decomposed (exactly) into binary relationships. In converting an ER design to a relational one, a relationship is sometimes translated into a relational table, and sometimes not. (We will have more to say about this in the next section.) For example, the yearlies relationship (a ternary relationship) is translated into a relational table named yearlies. However, the manages relationship between Employees and Employees, shown in Figure 2.3, does not translate into a table of its own. Instead, this relationship is usually translated into a column in employees identifying the mgrid to whom the employee reports. This table is shown again in Figure 2.4.

Note the surprising fact that mgrid is *not* considered an attribute of the Employees entity, although it exists as a column in the employees table. The mgrid column is what is known as a *foreign key* in the relational model, and it corresponds to the actual manages relationship in the ER diagram of Figure 2.3. We deal more with this in the next section, after we have had an opportunity to consider some of the properties of relationships. To summarize this section, Figure 2.5(a) and (b) lists the concepts introduced up to now.

2.2 FURTHER DETAILS OF ER MODELING

Now that we've defined some fundamental means of classification, let's discuss properties of relationships in the ER method of database design.

Classification	Description	Example
Entity	A collection of distinguishable real-world objects with common properties	`Customers, Agents, Products, Employees`
Attribute	A data item that describes a property of an entity or relationship	See below
Identifier (set of attributes)	Uniquely identifies an entity or relationship occurrence	customer identifier: `cid`, employee identifier: `eid`
Descriptor	Non-key attribute, describing an entity or relationship	`city` (for `Customers`), `capacity` (for `Class_rooms`)
Composite attribute	A group of simple attributes that together describe a property of an object	`emp_address` (see Figure 2.2)
Multi-valued attribute	An entity attribute that takes on multiple values for a single entity instance	`hobbies` (see Figure 2.2)

(a)

Classification	Description	Example
Relationship	Named set of m-tuples, identifies subset of the Cartesian product $E_1 \times E_2 \times \ldots \times E_m$	
Binary relationship	A relationship on two distinct entities	`teaches, works_on` (see Figure 2.3)
Ring, recursive relationship	A relationship relating an entity to itself	`manages` (see Figure 2.4)
Ternary relationship	A relationship on three distinct entities	`yearlies` (see Example 2.4)

(b)

FIGURE 2.5

Basic ER concepts: (a) entities and attributes, and (b) relationships.

2.2.1 Cardinality of Entity Participation in a Relationship

Figure 2.6 illustrates the concepts of *minimum* and *maximum cardinality* with which an entity participates in a relationship. Figure 2.6(a), (b), and (c) represent entities E and F on the left and right, respectively, by two sets; elements of the two sets are connected by a line exactly when a relationship R relates the two entity occurrences represented. Thus, the connecting lines themselves represent instances of the relation R. Note that the diagrams of Figure 2.6 are *not* what we refer to as ER diagrams.

The minimum cardinality with which an entity takes part in a relationship is the minimum number of lines that the DBA allows to be connected to each entity instance. Note that the diagrams of Figure 2.6 would normally only give examples of relationships at a given moment, and the line connections might change, just

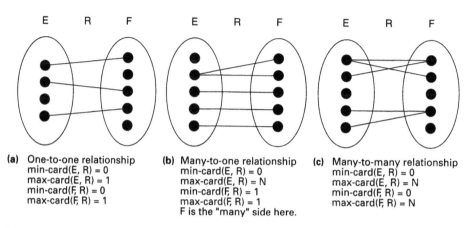

(a) One-to-one relationship
min-card(E, R) = 0
max-card(E, R) = 1
min-card(F, R) = 0
max-card(F, R) = 1

(b) Many-to-one relationship
min-card(E, R) = 0
max-card(E, R) = N
min-card(F, R) = 1
max-card(F, R) = 1
F is the "many" side here.

(c) Many-to-many relationship
min-card(E, R) = 0
max-card(E, R) = N
min-card(F, R) = 0
max-card(F, R) = N

FIGURE 2.6

Examples of relationships R between two entities E and F.

as the row content of a table can change, until some entity instances have different numbers of lines connected. On the other hand, the minimum and maximum cardinality properties of an entity are meant to represent rules laid down by the DBA for all time, rules that cannot be broken by normal database changes affecting the relationship. In Figure 2.6(a), the DBA clearly permits both entity sets E and F to take part in relationship R with minimum cardinality 0; that is to say, the DBA does not *require* a connecting line for each entity instance, since some elements of both sets have no lines connected to them. We symbolize this by writing min-card(E, R) = 0 and min-card(F, R) = 0. The maximum cardinality with which E and F take part in R is not obvious from Figure 2.6(a), however. No entity instance has more than one line connected to it, but from an example as of a given moment we have no guarantee that the line connections won't change in the future so that some entity instances will have more than one line connected. However, we will assume for purposes of simple explanation that the diagrams of this figure are meant to represent exactly the cardinalities intended by the DBA. Thus, since no entity instance of E and F in Figure 2.6(a) has more than one incident connecting line, we record this fact using the notation max-card(E, R) = 1 and max-card(F, R) = 1.

In Figure 2.6(b), assuming once again that this set of lines is representative of the designer's intention, we can write min-card(E, R) = 0, since not every element of E is connected to a line, but min-card(F, R) = 1, since at least one line is connected to every element of F, and our assumption implies that this won't change. We also write max-card(E, R) = N, where N means "more than one"; this means that the designer does not intend to limit to one the number of lines connected to each entity instance of E. However, we write max-card(F, R) = 1, since every element of F has exactly one line leaving it. Note that the two meaningful values for min-card are 0 and 1 (where 0 is not really a limitation at all, but 1 stands for the constraint "at least one"), and the two meaningful values for max-card are 1 and N (N is not really a limitation, but 1 represents the constraint "no more than one"). We don't try to differentiate numbers other than 0, 1, and many. Since max-card(E, R) = N, there are multiple entity instances of F connected to one of E by the relationship. For this reason, F is called the "many" side and E is called the "one" side in this many-to-one relationship.

Note particularly that the "many" side in a many-to-one relationship is the side that has *max-card value 1!* In Figure 2.6(b), the entity F corresponds to the "many" side of the many-to-one relationship, even though it has min-card(F, R) = max-card(F, R) = 1. As just explained, the "one" side of a many-to-one relationship is the side where some entity instances can participate in multiple relationship instances, "shooting out multiple lines" to connect to *many* entity instances on the "many" side! Phrased this way the terminology makes sense, but this seems to be an easy idea to forget, and forgetting it can lead to serious confusion.

In Figure 2.6(c) we have min-card(E, R) = 0, min-card(F, R) = 0, max-card(E, R) = N, and max-card(F, R) = N. The meaning of the terms used for the three diagrams—one-to-one relationship, many-to-one relationship, and many-to-many relationship—are defined later.

EXAMPLE 2.5

In the relationship `teaches` of Figure 2.3, `Instructors teaches Course_sections`, the DBA would probably want to make a rule that each course section needs to have at least one instructor assigned to teach it by writing min-card(`Course_sections`, `teaches`) = 1. However, we need to be careful in making such a rule, since it means that we will not be able to create a new course section, enter it in the database, assign it a room and a class period, and allow students to register for it, while putting off the decision of who is going to teach it. The DBA might also make the rule that at most one instructor can be assigned to teach a course section by writing max-card(`Course_sections`, `teaches`) = 1. On the other hand, if more than one instructor were allowed to share the teaching of a course section, the DBA would write max-card(`Course_sections`, `teaches`) = N. This is clearly a significant difference. We probably don't want to make the rule that every instructor teaches some course section (written as min-card(`Instructors`, `teaches`) = 1), because an instructor might be on leave, so we settle on min-card(`Instructors`, `teaches`) = 0. And in most universities the course load per instructor is greater than one in any given term, so we would set max-card(`Instructors`, `teaches`) = N.

Definition. When an entity E takes part in a relationship R with min-card(E, R) = x (x is either 0 or 1) and max-card(E, R) = y (y is either 1 or N), then in the ER diagram the connecting line between E and R can be labeled with the ordered cardinality pair (x, y). We use a new notation to represent this minimum-maximum pair (x, y): card(E, R) = (x, y).

According to the above definition and the assignments of Example 2.5, the edge connecting the entity `Course_sections` to the relationship `teaches` should be

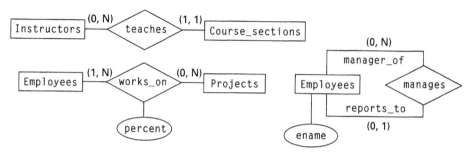

FIGURE 2.7

An ER diagram with labels (x, y) on ER connections.

labeled with the pair (1, 1). In Figure 2.7 we repeat the ER diagrams of Figure 2.3, with the addition of ordered pairs (x, y) labeling line connections, to show the minimum and maximum cardinalities for all ER pairs. The cardinality pair for the Instructors teaches Course_sections diagram follows the discussion of Example 2.5, and other diagrams are filled in with reasonable pair values. We make a number of decisions to arrive at the following rules: Every employee must work on at least one project (but may work on many); a project might have no employees assigned during some periods (waiting for staffing), and of course some projects will have a large number of employees working on them; an employee who acts in the manager_of role (see discussion below) may be managing no other employees at a given time and still be called a manager; and an employee reports to at most one manager, but may report to none (this possibility exists because there must always be a highest-level employee in a hierarchy who has no manager).

In the Employees-manages diagram shown in Figure 2.7, the normal notation, card(Employees, manages), would be ambiguous. We say that there are two different *roles* played by the Employees entity in the relationship: the manager_of role and the reports_to role. Each relationship instance in manages connects a *managed employee* (Employees instance in the reports_to role) to a *manager employee* (Employees instance in the manager_of role). We use the cardinality notation with entities having parenthesized roles to remove ambiguity.

    card(Employees(reports_to). manages) = (0. 1)

and

    card(Employees(manager_of). manages) = (0. N)

And from these cardinalities we see that an employee who acts in the manager_of role may be managing no other employees at a given time and still be called a manager; and an employee reports to at most one manager, but may report to none (because of the highest-level employee in a hierarchy who has no manager— if it weren't for that single person, we could give the label (1, 1) to the reports_ to branch of the Employees-manages edge).

Definition. When an entity E takes part in a relationship R with max-card(E, R) = 1, then E is said to have *single-valued* participation in the relationship R. If max-card(E, R) = N, then E is said to be *multivalued* in this relationship. A binary relationship R between entities E and F is said to be *many-to-many*, or N-N, if both entities E and F are multi-valued in the relationship. If both E and F are single-valued, the relationship is said to be *one-to-one*, or 1-1. If E is single-valued and F is multivalued, or the reverse, the relationship is said to be many-to-one, or N-1. (We do not normally speak of a 1-N relationship as distinct from an N-1 relationship.)

2.2.2 One-to-One, Many-to-Many, and Many-to-One Relationships

Recall that the "many" side in a many-to-one relationship is the side that has single-valued participation. This might be better understood by considering the relationship in Figure 2.7, Instructors teaches Course_sections, where card (Course_sections, teaches) = (1, 1), and the Course_sections entity represents the "many" side of the relationship. This is because one instructor teaches "many" course sections, while the reverse is not true.

In the last definition, we see that the values max-card(E, R) and max-card(F, R) determine whether a binary relationship is many-to-many, many-to-one, or one-to-one. On the other hand, the values min-card(E, R) and min-card(F, R) are not mentioned, and they are said to be independent of these characterizations. In particular, the fact that min-card(F, R) = 1 in Figure 2.6(b) is independent of the fact that that figure represents a many-to-one relationship. If there were additional elements in entity F that were not connected by any lines to elements in E (but all current connections remained the same), this would mean that min-card(F, R) = 0, but the change would not affect the fact that R is a many-to-one relationship. We would still see one element of E (the second from the top) related to two elements of F; in this case, the entity F is the "many" side of the relationship.

Although min-card(E, R) and min-card(F, R) have no bearing on whether a binary relationship R is many-to-many, many-to-one, or one-to-one, a different characterization of entity participation in a relationship is determined by these quantities.

Definition. When an entity E that participates in a relationship R has min-card(E, R) = 1, E is said to have mandatory participation in R, or is simply called mandatory in R. An entity E that is not mandatory in R is said to be optional, or to have optional participation.

2.2.3 Transforming Binary Relationships to Relations

We are now prepared to give the transformation rule for a binary many-to-many relationship.

Transformation Rule 3. N–N Relationships: When two entities E and F take part in a many-to-many binary relationship R, the relationship is mapped to a representative table T in the related relational database design. The table contains columns for all attributes in the primary keys of both tables transformed from entities E and F, and this set of columns forms the primary key for the table T. Table T also contains columns for all attributes attached to the relationship. Relationship occurrences are represented by rows of the table, with the related entity instances uniquely identified by their primary key values as rows. ∎

EXAMPLE 2.6

In Figure 2.7, the relationship works_on is many-to-many between the entities Employees and Projects. The relational design in Figure 2.8 follows Transformation Rule 1 to provide a table for the entity Employees (as specified in Example 2.2) and a table for the entity Projects; it also follows Transformation Rule 3, to provide a table for the relationship works_on.

We generally assume that the eid column in the employees table and prid column for the projects table cannot take on null values, since they are the primary keys for their tables and must differentiate all rows by unique values. Similarly, the (eid, prid) pair of columns in the works_on table cannot take on null values in either component, since each

employees

eid	straddr	city	state	zipcode
197	7 Beacon St	Boston	MA	02102
221	19 Brighton St	Boston	MA	02103
303	153 Mass Ave	Cambridge	MA	02123
...	...	...	...	...

works_on

eid	prid	percent
197	p11	50
197	p13	25
197	p21	25
221	p21	100
303	p13	40
303	p21	60
...	...	...

projects

prid	proj_name	due_date
p11	Phoenix	3/31/99
p13	Excelsior	9/31/99
p21	White Mouse	6/30/00
...	...	...

FIGURE 2.8

Relational design for Employees works_on Projects of Figure 2.7.

row must uniquely designate the employee–project pair related. Note that no primary key column of a relational table can take on null values. Note that although we refer to this as the *entity integrity rule*, it applies as well to tables arising out of the relationships in the ER model. Note also that the SQL Create Table command provides syntax to impose an integrity constraint on a table that guarantees this rule will not be broken, that no nulls will be assigned. For example, the SQL statement

```
create table projects (prid char(3) not null . . .);
```

guarantees that the prid column of the projects table cannot take on null values as a result of later Insert, Delete, or Update statements. There are other constraints as well that have this effect.

Transformation Rule 4. N–1 Relationships: When two entities E and F take part in a many-to-one binary relationship R, the relationship will not be mapped to a table of its own in a relational database design. Instead, if we assume that the entity F has max-card(F, R) = 1 and thus represents the "many" side of the relationship, the relational table T transformed from the entity F should include columns constituting the primary key for the table transformed from the entity E; this is known as a *foreign key* in T. Since max-card(F, R) = 1, each row of T is related by a foreign key value to at most one instance of the entity E. If F has mandatory participation in R, then it must be related to exactly one instance of E, and this means that the foreign key in T cannot take on null values. If F has optional participation in R, then each row of T that is not related can have null values in all columns of the foreign key. ■

EXAMPLE 2.7

Figure 2.9 shows a relational transformation of the Instructors teaches Course_sections ER diagram of Figure 2.7. Recall that we made the rule that one instructor can teach multiple course sections, but each course section can have only one instructor. The insid column in the Course_sections table is a foreign key, relating a course_sections instance (row) to a unique instructors instance (row).

The Create Table command in SQL can require a column not to take on null values; therefore, it is possible to guarantee a faithful representation for mandatory participation by the "many" side entity in a many-to-one relationship. Here we can create the course_sections table so no nulls are allowed in the insid column. What we mean by "faithful" is that it becomes impossible for a user to corrupt the data by a thoughtless update, because SQL does not allow a course_sections row with a null value for insid. SQL can also impose a constraint that the foreign key insid value in a row of the course_sections table actually exists as a value in the insid primary key column in the instructors table. This constraint is known as *referential integrity*.

Unfortunately, it is not possible in standard SQL to guarantee a mandatory participation by the "one" side of a many-to-one relationship, or by either side of a many-to-many relationship. Thus, in Example 2.7 there would be no way to instructors

insid	lname	office_no	ext
309	O'Neil	S-3-223	78543
123	Bergen	S-3-547	78413
113	Smith	S-3-115	78455
...	...	...	...

course_sections

secid	insid	course	room	period
120	309	CS240	M-1-213	MW6
940	309	CS630	M-1-214	MW7:30
453	123	CS632	M-2-614	TTH6
...	...	...	...	...

FIGURE 2.9

Relational design for Instructors teaches Course_sections of Figure 2.7.

provide a faithful representation in an SQL table definition that would guarantee that every instructor teaches at least one course.

Note that there are differences of opinion among texts on some of these ER transformation rules for relationships. Teorey (1994) gives the equivalent to Transformation Rule 4 for N-1 relationships, but Batini et al. (1992) provides an alternate transformation where the relationship is mapped onto a table of its own if the entity at the "many" side of the relationship has an optional participation. The reason for this is to avoid possibly heavy use of null values in the foreign key (insid in course_sections in Example 2.7); but since there seems to be nothing wrong with using null values, we follow the transformation of Teorey (1994).

Transformation Rule 5. 1-1 Relationships, Optional Participation: Given two entities E and F that take part in a one-to-one binary relationship R, where participation is optional on either side, we wish to translate this situation into a relational design. To do this, we create a table S to represent the entity E, following the prescription of Transformation Rule 1, and similarly a table T to represent the entity F. Then we adjoin to the table T a set of columns (as a foreign key) constituting the primary key for table S. If we wish, we may also adjoin to table S a foreign key set of columns referring to the primary key of table T. For any relationship instance in R, a unique entity instance in E is related to a unique instance in F—in the corresponding rows of S and T, the foreign key column values filled in to reference the row in the other table arising from the instances related by R. ∎

Transformation Rule 6. 1-1 Relationships, Mandatory Participation on Both Sides: In the case of a one-to-one relationship with mandatory participation on both sides, it is most appropriate to combine the tables for the two entities into one, and in this way avoid any foreign keys. ∎

We do not present transformation rules for all possible *n*-ary relationships with *n* > 2. Usually such an *n*-ary relationship is transformed into a table of its own, but if all but one of the entities of the relationship participate with max-card = 1, then it is possible to represent the relationship with *n* − 1 foreign keys in the one table that participates with greater cardinality.

2.3 ADDITIONAL ER CONCEPTS

In this section we introduce a number of additional concepts useful for ER modeling.

2.3.1 Cardinality of Attributes

To begin with, we note that the min-card/max-card notation can be used to describe the cardinality of attributes attached to entities.

Definition. Given an entity E and an attached attribute A, we write min-card(A, E) = 0 to indicate that the attribute A is optional, and min-card(A, E) = 1 to indicate that the attribute A is mandatory. An attribute that is mandatory should correspond to a column declared in the table representing the entity E with no nulls allowed. We write max-card(A, E) = 1 to indicate that the attribute is single valued, and max-card(A, E) = N to indicate that the attribute is multivalued. An attribute A is said to have card(A, E) = (x, y) when min-card(A, E) = x and max-card(A, E) = y. The (x, y) pair can be used to label an attribute–entity connection in an ER diagram to indicate the cardinality of the attribute.

Attributes that have unlabeled connectors in an ER diagram can be assumed to have cardinality (0, 1) if they are descriptor attributes, and cardinality (1, 1) if they are identifier attributes. Figure 2.10 recapitulates Figure 2.2 with labeled attribute–entity connectors. (Note that these are not the default cardinalities only because of lack of notation.)

In Figure 2.10 we note that the attribute midinitial is optional (some people don't have middle names). The composite attribute student_names is mandatory for Students, but emp_address is optional for Employees. However, given that emp_address exists, all four simple attributes making up the address are mandatory. Both sid and eid have cardinality (1, 1); this is always the case for entity identifiers. The multivalued hobbies attribute has max-card N, as we can also tell

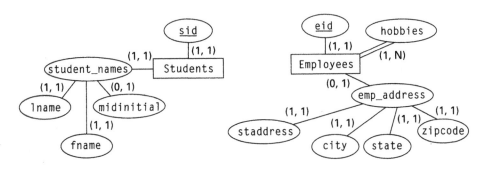

FIGURE 2.10

ER diagrams with labeled attribute–entity connectors.

from the fact that it is connected to its entity by a double line. The fact that min-card(hobbies, Employees) = 1 is somewhat surprising and indicates that the employee *must* name at least one hobby for inclusion in the database.

Definition: Weak Entity. A weak entity is an entity whose occurrences are dependent for their existence, through a relationship R, on the occurrence of another (strong) entity.

2.3.2 Weak Entities

As an example, we have been assuming in our CAP design that an order specifies a customer, agent, product, quantity, and dollar cost. A common design variant that allows multiple products to be ordered at once will create an orders table that relates to customers and agents rows, as well as a line_items table containing individual product purchases; a number of rows in the line_items table relate to one master orders occurrence. The design of this in the ER model is given in Figure 2.11.

As we see, the entity Orders is optional in its relationship to Line_items, since each order must start without any line items. Line_items is mandatory in the relationship, because a line-item order for a product cannot exist without a master order containing it to specify the customer and agent for the order. If the Orders occurrence goes away (the customer cancels it), all occurrences of the weak entity Line_items will likewise disappear. A dead giveaway for a weak entity is the fact that the primary identifier for Line_items (lineno) is only meaningful within some order. In fact, what this implies is that the primary identifier for the weak entity Line_items must include the attributes in the primary identifier for the

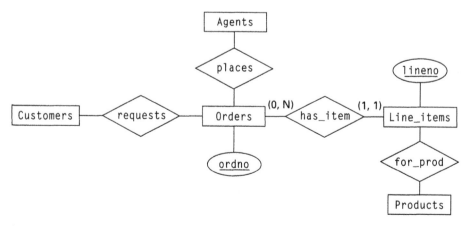

FIGURE 2.11

A weak entity, Line_items, dependent on the entity Orders.

Orders entity. Attributes such as Line_items are known as *external identifier* attributes.

When the Line_items weak entity is mapped to a relational table line_items, an ordno column is included by Transformation Rule 4 to represent the N-1 has_item relationship; thus, the primary key for the line_items table is constructed from the external attribute ordno and the weak entity identifier lineno. Note that it is also sometimes difficult to distinguish between a weak entity and a multivalued attribute. For example, hobbies in Example 2.2 could be identified as a weak entity Hobbies, with an identifier hobby_name. However, Figure 2.11 obviously implies Line_items is a weak entity rather than a multivalued attribute, since Line_items is separately related to another entity, Products.

2.3.3 Generalization Hierarchies

Finally, we introduce the concept of a *generalization hierarchy* or *generalization relationship*. The idea is that several entities with common attributes can be generalized into a higher-level *supertype entity*, or, alternatively, a general entity can be decomposed into lower-level *subtype entities*. The purpose is to attach attributes at the proper level and thus avoid having attributes of a common entity that require a large number of null values in each entity instance. For example, assume that we distinguish between Managers and Non_managers as *subtype* entities of the *supertype* Employees (see Figure 2.12). Then attributes such as expenseno (for expense reports) can be attached only to the Managers entity, while nonmanager attributes such as union status can be attached to Non_managers. Consultants might form another entity type sharing many properties with Employees, and we could create a new supertype entity named Persons to contain them both. An ER diagram showing a generalization hierarchy normally has arrows (unnamed) directed from the subtype to the supertype entities.

The arrow relationship between the subtype entity and the supertype entity is often referred to as an *is-a relationship*, since a consultant *is a* person, a manager *is an* employee, and so forth. Object-relational database systems express

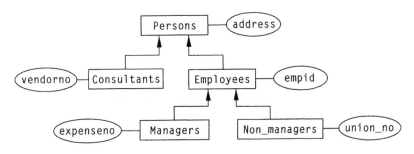

FIGURE 2.12

A generalization hierarchy with examples of attributes attached.

these concepts using *type inheritance*, where objects (rows) of a given subtype contain specific attributes but *inherit* all attributes of their *supertype*. In particular, INFORMIX and SQL-99 support inheritance of object types.

The relational model provides no support for the concept of generalization hierarchy, so it is necessary to reconfigure such a design element into simpler concepts. This can happen either prior to transformation into relational tables or as part of the transformation. Here we give an idea of how to perform such a reconfiguration while remaining in the ER model, before transformation into a relational representation. We consider one level of generalization hierarchy at a time and give two alternatives.

1. We can collapse a one-level generalization hierarchy of subtype and supertype entities into a single entity by adding all attributes of the subtype entities to the supertype entity. An additional attribute must be added to this single entity, which will discriminate among the various types. As an example, the Employees entity in Figure 2.12 could be augmented to represent managers and nonmanagers as well, by affixing the attributes union_no, expenseno, and emptype to the Employee entity. Now the union_no attribute will be null when emptype has value "Manager," and similarly expenseno will be null when emptype is "Nonmanager." The emptype attribute might also designate the supertype case, an important alternative when some entity instances in the supertype fall in none of the named subtypes.

2. We can retain the supertype entity and all subtype entities as full entities and create explicit named relationships to represent the is-a relationships.

Alternative 2 is particularly useful when the various subtypes and supertype are quite different in attributes and are handled differently by application logic.

We do not investigate all concepts of the ER model in full depth here. See the references at the end of this chapter for a list of texts devoted to complete coverage of the ER model and logical database design.

2.4 CASE STUDY

Let us try to perform an ER design from the beginning, ending up with a set of relational tables. Consider a simple airline reservation database handling (only) outgoing flights from one airline terminal. We need to keep track of passengers, flights, departure gates, and seat assignments. We could get almost arbitrarily complex in a real design, since a "flight" actually brings together a flight crew and an airplane, serviced by a ground crew, slotted into a regularly scheduled departure time with an assigned flight number on a specific date. But for simplicity, we will assume that we can represent flights with an entity Flights, having primary identifier flightno (unique identifier values, not repeated on successive days) and descriptive attribute depart_time (actually made up of date and time); other details will be hidden from us. Passengers are represented by another entity,

Passengers, with primary identifier attribute ticketno; a passenger has no other attribute that we care about. We also need to keep track of seats for each flight. We assume that each seat is an entity instance in its own right, an entity Seats, identified by a seat number, seatno, valid only for a specific flight (different flights might have different airplane seat layouts, and therefore different sets of seat numbers). We see therefore that seat assignment is a relationship between Passengers and Seats, which we name seat_assign.

Now think about this specification for a moment. The Passengers entity is easy to picture, and so is the Flights entity. The depart_time attribute for Flights is composite, consisting of simple attributes dtime and ddate. We can add another entity Gates, with primary identifier gateno. We have already defined a Seats entity, but the entity seems to be a little strange: The seatno primary identifier for Seats is only meaningful when related to a Flights instance. This is what is referred to in the previous section as a weak entity, and thus there must be a relationship between Flights and Seats, which we name has_seat. The identifier for Seats is partially external, encompassing the identifier of the containing flight.

What other relationships do we have? If we draw the ER diagram for what we have named up to now, we notice that the Gates entity is off by itself. But clearly passengers go to a gate to meet a flight. We model this as two binary relationships rather than as a ternary relationship: each passenger is related to a specific flight through the relationship Passengers travels_on Flights, and gates normally act as marshaling points for multiple flights (at different times) through the relationship Gates marshals Flights. Figure 2.13 shows the ER diagram so far. The arrow from seatno to flightno symbolizes the fact that the primary identifier for Seats includes the identifier for the master entity Flights.

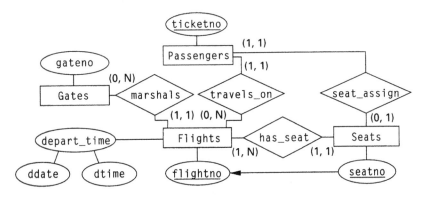

FIGURE 2.13

Early ER design for a simple airline reservation database.

Now we need to work out the cardinalities with which the various entities participate in their relationships. Considering the `marshals` relationship first, clearly there is exactly one gate for each flight, so card(`Flights`, `marshals`) = (1, 1). A single gate might be used for multiple flights at different times, but there is no rule that a gate must be used at all, so card(`Gates`, `marshals`) = (0, N). Now each passenger must travel on exactly one flight, so card(`Passengers`, `travels_on`) = (1, 1). A flight must have multiple passengers to fly (the flight will be canceled and the gate reassigned if there are too few), but the database needs to hold information starting from no passengers, so we set a minimum of 0, and card(`Flights`, `travels_on`) = (0, N). A flight must have numerous seats for passengers, so card(`Flights`, `has_seat`) = (1, N), and each seat is on a unique flight, so card(`Seats`, `has_seat`) = (1, 1). Each passenger must have a seat, and only one, so card(`Passengers`, `seat_assign`) = (1, 1), and seats can be used by at most one passenger and may go empty, so card(`Seats`, `seat_assign`) = (0, 1). The ER diagram with these cardinality pairs added is pictured in Figure 2.14.

Now the ER design is complete, and we need to transform the design into relational tables. We can begin by creating tables to map entities, even though this means that we might overlook some attributes that will be needed to represent foreign keys for relationships. We will simply have to return later when we consider the relationships and add attributes to these tables. To begin with, we notice with the `Flights` entity that we don't have multivalued attributes in relational tables, so following the hint of Transformation Rule 1, we create columns for `ddate` and `dtime` in the `flights` table. All other tables are easily mapped, except for the `seats` table, where we take the easy way out and use the single column `seatno`, even though this is not a complete key for the table. Here are the tables so far:

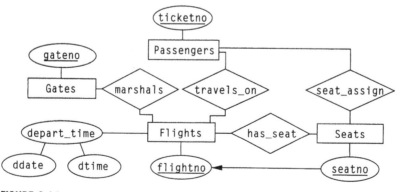

FIGURE 2.14

ER design with cardinalities for a simple airline reservation database.

passengers	gates	flights				seats
ticketno	gateno	flightno	ddate	dtime		seatno
...						

Now consider the relationship has_seat, which is N-1 in Figure 2.14, with Seats on the "many" side. By Transformation Rule 4, a foreign key in the seats table will connect each seats row to the appropriate flights row. This completes the primary key for the seats table, which represents a weak entity and therefore needs a foreign key to identify each row.

passengers	gates	flights				seats	
ticketno	gateno	flightno	ddate	dtime		seatno	flightno
...							

The seat_assign relationship is 1-1, with optional participation by Seats, so by Transformation Rule 5 we can represent this by adjoining to the passengers table a foreign key for seats (this requires two additional columns). We don't expect that we will ever need to look up the passenger for a given seat, so we place no additional foreign key on the seats table. The resulting table definitions are as follows:

passengers			gates
ticketno	seatno	flightno	gateno
...			

flights			seats	
flightno	ddate	dtime	seatno	flightno

Now consider the marshals relationship. This is N-1, with Flights on the "many" side, so by Transformation Rule 4 a foreign key in the flights table, gateno, will connect each flights row to the appropriate gates row:

passengers			gates
ticketno	seatno	flightno	gateno
...			

flights				seats	
<u>flightno</u>	gateno	ddate	dtime	<u>seatno</u>	<u>flightno</u>

Similarly the travels_on relationship is N-1, with Passengers on the "many" side, so by Transformation Rule 4 a foreign key, flightno, in the passengers table will connect each passengers row to the appropriate flights row. This column already exists in the passengers table, however, so the relational table design is complete.

2.5 NORMALIZATION: PRELIMINARIES

Normalization is another approach to logical design of a relational database, which seems to share little with the ER model. However, it will turn out that a relational design based on normalization and a careful ER design transformed into relational form have nearly identical results, and in fact the two approaches reinforce each other. In the normalization approach, the designer starts with a real-world situation to be modeled and lists the data items that are candidates to become column names in relational tables, together with a list of rules about the relatedness of these data items. The aim is to represent all these data items as attributes of tables that obey restrictive conditions associated with what we call *normal forms*. These normal form definitions limit the acceptable form of a table so that it has certain desirable properties, thus avoiding various kinds of anomalous behavior. There is a series of normal form definitions, each more restrictive than the one before; the forms covered in this chapter are first normal form (1NF), second normal form (2NF), third normal form (3NF), and Boyce-Codd normal form (BCNF). Other types of normalization, 4NF and 5NF, are less commonly considered and are not covered in detail in this chapter.

To begin with, a table in 1NF is simply one that has no multivalued (repeating) fields. SQL language accepts this rule as basic. *In what follows we assume that tables are in 1NF unless otherwise specified.* 2NF turns out to be of mainly historical interest, since no sensible designer would leave a database in 2NF but would always continue normalization until the more restrictive 3NF was reached. From an initial database containing data items that are all in the same table (sometimes referred to as a *universal table*) and relatedness rules on these data items, there is a procedure to create an equivalent database with multiple tables, all of which are in 3NF. (This is what we mean by having a database in 3NF—that all of its tables have 3NF form.) As we proceed through this chapter we will find that any table that does not obey 3NF can be factored into distinct tables in such a way that (1) each of the factored tables is in a valid 3NF, and (2) the join of all these factored tables contains exactly the information in the table from which they were factored. The set of 3NF tables resulting from the initial universal table is known as a 3NF *lossless decomposition* of the database.

There is a third desirable property that we can always provide with a 3NF decomposition. Note that when a new row is added to one of the tables in the 3NF decomposition (or an old row is updated), it is possible that an erroneous change might break one of the rules of data item relatedness, mentioned earlier as part of the design input. We wish to impose a constraint on Insert and Update operations so that such errors will not corrupt the data. The third property that we consider important in a decomposition, then, is (3) when a table Insert or Update occurs, the possible relatedness rules that might be broken can be tested by validating data items in the single table affected; there is no need to perform table joins in order to validate these rules. A 3NF decomposition constructed to have the three desirable properties just mentioned is generally considered an acceptable database design. It turns out that a further decomposition of tables in 3NF to the more restrictive BCNF is often unnecessary (many real-world databases in 3NF are also in BCNF), but in cases where further decomposition results, property (3) no longer holds in the result. Many database designers therefore settle on 3NF design.

We will need a good deal of insight into the details of the normalization approach before we are able to properly deal with some of these ideas. Let us begin to illustrate them with an example.

2.5.1 A Running Example: Employee Information

We need an example to clarify some of the definitions of database design that follow. Consider the data items listed in Figure 2.15, representing the employee information that must be modeled by the personnel department of a very large company.

```
emp_id
emp_name
emp_phone
dept_name
dept_phone
dept_mgrname
skill_id       ⎫
skill_name     ⎬  From one up to a large number
skill_date     ⎪  of skills useful to the company
skill_lvl      ⎭
```

FIGURE 2.15

Unnormalized data items for employee information.

The data items beginning with emp_all represent attributes of what we would refer to in the ER approach as the entity Employees. Other entities underlying the data items of Figure 2.15 include Departments where employees in the company work and Skills that the various employees need to perform their jobs. In the normalization approach, we leave the entity concept unnamed but reflect it in the data item interrelatedness rules that will be explained shortly, rules known as *functional dependencies*. The data item emp_id has been created to uniquely identify employees. Each employee works for some single department in the company, and the data items beginning with dept_ describe the different departments; the data item dept_name uniquely identifies departments, and each department normally has a unique manager (also an employee) with a name given in dept_mgrname. Finally, we assume that the various employees each possess some number of skills, such as typing or filing, and that data items beginning with skill_ describe the skills that are tested and used for job assignment and salary determination by the company. The data item skill_id uniquely identifies the skill, which also has a name, skill_name. For each employee who possesses a particular skill, the skill_date describes the date when the skill was last tested, and skill_lvl describes the level of skill the employee displayed at that test.

Figure 2.16 provides a universal table, emp_info, containing all the data items of employee information from Figure 2.15. Because of 1NF, there can only be atomic values in each row and column position of a table. This poses a difficulty, because each individual employee might have any number of skills. It is inappropriate to design a table with unique rows for each emp_id and a distinct column for each piece of skill information—we don't even know the maximum number of skills for an employee, so we don't know how many columns we should use for skill_id-1, ..., skill_id-n. The only solution that will work in a single

emp_info

emp_id	emp_name	...	skill_id	skill_name	skill_date	skill_lvl
09112	Jones	...	44	librarian	03-15-99	12
09112	Jones	...	26	PC-admin	06-30-98	10
09112	Jones	...	89	word-proc	01-15-00	12
12231	Smith	...	26	PC-admin	04-15-99	5
12231	Smith	...	39	bookkeeping	07-30-97	7
13597	Brown	...	27	statistics	09-15-99	6
14131	Blake	...	26	PC-admin	05-30-98	9
14131	Blake	...	89	word-proc	09-30-99	10
...	...	...	...	...	...	...

FIGURE 2.16

Single employee information table, emp_info, in 1NF.

(universal) table is to give up on having a unique row for each employee and replicate information about the employee, pairing the employee with different skills on different rows.

The intention of the database designer in the emp_info table of Figure 2.16 is that there is a row for every employee-skill pair existing in the company. From this, it should be clear that there cannot be two rows with the same values for the pair of attributes emp_id and skill_id. The table emp_info has a (candidate) key consisting of the set (pair) of attributes emp_id and skill_id. We confirm that these attributes form a key by noting that the values they take on distinguish any pair of rows in any permissible content of the table (i.e., for any rows u and v, either u(emp_id) ≠ v(emp_id) or u(skill_id) ≠ v(skill_id)), and that no subset of this set of attributes does the same (there can be two rows u and v such that u(emp_id) = v(emp_id), and there can be two rows r and s such that r(skill_id) = s(skill_id)). We assume in what follows that emp_id and skill_id is the primary key for the emp_info table.

It turns out that the database design of Figure 2.16 is a bad one, because it is subject to certain anomalies that can corrupt the data when data manipulation statements are used to update the table.

2.5.2 Anomalies of a Bad Database Design

It appears that there might be a problem with the emp_info table of Figure 2.16 because there is replication of employee data on different rows. It seems more natural, with the experience we have had up to now, to have a unique row for each distinct employee. Do we have a good reason for our feeling? Let us look at the behavior of this table as SQL updates are applied.

If some employee were to get a new phone number, we would have to update multiple rows (all rows with different skills for that employee) in order to change the emp_phone value in a uniform way. If we were to update the phone number of only one row, we might *corrupt* the data, leaving some rows for that employee with different phone numbers than others. This is commonly known as an *update anomaly*, and it arises because of *data redundancy*, duplication of employee phone numbers and other employee attributes on multiple rows of emp_info. Calling this an "anomaly," with the implication of irregular behavior under update, may seem a bit extreme, since the SQL language is perfectly capable of updating several rows at once with a Searched Update statement such as:

```
update emp_info set emp_phone = :newphone where emp_id = :
   eidval;
```

In fact, the consideration that several rows will be updated is not even apparent from this syntax—the same Searched Update statement would be used if the table had a unique row for each emp_id value. However, with this replication of phone numbers on different rows, a problem can still arise in performing an update with a Positioned Update statement. If we encountered a row of the emp_info table in fetching rows from a cursor created for an entirely different purpose, the program might execute the following statement to allow the user to correct an invalid phone number:

```
update emp_info set emp_phone = :newphone
    where current of cursor_name;
```

This would be a *programming error*, since an experienced programmer would realize that multiple rows need to be updated in order to change an employee phone number. Still, it is the kind of error that could easily occur in practice, and we would like to be able to create a *constraint* on the table that makes such an erroneous update impossible. It turns out that the best way to provide such a constraint is to reconfigure the data items into different tables so as to eliminate the redundant copies of information. This is exactly what is achieved during the process of normalization. We sum up the idea of an update anomaly in a definition that makes reference to our intuitive understanding of the ER model.

Definition: Update Anomaly. A table T is subject to an update anomaly when changing a single attribute value for an entity instance or relationship instance represented in the table that may require that several rows of T be updated.

A different sort of problem, known as the *delete anomaly*, is reflected by the following definition.

Definition: Delete Anomaly, Insert Anomaly. A table T is subject to a delete anomaly when deleting some row of the table to reflect the disappearance of some instance of an entity or relationship that can cause us to lose information about some instance of a different entity or relationship that we do not wish to forget. The insert anomaly is the other face of this problem for inserts, where we cannot represent information about some entity or instance without including information about some other instance of an entity or relationship that does not exist.

For example, assume that a skill possessed by an employee must be retested after five years to remain current for that employee. If the employee fails to have the skill retested (and the skill_date column updated), the skill will drop off the emp_info list (an automatic process deletes the row with this emp_id and skill_id). Now consider what happens if the number of skills for some employee goes to zero in the emp_info table with columns of Figure 2.16: *No row of any kind will remain for the employee!* We have lost the phone number and the department the employee works in because of this delete! This is clearly inappropriate design. The *insert anomaly* exists in the emp_info table because we cannot enter a new employee into the table until the employee has acquired some skill; thus it becomes impossible to hire an employee trainee. Clearly this is just the other face of the delete anomaly, where information about an employee is lost when the employee loses his or her last skill.

Let us jump ahead to a solution for some of the problems mentioned so far. We simply factor the emp_info table and form two tables, the emps table and the

```
emps
emp_id
emp_name
emp_phone
dept_name
dept_phone
dept_mgrname
```

```
skills
emp_id
skill_id
skill_name
skill_date
skill_lvl
```

FIGURE 2.17

The emp_info database with two tables.

skills table, whose column names are listed in Figure 2.17. Notice that the emps table has a unique row for each emp_id (and emp_id is the key for this table), while the skills table has a unique row for each emp_id and skill_id pair, and this pair forms a key for the table. Since there are multiple skills associated with each employee, the emp_id column that we have included in the skills table acts as a foreign key, relating skills back to employees. When we form the natural join of these two tables, the result is exactly the emp_info table we started with. (We will need to demonstrate this fact in what follows, but for now you should take it on faith.) However, the delete anomaly is no longer a problem, since if we delete all rows corresponding to skills for any individual employee, this merely deletes rows in the skills table; the emps table still contains the information we want to retain about the employee, such as emp_phone, dept_name, and the like.

In the sections that follow we will learn how to perform normalization, to factor tables so that all anomalies are removed from our representation. Note that we haven't yet achieved this with the tables of Figure 2.17; as we will see shortly, a number of anomalies still exist. We will need a good deal of insight into the details of the normalization approach before we are able to properly deal with fundamental normalization concepts. In the following sections we present some needed mathematical preliminaries to database normalization. Because it is not always possible to show a real-life application for all these concepts as they are introduced, we ask the reader to be patient. The value of the concepts will become clear in the end.

2.6 FUNCTIONAL DEPENDENCIES

A *functional dependency* (FD) defines the most commonly encountered type of relatedness property between data items of a database. We usually only need to consider relatedness between column attributes of a single relational table, and our definition reflects this. We represent rows of a table T by the notation

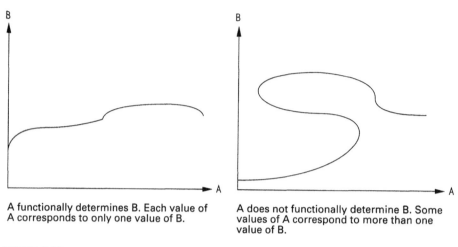

A functionally determines B. Each value of A corresponds to only one value of B.

A does not functionally determine B. Some values of A correspond to more than one value of B.

FIGURE 2.18

Graphical depiction of functional dependency.

r_1, r_2, ... , and follow standard convention by referring to attributes, rather than columns, of the table T. Individual attributes of a table will be represented by letters such as A, B, ... , and the letters X, Y, ... will refer to subsets of attributes. We follow the notation that $r_i(A)$ represents the value of row r_i at attribute A.

Definition. Given a table T containing at least two attributes designated by A and B, we say that A → B (read "A functionally determines B" or "B is functionally dependent on A"), if and only if it is the intent of the designer, for any set of rows that might exist in the table, that two rows in T cannot agree in value for A and disagree in value for B. A more formal way of saying this is: Given two rows r_1 and r_2 in T, if $r_1(A) = r_2(A)$, then $r_1(B) = r_2(B)$. We will usually try to use the less formal statement in what follows.

This definition is comparable to the definition of a *function* in mathematics: For every element in attribute A (which appears on some row), there is a unique corresponding element (on the same row) in attribute B. See Figure 2.18 for a graphical representation of the functional dependency concept.

EXAMPLE 2.8

In the emp_info table of Figure 2.16, the following functional dependencies hold:

emp_id → emp_name
emp_id → emp_phone
emp_id → dept_name

In ER terms, we know this is true because `emp_id` is an identifier for the `Employee` entity, and the other data items simply represent other attributes of the entity; once the entity is identified, all the other attributes follow. But we also recognize these facts intuitively.

If we saw two rows in the single table `emp_info` design of Figure 2.16 with the same `emp_id` value and different `emp_phone` values, we would believe that the data are corrupted (assuming that every employee has a unique phone), but if we saw two rows with the same `emp_phone` value and different `emp_id` values, our first thought would be that they represented different employees who shared a phone. But the two situations are symmetric; it is simply our understanding of the data that makes the first one seem to imply corrupted data. We look to `emp_id` to break ties and uniquely identify employees. Note that what we are saying implies that, while `emp_id` functionally determines `emp_phone`, `emp_phone` does *not* functionally determine `emp_id`. We sometimes express this second fact with this notation:

$$emp\_phone \nrightarrow emp\_id$$

EXAMPLE 2.9

Following are three tables to investigate for functional dependencies between attributes (note that some of the tables break the unique row rule, but we accept them as valid tables for purposes of illustration). In these tables we assume that it is the intent of the designer that *exactly* this set of rows should lie in each table—no changes will ever occur in the tables. Thus, we can determine what functional dependencies exist by examining the data. This is a *very unusual situation*. Normally we determine functional dependencies from understanding the data items and rules of the enterprise (e.g., each employee has a single phone number, employees can share a phone, etc.), as in Example 2.8. These rules exist before any data have been placed in the tables.

Row #	T1 A	T1 B	T2 A	T2 B	T3 A	T3 B
1	x1	y1	x1	y1	x1	y1
2	x2	y2	x2	y4	x2	y4
3	x3	y1	x1	y1	x1	y1
4	x4	y1	x3	y2	X3	y2
5	x5	y2	x2	y4	X2	y4
6	x6	y2	x4	y3	X4	y4

In table T1 we can easily see that A → B; we merely need to check that for every pair of rows r_1 and r_2, if $r_1(A) = r_2(A)$, then $r_1(B) = r_2(B)$. However, there is no pair of rows in T1 with equal values for column A, so the condition is trivially satisfied. At the same time, in T1, B $\nrightarrow$ A (read "column B does *not* functionally determine column A"), since, for example, if r_1 is row 1 and r_2 is row 3, then $r_1(B) = r_2(B) = y1$, but $r_1(A) = x1 \neq r_2(A) = x3$. In table T2, we have A → B (we just need to check that rows 1 and 3, which have matching pairs of A values, also have matching B values, and similarly check rows 2 and 5), and B → A. Finally, in table T3, A → B but B $\not\to$ A (note that if r_1 is row 2 and r_2 is row 6, then $r_1(B) = r_2(B) = y4$, but $r_1(A) = x2 \neq r_2(A) = x4$).

It is obvious how to extend the definition for functional dependency to its full generality, dealing with *sets* of attributes.

Definition. We are given a table T with two sets of attributes, designated by X = $A_1 A_2, \ldots, A_k$ and Y = $B_1 B_2, \ldots, B_m$, where some of the attributes from X may overlap with some of the attributes from Y. We say that X → Y (read "X functionally determines Y" or "Y is functionally dependent on X"), if and only if it is the intent of the designer, for any set of rows that might exist in the table, that two rows in T cannot agree in value on the attributes of X and simultaneously disagree in value on the attributes of Y. Note that two rows agree in value on the attributes of X if they agree on *all of* the attributes of X, and they disagree in value on the attributes of Y if they disagree on *any of* the attributes of Y. More formally, given any two rows r_1 and r_2 in T, if $r_1(A_i) = r_2(A_i)$ for every A_i in X, then $r_1(B_j) = r_2(B_j)$ for every B_j in Y.

EXAMPLE 2.10

We list here what we claim are all the functional dependencies for the `emp_info` table of Figure 2.16 (with missing attributes in Figure 2.15). With this FD list, all the information needed for the normalization procedure has been provided.

1. `emp_id → emp_name emp_phone dept_name`
2. `dept_name → dept_phone dept_mgrname`
3. `skill_id → skill_name`
4. `emp_id skill_id → skill_date skill_lvl`

You should be able to interpret each of these functional dependencies and see if you agree with them. For example, FD 1 states that if we know the `emp_id`, then the `emp_name`, `emp_phone`, and `dept_name` are determined. Note that FD 1 is just another way of stating the FDs of Example 2.8. That is, if we know the FDs given there,

`emp_id → emp_name, emp_id → emp_phone, and emp_id → dept_name,`

we can conclude that FD 1 holds.

To say this in yet another way, the three FDs of Example 2.8 together imply FD 1. Similarly, from FD 1 we can conclude that the three FDs of Example 2.8 hold. A simple rule of FD implication is used to arrive at these conclusions, based on the FD definition. We will learn more about such rules shortly.

Because the FDs given in 1–4 are *all* the FDs for the `emp_info` table, we can conclude, for example, that the designer does *not* intend that `skill_name` be unique for a specific skill. Since `skill_id` is a unique identifier for the skill, to have a unique `skill_name` would presumably mean that `skill_name → skill_id`, the reverse of FD 3. However, this FD does not exist in the set, nor is it implied. (A quick test to see that it isn't implied is to note that `skill_name` does not occur on the left side of any FD in the set.) We also note that we do not have the FD `dept_mgrname` → `dept_name`, which presumably means that although each department has a unique manager, one manager might simultaneously manage more than one department. Finally, note that `skill_lvl` and `skill_date` are only meaningful as attributes of the *relationship* between an `Employee` entity and a `Skill` entity. If we said that a given employee had a skill level of 9, it would be necessary to ask, "For what skill?"; and if we said that we know there is a skill level of 9 for "typing," we would wonder, "What employee?" Thus, we need to name both the `emp_id` and the `skill_id` to determine these attributes.

2.6.1 Logical Implications among Functional Dependencies

In Example 2.10 a number of conclusions were drawn that depended on understanding implications among functional dependencies. In what follows, we will derive certain rules of implication among FDs that follow directly from previous definition. The reader needs to understand many such rules at both a rigorous and an intuitive level to properly appreciate some of the techniques of normalization that are presented in later sections. We begin with a very basic rule.

Theorem 2.1: Inclusion Rule. We are given a table T with a specified heading (set of attributes), Head (T). If X and Y are sets of attributes contained in Head(T), and $Y \subseteq X$, then $X \rightarrow Y$.

PROOF. To show that $X \rightarrow Y$, we need only demonstrate that there is no pair of rows u and v that agree in value on the attributes of X and simultaneously disagree in value on the attributes of Y. But this is obvious, since two rows can never agree in value on the attributes of X and simultaneously disagree on a subset of those attributes. ∎

The inclusion rule provides us with a large number of FDs that are true for any table of attributes, irrespective of the intended content.

Definition: Trivial Dependency. A trivial dependency is an FD of the form $X \rightarrow Y$, in a table T where $X \cup Y \subseteq$ Head(T), that will hold for any possible content of the table T.

We can prove that trivial dependencies always arise as a result of the inclusion rule.

Theorem 2.2. Given a trivial dependency $X \rightarrow Y$ in T, it must be the case that $Y \subseteq X$.

PROOF. Given the table T with a heading containing the attributes in $X \cup Y$, consider the set of attributes $Y - X$ (attributes in Y that are not in X). Since $X \rightarrow Y$ is a trivial dependency, it must hold for any possible content of the table T. We will assume $Y - X$ is nonempty and reach a contradiction. If the set

Y – X is nonempty, let A be an attribute contained in Y – X. Since A ∉ X, it is possible to construct two rows, u and v, in the table T, alike in values for all attributes in X, but having different values for the attribute A. But with these two rows in T, the dependency X → Y does not hold, since rows u and v agree in value on attributes of X and disagree on attributes of Y (because A ∈ Y). Since a trivial dependency is supposed to hold for any possible content of the table T, we have created a contradiction, and from this we conclude that the set Y – X cannot contain an attribute A, and therefore Y ⊆ X.   ■

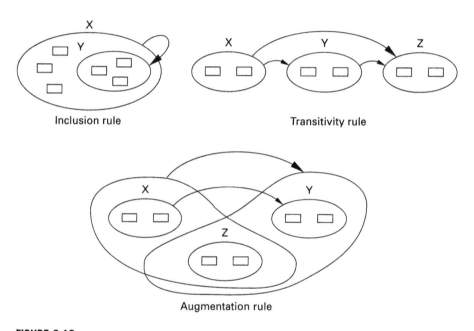

Inclusion rule   Transitivity rule

Augmentation rule

FIGURE 2.19

Armstrong's Axioms.

2.6.2 Armstrong's Axioms

The inclusion rule is one rule of implication by which FDs can be generated that are guaranteed to hold for all possible tables. It turns out that from a small set of basic rules of implication, we can derive all others. We list here three basic rules that we call Armstrong's Axioms (Figure 2.19).

Definition: Armstrong's Axioms. Assume in what follows that we are given a table T, and that all sets of attributes X, Y, Z are contained in Head(T). Then we have the following rules of implication.

1. *Inclusion rule:* If $Y \subseteq X$, then $X \rightarrow Y$.
2. *Transitivity rule:* If $X \rightarrow Y$ and $Y \rightarrow Z$, then $X \rightarrow Z$.
3. *Augmentation rule:* If $X \rightarrow Y$, then $X Z \rightarrow Y Z$.

Just as we list attributes with spaces between them in a functional dependency to represent a set containing those attributes, two sets of attributes in sequence imply a union operation. Thus, the augmentation rule could be rewritten: If $X \rightarrow Y$, then $X \cup Z \rightarrow Y \cup Z$.

We have already proved the inclusion rule, in Theorem 2.1, so let us prove the augmentation rule now in Theorem 2.3.

Theorem 2.3: Augmentation Rule. We wish to show that if $X \rightarrow Y$, then $X Z \rightarrow Y Z$. Assume that $X \rightarrow Y$, and consider any two rows u and v in T that agree on the attributes of $X Z$ (i.e., $X \cup Z$). We need merely show that u and v cannot disagree on the attributes of $Y Z$. But since u and v agree on all attributes of $X Z$, they certainly agree on all attributes of X; and since we are assuming that $X \rightarrow Y$, then u and v must agree on all attributes of Y. Similarly, since u and v agree on all attributes of $X Z$, they certainly agree on all attributes of Z. Therefore, u and v agree on all attributes of Y and all attributes of Z, and the proof is complete. ∎

From Armstrong's Axioms we can prove a number of other rules of implication among FDs. Furthermore, we can do this without any further recourse to the FD definition, using only the axioms themselves.

Theorem 2.4: Some Implications of Armstrong's Axioms. Again we assume that all sets of attributes below—W, X, Y, and Z—are contained in the heading of a table T.

1. *Union rule:* If $X \rightarrow Y$ and $X \rightarrow Z$, then $X \rightarrow Y Z$.
2. *Decomposition rule:* If $X \rightarrow Y Z$, then $X \rightarrow Y$ and $X \rightarrow Z$.
3. *Pseudotransitivity rule:* If $X \rightarrow Y$ and $W Y \rightarrow Z$, then $X W \rightarrow Z$.
4. *Set accumulation rule:* If $X \rightarrow Y Z$ and $Z \rightarrow W$, then $X \rightarrow Y Z W$.

PROOF. We prove only 2 and 4 here. For 2, note that $Y Z = Y \cup Z$. Thus, $Y Z \rightarrow Y$ by the inclusion rule (axiom 1). By transitivity (axiom 2), $X \rightarrow Y Z$ and $Y Z \rightarrow Y$ implies $X \rightarrow Y$. Similarly, we can show $X \rightarrow Z$, and the decomposition rule (2) has been demonstrated. For 4, we are given that (a) $X \rightarrow Y Z$ and (b) $Z \rightarrow W$. Using axiom 3, we augment (b) with $Y Z$ to obtain $Y Z Z \rightarrow Y Z W$. Since $Z Z = Z$, we have (c) $Y Z \rightarrow Y Z W$. Finally, by transitivity, using (a) and (c), we have $X \rightarrow Y Z W$, and the set accumulation rule (4) has been demonstrated. ∎

We state without proof the rather startling result that *all* valid rules of implication among FDs can be derived from Armstrong's Axioms. In fact, if F is any set of FDs, and $X \rightarrow Y$ is an FD that cannot be shown by Armstrong's Axioms to be implied by F, then there must be a table T in which all of the FDs in F hold but X → Y is false. Because of this result, Armstrong's Axioms are often referred to as being *complete*, meaning that no other rule of implication can be added to increase their effectiveness.

Recall that in Example 2.10 we pointed out that the three FDs from Example 2.8,

emp_id → emp_name, emp_id → emp_phone, and emp_id → dept_name,

allowed us to conclude that FD 1 holds:

1. emp_id → emp_name emp_phone dept_name.

This fact follows from two applications of the union rule of Theorem 2.4. The inverse implication, that FD 1 implies the first three, follows from two applications of the decomposition rule in the same theorem. Whenever we have some set of attributes X on the left of a set of FDs, we can take a union of all sets of attributes on the right of these FDs and combine the FDs into one. For example, assume we have the attributes A, B, C, D, E, F, and G in the heading of a table T, and we know that the following FDs hold:

$$B D \rightarrow A, B D \rightarrow C, B D \rightarrow E, B D \rightarrow F, \text{ and } B D \rightarrow G.$$

Then we can combine these FDs into one by successive applications of the union rule:

$$B D \rightarrow A C E F G$$

As a matter of fact, we can add the trivial dependency B D → B D and conclude

$$B D \rightarrow A B C D E F G$$

However, we normally try to avoid including information in a set of dependencies that can be derived using Armstrong's Axioms from a more fundamental set. Thus, we might want to return to the FD form of B D → A C E F G. Note that if we had another attribute H in the heading of the table T not mentioned in any FD, we could conclude that in addition to this FD, the following FD holds:

$$B D H \rightarrow A C E F G H$$

But since this FD can be derived from B D → A C E F G by using the augmentation rule, we would once again prefer this shorter FD.

EXAMPLE 2.11

List a minimal set of functional dependencies satisfied by the following table T, where we assume that it is the intent of the designer that *exactly* this set of rows lies in the table. Once again, we point out that it is unusual to derive FDs from the content of a table. Normally we determine functional dependencies from understanding the data items and rules of the enterprise. Note that we do not yet have a rigorous definition of a minimal set of FDs, so we simply try to arrive at a minimal set in an intuitive way.

T

Row #	A	B	C	D
1	a1	b1	c1	d1
2	a1	b1	c2	d2
3	a2	b1	c1	d3
4	a2	b1	c3	d4

Analysis

Let us start by considering FDs with a single attribute on the left. Clearly we always have the trivial FDs, $A \rightarrow A$, $B \rightarrow B$, $C \rightarrow C$, and $D \rightarrow D$, but we are asking for a minimal set of dependencies, so we won't list them. From the specific content of the table we are able to derive the following. (a) All values of the B attribute are the same, so it can never happen for any other attribute P (i.e., where P represents A, C, or D) that $r_1(P) = r_2(P)$, while $r_1(B) \neq r_2(B)$; thus, we see that $A \rightarrow B$, $C \rightarrow B$, and $D \rightarrow B$. At the same time no other attributes P are functionally dependent on B, since they all have at least two distinct values, and so there are always two rows r_1 and r_2 such that $r_1(P) \neq r_2(P)$, while $r_1(B) = r_2(B)$; thus, $B \nrightarrow A$, $B \nrightarrow C$, and $B \nrightarrow D$. (b) Because the D values are all different, in addition to $D \rightarrow B$ of part (a), we also have $D \rightarrow A$ and $D \rightarrow C$; at the same time D is not functionally dependent on anything else since all other attributes have at least two duplicate values. So in addition to $B \nrightarrow D$ of part (a), we have $A \nrightarrow D$ and $C \nrightarrow D$. (c) We have $A \nrightarrow C$ (because of rows 1 and 2) and $C \nrightarrow A$ (because of rows 1 and 3). Therefore, we can list all FDs (and failed FDs) with a single attribute on the left. (Letters in parentheses are keyed to the parts above that give us each fact.)

(a) $A \rightarrow B$	(a) $B \nrightarrow A$	(c) $C \nrightarrow A$	(b) $D \rightarrow A$
(c) $A \nrightarrow C$	(a) $B \nrightarrow C$	(a) $C \rightarrow B$	(a) $D \rightarrow B$
(b) $A \nrightarrow D$	(a) $B \nrightarrow D$	(b) $C \nrightarrow D$	(b) $D \rightarrow C$

By the union rule, whenever a single attribute on the left functionally determines several other attributes, as with D above, we can combine the attributes on the right: $D \rightarrow A\,B\,C$. From the analysis so far, we have the following set of FDs (which we believe to be minimal):

1. $A \rightarrow B$ 2. $C \rightarrow B$ 3. $D \rightarrow A\,B\,C$

Now consider FDs with *pairs* of attributes on the left. (d) Any pair containing D determines all other attributes, by FD 3 above and the augmentation rule, so there is no new FD with D on the left that is not already implied. (e) The attribute B, combined with any other attribute P on the left, still functionally determines only those attributes already determined by P, as we see by the following argument. If $P \nrightarrow Q$, this means there are rows r_1 and r_2 such that $r_1(Q) \neq r_2(Q)$, while $r_1(P) = r_2(P)$. But because B has equal values on all rows, we know that $r_1(B\ P) = r_2(B\ P)$ as well, so B P $\nrightarrow$ Q. Thus, we get no new FDs with B on the left.

(f) Now the only pair of attributes that does not contain B or D is A C, and since A C has distinct values on each row (examine table T again!), we know that A C $\rightarrow$ A B C D. This is new. We can show most of this by inference rules: It is trivial that A C $\rightarrow$ A and AC $\rightarrow$ C, by inclusion, and we already knew that A $\rightarrow$ B, so it is easy to show that A C $\rightarrow$ B. Thus, the only new fact we get from A C $\rightarrow$ A B C D is that A C $\rightarrow$ D, and we are searching for a minimal set of FDs, so that is all we include as FD 4 in the list below. If we now consider looking for FDs with triples of attributes on the left, we see that we can derive from the FDs we already have that any triple functionally determines all other attributes. Any triple that contains D clearly does, and the only triple not containing D is A B C, where A C alone functionally determines all other attributes. Clearly the same holds for any set of four attributes on the left.

The complete set of FDs implicit in table T is therefore the following:

$$1.\ A \rightarrow B \quad 2.\ C \rightarrow B \quad 3.\ D \rightarrow A\ B\ C \quad 4.\ A\ C \rightarrow D$$

The first three FDs come from the earlier list of FDs with single attributes on the left, while the last FD, A C $\rightarrow$ D, is the new one generated with two attributes listed on the left. It will turn out that this set of FDs is not quite minimal, despite all our efforts to derive a minimal set. We will see this after we have had a chance to define what we mean by a minimal set of FDs.

2.6.3 Closure, Cover, and Minimal Cover

The implication rules for FDs derived from Armstrong's Axioms mean that whenever a set F of functional dependencies is given, a much larger set may be implied.

Definition: Closure of a Set of FDs. Given a set F of FDs on attributes of a table T, we define the closure of F, symbolized by F^+, to be the set of all FDs implied by F.

EXAMPLE 2.12

Consider the set F of FDs given by

$$F = \{A \rightarrow B, B \rightarrow C, C \rightarrow D, D \rightarrow E, E \rightarrow F, F \rightarrow G, G \rightarrow H\}$$

By the transitivity rule, A $\rightarrow$ B and B $\rightarrow$ C together imply A $\rightarrow$ C, which must be included in F^+. Also, B $\rightarrow$ C and C $\rightarrow$ D imply B $\rightarrow$ D. Indeed, every single attribute appearing prior to the terminal one in the sequence A B C D E F G H can be shown by transitivity to functionally determine every single attribute on its right in the sequence. We also have trivial FDs such as A $\rightarrow$ A. Next, using the union rule, we can generate other FDs, such as A $\rightarrow$ A B C D E F G H. In fact, by using the union rule in different combinations, we can show A $\rightarrow$ (any nonempty subset of A B C D E F G H). There are $2^8 - 1 = 255$ such nonempty subsets. All FDs we have just derived are contained in F^+.

Functional dependencies usually arise in creating a database out of common-sense rules. In terms of ER concepts, it is clear that data items corresponding to identifiers of entities functionally determine all other attributes of that entity. Similarly, attributes of relationships are uniquely determined by the identifiers of entities that take part in the relationship. We would normally expect to start with a manageable set F of FDs in our design, but as Example 2.12 shows, the set of FDs that is implied by F could conceivably grow exponentially. In what follows, we try to find a way to speak of what is implied by a set F of FDs without this kind of exponential explosion. What we are leading up to is a way to determine a *minimal set* of FDs that is equivalent to a given set F. We will also provide an algorithm to derive such a minimal set in a reasonable length of time.

Definition: FD Set Cover. A set F of FDs on a table T is said to cover another set G of FDs on T, if the set G of FDs can be derived by implication rules from the set F, or in other words, if $G \subseteq F^+$. If F covers G and G covers F, then the two sets of FDs are said to be equivalent, and we write $F \equiv G$.

EXAMPLE 2.13

Consider the two sets of FDs on the set of attributes A B C D E:

$$F = \{B \rightarrow C\,D, A\,D \rightarrow E, B \rightarrow A\}$$

and

$$G = B \rightarrow \{C\,D\,E, B \rightarrow A\,B\,C, A\,D \rightarrow E\}$$

We will demonstrate that F covers G, by showing how all FDs in G are implied by FDs in F. In what follows we derive implications of FDs in F using the various inference rules from previous definitions and Theorem 2.4. Since in F we have (a) $B \rightarrow C\,D$ and (b) $B \rightarrow A$, by the union rule we see that (c) $B \rightarrow A\,C\,D$. The trivial functional dependency $B \rightarrow B$ clearly holds, and in union with (c), we get (d) $B \rightarrow A\,B\,C\,D$. By the decomposition rule, $B \rightarrow A\,B\,C\,D$ implies (e) $B \rightarrow A\,D$, and since (f) $A\,D \rightarrow E$ is in F, by transitivity we conclude (g) $B \rightarrow E$. This, in union with (d), gives us $B \rightarrow A\,B\,C\,D\,E$. From this, by decomposition we can derive the initial two FDs of the set G, and the third one also exists in F. This demonstrates that F covers G.

In Example 2.8 a technique was used to find *all* the attributes functionally determined by the attribute B under the set F of FDs. (This turned out to be all the attributes there were.) In general, we can do this for any set X of attributes on the left, finding all attributes functionally determined by the set X.

Definition: Closure of a Set of Attributes. Given a set F of FDs on a table T and a set X of attributes contained in T, we define the closure of the set X, denoted by X^+, as the largest set Y of attributes functionally determined by X, the largest set Y such that X → Y is in F⁺. Note that the set Y contains all the attributes of X, by the inclusion rule, and might not contain any other attributes.

Here is an algorithm for determining the closure of any set of attributes X.

ALGORITHM 2.1: Set Closure. This algorithm determines X^+, the closure of a given set of attributes X, under a given set F of FDs.

```
I = 0; X[0] = X;                            /* integer I, attribute set X[0]   */
REPEAT                                      /* loop to find larger X[I]        */
    I = I + 1;                              /* new I                           */
    X[I] = X[I-1];                          /* initialize new X[I]             */
    FOR ALL Z → W in F                      /* loop on all FDs Z → W in F      */
        IF Z ⊆ X[I]                         /* if Z contained in X[I]          */
            THEN X[I] = X[I] ∪ W;           /* add attributes in W to X[I]     */
    END FOR                                 /* end loop on FDs                 */
UNTIL X[I] = X[I-1];                        /* loop until no new attributes    */
RETURN X⁺ = X[I];                           /* return closure of X             */
```

Note that the step in this algorithm that adds attributes to X[I] is based on the set accumulation rule, proved in Theorem 2.4: If X → Y Z and Z → W, then X → Y Z W.

In our algorithm we are saying that since X → X[I] (our induction hypothesis) and after finding Z → W in F with Z ⊆ X[I], X[I] can be represented as Y Z (Y = X[I] − Z), so we can write X → X[I] as X → Y Z. Now since F contains Z → W, we conclude by the set accumulation rule that X → Y Z W, or in other words, X → X[I] ∪ W, and our induction hypothesis is maintained.

Set closure is an important milestone in our development. It gives us a general way of deciding whether a given FD is implied by a set F of FDs, without worrying about the exponential explosion that Example 2.12 showed could occur in calculating F⁺. For example, suppose we need to know if the functional dependency X → A is implied by set F of FDs. We simply calculate X⁺ under F by the set closure in Algorithm 2.1, and determine if it contains A: If so, X → A is in F⁺; that is, it is implied by F.

We will see that a key for a table is just a minimal set of attributes that functionally determines all the attributes of the table. To determine if X is a key, we just compute X⁺ under F, the set of FDs for the table's attributes, and see if it includes all of them, then check that no subset of X does the same. ■

EXAMPLE 2.14

Set Closure and a Compact Derivational Notation for It

In Example 2.13 we were given a set F of FDs, which we number:

$$\text{F: 1. B} \rightarrow \text{C D} \quad \text{2. A D} \rightarrow \text{E} \quad \text{3. B} \rightarrow \text{A}$$

Given X = B, we determined that X⁺ = A B C D E. Using Algorithm 2.1, we start with X[0] = B. Then X[1] = B, and we begin to loop through the FDs. Because of (1) B → CD, we get X[1] = B C D. As a notational device to show that C and D were added after B because of FD 1, we write this as B C D (1). The next FD, (2) A D → E, does not apply at this time, since A D is not a subset of X[1]. Next, from (3) B → A, we get X[1] = A B C D (or, in our notation to reflect derivation order, B C D (1) A (3)). Now X[0] is strictly contained in X[1] (i.e., X[1 − 1] ⊂ X[1]), so X[1 − 1] ≠ X[1].

Thus, we've made progress in the prior pass of the loop and go on to a new pass, setting X[2] = X[1] = A B C D (i.e., B C D (1) A (3)). Looping through the FDs again, we see all of them can be applied (but we skip the ones that have been applied before, since they will have no new effect), with the only new FD, (2) A D → E, giving us X[2] = A B C D E, or in the derivational notation, B C D (2) A (3) E (2). At the end of this loop, the algorithm notes that X[1] ⊂ X[2]. Progress has been made, so we go on to create X[3] and loop through the FDs again, ending up this pass with X[3] = X[2]. Since all of the FDs had been applied already, we could omit this pass by noting that fact. Note that a different *ordering* of the FDs in F can change the details of execution for this algorithm. In exercises where the derivational notation is requested to demonstrate that the proper derivation was determined, the order is crucial; for example, the derivation above yields the compact notation

$$B\ C\ D(1)A(3)E(2)$$

and *not*

$$B\ C\ D(1)E(2)A(3).$$

Given a set F of FDs on a table T, we use the following algorithm to determine a minimal set of dependencies M that covers F. The set M will be minimal in the sense that none of its FDs can be dropped in their entirety or changed by dropping any attributes on the left-hand side, without losing the property that it covers F.

ALGORITHM 2.2: Minimal Cover. This algorithm constructs a minimal set M of FDs that covers a given set F of FDs. M is known as the minimal cover of F—or, in some texts, as the canonical cover of F.

Step 1. From the set F of FDs, we create an equivalent set H of FDs, with only single attributes on the right side.

```
H = Ø;                          /* initialize H to null set        */
FOR ALL X → Y in F              /* loop on FDs in F                */
    FOR ALL A IN Y              /* loop on attributes in Y         */
        H = H ∪ {X → A};        /* add FD to H                     */
    END FOR                     /* end loop on attributes in Y     */
END FOR                         /* end loop on FDs in F            */
```

Since step 1 derives H by successive applications of the decomposition rule, and F can be reconstructed from H by successive applications of the union rule, it is obvious that F ≡ H.

Step 2. From the set H of FDs, successively remove individual FDs that are *inessential* in H. An FD X → Y is inessential in a set H of FDs, if X → Y can be removed from H, with result J, so that $H^+ = J^+$, or H ≡ J. That is, removal of the FD from H has no effect on H^+. See Figure 2.20 for an example of an inessential FD.

```
FOR ALL X → A in H              /* loop on FDs in H                */
    J = H − {X → A};            /* try removing this FD            */
    DETERMINE X⁺ UNDER J;       /* set closure algorithm 2.6.12    */
    IF A ∈ X⁺                   /* X → A is still implied by J     */
        H = H − {X → A};        /* . . . so it is inessential in H */
END FOR                         /* end loop on FDs in H            */
```

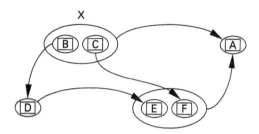

FIGURE 2.20

Example of an inessential FD: X → A.

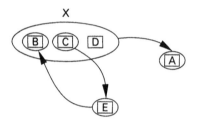

FIGURE 2.21

Example of a functional dependency X → A, where B can be dropped from the left-hand side.

Each time an FD is removed from H in step 2, the resulting set is equivalent to the previous, larger H. It is clear from this that the final resulting H is equivalent to the original. However, a number of FDs might have been removed.

Step 3. From the set H of FDs, successively replace individual FDs with FDs that have a smaller number of attributes on the left-hand side, as long as the result does not change H⁺. See Figure 2.21 for an example of an FD that can be simplified in this manner.

```
HO = H                              /* save original H                          */
FOR ALL X → A in H with #X > 1      /* loop on FDs with multiple attribute lhs  */
    FOR ALL B ∈ X                   /* loop on attributes in X                  */
        Y = X – {B}                 /* try removing one attribute               */
        J = (H – {X → A} ∪ {Y → A}; /* left-reduced FD                          */
        GENERATE Y⁺ UNDER J, Y⁺ UNDER H;  /* set closure algorithm 2.6.12       */
        IF Y⁺ UNDER H = Y⁺ UNDER J  /* if Y⁺ is unchanged                       */
            UPDATE CURRENT X → A in H  /* this is X → A in outer loop           */
                SET X = Y;          /* change X, continue outer loop            */
    END FOR                         /* end loop of attributes in X              */
END FOR                             /* end loop on FDs in H                     */
IF H <>HO                           /* if FD set changed in Step 3              */
    REPEAT STEP 2 AND THEN GOTO STEP 4  /* retest: some FDs may be inessential now */
```

Step 4. From the remaining set of FDs, gather all FDs with equal left-hand sides and use the union rule to create an equivalent set of FDs M where all left-hand sides are unique.

```
M = Ø;                                    /* initialize M to null set        */
FOR ALL X → A in H                        /* loop on FDs in H                */
    IF THIS FD IS FLAGGED, CONTINUE;      /* if already dealt with, loop     */
    FLAG CURRENT FD;                      /* deal with FDs with X on left    */
    Y = {A};                              /* start with right-hand side A    */
    FOR ALL SUCCESSIVE X → B in H         /* nested loop                     */
        FLAG CURRENT FD;                  /* deal with all FDs, X on left    */
        Y = Y ∪ {B};                      /* gather attributes on right      */
    END FOR                               /* gathering complete              */
    M = M ∪ {X → Y};                      /* combine right sides of X → ?    */
END FOR                                   /* end outer loop on FDs in H      */
```

We state without proof that this algorithm grows in execution time only as a polynomial in n, the number of attributes in the listed FDs of F (counting repetitions). Step 3 is the most costly, since we need to perform the set closure algorithm once for each attribute on the left-hand side of some FD in H. Note that if we performed step 3 before step 2, we would not have to go back and repeat step 2, as prescribed at the end of step 3 above; however, in general it would take more work for the costly step 3 without the cleanup action of step 2 occurring first. ∎

EXAMPLE 2.15

Construct the minimal cover M for the set F of FDs, which we number and list:

  F: 1. A B D → A C, 2. C → B E, 3. A D → B F, 4. B → E

Note that it is important to *rewrite* the set of FDs as you begin each new step where the FDs have changed, so you can refer to individual ones easily in the next step.

Step 1. We apply the decomposition rule to FDs in F, to create an equivalent set with singleton attributes on the right-hand sides (rhs) of all FDs. H =

  1. A B D → A, 2. A B D → C, 3. C → B, 4. C → E

  5. A D → B, 6. A D → F, 7. B → E

Step 2. We consider cases corresponding to the seven numbered FDs in H.

1. A B D → A is trivial and thus clearly inessential (since A B D^+ contains A), so it can be removed. The FDs remaining in H are (2) A B D → C, (3) C → B, (4) C → E, (5) A D → B, (6) A D → F, and (7) B → E.

2. A B D → C cannot be derived from the other FDs in H by the set closure algorithm, Algorithm 2.1, because there is no other FD with C on the right-hand side. (A B D^+, with FD (2) missing, will not contain C. We could also go through the steps of Algorithm 2.1 to demonstrate this fact. See also substep 6, below.)

3. Is C → B inessential? Is it implied under the set of other FDs that would remain if this were taken out: {(2) A B D → C, (4) C → E, (5) A D → B, (6) A D → F, (7) B → E}? To see if C → B is inessential, we generate C^+ under this smaller set of FDs. (We use the set closure Algorithm, 2.1, to generate X^+ in what follows, and use the derivational notation introduced in Example 2.14.) Starting with C^+ = C, FD (4) gives us C^+ = CE. To indicate the use of FD (4) notationally, we write C^+ = CE (4). Now with FD (3) removed, no other left side of an FD is contained in the set C E, so we have reached the full closure of the attribute C. Since C^+ doesn't contain B, (3) C → B is essential and remains in H.

4. C → E is inessential as shown by the working out of set closure on C with FD (4) missing. We get C^+ = C B (3) E (7). Thus, since E is in C^+ after FD (4) is removed, we can drop FD (4). The FDs remaining in H are (2) A B D → C, (3) C → B, (5) A D → B, (6) A D → F, and (7) B → E.

5. Is A D → B inessential under the set of FDs that remain with (5) missing: {(2) A B D → C, (3) C → B, (6) A D → F, and (7) B → E}? In the set closure algorithm, A D^+ = A D F (6) and nothing more. So FD (5) is essential and cannot be removed.

6. Is A D → F inessential given the set of other FDs that would remain: {(2) A B D → C, (3) C → B, (5) A D → B, (7) B → E}? Clearly with this set of FDs we can derive A D^+ to contain A D B (3) C (2) E (7), all the attributes there are on the right except F, so we cannot derive A D → F without FD (6). Another way to say this is that with FD (6) removed, no FD has F on its right-hand side, so A D → F cannot be implied.

7. Is B → E inessential under the set of other FDs that remains: {(2) A B D → C, (3) C → B, (5) A D → B, (6) A D → F}? The answer is no, since deriving B^+ with this set of FDs gives only B.

   We end step 2 with the set H = {(2) A B D → C, (3) C → B, (5) A D → B, (6) A D → F, (7) B → E}, which should be renumbered for ease of reference in step 3.

   H = 1. A B D → C,   2. C → B,   3. A D → B,   4. A D → F,   5. B → E

Step 3. We start with FD (1) and note that there are multiple attributes on the left-hand side; we call this set on the left side of FD (1), X = A B D. Therefore, we need to try to reduce this set X by removing any single attributes and creating a new set J of FDs each time.

Drop A? We try to do away with the attribute A in FD (1), so the new set J is given by: (1) B D → C, (2) C → B, (3) A D → B, (4) A D → F, (5) B → E. To show that this reduction gives an equivalent set of FDs, we need to show that B D^+ (under H) is the same as B D^+ (under J). The risk here is that B D+ under J will functionally determine more than B D^+ under H, since J has an FD with only B D on the left that H does not. We claim that the two sets H and J are equivalent FD sets if and only if B D^+ (under H) is the same as B D^+ (under J). So we calculate B D^+ under H to be B D E (5), and that's all. Under J, B D+ is B D C (1) E (5). Since these are different, we can't replace (1) A B D → C with (1) B D → C.

Drop B? We repeat the method. Now J contains (1) A D → C, (2) C → B, (3) A D → B, (4) A D → F, (5) B → E, and A D^+ under J is A D C (1) B (2) F (4) E (5). But under H, A D^+ = A D B (3) F (4) E (5) C (1). These are the same sets, but note the different order of generation. You need to use derivational notation with the proper order to show that the set closure algorithm is being applied on the proper FD set. Under H, FD (3) is the first one that expands the A D^+ closure, and FD (1) comes in the second pass. Under J, we can use each FD as we come to it in order on the first pass. In any event, since A D^+ under H is the same as A D^+ under J, we can reduce FD (1) to A D on the left-hand side, and the FD set H is now

   H = 1. A D → C,   2. C → B,   3. A D → B,   4. A D → F,   5. B → E

Drop D? We have already considered dropping A from the left side of FD (1), A B D → C, and we don't need to repeat this now that B is dropped. But we must consider dropping D. Now J will contain: (1) A → C, (2) C → B, (3) A D → B, (4) A D → F, and (5) B → E, and we need to consider taking A^+ under H(A^+ = A) and under J(A^+ = A C (1) B (2) E (5)). Since they are different, we cannot remove D from FD (1).

We note FD (2), C → B, cannot be reduced on the left side, and (3) A D → B also cannot be reduced on the left side, since A⁺ and D⁺ under H will contain only these attributes, whereas under the relevant J the closures will contain B. The argument that (4) A D → F cannot be reduced is similar.

Now since the set of FDs in H has changed in this pass through step 3, we need to return to step 2. When we reach FD (3) and consider dropping it, (3) A D → B, we find now that A D⁺ under {(1) A D → C, (2) C → B, (4) A D → F, (5) B → E} gives A D C (1) B (2), so since A D⁺ contains B with FD 3 missing, this FD is inessential and may be dropped. (Surprised? Repeating step 2 is a crucial step!) The final answer out of step 3 is

H = 1. A D → C,   2. C → B,   3. A D → F,   4. B → E

This set is minimal. If you wish, you can perform step 2 and step 3 a final time to assure yourself there are no other changes.

Finally, step 4 leads to the final set of FDs.

H = 1. A D → C F,   2. C → B,   3. B → E

To understand what we have accomplished, you might go through Example 2.15 and think about each change that was made in the set of FDs, then try to use Armstrong's Axioms to demonstrate that each change that was actually performed will result in the same FD closure. (Don't duplicate the set closure argument, but instead find a direct proof that the change is legal.)

EXAMPLE 2.16

The set of functional dependencies stated in Example 2.10 for the emp_info database,

1. emp_id → emp_name emp_phone dept_name
2. dept_name → dept_phone dept_mgrname
3. skill_id → skill_name
4. emp_id skill_id → skill_date skill_lvl

already forms a minimal set; that is, the minimal cover Algorithm 2.2 will not reduce it further. We leave this derivation as an exercise.

The algorithm for finding a minimal cover of a set F of FDs will be crucial in later sections for algorithms to perform appropriate design by the method of normalization.

2.7 LOSSLESS DECOMPOSITIONS

The process of normalization depends on being able to *factor* or *decompose* a table into two or more smaller tables, in such a way that we can recapture the precise content of the original table by joining the decomposed parts.

Definition: Lossless Decomposition. For any table T with an associated set of functional dependencies F, a *decomposition* of T into k tables is a set of tables {T₁,

$T_2, \ldots, T_k$} with two properties: (1) for every table T_i in the set, Head(T_i) is a proper subset of Head(T); (2) Head(T) = Head(T_1) $\cup$ Head(T_2) $\cup \ldots \cup$ Head(T_k).

Given any specific content of T, the rows of T are projected onto the columns of each T_i as a result of the decomposition. A decomposition of a table T with an associated set F of FDs is said to be a *lossless decomposition*, or sometimes a *lossless-join decomposition* if, for any possible future content of T, the FDs in F guarantee that the following relationship will hold:

$$T = T_1 \bowtie T_2 \bowtie \ldots \bowtie T_k$$

When a table T is decomposed, it is sometimes not possible to recover all the information that was originally present in some specific content of table T by joining the tables of the decomposition, not because we don't get back all the rows we had before, but because we get back other rows that were not originally present.

EXAMPLE 2.17

A Lossy Decomposition

Consider the following table ABC:

ABC

A	B	C
a1	100	c1
a2	200	c2
a3	300	c3
a4	200	c4

If we factor this table into two parts, AB and BC, we get the following table contents:

AB

A	B
a1	100
a2	200
a3	300
a4	200

BC

B	C
100	c1
200	c2
300	c3
200	c4

However, the result of joining these two tables is

AB Join BC

A	B	C
a1	100	c1
a2	200	c2
a2	200	c4
a3	300	c3
a4	200	c2
a4	200	c4

This is *not* the original table content for ABC! Note that the same decomposed tables AB and BC would have resulted if the table we had started with was ABCX, with content equal to AB Join BC above, or either of two other tables, ABCY or ABCZ.

ABCY

A	B	C
a1	100	c1
a2	200	c2
a2	200	c4
a3	300	c3
a4	200	c4

ABCZ

A	B	C
a1	100	c1
a2	200	c2
a3	300	c3
a4	200	c2
a4	200	c4

Since we can't tell what table content we started from, information has been lost by this decomposition and the subsequent join. This is known as a *lossy decomposition*, or sometimes a *lossy-join decomposition*.

The reason we lost information in the decomposition of Example 2.17 is that attribute B has duplicate values (200) on distinct rows of the factored tables (with a2 and a4 in table AB and with c2 and c4 in table BC). When these factored tables are joined again, we get cross-product rows that did not (or might not) exist in the original:

a2	200	c4

and

a4	200	c2

EXAMPLE 2.18

A Different Content for Table ABC

Now let's say that table ABC started with a different content, one that had no duplicate values in column B.

ABC

A	B	C
A1	100	c1
A2	200	c2
A3	300	c3

The question is this: If we decompose this table ABC into the two tables AB and BC as we did in Example 2.17, is the resulting decomposition lossless? The answer is no, because the definition of a lossless decomposition requires that the join of the factored tables recapture the original information for *any possible future content* of the original table. But the table ABC content we have just shown could change with the insert of a single row to give the content of Example 2.17. There doesn't seem to be any rule that would keep this from happening.

What sort of rule would we need to limit all possible future content for table ABC so that the decomposition into tables AB and BC would be lossless? Of course, functional dependencies spring to mind, because they represent rules that govern future content of a table. Notice that in the previous definition of a lossless decomposition, a set F of FDs is considered to be part of the table T definition.

Definition: Database Schema. A database schema is the set of headings of all tables in a database, together with the set of all FDs that the designer wishes to hold on the join of those tables.

EXAMPLE 2.19

Table ABC with a Functional Dependency

Assume that table ABC is defined, which obeys the functional dependency $B \rightarrow C$. Now the table content of Example 2.18 is perfectly legal:

ABC

A	B	C
a1	100	c1
a2	200	c2
a3	300	c3

But if we tried to insert a fourth row to achieve the content of Example 2.17,

| a4 | 200 | c4 |

this insert would fail because it would break the functional dependency B → C. A new row with a duplicate value for B must also have a duplicate value for C in order for B → C to remain true:

| a4 | 200 | c2 |

Is it true, then, that this new content for ABC can be decomposed and then rejoined losslessly? The answer is yes. Starting with:

ABC

A	B	C
a1	100	c1
a2	200	c2
a3	300	c3
a4	200	c2

if we factor this table into two parts, AB and BC, we get the following table contents:

AB

A	B
a1	100
a2	200
a3	300
a4	200

BC

B	C
100	c1
200	c2
300	c3

Note that four rows are projected onto three in table BC because of duplicate values. Now when these two tables are joined again, the original table ABC with the functional dependency B → C results.

Because of the functional dependency B → C in table ABC of Example 2.19, the projection of ABC on BC will always have *unique values* for attribute B. Recall that this means attribute B is a *key* for table BC. The reason that the decomposition of ABC into AB and BC is lossless is that no cross terms can ever arise in joining them: Although duplicate values for column B can occur in table AB, every row in table AB joins with a *unique* row in table BC (assuming that this B value exists in table BC, as it always would in an initial decomposition that projects rows from ABC). This is reminiscent of what happened with our CAP database when we joined `orders` with `customers`. We simply extended rows of `orders` with more information about individual customers. Although duplicate values can exist in the `cid` column of the `orders` table, the `cid` values in the `customers` table are unique, so every row in `orders` joins to exactly one row in `customers`.

We generalize the preceding discussion somewhat to deal with sets of attributes.

Theorem 2.5. Given a table T and a set of attributes $X \subseteq \text{Head}(T)$, the following two statements are equivalent: (1) X is a superkey of T; (2) $X \to \text{Head}(T)$; that is, the set of attributes X functionally determines *all* attributes in T. Equivalently: $X^+ = \text{Head}(T)$.

PROOF. (1) implies (2). If X is a superkey of table T, then for any content of table T, two distinct rows of T must always disagree on X; that is, distinct rows cannot agree in value on all attributes of X. But from this it is clear that two rows u and v cannot agree on X and disagree on some other column in Head(T) (since if two rows agree in X, then they both represent the same row), and this means that $X \to \text{Head}(T)$.

   (2) implies (1). Similarly if $X \to \text{Head}(T)$, then for any possible content of T, two rows in T cannot agree in value on X and simultaneously disagree on Head(T). But if the two rows u and v don't disagree on any attributes of Head(T), then they must be the same row. Therefore, this argument has shown that two distinct rows cannot agree in value on X, and therefore X is a superkey for T. ∎

We have reached a point where we can give a general rule for the kind of lossless decomposition we will need in performing normalization.

Theorem 2.6. Given a table T with an associated set F of functional dependencies valid on T, a decomposition of T into two tables $\{T_1, T_2\}$ is a lossless decomposition of T if and only if $\text{Head}(T_1)$ and $\text{Head}(T_2)$ are both proper subsets of $\text{Head}(T)$, $\text{Head}(T) = \text{Head}(T_1) \cup \text{Head}(T_2)$ (i.e., all attributes of T are duplicated either in T_1 or T_2), and one of the following functional dependencies is implied by F:

   1. $\text{Head}(T_1) \cap \text{Head}(T_2) \to \text{Head}(T_1)$

or

   2. $\text{Head}(T_1) \cap \text{Head}(T_2) \to \text{Head}(T_2)$.

PROOF. We take as given table T, its decomposition into T1 and T2, and FD 1, $\text{Head}(T1) \cap \text{Head}(T_2) \to \text{Head}(T_2)$. (The case with FD 2 is proven similarly.)

In what follows, we denote by X the set of attributes $\text{Head}(T_1) \cap \text{Head}(T_2)$; Y is the set of attributes in $\text{Head}(T_1) - \text{Head}(T_2)$, and Z is the set of attributes in $\text{Head}(T_2) - \text{Head}(T_1)$. To begin, we note by the definition of decomposition that T_1 and T_2 are projections of T, and $\text{Head}(T_1) \cup \text{Head}(T_2) = \text{Head}(T)$. From this we can demonstrate that $T \subseteq T_1 \bowtie T_2$. Every column of T appears in $T_1 \bowtie T_2$, and if u is a row in T, we say that the projection of u on $\text{Head}(T_1)$ is given by y_1x_1, a concatenation of attribute values, where y_1 represents values for attributes in Y and x_1 represents values for attributes in X; similarly, x_1z_1 is the projection of u on $\text{Head}(T_2)$. Clearly the projection of u on $\text{Head}(T_1)$ has the same values as the projection of u on $\text{Head}(T_2)$ on all attributes in $X = \text{Head}(T_1) \cap \text{Head}(T_2)$, and by the definition of join, row u, a concatenation $y_1x_1z_1$, will appear in $T_1 \bowtie T_2$.

Now we show under the given assumptions that $T1 \bowtie T_2 \subseteq T$. Assume that from row u in T, we get by projection a row y_1x_1 in T_1. Similarly assume that from row v in T, we get row x_2z_2 in T_2, with x_2 representing values for attributes in X. Now assume that the two rows y_1x_1 and x_2z_2 in T_1 and T_2 are joinable so that x_1 is identical in all attribute values to x_2, and $y_1x_1z_2$ is in $T_1 \bowtie T_2$. This is the most general possible form for a row in $T_1 \bowtie T_2$, and we have only to show that the row is also in T. We denote the additional attribute values of u that project on y_1x_1 in T by z_1, so that $u = y_1x_1z_1$, and claim that $z_1 = z_2$. This is because the row u is identical to v in the attributes of X, and $X \rightarrow \text{Head}(T_2)$, so in particular $X \rightarrow \text{Head}(T_2) - \text{Head}(T_1) = Z$, and since u and v are alike on X, they must be alike on attributes of Z. Thus, $z_1 = z_2$ and row $y_1x_1z_2$ that is in $T_1 \bowtie T_2$ is identical to row $y_1x_1z_2$ in T.   ∎

EXAMPLE 2.20

In Example 2.19, we demonstrated a decomposition of table T with heading A B C and functional dependency $B \rightarrow C$, into two tables T_1 and T_2 with $\text{Head}(T_1) = A B$ and $\text{Head}(T_2) = B C$. If we apply Theorem 2.6, we have $\text{Head}(T_1) \cap \text{Head}(T_2) \rightarrow \text{Head}(T_2)$; that is, A B $\cap$ B C $\rightarrow$ B C, or $B \rightarrow B C$, which is clear from $B \rightarrow C$.

EXAMPLE 2.21

Consider the table custords from Example 2.18, created by joining customers with orders. Clearly ordno is a key for custords, since it has unique values, and the reader can also verify that we have the FD cid $\rightarrow$ Head(customers). Now we note that Head(customers) $\cap$ Head(orders) = cid, the key for customers, so Head(customers) $\cap$ Head(orders) $\rightarrow$ Head(customers). Thus, by Theorem 2.6, custords has a lossless join decomposition into custs and ords, with the same headings as customers and orders, respectively (we would need to verify that the rows projected from custords onto custs and ords give the same rows that we're used to in customers and orders). The reason that this decomposition seems intuitive is that by joining customers and orders, we extend each of the rows in the orders table with columns from customers associated with the unique cid value in that row. It seems clear, therefore, that we don't lose any information by decomposing the join back onto the headings of customers and orders. Of course, we might have lost some information originally in creating custords—if there were some customers who didn't place any orders, for example. But our lossless decomposition starts with the table custords and guarantees that no information is lost in the decomposition.

Theorem 2.6 shows how to demonstrate that a decomposition of a table T into two tables $\{T_1, T_2\}$ is a lossless decomposition. In cases where three or more tables exist in the decomposition, $\{T_1, T_2, \ldots, T_k\}$, with $k \geq 3$, we can demonstrate losslessness by using the two-table result in a recursive manner.

EXAMPLE 2.22

Lossless Join Decomposition with Multiple Tables

Assume that we are given the table T with Head(T) = A B C D E F and the FD set given by (1) A B $\rightarrow$ C, (2) A $\rightarrow$ D, and (3) B $\rightarrow$ E. Notice there is no FD for the attribute F, but A B forms a key for A B C D E, since its closure includes all these attributes. Therefore, the key for table T must be A B F, since the key must functionally determine everything in Head(T). A perfectly acceptable lossless decomposition of T is $\{T_1, T_2, T_3, T_4\}$, where Head(T_1) = A B C (the keys for these tables are underlined), Head(T_2) = A D, Head(T_3) = B E, and Head(T_4) = A B F. The union of these tables contains all the attributes in T, so we merely need to demonstrate losslessness. Note that if we join tables in the following order by pairs, each parenthesized table join so far will ensure a lossless decomposition with the table that is joined next by Theorem 2.6.

$$((T_1 \bowtie T_2) \bowtie T_3) \bowtie T_4$$

We note that Head(T_1) = A B C, Head(T_2) = A D, Head($T_1 \bowtie T_2$) = A B C D, Head(T_3) = B E, and Head(($T_1 \bowtie T_2$) $\bowtie T_3$) = A B C D E. Thus, the following FDs yield losslessness for the multitable join desired.

Head(T_1) $\cap$ Head(T_2) = A $\rightarrow$ Head(T_2) = A D, because of (2) A $\rightarrow$ D
Head($T_1 \bowtie T_2$) $\cap$ Head(T_3) = B $\rightarrow$ Head(T_3) = B E, because of (3) B $\rightarrow$ E
Head(($T_1 \bowtie T_2$) $\bowtie T_3$) $\cap$ Head(T_4) = A B $\rightarrow$ Head(T_1) = A B C, because of
   (1) A B $\rightarrow$ C

Since the join operator is associative, losslessness does not require a specific order of join and we can remove the parentheses in the expression (($T_1 \bowtie T_2$) $\bowtie T_3$) $\bowtie T_4$.

In the last few sections we have developed algorithms to determine a minimal set of FDs for a given set F and defined what is meant by a lossless decomposition. In the coming section, we learn how a minimal set of FDs helps us create an appropriate normal form decomposition for a database.

```
emp_id        dept_name       skill_id
emp_name      dept_phone      skill_name
emp_phone     dept_mgrname    skill_date
                              skill_lvl


(1) emp_id → emp_name emp_phone dept_name
(2) dept_name → dept_phone dept_mgrname
(3) skill_id → skill_name
(4) emp_id skill_id → skill_date skill_lvl
```

FIGURE 2.22

Data items and FDs for the employee information database.

2.8 NORMAL FORMS

Let us return now to the example of bad database design from Section 2.5 that motivated the long mathematical digression of the last two sections. Recall that we wish to create a database on a set of data items given in Figure 2.15, with rules of interrelatedness stated in the set of functional dependencies in Example 2.1. We repeat these here as Figure 2.22.

    We started with a 1NF table, emp_info, that combined all these data items (see Figure 2.16) and noted a number of design problems, referred to as *anomalies*. In the following section, we perform a sequence of table factorizations, which are in fact lossless decompositions, to eliminate redundancies from the employee information database.

    As explained earlier, a database schema is the set of headings of all tables in a database together with a set of all FDs intended by the designer. The emp_info table in Figure 2.23, together with the FDs given, make up such a database schema.

2.8.1 A Succession of Decompositions to Eliminate Anomalies

One anomaly of the database represented in Figure 2.23 is that if the number of skills for some employee goes to zero in the emp_info table, no row of any kind will remain for the employee. We have lost the phone number and the department the employee works in because of deleting this skill. At the end of Section 2.5, we proposed a solution for this anomaly by factoring the emp_info table into two tables, the emps table and the skills table, whose column names were given in Figure 2.17 and are repeated in Figure 2.24.

    When the emps and skills tables were originally proposed, a number of features of this factorization were mentioned without justification. We are now in a position to demonstrate these points.

emp_info

emp_id	emp_name	...	skill_id	skill_name	skill_date	skill_lvl
09112	Jones	...	44	librarian	03-15-99	12
09112	Jones	...	26	PC-admin	06-30-98	10
09112	Jones	...	89	word-proc	01-15-97	12
14131	Blake	...	26	PC-admin	05-30-98	9
14131	Blake	...	89	word-proc	09-30-99	10
...	...	...	...	...	...	...

(1) emp_id → emp_name emp_phone dept_name
(2) dept_name → dept_phone dept_mgrname
(3) skill_id → skill_name
(4) emp_id skill_id → skill_date skill_lvl

FIGURE 2.23

Employee information schema with a single table, emp_info.

emps		skills
emp_id		emp_id
emp_name		skill_id
emp_phone		skill_name
dept_name		skill_date
dept_phone		skill_lvl
dept_mgrname		

(1) emp_id → emp_name emp_phone dept_name
(2) dept_name → dept_phone dept_mgrname
(3) skill_id → skill_name
(4) emp_id skill_id → skill_date skill_lvl

FIGURE 2.24

Employee information schema with two tables, emps and skills.

Proposition 2.1. The key for the emp_info table is the attribute set emp_id and skill_id. This is also key for the skills table, but the emps table has a key consisting of the single attribute emp_id.

PROOF. By Theorem 2.5 we can determine a superkey for a table T by finding a set of attributes $X \subseteq Head(T)$ such that $X \to Head(T)$. Then, to show the set X is a key, we need merely show that no properly contained subset Y of X has this property. We start our search by finding the set closure of X for all attribute sets X found on the left-hand side of any of the FDs in Figure 2.23, repeated here.

1. `emp_id → emp_name emp_phone dept_name`
2. `dept_name → dept_phone dept_mgrname`
3. `skill_id → skill_name`
4. `emp_id skill_id → skill_date skill_lvl` ∎

Starting with X = `emp_id skill_id` (the left side of FD 4 above), we use Algorithm 2.1 and the FD set F given to determine X^+. Starting from X^+ = `emp_id skill_id` and applying FD 4, we get X^+ = `emp_id skill_id skill_date skill_lvl`. Next, applying FD 3, since `skill_id` is in X^+, we add `skill_name` to X^+. Applying FD 1, since `emp_id` is in X^+, we add the right-hand side of FD 1 to get X^+ = `emp_id skill_id skill_date skill_lvl skill_name emp_name emp_phone dept_name`. Finally, we apply FD 2, and since `dept_name` is now in X^+, we add the right-hand side of FD 2 to get X^+ = `emp_id skill_id skill_date skill_lvl skill_name emp_name emp_phone dept_name dept_phone dept_mgrname`. This final list contains all the attributes in `emp_info`—that is, Head(`emp_info`). By the definition of X^+, this means that

(2.1) `emp_id skill_id → Head(emp_info)`

By Theorem 2.75 then, `emp_id skill_id` is a superkey for `emp_info`.

To show that `emp_id skill_id` is in fact a key for `emp_info`, we need only show that no subset (either `emp_id` or `skill_id` alone) functionally determines all these attributes. Let us take the closure of the set `emp_id` to find what attributes are functionally determined. We can immediately apply FD 1 to get `emp_id → emp_id emp_name emp_phone dept_name`. Next we can apply FD 2, and derive

(2.2) `emp_id → emp_id emp_name emp_phone dept_name dept_phone dept_mgrname`

Since `skill_id` is not in the right-hand set of (2.2), no other FDs can be applied, so this is the maximum right-hand set that is functionally determined by `emp_id`.

Finally, starting with `skill_id` alone in the set X to be closed, FD 3 is the only one that can be applied, and we see that the maximum right-hand set functionally determined by `skill_id` is given as

(2.3) `skill_id → skill_id skill_name`

Neither (2.2) nor (2.3) contains all attributes of `emp_info`, and thus we can conclude from (2.1) that

(2.4) `emp_id skill_id` is a key for the `emp_info` table

In addition, we note from (2.2) that `emp_id` functionally determines all attributes in the `emps` table of Figure 2.24, and since no subset of a singleton set can be on the left side of an FD,

(2.5) `emp_id` is a key for the `emps` table

Finally, we note that the `skills` table has attributes that are not functionally determined by either `emp_id` or `skill_id` individually, `skill_lvl` is not on the right-hand side in either (2.2) or (2.3), and therefore the only possible key for the `skills` table is `emp_id skill_id`:

(2.6) `emp_id skill_id` is a key for the `skills` table

Proposition 2.2. The factorization of the `emp_info` table into the `emps` and `skills` tables is a true lossless decomposition.

PROOF. To see that this is a valid decomposition, we note that Head(emps) $\cup$ Head(skills) = Head(emp_info). Furthermore, Head(emps) $\cap$ Head(skills) = `emp_id`, and since functional dependency (2.2) shows that `emp_id` $\rightarrow$ Head(emps), by Theorem 2.6, the decomposition is lossless. ∎

From Proposition 2.2, we see that the decomposition that brings us from the `emp_info` table of Figure 2.23 to the `emps` and `skills` tables of Figure 2.24 will always allow us to recapture any content of `emp_info` by a join of the two factored tables. But the real motivation for this decomposition was to deal with the various anomalies mentioned earlier.

How did the delete anomaly mentioned in Section 2.5 arise in the `emp_info` table of Figure 2.23? The basic reason is that the pair of attributes `emp_id skill_id` form the key for that table, but there are attributes that we wish to keep track of that are functionally determined by a single one of those two attributes, `emp_id`. If we delete the last `skill_id` value for some specific `emp_id`, we no longer have any (`emp_id skill_id`) pairs with that specific `emp_id`, *but we still have information that is dependent only on* `emp_id`, *which we don't want to lose!* Putting this in terms of the ER model, employees are real entities whose attributes we want to keep track of (and so the employee identifier, `emp_id`, shows up on the left of a functional dependency).

In the decomposition of Figure 2.24, we factored the `emps` table out of the `emp_info` table so that we wouldn't lose information in this way. With this new schema, we can keep a row for a given employee in the `emps` table even if the employee has no skills. Recall that the insert anomaly is the inverse face of the delete anomaly, making it impossible to insert a new employee without skills—a trainee—into the `emp_info` table. As before, this problem is solved by factoring out the `emps` table, since a new row can be inserted into `emps` that doesn't have any join to a row of the `skills` table. As far as the update anomaly is concerned, this problem arises in the `emp_info` table once again because attributes dependent only on `emp_id` are in a table with key `emp_id skill_id`; we can therefore have multiple rows with the same employee phone number in this table that must all be updated at once. Once again, factoring out the `emps` table solves this problem, because each employee is now represented by a single row.

The question now is this: Are there any more anomalies remaining in the database schema of Figure 2.24? The answer, perhaps unsurprisingly, is yes. There is another anomaly of the kind we have just analyzed in the `skills` table. This table has the primary key (`skill_id emp_id`), and we recall FD 3 of Figure 2.22:

(2.7) `skill_id → skill_name`

What this FD seems to be saying is that `skills` is an entity in its own right, that `skill_id` is an identifier for the entity, and that `skill_name` is a descriptor. (There might be two distinct skills with different `skill_id` values but the same `skill_name`, since `skill_name → skill_id` is not an FD that is implied by the list we presented.) But recall that the key we have discovered for the skills table is `emp_id skill_id`. This situation seems to be symmetric with the one that caused us to factor out the table `emps` from `emp_info`. Can we construct (for example) a delete anomaly of the kind that led to this step? The answer is yes, for if we assume that some skill is rare and difficult to master, and we suddenly lose the last employee who had it, we would no longer have any information about the skill at all, neither the `skill_id` nor the `skill_name`. We therefore need to factor out another table to solve this anomaly, and we see the result in Figure 2.25.

From examination of the new `emp_skills` table and `skills` table of Figure 2.25, it should be clear that these two tables form a lossless decomposition of the `skills` table of Figure 2.24. Indeed, the three tables of Figure 2.25 form a lossless decomposition of the single `emp_info` table we started with in Figure 2.23. Most importantly, we have dealt with the anomalies that arise from keeping attributes of skills entities in a table with a key of two attributes. In terms of the ER model,

emps	emp_skills	skills
emp_id	emp_id	skill_id
emp_name	skill_id	skill_name
emp_phone	skill_date	
dept_name	skill_lvl	
dept_phone		
dept_mgrname		

(1) `emp_id → emp_name emp_phone dept_name`

(2) `dept_name → dept_phone dept_mgrname`

(3) `skill_id → skill_name`

(4) `emp_id skill_id → skill_date skill_lvl`

FIGURE 2.25

Employee information schema with three tables.

what we have just done is to factor out the relationship emp_skills from the two entities Emps and Skills.

Consider now the three tables of Figure 2.25. Everything in the emps table, as we showed earlier in Proposition 2.1, is functionally determined by the singleton attribute emp_id; a similar situation holds with the skills table, as we see from the FD in (2.7); in the emp_skills table, a glance at (2.2) and (2.3) makes it clear that no remaining attributes in this table are dependent on a subset of the (emp_id skill_id) key. We ask then if any further anomalies can remain in these tables. Once more, the answer is yes!

To see how this is possible, consider what would happen if we had a large reorganization in the company, so that every employee in one department are to be transferred to other departments (even the manager will be transferred—presumably, at some later time, different employees will take their place in the department that has just been emptied). Now notice that when the last employee is removed, there remains no row in the emps table containing information about the department: We have lost even the phone number of the department and the name it goes under! The solution to this problem is obvious: We must factor out a separate table for departments. This will result in the emp_info database of Figure 2.26; this database is in 3NF, or equivalently in this case, in BCNF. We will give definitions for these normal forms shortly.

With the factorization of the depts table of Figure 2.26, the update anomaly relating to department information will no longer trouble us. In terms of the ER model, what we have done is to differentiate between the two entities Emps and Depts, between which there is a many-to-one relationship (represented by the foreign key dept_name in the emps table).

At this point, we claim that the database schema of Figure 2.26 is in some sense a final result—no anomalies remain in the representation to trouble us. For the

emps	depts	emp_skills	skills
emp_id	dept_name	emp_id	skill_id
emp_name	dept_phone	skill_id	skill_name
emp_phone	dept_mgrname	skill_date	
dept_name		skill_lvl	

(1) emp_id → emp_name emp_phone dept_name
(2) dept_name → dept_phone dept_mgrname
(3) skill_id → skill_name
(4) emp_id skill_id → skill_date skill_lvl

FIGURE 2.26

Employee information database schema in 3NF (also in BCNF).

rationale to justify this statement, we look to the four FDs listed that must be maintained in the database, which we refer to in what follows as the set F of FDs. In every case where we have noted an anomaly in earlier schemas, the underlying reason for the anomaly has turned out to hinge on the fact that some attribute (it could have been a set of attributes in a different schema) on the left-hand side of an FD in F might have multiple duplicate occurrences (or possibly zero occurrences) in the table where it appeared. The solution was to create a separate table, placing the attributes on the left-hand side of this FD, together with all attributes on the right-hand side in that table, while the attributes on the right-hand side were removed from the table where they previously appeared. Look carefully at the successive decompositions presented in Figures 2.23 through 2.26 to see that this is an accurate description of what was done. Since the attributes on the left-hand side of the FD are in both the old and the new tables and determine all other attributes in the new table, the decomposition is lossless. Thus, FD 1 generates the emps table, FD 2 the depts table, FD 3 the skills table, and FD 4 the emp_skills table. Since no more FDs exist in F, we maintain that no more anomalies will arise, and therefore no further decomposition is necessary. Thus, we have reached a final form.

2.8.2 Normal Forms: BCNF, 3NF, and 2NF

The tables in the final schema of Figure 2.26 each have unique candidate keys, which we may think of as primary keys for the tables. One way to characterize why no further decomposition is needed to address anomalies in these tables is to say that all functional dependencies involving attributes of any single table in this schema arise from the table keys alone. We provide definitions to make this idea precise.

Definition. Given a database schema with a universal table T and a set of functional dependencies F, let $\{T_1, T_2, \ldots, T_k\}$ be a lossless decomposition of T. Then a functional dependency $X \rightarrow Y$ of F is said to be preserved in the decomposition of T, or alternatively the decomposition of T preserves the functional dependency $X \rightarrow Y$, if for some table T_i of the decomposition, $X \cup Y \subseteq \text{Head}(T_i)$. When this is the case, we also say that the FD $X \rightarrow Y$ is preserved in T_i or that it lies in T_i or is in T_i.

EXAMPLE 2.23

We have derived a number of successive decompositions of the employee information schema of Figure 2.23 with a universal table and a set F of FDs: a decomposition with two tables (Figure 2.24), three tables (Figure 2.25), and four tables (Figure 2.26). Each of these decompositions preserves all dependencies in F. For example, in the four-table decomposition of Figure 2.26, FD 1 lies in the emps table, FD 2 lies in the depts table, FD 3 lies in the skills table, and FD 4 lies in the emp_skills table.

Because every FD in F is preserved in one of the four tables of Figure 2.26, whenever any single table in the schema is updated, it is possible to verify that any FD affected by the update is still valid by testing its validity in that single table, without any need for a join. This is the motivation for seeking to preserve functional dependencies in a decomposition.

Definition: Boyce-Codd Normal Form. A table T in a database schema with FD set F is said to be in Boyce-Codd normal form (BCNF) when the following property holds. For any functional dependency $X \rightarrow A$ implied by F that lies in T, where A is a single attribute that is not in X, X must be a superkey for T. A database schema is in BCNF when all the tables it contains are in BCNF.

Consider a table T, and let $X \rightarrow A$ be a functional dependency in T. If the BCNF property holds for this case, then X is a superkey, so for some set K of attributes representing a key for T, $K \subseteq X$. (Note that there might be a number of different sets $K_1, K_2, \ldots$ that are candidate keys for T, as we consider in Example 2.26 below.) If the BCNF property fails, then X does not contain a key set K, and $K - X$ is nonempty for all K. Then two cases are possible: either (1) $X - K$ is empty for some K—that is, $X \subset K$, and we say that some attributes of T are functionally determined by a *proper subset* X of a key K; or (2) $X - K$ is nonempty for all K, so some attributes are determined by a set X at least partially outside each K. In the second case, we say that some attributes of T are functionally determined by a *different* set of attributes that does not contain and is not contained in any key set.

EXAMPLE 2.24

In the `emp_skills` table of Figure 2.26, the only key consists of the set `emp_id skill_id`, as we can easily demonstrate by set closure arguments: Any set of attributes that functionally determine all attributes in the `emp_skills` table must contain both of these attributes. We claim that the table is in BCNF and will demonstrate this in Example 2.25. As we just pointed out, the BCNF property implies that no attributes of this table are functionally determined by any *subset* of this key set, or any *different* set of attributes that does not contain this key set.

In the `skills` table of Figure 2.24, the unique key for this table consists of the two attributes `emp_id skill_id`, while the FD `skill_id → skill_name` also lies in the table. Clearly the left-hand side of this FD is a *subset* of the key `emp_id skill_id`. Because of this, the BCNF property fails for this table (and we pointed out that an anomaly arose requiring us to perform further decomposition).

In the `emps` table of Figure 2.24 (identical to the `emps` table in Figure 2.25), the unique key for the table consists of the attribute `emp_id`, while the FD `dept_name → dept_phone` is implied by FD 2 of F and lies in the table. Since the left side of this FD is *different* from the key set (neither a subset nor a superset), the BCNF property fails, and further decomposition is necessary. Note, by the way, that a table `emps2` containing all the attributes of `emps` except the attribute `dept_phone` would still not obey the BCNF property. Although the FD `dept_name → dept_phone` does not lie in the table `emps2`, the FD `dept_name → dept_mgrname`, which is also implied by FD 2, does lie in `emps2`.

EXAMPLE 2.25

We claim that the database schema of Figure 2.26 is in BCNF. We need to show that for any functional dependency X → A implied by F that lies in one of the tables of Figure 2.26, where A is an attribute not in X, then X contains a key for that table. We have shown in Example 2.23 that for the set of tables in Figure 2.26, one FD of F lies in each table, and this FD has as its left side the key for the table. This does not quite conclude the issue, however, because we also need to consider all FDs that are implied by F; that is, all FDs that are true in the schema. In Proposition 2.1, FDs (2.1), (2.2), and (2.3), we determined the closure of all sets X of attributes that fall on the left side of three FDs of F, and showed that these three sets form keys for three of the tables. For the fourth FD, we need merely take the closure of dept_name, which is easily seen to consist of the set dept_name, dept_phone, dept_mgrname, or Head(depts):

(2.8) dept_name → Head(depts)

Now we claim that all attribute sets Z that do not contain one of the sets X, the left side of an FD in F and therefore a key for one of the Figure 2.26 tables, must have trivial closure $Z^+ = Z$. This follows from the fact that no FDs of the form X → Y exist with $X \subseteq Z$, and by Algorithm 2.1, no attributes will ever be added to Z's set closure.

From this we can easily see that all of the tables in Figure 2.26 are BCNF, because if X → A holds and A is an attribute not contained in the attribute set X, then X → A X, and therefore X^+ is not identical to X. But we have just shown that any attribute set that does not contain a table key has a trivial closure, and this must mean that X contains some table key K. In that table, we have also included all attributes functionally determined by K, and therefore A is in that table as well.

EXAMPLE 2.26

Suppose we changed the rules in the employee information database so that dept_mgrname was a second identifier of the Departments entity duplicating the effect of dept_name. This would add a new FD to the set F: dept_mgrname → dept_name; by transitivity, since dept_name is a key for the depts table in Figure 2.26, dept_mgrname would also be a key. The question now is whether the depts table is still in BCNF. And the answer is yes, because the BCNF property was specially constructed not to require a unique key for the table. The only thing that has changed in the depts table is that there are now two keys, but any FD of the form X → Y in this table has the necessary property that X contains dept_mgrname or X contains dept_name.

Recall that every FD in F is *preserved* in one of the four tables of Figure 2.26, so that whenever any table in the schema is updated, it is possible to verify that an affected FD still holds by testing data items in that table alone. We would like to be able to guarantee that this property, preservation of FDs, can always be achieved starting from a universal table and proceeding to a lossless decomposition into BCNF. Unfortunately this is not true, because the BCNF criterion for a table is too strict.

EXAMPLE 2.27

We wish to add a number of attributes to the employee information database of Figure 2.22 to keep track of the full addresses of all employees (assumed to be living in the United States):

```
emp_cityst, emp_straddr, emp_zip
```

Here `emp_cityst` reflects the city and state, `emp_zip` the zip code, and `emp_straddr` the street name, number, and apartment, if any. We find that when we reach the decomposition of Figure 2.26, the `emps` table contains all of these attributes in addition to the ones that are already there, as we see in Figure 2.27.

We assume that each employee is required to provide a single address, so it is clear that the `emp_id` value functionally determines all these new attributes, and FD (1) is modified accordingly:

1. `emp_id → emp_name emp_phone dept_name emp_straddr emp_cityst emp_zip`

No keys for any other tables of Figure 2.26 are affected, and the key for the `emps` table is still `emp_id`.

But the post office has assigned zip codes to cover regions of a city (determined by street address) and never to cross city boundaries, so we also have the following new FDs to add to the set F:

5. `emp_cityst emp_straddr → emp_zip` regions of city determine the zip code
6. `emp_zip → emp_cityst` zip codes never cross city boundaries

Since the left side of FD 5, `emp_cityst emp_straddr`, is not a superkey of the `emps` table, we need to perform a further decomposition to achieve the BCNF property. If we did not do this and deleted the last employee in some zip code, we would lose what information we have about that zip code—namely, what city and state it is associated with. After the prescription explained in the discussion following Figure 2.26, we place the attributes on the left side of FD 5, together with all attributes on the right side of this FD in a separate

emps
emp_id
emp_name
emp_phone
dept_name
emp_cityst
emp_straddr
emp_zip

FIGURE 2.27

The `emps` table extended to contain employee addresses.

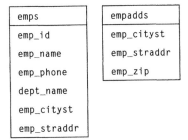

FIGURE 2.28

A 3NF decomposition of Figure 2.27.

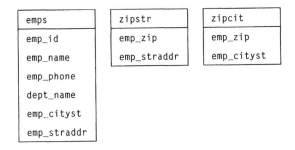

FIGURE 2.29

A BCNF decomposition of Figure 2.28.

table (`empadds`), while the attributes on the right side are removed from the table where they previously appeared (`emps`). The result is given in Figure 2.28. This is a perfectly reasonable lossless decomposition of the previous table (lossless because of Theorem 2.6, since `emp_cityst emp_straddr` is a key for `empadds`, and this is also the intersection of the headings of the two tables). We note too that `emp_zip emp_straddr` is an alternate candidate key for `empadds`, since taking the closure of this set, we get `emp_cityst` by FD 6. Thus, we have the new derived FD 7. It is easy to see by closure that no other candidate keys exist for empadds.

7. `emp_zip emp_straddr → emp_cityst` (FD derived from (5) and (6))

The `emps` table of Figure 2.28 is now in BCNF, since neither FD 5 nor 6 lies in `emps`, and the only remaining FD, FD 1, requires that any superkey for the table will contain `emp_id`. This decomposition also preserves FDs 5 and 6, which both lie entirely in the `empadds` table. However, at this point FD 6 forces us to perform further decomposition of `empadds` to achieve BCNF, since `emp_zip → emp_cityst`, and `emp_zip` does not contain either candidate key of `empadds`. Clearly this new decomposition must contain at most two attributes in each table, and we require one table (`zipcit` in Figure 2.29) to have heading `emp_zip emp_cityst` to contain FD 6. The other table only has two possible pairs of attributes for a heading, the left-hand side of FD 5 or the left-hand side of FD 7, both keys for the `empadds` table. Choosing the left-hand side of FD 5, `emp_cityst emp_straddr`, would not result in a lossless decomposition, since the only attribute it would have in common with zipcit is emp_cityst, and this wouldn't contain a key for either table. We therefore choose BCNF decomposition shown in the figure.

The decomposition of Figure 2.29 is lossless for the following reasons: emp_zip is the key for the zipcit table, the intersection of Head(zipstr) and Head(zipcit), so that join is lossless; the union of the zipstr and zipcit table headings contains all the attributes of the previous empadds table, so zipstr and zipcit join to form the empadds table of Figure 2.28; the empadds table formed a lossless join with the emps table, so the three tables join losslessly. Furthermore, both new tables in Figure 2.29 are in BCNF form. The only FD in the zipcit table is FD 6, and emp_zip is the key. The zipstr table has no FD in it, so the unique key includes both attributes, emp_zip emp_straddr, which was also an alternate candidate key for the empadds table of Figure 2.28.

But the decomposition in Figure 2.29 does *not* preserve dependencies of the extended set F, since FD 5 does not lie in either table. This can have an unfortunate effect, in that we must perform programmatic checking to ensure that a given street address, city, state, and zip code being entered conform with the post office assignment.

It seems that we have gone too far in decomposition if we really want to preserve functional dependencies. What we'd like is a definition for normal form that allows us to stop at Figure 2.28 and not press on to Figure 2.29. In order to do this, we have to come up with a new definition for normal form (3NF, as it turns out). We achieve this with the following definitions.

Definition: Prime Attribute. In a table T, an attribute A is said to be prime if and only if the attribute A exists in some key K for the table.

Definition: Third Normal Form. A table T in a database schema with FD set F is said to be in third normal form (3NF) under the following condition. For any functional dependency X → A implied by F that lies in T, where A is a single attribute that is not in X, one of the two following properties must hold: either (1) X is a superkey for T; or (2) A is a prime attribute in T. A database schema is in 3NF when all the tables it contains are in 3NF.

EXAMPLE 2.28

Consider the database schema of Figure 2.29. Each of the tables in this schema is in BCNF, and therefore in 3NF. The BCNF prescription for a table requires that the table has property 1 of the 3NF definition, and it doesn't permit the "escape clause" of property 2. Therefore, any table in BCNF is also in 3NF, but the reverse doesn't hold.

EXAMPLE 2.29

Consider the empadds table of Figure 2.28. This table is in 3NF but not in BCNF. The reason we required a further decomposition of this table was that the empadds table of Figure 2.28 had as a key the attributes emp_cityst emp_straddr, and at the same time FD 6, emp_zip

→ `emp_cityst` lies in the table. This is an FD whose left-hand side does not contain a key of `empadds`, so the FD does not fulfill the BCNF property. However, we note that the attribute on the right of this FD does lie in some key and is therefore prime. Thus, the FD does fulfill property 2 of the 3NF definition.

EXAMPLE 2.30

We are given a table T with Head(T) = A B C D, and FD set F as follows:

1. A B → C D,   2. D → B

Clearly A B is a candidate key for T, and we see by closure that A D is another one: A D$^+$ = A D B (2) C (1). It is easy to confirm that there are no others. Now we maintain that table T is already in 3NF, because the only FD implied by F that does not contain A B on the left-hand side (and is not trivial) depends on FD 2, D → B, and since B is a prime attribute, table T is 3NF by the "escape clause" of property 2.

If we did wish to decompose T losslessly to a BCNF form, we would want to start by projecting on a table that contains FD 2—that is, table T_2 with Head(T_2) = B D. Then we will want table T_1 to contain a candidate key for T as well as the attribute C, but if we create T_1 with Head(T_1) = A B C, then the headings of T_1 and T_2 won't intersect in D and therefore won't join losslessly. Thus, we must create table T_1 with Head(T_1) = A D C. And so we have the BCNF decomposition {A D C, B D}.

In decomposing a database with a given set of functional dependencies F to achieve a normal form, the BCNF and 3NF forms are often identical, as we saw in Example 2.28. They differ exactly when there exist two nontrivial FDs implied by F, X → Y and Z → B, where Z ⊂ X ∪ Y and B ∈ X. In Example 2.30, FD 1 gave us A B → C D and FD 2 gave us D → B, with D ⊂ C D and B ∈ A B. Further decomposition to achieve BCNF will cause dependencies not to be preserved. Many database designers aim for a 3NF design that preserves dependencies.

Another definition for a table property, known as *second normal form* (2NF), is weaker than 3NF and of mainly historical interest, since no advantage arises from stopping short of 3NF. When a table fails to be 3NF, it must contain a valid nontrivial functional dependency X → A, where A is nonprime and X is not a superkey for T. Recall from the previous discussion of BCNF that if X is not a superkey for T, then two cases are possible: Either X ⊂ K for some K and we say that some attributes of T are functionally determined by a proper subset X of a key K, or else X − K is nonempty for all keys K in T, and we say that some attributes of T are functionally determined by a different set of attributes that does not contain and is not contained in any key set. This latter case is also known as a *transitive dependency*, since we have K → X for any key K, and given X → A, the functional dependency K → A is implied by transitivity. A table in 2NF is not allowed to have attributes that are functionally determined by a proper subset of a key K, but it may still have transitive dependencies.

Definition: Second Normal Form. A table T in a database schema with FD set F is said to be in second normal form (2NF) under the following condition: For any functional dependency X → A implied by F that lies in T, where A is a single attribute that is not in X and is nonprime, X is not a proper subset of any key K of T. A database schema is in 2NF when all the tables it contains are in 2NF.

2.8.3 An Algorithm to Achieve Well-Behaved 3NF Decomposition

For a number of technical reasons it turns out that the approach of successive decompositions to achieve a 3NF lossless join decomposition preserving functional dependencies is distrusted by many practitioners. This is the only approach we have seen, used in Figures 2.23 through 2.26. Problems can arise because the set F of functional dependencies used in the successive decompositions has not been carefully defined, and as we saw in Section 2.6, numerous equivalent sets F are possible. Algorithm 2.3 provides a straightforward method to create the desired decomposition.

ALGORITHM 2.3 This algorithm, given a universal table T and set F of FDs, generates a lossless join decomposition of T that is in 3NF and preserves all FDs of F. The output is a set S of headings (sets of attributes) for tables in the final database schema.

```
REPLACE F WITH MINIMAL COVER OF F;           /* use algorithm 2.6.13        */
S = Ø;                                        /* initialize S to null set    */
FOR ALL X → Y in F                            /* loop on FDs found in F      */
    IF. FOR ALL Z ∈ S, X ∪ Y ⊄ Z             /* no table contains X → Y     */
        THEN S = S ∪ Heading (X ∪ Y);        /* add new table Heading to S  */
END FOR                                       /* end loop on FDs             */
IF, FOR ALL CANDIDATE KEYS K FOR T            /* if no candidate Keys of T   */
        FOR ALL Z ∈ S, K ⊄ Z                  /* are contained in any table  */
    THEN CHOOSE A CANDIDATE KEY K AND         /* choose a candidate key      */
        SET S = S ∪ Heading(K);              /* and add new table to S      */
```

Note that the function Heading(K) generates a singleton set containing the set K of attributes, which can then be added to the set S, which is a set of sets of attributes. ∎

EXAMPLE 2.31

To see why the choice of a candidate key might sometimes be necessary in Algorithm 2.3, consider the following small school database. We are given a universal table T with heading.

    Head(T) = instructor class_no class_room text

and FD set F given by

    F = {class_no → class_room text}

In ER terms, there is an entity Classes, identified by class_no, and the actual class holds all its meetings in the same classroom with a unique text. Whether or not there is an entity Class_rooms with identifier class_room is a matter of opinion. Since there is no FD with class_room on the left, such an entity would have no descriptor attributes, and so no table exists for it in the relational model; thus, we can think of class_room as a descriptor attribute for Classes if we like. The same argument can be applied to the text attribute in Head(T). But the instructor attribute in Head(T) is a different situation. Since the instructor attribute is not functionally determined by class_no, there can be several instructors for the same class, and since instructor does not determine class_no, this means that one instructor might teach several classes. From this it is clear that instructors have independent existence from classes and in fact represent an entity, Instructors. Indeed, table T contains a relationship between Instructors and Classes.

By standard BCNF/3NF normalization, since the attributes class_room and text depend on class_no alone in table T, we need to factor T into two tables, T_1 and T_2, with

    Head(T_1) = class_no class_room text
    Head(T_2) = instructor class_no

But in Algorithm 2.3, only table T_1 will be created in the initial loop on FDs, since the instructor attribute does not figure in any FDs of F. However, it is clear from the standard set closure approach that the unique candidate key for T is class_no instructor. Therefore, the loop on candidate keys in Algorithm 2.3 is necessary to create table T_2 for set S.

It is commonly said that the normalization approach and the ER approach reinforce one another. Example 2.31 gives an example of this. Without considering functional dependencies, it is not clear why the instructor data item must represent an entity but the class_room data item might not. On the other hand, the ER approach gives the motivation for why the loop on candidate keys in Algorithm 2.3 is appropriate to create table T_2. We need table T_2 to represent the relationship between the Instructors and Classes entities.

2.8.4 A Review of Normalization

In the normalization approach to database design, we start out with a set of data items and a set F of functional dependencies that the designer wishes to see maintained by the database system for any future content of the database. The data items are all placed in a single universal table T, and the set F is replaced by an equivalent minimal cover; then the designer determines a decomposition of this table into a set of smaller tables $\{T_1, T_2, \ldots, T_k\}$, with a number of good properties, as follows.

1. The decomposition is lossless, so that $T = T_1 \bowtie T_2 \bowtie \ldots \bowtie T_n$.
2. To the greatest extent possible, the only FDs $X \to Y$ in table T_i arise because X contains some key K in T_i; this is the thrust of the BCNF/3NF definitions.
3. All FDs in F of the form $X \to Y$ are preserved in tables of the decomposition.

The value of property 2 is that we can avoid the various anomalies defined in Section 2.5. It is also important that with these normal forms we can guarantee that functional dependency will not be broken, so long as we guarantee the uniqueness of all keys for a table. The Create Table statement of SQL gives us a way to define such keys K for a table, and the uniqueness of these keys will then be guaranteed by the system for all SQL table Update statements that follow (an update that breaks such a uniqueness constraint will result in an error). As we will see a bit later, such a uniqueness condition is a particularly easy condition to check with an index on the key columns involved, whereas a general functional dependency $X \rightarrow Y$ in a table T_i, where multiple rows with the same value for X can exist, is more difficult. Standard SQL does not provide a constraint to guarantee such general dependencies against update errors.

The value of property 3 should also be clear, since we want to guarantee that all functional dependencies provided by the designer hold for any possible content of the database. Property 3 means that FDs won't cross tables in the final database schema, so that if an update of one table occurs, only FDs in that table need to be tested by the system. On the other hand, the very decomposition we are providing does result in a certain amount of join testing, since the standard lossless join decomposition into tables T_1 and T_2 leads to a key for one table with attributes in both—that is, a key consisting of $(Head(T_1) \cap Head(T_2))$. Standard SQL provides a constraint, known as *referential integrity*, that can be imposed with the Create Table statement to guarantee that these attribute values continue to make sense between the two tables they join, a constraint also known as a *foreign key condition*.

To sum up, the standard 3NF decomposition eliminates most anomalies and makes it possible to verify efficiently that desired functional dependencies remain valid when the database is updated.

Additional normal forms exist that are not covered here, 4NF and 5NF. In particular, fourth normal form, or 4NF, is based on an entirely new type of dependency, known as a *multivalued dependency*. You are referred to Teorey (1994) and Ullman (1988) for good descriptions of these.

We should mention at this point that *overnormalization*, factoring a database into more tables than are required in order to reach 3NF when this is the goal, is considered a bad practice. For example, if we factored the `depts` table into two tables, one with `dept_name` and `dept_phone` and a second with `dept_name` and `dept_mgrname`, we would certainly still have a 3NF database, but we would have gone further than necessary in decomposition. Unnecessary inefficiencies would arise in retrieving all department information together, because of the join that would now be required.

2.9 ADDITIONAL DESIGN CONSIDERATIONS

The ER and normalization approaches both have weaknesses. The ER approach, as it is usually presented, is extremely dependent on intuition, but if intuition fails there is little fallback. As we saw in Example 2.31, it can be difficult on the basis of intuition alone to determine whether a data item represents an entity or not. It helps to have the concept of functional dependency from normalization. Normalization is more mathematically based and mechanical in its application, but the idea that you can write down a complete set of FDs as a first step of logical database design is often a delusion; it may be found later that some have been missed. The intuitive exercise of trying to discover entities and relationships and weak entities and so on aids the designer in discovering FDs that might otherwise be overlooked.

Another factor affecting the normalization approach is that a certain amount of judgment might be needed to decide whether a particular functional dependency should be reflected in a final design. Consider the CAP database schema we discussed earlier in the chapter. It might seem that all functional dependencies that hold for the database are reflections of the table key dependencies, so that all the tables are in BCNF. However, there is a rather unexpected FD of the following form:

(2.9) `qty price discnt → dollars`

That is, for each order, from the order quantity, product price, and customer discount we can calculate the dollars charge for the order. This is expressed in the following SQL Insert statement (2.10). Clearly the FD as it stands crosses tables, and therefore the decomposition does not preserve dependencies. Note that we can create another table, `ddollars`, that contains all the attributes on both sides of FD (2.9), `qty price discnt dollars`, and simultaneously remove the `dollars` attribute from `orders`. The result, a five-table schema for CAP including the `ddollars` table, is a 3NF design that would be arrived at by Algorithm 2.3. The unique key for the `ddollars` table is `qty price discnt`, and the only FD is given in (2.9). There is a problem with this design, however. Whenever we want to retrieve the dollar cost for an order, we have to perform a join with `products` to get `price`, `customers` to get `discnt`, and `ddollars` to read off the `dollars` value for the given `qty`, `price`, and `discnt`. Is all this really necessary?

If we consider the original motivations for a decomposition such as this, we have two: to remove anomalies and to validate all FDs whenever changes are made in the data. But do we really want to validate this FD by a unique key constraint in normal form? Presumably when a new order is inserted, the program logic does a calculation of the dollars amount to store, something like this:

(2.10) `exec sql insert into orders`
`            values (:ordno, :month, :cid, :aid, :pid, :qty,`
`            qty*:price - .01*:discnt*:qty*:price:`

With this Insert statement we guarantee the FD (2.9); and more than that, we guarantee an exact numerical relationship that an FD is incapable of representing. The only validation that the `ddollars` table is capable of providing is this: If a previous row exists with a given `qty`, `price`, and `discnt`, then the calculated `dollars` value will be identical. This seems like a rather strange validation, since if there are a lot of products and customers, with real variation in order sizes and some limit on the number of orders tracked, we can expect to be adding many (qty, price, discnt) triples for the first time. Thus, the unique key constraint offers no real value in verification: There is no old row with the same key to compare with it. You would much rather depend on the Insert statement (2.10) to perform the correct calculation. In this regard, it certainly makes sense to provide this insert in a tested function that must be used by all logic-performing inserts of new orders.

Now the delete and insert anomalies amount to saying that we don't want to lose track of any (qty, price, discnt) triples, but this is a questionable proposition given that we don't really value this method of validation. As for the update anomaly, we consider the case of needing to update all dollars values at once for a given (qty, price, discnt). Presumably this might happen if the price or discnt value needed to be changed for orders that were previously entered, perhaps because that value was originally entered erroneously and now has to be corrected. But this change would be so unusual and have such major ramifications for a wholesale business that it is unreasonable to assume that an inexperienced programmer might write code to correct a single row in orders by mistake. Indeed many designers would model the dollars column as an insert-only quantity that should not be updated at all (except to correct input errors). We are therefore willing to forgo the protection from the update anomaly.

We have gone into detail here to exemplify a type of situation that arises with some frequency in commercial applications, a need for *denormalization* to improve performance. Most design practitioners will agree that there is frequently a need for this.

2.9.1 Database Design Tools

A number of commercial products are aimed at providing environments to support the DBA in performing database design. These environments are provided by *database design tools*, or sometimes as part of a more general class of products known as *computer-aided software engineering* (CASE) tools. Such tools usually have a number of components, chosen from the following kinds. It would be rare for a single product to offer all these capabilities.

ER Design Editor
A common component is an interface in which a designer can construct ER diagrams, editing and making changes to the diagrams using the graphical drag-and-drop methods common to products such as the Apple Macintosh and Microsoft Windows.

ER to Relational Design Transformer
Another common component of such tools is a transformer that automatically performs a transformation of an ER design to a set of relational table definitions,

following the steps outlined in Section 2.3 and exemplified in the case study of Section 2.4.

With database design tools, the flow of development usually starts with ER design and proceeds to a relational table definition. However, a number of products deal with functional dependencies. One tool advises loading a small universal table and abstracts from these data the possible functional dependencies that might hold for the data. A transformation to BCNF/3NF for this set of FDs can then be automatically generated.

FD to ER Design Transformer

Another type of component that is sometimes offered takes a set of FDs for the database and generates a valid ER diagram to reflect the rules of the data.

As indicated in the previous section, a design that is theoretically perfect may also be inefficient in terms of performance. Thus, a good design tool tries to analyze the performance implications of a design and accepts designer decisions to perform certain kinds of denormalization to improve performance. In addition, a tool must be forgiving of errors and omissions in FDs and entity classifications, in order to produce some kind of best guess at a design that the designer can picture while making corrections. This brings up another kind of standard tool component.

Design Analyzers

These components analyze design in the current stage and produce reports that might help the DBA to correct errors of various kinds.

For an excellent overview of database design tools, you are referred to the last chapter in Batini, Ceri, and Navathe (1992).

2.10 SUGGESTIONS FOR FURTHER READING

Many variations in terminology are prevalent in the field of logical database design. The ER approach is sometimes referred to as *semantic modeling*. The real-world objects known as *entity occurrences* in our notation are often referred to in the literature as *entities*, and the *entity* in our notation that makes up a category of entity occurrences then becomes an *entity type*. Attributes are also sometimes called *properties*.

Let us try to give an idea of what is meant by semantic modeling. In a programming language, the *syntax* of the language specifies how the statements are formed out of basic textual elements. The syntax does not associate any meaning with the statements, however. A specification of how programming language statements act under all possible conditions, what the statements mean in terms of their effect, is known as the *semantics* of the language. The term *semantic modeling* implies that in the ER approach, we are getting into the topic of what data items *really mean* in order to model their behavior in terms of database structures such as relational tables.

References 1, 2, and 4 cover the topic of logical database design. Reference 1 also contains as its final section an article by David Reiner on commercial products used for database design, known as database design tools. References 3 and 5 also contain excellent coverage of many normalization concepts that are not covered in the current chapter. Reference 3, in particular, is extremely advanced and represents the state of the art in this field. Reference 6 is at the same level as this text and covers both entity–relationship and normalization.

1. C. Batini, S. Ceri, and S. B. Navathe. *Conceptual Database Design*. Benjamin-Cummings, 1992.
2. C. J. Date. *An Introduction to Database Systems*, 6th ed. Addison-Wesley, 1995.
3. David Maier. *The Theory of Relational Databases*. Computer Science Press, 1983.
4. Toby J. Teorey. *Database Modeling and Design: The Fundamental Principles*, 2nd ed. Morgan Kaufmann, 1994.
5. Jeffrey D. Ullman. *Database and Knowledge-Base Systems*, Volume 1. Computer Science Press, 1988.
6. Jeffrey D. Ullman and Jennifer Widom. *A First Course in Database Systems*. Prentice-Hall, 1997.

Data Modeling in UML

3

3.1 INTRODUCTION

Although semantic approaches to information modeling appeared in the early 1970s, no single approach has yet achieved universal adoption. By and large, the history of information systems modeling has been characterized by a plethora of techniques and notations, with occasional religious wars between proponents of different approaches. Each year, many new approaches would be proposed, leading to groans from academics who were charged with teaching the state of the art. This is referred to as the "yama" (Yet Another Modeling Approach!) or "nama" (Not Another Modeling Approach!) syndrome. Figure 3.1 shows this as a mountain of modeling methods, piled on top of one another, which nicely ties in with the Japanese meaning of *yama* (mountain), depicted as a kanji that is high in the middle and low on the ends.

While diversity is often useful, the modeling industry would benefit if practitioners agreed to use just a few standard modeling approaches, individually suited for their modeling scope, and collectively covering the tasks needed to model a wide variety of applications. This would improve communication between modelers and reduce training costs, especially in an industry with a high turnaround of employees.

Recently, the rapid rise of the Unified Modeling Language (UML) has been accompanied by claims that UML by itself is an adequate approach for modeling any software application. Some UML proponents have even been so bold as to claim that "the modeling wars are over—UML has won." This claim has been strongly rejected by several experienced data modelers, including Dave Hay, who argues that "there is no such thing as 'object-oriented analysis'" (Hay 1999a), only object-oriented design, and that "UML is . . . not suitable for analyzing business requirements in cooperation with business people" (Hay 1999b).

To date, UML is mainly used in industry for designing object-oriented program code. Although it can be used for designing databases, UML has so far had little success in displacing other approaches such as entity–relationship (ER) for this purpose. Given UML's object-oriented focus, and the dominance of relational

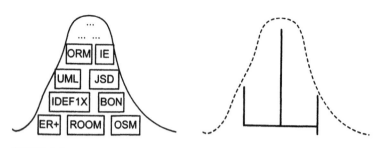

FIGURE 3.1

Yama—Japanese for "mountain."

database management systems (DBMSs), this is perhaps not surprising. Nevertheless, UML is a very important language that could well become popular for database design in the future.

Initially based on a combination of the Booch, Object Modeling Technique (OMT), and Object-Oriented Software Engineering (OOSE) methods, UML was further developed by a consortium of companies and individuals working within the Object Management Group (OMG). It includes adaptations of many other techniques (e.g., Harel's state charts) and is continually being refined and extended.

Version 1.1 of UML was adopted in November 1997 by the OMG as a language for object-oriented analysis and design. Versions 1.2, 1.3, 1.4, and 1.5 were approved in 1998, 1999, 2001, and 2003, respectively. Version 1.4.2 was accepted as a standard by the International Standards Organization (ISO). A major revision (2.0) was recommended in 2004, comprising infrastructure and superstructure specifications, plus related specifications on the Object Constraint Language (OCL) and diagram interchange. In 2007, UML 2.0 was updated to version 2.1.1 (see www.omg.org/technology/documents/formal/uml.htm). When using a UML tool, be aware that vendor support typically lags behind the latest OMG adopted version (e.g., some tools are still at UML 1.2).

As discussed later, the UML metamodel and notation have inconsistencies, with some unresolved problems being fundamental. Despite these issues, UML is the closest thing to a de facto standard in industry for object-oriented software design, and therefore is worthy of study.

The UML notation is really a set of languages rather than a single language. It includes a vast number of symbols, from which various diagrams may be constructed to model different perspectives of an application. The 9 main diagram types in UML 1.5 are use case (use case diagram); static structure (class diagram, object diagram); behavior (statechart, activity diagram); interaction (sequence diagram, collaboration diagram); and implementation (component diagram, deployment diagram). UML 2.0 extended these to 13 diagram types, as set out in Table 3.1.

Table 3.1   The 13 Predefined UML 2.0 Diagram Types

Structure	Class Object Component Deployment Package Composite Structure	
Behavior	Use Case State Machine Activity	
	Interaction	Sequence Collaboration Interaction Overview Timing

Some of these diagrams (e.g., collaboration diagrams) are useful only for designing object-oriented program code. Some (e.g., activity diagrams and use case diagrams) can be useful in requirements analysis, and some (e.g., class diagrams) have limited use for conceptual analysis and are best used for logical design.

The UML specification provides syntax and semantics for these diagram types, but not yet a process for developing UML models, other than to suggest that model development should be use case driven, iterative, and architecture centric. Various companies promote their own modeling process for UML, such as the Rational Unified Process (RUP).

Although all the UML diagram types are worth studying, this book focuses on information modeling for databases. This chapter addresses data modeling in UML, so it considers only the static structure (class and object) diagrams. Class diagrams are used for the data schema, and object diagrams provide a limited means to discuss data populations.

Like ER, UML uses attributes. Attributes are great for logical models, but are best modeled as relationships when performing conceptual analysis, since this facilitates validation and minimizes the impact of change. For such reasons, we believe the best way to develop UML data models is to first do an ORM model and then map it to UML. Since Object–Role Modeling (ORM) will be used to clarify the data modeling concepts in UML, to gain the full benefits of this clarification, you should be familiar with the ORM concepts.

No language is perfect, ORM included. Overall, UML provides a useful suite of notations for both data and process modeling, while ORM is currently focused on data modeling only.

3.2 OBJECT ORIENTATION

UML facilitates object-oriented (OO) code design because it covers both data and behavioral modeling, and lets you drill down into physical design details relevant to OO code. The class diagram in Figure 3.2 models a class whose instances are screen dialog boxes.

The class shape in Figure 3.2 has three compartments. The name compartment includes the class name, as well as a tagged value naming the author of the class. The attribute compartment lists the visibility, name, and type of each attribute. The visibility settings +, −, #, and ~ indicate whether the attribute is public, private, protected, or package. These visibility settings are software, not conceptual, issues. The size attribute is initialized to a given area value. The operation compartment specifies what operations are encapsulated in instances of the class. In this example, the operations may be implemented by methods to display the dialog box at a specific position, and to hide the dialog box.

Figure 3.3 shows another class diagram that depicts Employee and Car classes, as well as an association corresponding to the ORM fact type Employee drives Car. The association is depicted by a line between the classes. The role name "driver" on the left end of the association clarifies the intended semantics (an association reading could also be supplied). The open arrow at the right end of the association is a navigability setting indicating that fast access is required from employee instances to their car instances. This may be implemented by including

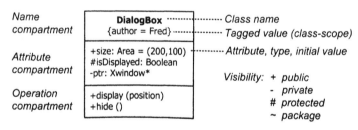

FIGURE 3.2

Example of a UML class.

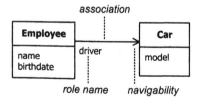

FIGURE 3.3

The navigability setting demands fast access from the Employee class to the Car class.

pointers from employee objects (software objects) to the car objects that model the cars that they drive. Navigability settings are implementation issues related to performance, not conceptual issues about the business domain.

By omitting implementation details such as attribute visibility and association navigability, class diagrams can be used for conceptual analysis. When used in this way, class diagrams are somewhat similar to ER models. But there is a significant difference arising from the OO perspective. If you look at the classes in Figures 3.2 and 3.3, what strikes you as missing?

You guessed it! No identification schemas are provided for the classes. In object-oriented programming, objects may be identified by their memory addresses or internal object identifiers (oids), so UML does not require that you provide a value-based identification scheme for use by humans in communicating about the objects. For conceptual analysis, however, such human-oriented reference schemes (e.g., dialog box numbers, employee numbers, car registration numbers) must be supplied. UML does allow you to add such attributes, but has no standard notation for declaring them to be preferred identifiers or even for declaring them to be unique. For this, we choose "{P}" for preferred reference and "{Un}" for uniqueness ($n > 0$), where n is used to disambiguate cases where the same U constraint might apply to a combination of attributes. Various UML tool vendors choose different notations for such constraints.

In Figure 3.4, for example, employee number (nr) and car registration number (regNr) attributes have been added as the primary identifiers of the Employee and Car classes, respectively. This entails that they are mandatory and unique. Additionally, the combination of employee name and birth date has been declared unique. We also dropped the navigation arrow, as it is irrelevant to the business semantics.

The requirement that each class has a value-based identification scheme distinguishes both ORM and ER from UML. ORM classifies objects into entities (non-lexical objects) and values (lexical objects) and requires each entity to be identified by a reference scheme used by humans to communicate about the entity. ORM uses *object, entity*, and *value* to mean *object instance, entity instance*, and *value instance*, respectively, appending "type" for the relevant set of all possible instances. Entities may be referenced in different ways, and typically change their state over time. Glossing over some subtle points, values are constants (e.g.,

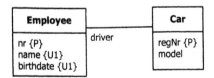

FIGURE 3.4

Adding nonstandard notations for preferred reference and uniqueness.

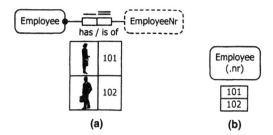

FIGURE 3.5

A simple reference scheme in ORM, shown (a) explicitly and (b) implicitly.

character strings) that basically denote themselves, so they do not require a reference scheme to be declared.

Figure 3.5(a) depicts explicitly a simple reference scheme in ORM. If an entity type has more than one candidate reference scheme, one may be declared preferred to assist verbalization of instances (or to reflect the actual business practice). A preferred reference scheme for an entity type maps each instance of it onto a unique, identifying value (or a combination of values). In Figure 3.5(a), the reference type has a sample population shown in a reference table (one column for each role). Here icons are used to denote the real-world employee entities.

Simple reference schemes may be abbreviated by enclosing the reference mode in parentheses, as in Figure 3.5(b), and an object type's reference table includes values but no icons. References verbalize as existential sentences—for example, "There is an Employee who has the `EmployeeNr 101`." Entity instances are referenced elsewhere by definite descriptions—for example, "The Employee who has the `EmpNr 101`."

In a relational database, we might use the preferred reference scheme to provide value-based identity or instead use system-generated row-ids. In an object-oriented implementation, we might use oids (hidden, system-generated object identifiers). Such choices can be added later as annotations to the model. For analysis and validation purposes, however, we need to ensure that humans have a way to identify objects in their normal communication. It is the responsibility of humans (not the system) to enforce constraints on preferred reference types. Assuming humans do enforce the reference type constraints, the system may be used to enforce the elementary fact type constraints.

UML classifies instances into objects and data values. UML *objects* basically correspond to ORM entities, but are assumed to be identified by oids. Although UML does not require entities to have a value-based reference scheme, we should include value-based reference in any UML class intended to capture all the conceptual semantics. UML *data values* basically correspond to ORM values: They are constants (e.g., character strings or numbers) and therefore require no oids to establish their identity. Entity types in UML are called *classes*, and value types are basically *data types*. Note that "object" means "object instance," not "object type." A relationship instance in UML is called a *link*, and a relationship type is called an *association*.

3.3 ATTRIBUTES

Like other ER notations, UML allows relationships to be modeled as attributes. For instance, in Figure 3.6(a) the `Employee` class has eight attributes. The corresponding ORM diagram is shown in Figure 3.6(b).

In UML, *attributes are mandatory and single valued by default.* So the employee number, name, title, gender, and smoking status attributes are all mandatory. In the ORM model, the unary predicate `smokes` is optional (not everybody smokes). UML does not support unary relationships, so it models this instead as the Boolean attribute `isSmoker` with possible values `True` or `False`. In UML, the domain (i.e., type) of any attribute may optionally be displayed after it (preceded by a colon). In this example, the domain is displayed only for the `isSmoker` attribute. By default, ORM tools usually take a closed-world approach to unaries, which agrees with the `isSmoker` attribute being mandatory.

The ORM model also indicates that `Gender` and `Country` are identified by codes (rather than names, for example). We could convey some of this detail in the UML diagram by appending domain names. For example, `Gender.code` and `Country.`

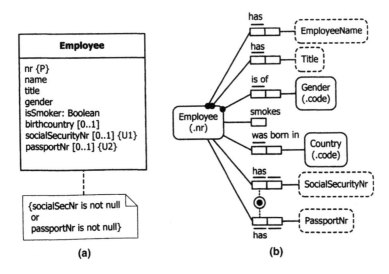

(a)   (b)

FIGURE 3.6

UML attributes (a) depicted as ORM relationship types (b).

Table 3.2 Multiplicities

Multiplicity	Abbreviation	Meaning	Note
0..1		0 or 1 (at most one)	
0..*	*	0 to many (zero or more)	
1..1	1	exactly 1	Assumed by default
1..*		1 or more (at least one)	
n..*		n or more (at least n)	$n \geq 0$
n..m		at least n and at most m	$m \geq n \geq 0$

code could be appended to gender: and birthcountry: to provide syntactic domains.

In the ORM model it is *optional* whether we record birth country, social security number, or passport number. This is captured in UML by appending [0..1] to the attribute name (each employee has zero or one birth country, and zero or one social security number). This is an example of an *attribute multiplicity constraint*. The main multiplicity cases are shown in Table 3.2. If the multiplicity is not declared explicitly, it is assumed to be 1 (exactly one). If desired, we may indicate the default multiplicity explicitly by appending [1..1] or [1] to the attribute.

In the ORM model, the uniqueness constraints on the right-hand roles (including the EmployeeNr reference scheme shown explicitly in Figure 3.5(a)) indicate that each employee number, social security number, and passport number refer to at most one employee. As mentioned earlier, UML has no standard graphic notation for such "*attribute uniqueness constraints*," so we've added our own {P} and {Un} notations for preferred identifiers and uniqueness. UML 2.0 added the option of specifying {unique} or {nonunique} as part of a multiplicity declaration, but this is only to declare whether instances of collections for multivalued attributes or multivalued association roles may include duplicates, so it can't be used to specify that instances of single-valued attributes or combinations of such attributes are unique for the class.

UML has no graphic notation for an inclusive-OR constraint, so the ORM constraint that each employee has a social security number or passport number needs to be expressed textually in an attached *note*, as in Figure 3.6(a). Such *textual constraints* may be expressed informally, or in some formal language interpretable by a tool. In the latter case, the constraint is placed in *braces*.

In our example, we've chosen to code the inclusive-OR constraint in SQL syntax. Although UML provides OCL for this purpose, it does not mandate its use, allowing users to pick their own language (even programming code). This of course weakens the portability of the model. Moreover, the readability of the constraint is typically poor compared with the ORM verbalization.

The ORM fact type `Employee was born in Country` is modeled as a `birthcountry` attribute in the UML class diagram of Figure 3.6(a). If we later decide to record the population of a country, then we need to introduce `Country` as a class, and to clarify the connection between `birthcountry` and `Country`, we would probably reformulate the `birthcountry` attribute as an association between `Employee` and `Country`. This is a significant change to our model. Moreover, any object-based queries or code that referenced the `birthcountry` attribute would also need to be reformulated. ORM avoids such semantic instability by always using relationships instead of attributes.

Another reason for introducing a `Country` class is to enable a listing of countries to be stored, identified by their country codes, without requiring all of these countries to participate in a fact. To do this in ORM, we simply declare the `Country` type to be independent. The object type `Country` may be populated by a reference table that contains those country codes of interest (e.g., "AU" denotes Australia).

A typical argument in support of attributes runs like this: "Good UML modelers would declare `Country` as a class in the first place, anticipating the need to later record something about it, or to maintain a reference list; on the other hand, features such as the title and gender of a person clearly are things that will never have other properties, and therefore are best modeled as attributes." This argument is flawed. In general, you can't be sure about what kinds of information you might want to record later, or about how important some model feature will become.

Even in the title and gender case, a complete model should include a relationship type to indicate which titles are restricted to which gender (e.g., "Mrs.," "Miss," "Ms.," and "Lady" apply only to the female sex). In ORM this kind of constraint can be captured graphically as a join-subset constraint or textually as a constraint in a formal ORM language (e.g., If $Person_1$ has a `Title` that is restricted to $Gender_1$ then $Person_1$ is of $Gender_1$). In contrast, attribute usage hinders expression of the relevant restriction association (try expressing and populating this rule in UML).

ORM includes algorithms for dynamically generating ER and UML diagrams as attribute views. These algorithms assign different levels of importance to object types depending on their current roles and constraints, redisplaying minor fact types as attributes of the major object types. Modeling and maintenance are iterative processes. The importance of a feature can change with time as we discover more of the global model, and the domain being modeled itself changes.

To promote semantic stability, ORM makes no commitment to relative importance in its base models, instead supporting this dynamically through views. Elementary facts are the fundamental units of information, are uniformly represented as relationships, and how they are grouped into structures is not a conceptual

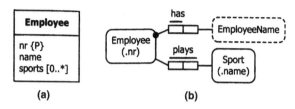

FIGURE 3.7

(a) Multivalued UML sports attribute depicted as (b) ORM $m:n$ fact type.

issue. You can have your cake and eat it too by using ORM for analysis; and if you want to work with UML class diagrams, you can use your ORM models to derive them.

One way of modeling this in UML is shown in Figure 3.7(a). Here the information about who plays what sport is modeled as the *multivalued attribute* sports. The [0..*] multiplicity constraint on this attribute indicates how many sports may be entered here for each employee. The 0 indicates that it is possible that no sports might be entered for some employees. UML uses a *null value* for this case, just like the relational model. The presence of nulls exposes users to implementation rather than conceptual issues and adds complexity to the semantics of queries. The "*" in [0..*] indicates there is *no upper bound* on the number of sports of a single employee. In other words, an employee may play many sports, and we don't care how many. If * is used without a lower bound, this is taken as an abbreviation for 0..*.

An equivalent ORM schema is shown in Figure 3.7(b). Here an optional, many: many fact type is used instead of the multivalued sports attribute. As discussed in the next section, this approach may also be used in UML using an $m:n$ association.

To discuss *class instance populations*, UML uses *object diagrams*. These are essentially class diagrams in which each object is shown as a separate instance of a class, with data values supplied for its attributes. As a simple example, Figure 3.8(a) includes object diagrams to model three employee instances along with their attribute values. The ORM model in Figure 3.8(b) displays the same sample population, using fact tables to list the fact instances.

For simple cases like this, object diagrams are useful. However, they rapidly become unwieldy if we wish to display multiple instances for more complex cases. In contrast, fact tables scale easily to handle large and complex cases.

ORM constraints are easily clarified using sample populations. For example, in Figure 3.8(b) the absence of employee 101 in the plays fact table clearly shows that playing sports is optional, and the uniqueness constraints mark out which column or column-combination values can occur on at most one row. In the EmployeeName fact table, the first column values are unique, but the second column includes duplicates. In the plays table, each column contains duplicates;

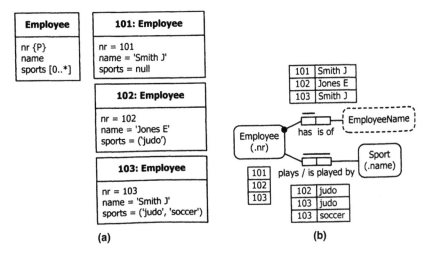

FIGURE 3.8

Populated models in (a) UML and (b) ORM.

only the whole rows are unique. Such populations are very useful for checking constraints with the subject matter experts. This validation-via-example feature of ORM holds for all its constraints, not just mandatory roles and uniqueness, since all its constraints are role based or type based, and each role corresponds to a fact table column.

As a final example of multivalued attributes, suppose that we wish to record the nicknames and colors of country flags. Let us agree to record at most two nicknames for any given flag and that nicknames apply to only one flag. For example, "Old Glory" and perhaps "The Star-Spangled Banner" might be used as nicknames for the United States' flag. Flags have at least one color.

Figure 3.9(a) shows one way to model this in UML. The [0..2] indicates that each flag has at most two (from zero to two) nicknames. The [1..*] declares that a flag has one or more colors. An additional constraint is needed to ensure that each nickname refers to at most one flag. A simple attribute uniqueness constraint (e.g., {U₁}) is not enough, since the nickname's attribute is set valued. Not only must each nickname's set be unique for each flag, but each element in each set must be unique (the second condition implies the former). This more complex constraint is specified informally in an attached note.

Here the attribute domains are hidden. Nickname elements would typically have a data type domain (e.g., `String`). If we don't store other information about countries or colors, we might choose `String` as the domain for country and color as well (although this is subconceptual, because real countries and colors are not character strings). However, since we might want to add information about these later, it is better to use classes for their domains (e.g., `Country` and `Color`). If we do this, we need to define the classes as well.

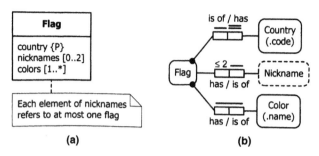

FIGURE 3.9

A flag model in (a) UML and (b) ORM.

Figure 3.9(b) shows one way to model this in ORM. For verbalization we identify each flag by its country. Since `country` is an entity type, the reference scheme is shown explicitly (reference models may abbreviate reference schemes only when the referencing type is a value type). The ≥2 frequency constraint indicates that each flag has at most two nicknames, and the uniqueness constraint on the role of `Nickname` indicates that each nickname refers to at most one flag.

UML gives us the choice of modeling a feature as an attribute or an association. For conceptual analysis and querying, explicit associations usually have many advantages over attributes, especially multivalued attributes. This choice helps us verbalize, visualize, and populate the associations. It also enables us to express various constraints involving the "role played by the attribute" in standard notation, rather than resorting to some nonstandard extension. This applies not only to simple uniqueness constraints (as discussed earlier) but also to other kinds of constraints (frequency, subset, exclusion, etc.) over one or more roles that include the role played by the attribute's domain (in the implicit association corresponding to the attribute).

For example, if the association `Flag is of Country` is depicted explicitly in UML, the constraint that each country has at most one flag can be captured by adding a multiplicity constraint of "0..1" on the left role of this association. Although `Country` and `Color` are naturally conceived as classes, `Nickname` would normally be construed as a data type (e.g., a subtype of `String`). Although associations in UML may include data types (not just classes), this is somewhat awkward; so in UML, `nicknames` might be best left as a multivalued attribute. Of course, we could model it cleanly in ORM first.

Another reason for favoring associations over attributes is stability. If we ever want to talk about a relationship, it is possible in both ORM and UML to make an object out of it and simply attach the new details to it. If instead we modeled the feature as an attribute, we would need to first replace the attribute by an association. For example, consider the association `Employee plays Sport` in Figure 3.8(b). If we need to record a skill level for this play, we can simply objectify this association as `play`, and attach the fact type `Play has SkillLevel`. A similar move can be made in UML if the `play` feature has been modeled as an association. In Figure 3.8(a), however, this feature is modeled as the sports attribute, which needs to be replaced by the equivalent association before we can add the new details about skill level. The notion of objectified relationship types or association classes is covered later.

Another problem with multivalued attributes is that queries on them need some way to extract the components, and therefore complicate the query process for users. As a trivial example, compare queries Q1 and Q2, expressed in ConQuer (an ORM query language) with their counterparts in OQL (the Object Query Language proposed by the ODMG). Although this example is trivial, the use of multivalued attributes in more complex structures can make it harder for users to express their requirements.

(Q1) List each Color that is of Flag "USA".
(Q2) List each Flag that has Color "red".
(Q1a) select x.colors from x in Flag where x.country = "USA"
(Q2a) select x.country from x in Flag where "red" in x.colors

For such reasons, multivalued attributes should normally be avoided in analysis models, especially if the attributes are based on classes rather than data types. If we avoid multivalued attributes in our conceptual model, we can still use them in the actual implementation. Some UML and ORM tools allow schemas to be annotated with instructions to override the default actions of whatever mapper is used to transform the schema to an implementation. For example, the ORM schema in Figure 3.9(b) might be prepared for mapping by annotating the roles played by `Nickname` and `Color` to map as sets inside the mapped `Flag` structure. Such annotations are not a conceptual issue, and can be postponed until mapping.

3.4 ASSOCIATIONS

UML uses Boolean attributes instead of unary relationships, but allows relationships of all other arities. Optionally, each association may be given at most one name. Association names normally start with a capital letter. *Binary associations are depicted as lines* between classes. Association lines may include elbows to assist with layout or when needed (e.g., for ring relationships). Association roles appear simply as line ends instead of boxes, but may be given role names. Once added, role names may not be suppressed. Verbalization into sentences is possible only for infix binaries, and then only by naming the association with a predicate reading (e.g., `Employs`) and using an optional marker (e.g., ▶) to denote the direction.

Figure 3.10 depicts two binary associations in both UML and ORM. On the UML diagram, the association names, their directional markers, and some role names are displayed. In UML, association names are optional, but role names are

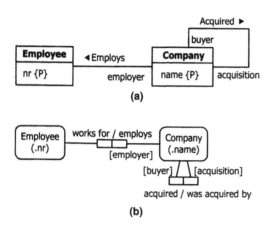

(a)

(b)

FIGURE 3.10

Binary associations in (a) UML and (b) ORM.

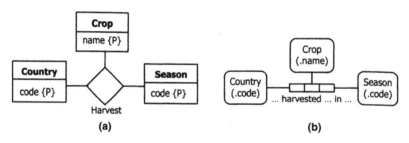

(a)   **(b)**

FIGURE 3.11

Ternary associations in (a) UML and (b) ORM.

mandatory. If a role name is not supplied, the role's name is assumed to be the name of its class (e.g., Employee). *If two or more roles are played by the same class, the roles must be given different names to distinguish them* (e.g., buyer or acquisition). In the ORM diagram, forward and inverse predicate readings are shown; at most, one of these may be omitted. Role names are optional in ORM, and their display (in square brackets) may be toggled on or off.

Ternary and higher arity associations in UML are depicted as a diamond connected by lines to the classes, as shown in Figure 3.11(a). Because many lines are used with no reading direction indicator, directional verbalization is ruled out, so the diagram can't be used to communicate in terms of sentences. This nonlinear layout also often makes it impractical to conveniently populate associations with multiple instances, unless we use role names for column names. Add to this the impracticality of displaying multiple populations of attributes, and it is clear that class diagrams are of little use for population checks.

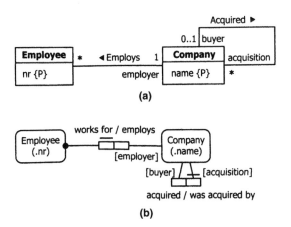

FIGURE 3.12

UML multiplicity constraints (a) and equivalent ORM constraints (b).

As discussed earlier, UML does provide object diagrams for instantiation, but these are convenient only for populating associations with a *single* instance. Adding multiple instances leads to a mess (e.g., Blaha and Premerlani, 1998, p. 31). Therefore, as noted in the *UML Notation Guide*, "the use of object diagrams is fairly limited."

The previous section discussed how UML depicts multiplicity constraints on attributes. A similar notation is used for associations, where the relevant multiplicities are written next to the relevant roles. Figure 3.12(a) adds the relevant multiplicity constraints to Figure 3.10(a). A "*" abbreviates "0..*," meaning "zero or more"; "1" abbreviates "1..1," meaning "exactly one"; and "0..1" means "at most one." If no multiplicity is supplied for an association role, "*" is assumed by default (unlike attributes, where 1 is the default multiplicity).

UML places each multiplicity constraint on the "far role," in the direction in which the association is read. Therefore, the constraints in this example mean that each company employs zero or more employees, each employee is employed by exactly one company, each company acquired zero or more companies, and each company was acquired by at most one company.

The corresponding ORM constraints are depicted in Figure 3.12(b). Recall that multiplicity covers both cardinality (frequency) and optionality. Here the mandatory role constraint indicates that each employee works for at least one company, and the uniqueness constraints indicate that each employee works for at most one company, and each company was acquired by at most one company.

For comparison purposes, Figure 3.13 depicts the $n:1$ association Moon orbits Planet in various notations. The instance diagram in Figure 3.13(a) includes a sample population of moons (p = Phobos, d = Deimos, c = Callisto) and planets (v = Venus, m = Mars, j = Jupiter). For illustration purposes, the ORM diagram in

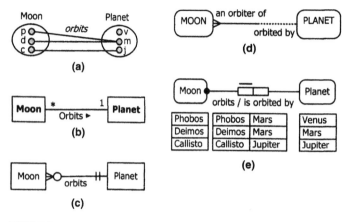

FIGURE 3.13

A mandatory:optional, n:1 association in various notations.

Figure 3.13(e) also includes the sample object and fact populations. The population is significant with respect to multiplicity constraints. Each planet orbits exactly one moon, and the same planet may be orbited by zero or more moons.

The UML (Figure 3.13(b)) and Information Engineering (Figure 3.13(c)) approaches are similar because both express the constraints in terms of multiplicities/cardinalities. In contrast, Barker ER (Figure 3.13(d)) and ORM (Figure 3.13(e)) capture some constraints in terms of mandatory/optional roles and other constraints in terms of cardinality/uniqueness constraints. As shown later, the failure of UML to separate out these two kinds of constraint prevents it from graphically capturing various cases it might otherwise have handled.

For binary associations, there are 4 possible uniqueness constraint patterns (n:1, 1:n, 1:1, m:n) and 4 possible mandatory role patterns (only the left role mandatory, only the right role mandatory, both roles mandatory, both roles optional). Therefore, if we restrict ourselves to a maximum frequency of one, there are 16 possible multiplicity combinations for binary associations. The 16 cases are shown in Figure 3.14, in both UML and ORM.

UML allows multiplicity constraints with whole numbers other than zero or one, and also supports multiplicity lists or ranges (e.g., "1..7, 10"). For such cases, ORM uses frequency constraints instead of uniqueness constraints. ORM is more expressive in this regard, since it can apply such constraints to arbitrary collections of roles, not just single roles.

For an elementary n-ary association, each internal uniqueness constraint in ORM must span at least $n - 1$ roles. In UML, a multiplicity constraint on a role of an n-ary association effectively constrains the population of the other roles combined. For example, Figure 3.15(a) is a UML diagram for a ternary association in which both Room-HourSlot and HourSlot-Activity pairs are unique. For simplicity, reference schemes are omitted.

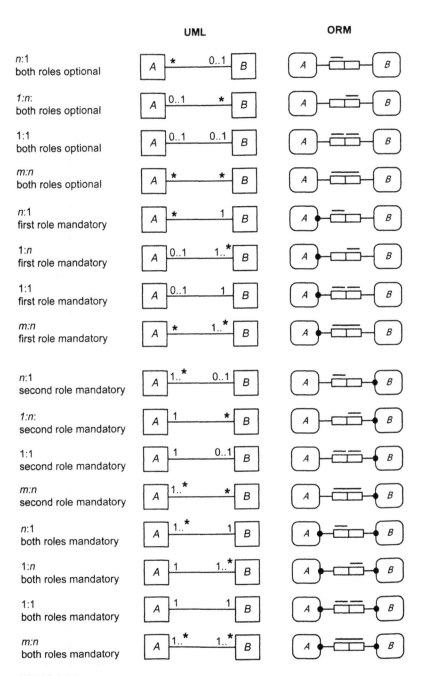

FIGURE 3.14

Equivalent constraint patterns in UML and ORM.

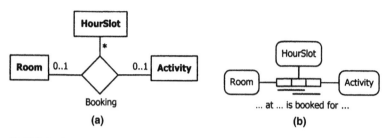

FIGURE 3.15

Constraints on a ternary in (a) UML and (b) ORM.

An ORM depiction of the same association is shown in Figure 3.15(b). The left-hand uniqueness constraint indicates that Room-HourSlot is unique (i.e., for any given room and hour slot, at most one activity is booked). The right-hand uniqueness constraint indicates that HourSlot-Activity is unique (i.e., for any given hour slot and activity, at most one room is booked). An extended version of this example was discussed in Section 1.2, where the ORM diagram better facilitated constraint checking by verbalization and population.

Because it covers some *n*-ary cases like this, UML's multiplicity constraint notation is richer than the optionality/cardinality notation of typical ER. However, there are many cases with *n*-ary associations where the multiplicity notation of UML is incapable of capturing even a simple mandatory role constraint, or a minimum frequency constraint above 1. In contrast, the mandatory, uniqueness, and frequency constraint notation of ORM can capture any possible constraint of this nature, on roles or role sequences, on predicates of any arity. So ORM is far richer in this regard.

For example, suppose we modify our room-booking example to indicate that all activities have a Room-HourSlot booking and also have unique names as well as their identifying codes. The modified example, including reference schemes, is shown in Figure 3.16 in both UML and ORM. Because UML bundles both mandatory and uniqueness into a single notion of multiplicity, it cannot capture the constraint that each activity has a booking graphically. The best we can do is add a note, as shown in Figure 3.16(a). This constraint may be expressed graphically in ORM using a mandatory role constraint, as shown in Figure 3.16(b).

This deficiency in UML is a direct consequence of choosing to attach minimum multiplicity to a role other than the immediate role. For the same reason, UML multiplicity constraints are also unable to capture various ORM frequency constraints. In general, *given any n-ary (n > 2) association, if an ORM mandatory or frequency constraint applies to at least 1 and at most n − 2 roles, this cannot be captured by a UML multiplicity constraint.* Some examples of such cases are shown in Figure 3.17. Further discussion on such cases may be found in Halpin (2000c).

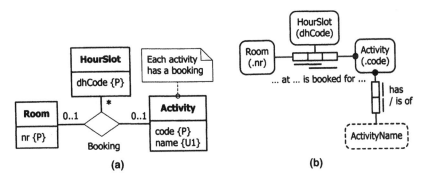

FIGURE 3.16

(a) UML resorts to a note to capture (b) a mandatory constraint in ORM.

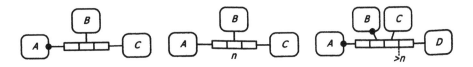

FIGURE 3.17

Some ORM constraints that can't be captured by UML multiplicities.

Unlike many ER versions, both UML and ORM allow associations to be objectified as first-class object types, *called association classes* in UML and *objectified associations* or *nested object types* in ORM. UML requires the same name to be used for the original association and the association class, impeding natural verbalization of at least one of these constructs. In contrast, ORM nesting is based on linguistic *nominalization* (a verb phrase is objectified by a noun phrase), thus allowing both to be verbalized naturally, with different readings for each.

Although UML identifies an association class with its underlying association, it displays them separately, connected by a dashed line (see Figure 3.18(a)). Each person may write many papers, and each paper is written by at least one person. Since authorship is *m:n,* the association class Writing has a primary reference scheme based on the combination of Person and Paper (e.g., the writing by person "Norma Jones" of paper 33). The optional period attribute stores how long that person took to write that paper.

Figure 3.18(b) shows an ORM schema for this domain. The objectified association Writing is marked independent (by the !) to indicate that a writing object may exist, independently of whether we record its period. ORM displays Period as an object type, not an attribute, and includes its unit.

UML allows any association (binary and above) to be objectified into a class, regardless of its multiplicity constraints. In particular, UML allows objectification of *n:1* associations, as shown in Figure 3.19(a). While this is allowed in ORM 2.0,

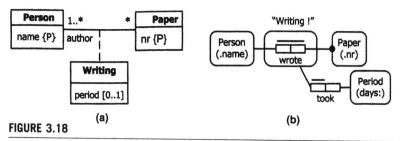

FIGURE 3.18

Writing depicted as an objectified association in (a) UML and (b) ORM.

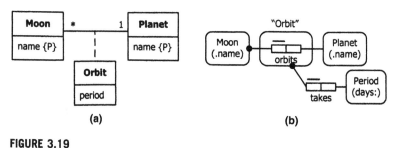

FIGURE 3.19

Objectification of an n:1 association in (a) UML and (b) ORM.

it is often a case of poor modeling. For example, given that a moon orbits only one planet, an orbital period may be related directly to the moon without including the planet. So instead of objectifying, we could model the orbital period in UML as an attribute of Moon, or in ORM as an association between Moon and Period.

Earlier we saw that UML has no graphic notation to capture ORM external uniqueness constraints across roles that are modeled as attributes in UML. Therefore, we introduced a {Un} notation to append textual constraints to the constrained attributes. Simple cases where ORM uses an external uniqueness constraint for *coreferencing* can also be modeled in UML using *qualified associations*. Here, instead of depicting the relevant ORM roles or object types as attributes, UML uses a class, adjacent to a *qualifier,* through which connection is made to the relevant association role. A qualifier in UML is a set of one or more attributes whose values can be used to partition the class, and is depicted as a rectangular box enclosing its attributes. Figure 3.20 is based on an example from the official UML specification, along with the ORM counterpart.

Here each bank account is used by at most one client, and each client may use many accounts. In the UML model, the attribute accountNr is a qualifier on the association, effectively partitioning each bank into different accounts. In the ORM model, an Account object type is explicitly introduced and referenced by combining its bank with its (local) account number.

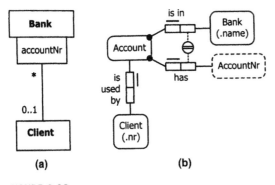

FIGURE 3.20

(a) Qualified association in UML, and (b) coreferenced type in ORM.

The UML notation is less clear and less adaptable. For example, if we now want to record something about the account (e.g., its balance) we need to introduce an Account class, and the connection to accountNr is unclear. For a similar example, see Fowler (1997, p. 92), where product is used with Order to qualify an order line association; again, this is unfortunate, since we would normally introduce a Product class to record data about products, and relevant connections are then lost.

As a complicated example of this deficiency, see Blaha and Premerlani (1998, p. 51), where the semantic connection between Node and nodeName is lost. The problem can be solved in UML by using an association class instead, although this is not always natural. The use of qualified associations in UML is hard to motivate, but may be partly explained by their ability to capture some external uniqueness constraints in the standard notation, rather than relying on nonstandard textual notations (such as our {Un} notation).

ORM's concept of an external uniqueness constraint that may be applied to a set of roles in one or more predicates provides a simple, uniform way to capture all of UML's qualified associations and unique attribute combinations, as well as other cases not expressible in UML graphical notation (e.g., cases with $m:n$ predicates or long join paths). As always, the ORM notation has the further advantage of facilitating validation through verbalization and multiple instantiation.

3.5 SET-COMPARISON CONSTRAINTS

Set-comparison constraints declare a subset, equality, or exclusion relationship between the populations of role sequences. This section compares support for these constraints in UML and ORM.

As an extension mechanism, UML allows subset constraints to be specified between *whole associations* by attaching the constraint label {subset} next to a

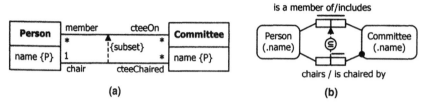

(a)   **(b)**

FIGURE 3.21

A subset constraint in (a) UML and (b) ORM.

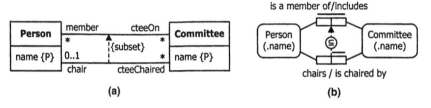

(a)   **(b)**

FIGURE 3.22

(a) A misleading UML diagram, and (b) a misleading ORM diagram.

dashed arrow between the associations. For example, the subset constraint in Figure 3.21(a) indicates that any person who chairs a committee must be a member of that committee. Figure 3.21(b) shows the same example in ORM.

ORM has a mature formalization, including a rigorous theory of schema consistency, equivalence, and implication. Since formal guidelines for working with UML are somewhat immature, care is needed to avoid logical problems. As a simple example, consider the modified version of our committee example shown in Figure 3.22(a), which comes directly from an earlier version of the UML specification, with reference schemes added. Do you spot anything confusing about the constraints?

You probably noticed the problem. The multiplicity constraint of 1 on the chair association indicates that each committee must have at least one chair. The subset constraint tells us that a chair of a committee must also be a member of that committee. Taken together, these constraints imply that each committee must have a member. Therefore, we would expect to see a multiplicity constraint of 1..* (one or more) on the Person end of the membership association. However, we see a constraint of * (zero or more) instead, which at best is misleading. An equivalent, misleading ORM schema is shown in Figure 3.22(b), where the upper role played by Committee appears optional when in fact it is mandatory.

One might argue that it is okay to leave these schemas unchanged, as the constraint that each committee includes at least one person is implied by other constraints. However, while display options for implied constraints may sometimes be a matter of taste, practical experience has shown that in cases like this

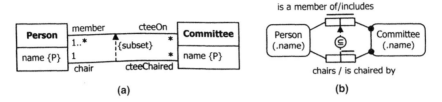

(a)   (b)

FIGURE 3.23

All constraints are now shown explicitly in (a) UML and (b) ORM.

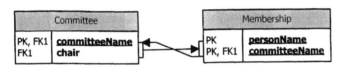

FIGURE 3.24

The relational schema mapped from Figure 3.23.

it is better to show implied constraints explicitly, as in Figure 3.23, rather than expect modelers or domain experts to figure them out for themselves.

Some ORM tools can detect the misleading nature of constraint patterns like that of Figure 3.22(b) and ask you to resolve the problem. Human interaction is the best policy here, since there is more than one possible mistake; for example, is the subset constraint correct leading to Figure 3.23, or is the optional role correct resulting in Figure 3.21?

If a schema in Figure 3.23 is mapped to a relational database, it generates a referential cycle, since the mandatory fact types for Committee map to different tables (so each committee must appear in both tables). The relational schema is shown in Figure 3.24 (arrows show the foreign key references, one simple and one composite, which correspond to the subset constraints).

Although referential cycles are sometimes unavoidable, they are awkward to implement. In this case, the cycle arose from applying a mandatory role constraint to a nonfunctional role. Unless the business requires it, this should be avoided at the conceptual level (e.g., by leaving the upper role of Committee optional, as in Figure 3.21).

Since UML does not allow unary relationships, subset constraints between ORM unaries need to be captured textually, using a note to specify an equivalent constraint between Boolean attributes. For example, the ORM subset constraint in Figure 3.25(b), which verbalizes as Each Patient who smokes is cancer prone, may be captured textually in UML by the note in Figure 3.25(a).

UML 2.0 introduced a *subsets property* to indicate that the population (extension) of an attribute or association role must be a subset of the population of another compatible attribute or association role, respectively. For example,

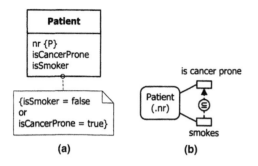

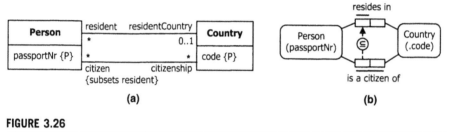

FIGURE 3.25

(a) UML note for (b) ORM subset constraint between unaries.

FIGURE 3.26

A single role subset constraint in (a) UML and (b) ORM.

adorning the citizen role in Figure 3.26(a) with {subsets resident} means that all citizens are residents (not necessarily of the same country). Figure 3.26(b) shows the equivalent ORM schema.

However, there are still many subset constraint cases in ORM that cannot be represented graphically as a subset constraint in UML. For example, the subset constraint in Figure 3.27(b) that each student with a second given name must have a first given name is captured as a note in Figure 3.27(a) because the relevant ORM fact types are modeled as attributes in UML, and the required subset constraint applies between student sets, not name sets. The subset constraint in Figure 3.25(b) is another example.

Moreover, UML does not support subset constraints over arguments that are just parts of relationships, such as the subset constraint in Figure 3.27(b) that students may pass tests in a course only if they enrolled in that course. Figure 3.27(a) models this constraint in UML by transforming the ternary into a binary association class (Enrollment) that has a binary association to Test. Although in this situation an association class provides a good way to cater for a compound subset constraint, sometimes this nesting transformation leads to a very unnatural view of the world. Ideally the modeler should be able to view the world

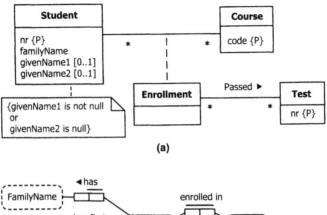

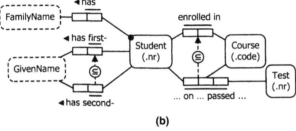

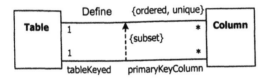

FIGURE 3.27

(a) UML model capturing (b) some subset constraints in ORM.

FIGURE 3.28

Spot anything wrong?

naturally, while having any optimization transformations that reduce the clarity of the conceptual schema performed under the covers.

As another constraint example in UML, consider Figure 3.28, which is the UML version of an OMT diagram used in Blaha and Premerlani (1998, p. 68) to illustrate a subset constraint (if a column is a primary key column of a table, it must belong to that table). Can you spot any problems with the constraints?

One obvious problem is that the 1 on the primary key association should be 0..1 (not all columns belong to primary keys), as in Figure 3.29(a). If we allow tables to have no columns (e.g., the schema is to cater for cases where the table is under construction), then the * on the define association is fine; otherwise it should be 1..*. Assuming that tables and columns are identified by oids or artificial

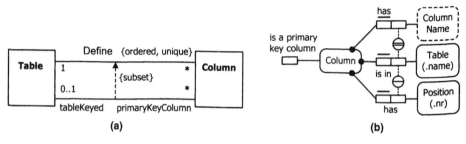

FIGURE 3.29

A corrected UML schema (a) remodeled in ORM (b).

identifiers, the subset constraint makes sense, but the model is arguably subopti-mal, since the primary key association and subset constraint could be replaced by a Boolean `is-aPKfield` attribute on `Column`.

From an ORM perspective, heuristics lead us to initially model the situation using natural reference schemes as shown in Figure 3.29(b). Here `ColumnName` denotes the local name of the column in the table. We've simplified reality by assuming that tables may be identified just by their name. The external uniqueness constraints suggest two natural reference schemes for `Column`: `Name` plus `Table`, or `Position` plus `Table`. We chose the first of these as preferred, but could have introduced an artificial identifier. The unary predicate indicates whether a column is, or is part of, a primary key. If desired, we could derive the association `Column is a primary key field of Table` from the path: `Column is in Table` and `Column is a primary key column` (the subset constraint in the UML model is then implied).

What is interesting about this example is the difference in modeling approaches. Most UML modelers seem to assume that oids will be used as identifiers in their initial modeling, whereas ORM modelers like to expose natural reference schemes right from the start and populate their fact types accordingly. These different approaches often lead to different solutions.

The main thing is to first come up with a solution that is natural and under-standable to the domain expert, because here is where the most critical phase of model validation should take place. Once a correct model has been determined, optimization guidelines can be used to enhance it.

One other feature of the example is worth mentioning. The UML solution in Figure 3.29(a) uses the annotation {ordered, unique} to indicate that a table is composed of an ordered set (i.e., a sequence with no duplicates) of columns. UML 2.0 allows the unique property to be specified with or without the ordered property. By default, `ordered` = false and `unique` = true. So either of the settings {ordered} or {ordered, unique} may be used to indicate an ordered set. That is, either no setting or the single setting {unique} indicates a set (the default). If {nonunique} is allowed in this context (this is unclear in the UML specification), one could specify a bag or sequence with the settings {nonunique} or {ordered, nonunique}, respectively.

In the ORM community, a debate has been going on for many years regarding the best way to deal with constructors for collection types (e.g., set, ordered set, bag, sequence) at the conceptual level. Our view is that such constructors should not appear in the base conceptual model, thus the use of Position in Figure 3.29(b) to convey column order (the uniqueness of the order is conveyed by the uniqueness constraint on Column has Position). Keeping fact types elementary has so many advantages (e.g., validation, constraint expression, flexibility, and simplicity) that it seems best to relegate constructors to derived views.

In ORM, an *equality constraint* between two compatible role sequences is shorthand for two subset constraints (one in either direction) and is shown as a circled "=." Such a constraint indicates that the populations of the role sequences must always be equal. If two roles played by an object type are mandatory, then an equality constraint between them is implied (and therefore not shown). UML has no graphic notation for equality constraints. For whole associations we could use two separate subset constraints, but this would be very messy. In general, equality constraints in UML may be specified as textual constraints in notes.

As a simple example, the equality constraint in Figure 3.30(b) indicates that if a patient's systolic blood pressure is measured, so is his or her diastolic blood pressure (and vice versa). In other words, either both measurements are taken or neither.

This kind of constraint is fairly common. Less common are equality constraints between sequences of two or more roles. Figure 3.30(a) models this in UML as a textual constraint between two attributes for blood pressure readings.

Subset and equality constraints enable various classes of schema transformations to be stated in their most general form, and ORM's more general support for these constraints allows more transformations to be easily visualized.

Although UML does not include a graphic notation for a pure exclusion constraint, it does include an *exclusive-OR constraint* to indicate that each instance of a class plays *exactly one* association role from a specified set of alternatives.

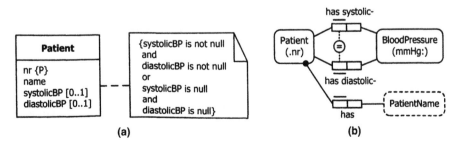

(a)   **(b)**

FIGURE 3.30

A simple equality constraint in (a) UML and (b) ORM.

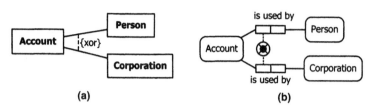

(a)   **(b)**

FIGURE 3.31

Exclusive-OR: each account is used by a person or corporation but not both.

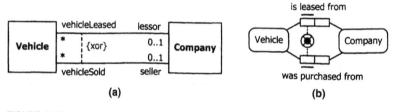

(a)   **(b)**

FIGURE 3.32

The exclusive-OR constraint should apply between association roles.

To indicate the constraint, {xor} is placed beside a dashed line connecting the relevant associations. Figure 3.31(a), which is based on an example from the UML specification, indicates that each account is used by a person or corporation but not both. For simplicity, reference schemes and other constraints are omitted.

Prior to UML 1.3, {or} was used for this constraint, which was misleading since "or" is typically interpreted in the inclusive sense. The equivalent ORM model is shown in Figure 3.31(b), where the exclusive-OR constraint is simply an orthogonal combination of a disjunctive mandatory role (inclusive-OR) constraint (circled dot) and an exclusion constraint (circled "X").

Although the current UML specification describes the exclusive-OR constraint as applying to a set of associations, we need to apply the constraint to a set of roles (association ends) to avoid ambiguity in cases with multiple common classes. Visually this could be shown by attaching the dashed line near the relevant ends of the associations, as shown in Figure 3.32(a). Unfortunately, UML attaches no significance to such positioning, so the exclusive-OR constraint could be misinterpreted to mean that each company must lease or purchase some vehicle rather than the intended constraint that each vehicle is either leased or purchased, a constraint captured unambiguously by the ORM schema in Figure 3.32(b).

UML has no symbols for exclusion or inclusive-OR constraints. If UML symbols for these constraints are ever considered, then {x} and {or}, respectively, seem appropriate; this choice also exposes the composite nature of {xor}.

UML exclusive-OR constraints are intended to apply between single roles. The current UML specification seems to imply that these roles must belong to different

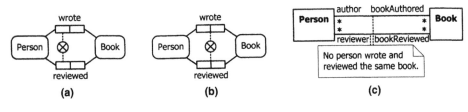

FIGURE 3.33

(a) Nobody wrote and reviewed a book; (b) nobody wrote and reviewed the same book; (c) UML version of (b).

associations. If so, UML cannot use an exclusive-OR constraint between roles of a ring fact type (e.g., between the husband and the wife roles of a marriage association). ORM exclusion constraints cover this case, as well as many other cases not expressible in UML graphic notation. As a trivial example, consider the difference between the following two constraints: No person both wrote a book and reviewed a book, and no person wrote and reviewed the same book. ORM clearly distinguishes these by noting the precise arguments of the constraint (compare Figure 3.33(a) with Figure 3.33 (b)).

The pair exclusion constraint in Figure 3.33(b) can be expressed in UML by a note connected by dotted lines to the two associations, as shown in Figure 3.33(c). Alternatively, one could attach a textual constraint to either the Person class (e.g., "bookAuthored and bookReviewed are disjoint sets") or the Book class (e.g. "author and reviewer are disjoint sets"), but the choice of class would be arbitrary.

UML has no graphic notation for exclusion between attributes, or between attributes and association roles. An exclusion constraint in such cases may often be captured as a textual constraint. For example, in Figure 3.34(a), the exclusion constraint that each employee is either tenured or is contracted until some date may be captured by the textual constraint shown.

Here the constraint is specified in OCL. The expressions -> isEmpty() and -> notEmpty() are equivalent to "is null" and "is not null" in SQL. Figure 3.34(b) depicts the exclusion constraint graphically in ORM. There are other ways to model this case in UML (e.g., using subtypes) that offer more chances to capture the constraints graphically.

3.6 SUBTYPING

Both UML and ORM support *subtyping,* using substitutability ("is-a") semantics, where each instance of a subtype is also an instance of its supertype(s). For example, declaring Woman to be a subtype of Person entails that each woman is a person, and therefore Woman inherits all the properties of Person. Given two object types, *A* and *B,* we say that *A* is a *subtype* of *B* if, for each database state, the

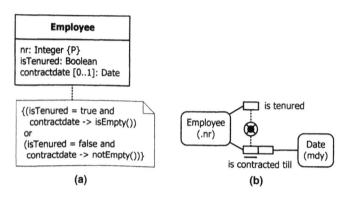

FIGURE 3.34

An exclusion constraint modeled in (a) UML and (b) ORM.

population of *A* is included in the population of *B*. For data modeling, the only subtypes of interest are *proper* subtypes. We say that *A* is a proper subtype of *B* if and only if *A* is a subtype of *B*, and there is a possible state where the population of *B* includes an instance not in *A*. From now on, we'll use "subtype" as shorthand for "proper subtype."

In both UML and ORM, *specialization* is the process of introducing subtypes, and *generalization* is the inverse procedure of introducing a supertype. Both UML and ORM allow single *inheritance*, as well as multiple inheritance (where a subtype has more than one direct supertype). For example, AsianWoman may be a subtype of both AsianPerson and Woman. In UML, "subclass" and "superclass" are synonyms of "subtype" and "supertype," respectively, and generalization may also be applied to things other than classes (e.g., interfaces, use case actors, and packages). This section restricts its attention to subtyping between object types (classes).

In ORM, a subtype inherits all the roles of its supertypes. In UML, a subclass inherits all the attributes, associations, and operations/methods of its supertype(s). An operation implements a service and has a signature (name and formal parameters) and visibility, but may be realized in different ways. A method is an implementation of an operation, and therefore includes both a signature and a body detailing an executable algorithm to perform the operation. In an inheritance graph, there may be many methods for the same operation (*polymorphism*), and scoping rules are used to determine which method is actually used for a given class. If a subclass has a method with the same signature as a method of one of its supertypes, this is used instead for that subclass (*overriding*). For example, if Rectangle and Triangle are subclasses of Shape, all three classes may have different methods for display(). This section focuses on data modeling, not behavior modeling, and covering inheritance of static properties (attributes and associations) but ignoring inheritance of operations or methods.

Subtypes are used in data modeling to assert typing constraints, encourage reuse of model components, and show a classification scheme (taxonomy). In this context, typing constraints ensure that subtype-specific roles are played only by the relevant subtype.

Since a subtype inherits the properties of its supertype(s), only its specific roles need to be declared when it is introduced. Apart from reducing code duplication, the more generic supertypes are likely to find reuse in other applications. At the coding level, inheritance of operations/methods augments the reuse gained by inheritance of attributes and association roles. Using subtypes to show taxonomy is of limited use, since taxonomy is often more efficiently captured by predicates. For example, the fact type `Person is of Gender {male, female}` implicitly provides the taxonomy for the subtypes MalePerson and FemalePerson.

Both UML and ORM display subtyping using *directed acyclic graphs.* A directed graph is a graph of nodes with directed connections, and "acyclic" means that there are no cycles (a consequence of proper subtyping). Figure 3.35 shows a subtype pattern in UML and ORM. An arrow from one node to another shows that the first is a subtype of the second. UML uses a thin arrow shaft with an open arrowhead, while ORM uses a solid shaft and arrowhead. As an alternative notation, UML also allows separate shafts to merge into one, with one arrowhead acting for all (e.g., E and F are subtypes of C). Since subtypehood is transitive, indirect connections are omitted (e.g., since E is a subtype of C, and C is a subtype of A, it follows that E is a subtype of A, so there is no need to display this implied connection).

UML includes four predefined constraints to indicate whether subtypes are exclusive or exhaustive. If subtype connections are shown with separate arrowheads, the constraints are placed in braces next to a dotted line connecting the subtype links, as in Figure 3.35(a) (top). We assume that this line may include elbows, as shown for the disjoint constraint, to enable such cases to be specified.

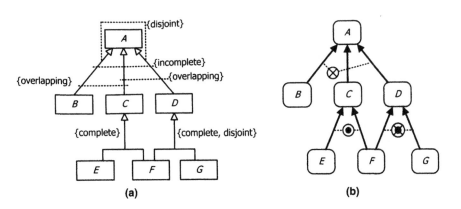

(a)   (b)

FIGURE 3.35

Subtyping displayed by directed acyclic graphs in (a) UML and (b) ORM.

If the subtype connections are shared, the constraints are placed near the shared arrowhead, as in Figure 3.35(a) (bottom). The {overlapping} and {disjoint} options, respectively, indicate that the subtypes overlap or are mutually exclusive. Originally {complete} simply meant that all subtypes were shown, but this was redefined to mean exhaustive (i.e., the supertype equals the union of its subtypes). The {incomplete} option means that the supertype is more than the union of its subtypes. The default is {disjoint, incomplete}. Users may add other keywords.

By default, ORM subtypes may overlap, and subtypes need not collectively exhaust their supertype. ORM allows graphic constraints to indicate that subtypes are mutually exclusive (a circled "X" connected to the relevant subtype links), collectively exhaustive (a circled dot), or both (a circled, crossed dot), as shown in Figure 3.35(b). ORM's approach is that exclusion and totality constraints are enforced on populations, not types. An overlapping "constraint" does not mean that the populations must overlap, just that they may overlap. Therefore, from an ORM viewpoint, this is not really a constraint at all, so there is no need to depict it. In ORM, subtype exclusion and totality constraints are often implied by other constraints in conjunction with formal subtype definitions.

For any subtype graph, the top supertype is called the *root,* and the bottom subtypes (those with no descendants) are called *leaves.* In UML this can be made explicit by adding {root} or {leaf} below the relevant class name. If we know the whole subtype graph is shown, there is little point in doing this, but if we were to display only part of a subtype graph, this notation makes it clear whether or not the local top and bottom nodes are also like that in the global schema. For example, from Figure 3.36 we know that globally Party has no supertype and that MalePerson and FemalePerson have no subtypes. Since Party is not marked as a leaf node, it may have other subtypes not shown here.

UML also allows an ellipsis "…" in place of a subclass to indicate that at least one subclass of the parent exists in the global schema, but its display is suppressed on the diagram. Currently ORM does not include a root/leaf notation or an ellipsis

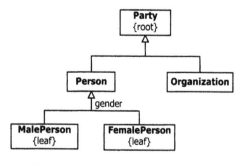

FIGURE 3.36

Party may have other subtypes not shown here.

notation for subtypes. Such notations could be a useful extension to ORM diagrams.

UML distinguishes between *abstract* and *concrete* classes. An abstract class cannot have any direct instances and is shown by writing its name in italics or by adding {abstract} below the class name. Abstract classes are realized only through their descendants. Concrete classes may be directly instantiated. This distinction seems to have little relevance at the conceptual level and is not depicted explicitly in ORM. For code design, however, the distinction is important (e.g., abstract classes provide one way of declaring interfaces, and in C++ abstract operations correspond to pure virtual operations, while leaf operations map to nonvirtual operations). For further discussion of this topic, see Fowler (1997, pp. 85–88) and Booch et al. (1999, pp. 125–126).

Like other ER notations, UML provides only weak support for defining subtypes. A *discriminator* label may be placed near a subtype arrow to indicate the basis for the classification. For example, Figure 3.37 includes a "gender" discriminator to specialize Patient into MalePatient and FemalePatient.

The UML specification says that the discriminator names "a partition of the subtypes of the superclass." In formal work, the term *partition* usually implies the division is both exclusive and exhaustive. In UML, the use of a discriminator does not imply that the subtypes are exhaustive or complete, but at least some authors argue that they must be exclusive (Fowler 1997, p. 78). If that is the case, there does not appear to be any way in UML of declaring a discriminator for a set of overlapping subtypes.

The same discriminator name may be repeated for multiple subclass arrows to show that each subclass belongs to the same classification scheme. This repetition can be avoided by merging the arrow shafts to end in a single arrowhead, as in Figure 3.37.

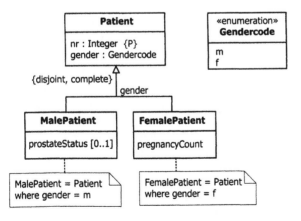

FIGURE 3.37

Gender is used as a discriminator to partition Patient.

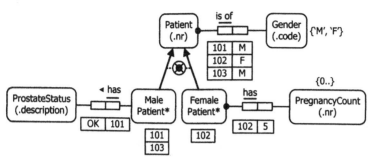

*Each MalePatient **is a** Patient **who** is of Gender 'M'.
*Each FemalePatient **is a** Patient **who** is of Gender 'F'.

FIGURE 3.38

With formal subtype definitions, subtype constraints are implied.

In Figure 3.37, the gender attribute of Patient is used as a discriminator. This attribute is based on the enumerated type Gendercode, which is defined using the stereotype «enumeration», and listing its values as attributes. The notes at the bottom are needed to ensure that instances populating these subtypes have the correct gender. For example, without these notes there is nothing to stop us populating MalePatient with patients that have the value f for their gender code.

ORM overcomes this problem by requiring that if a taxonomy is captured both by subtyping and a classifying fact type, these two representations must be synchronized, either by deriving the subtypes from *formal subtype definitions* or by deriving the classification fact type from asserted subtypes. For example, the populated ORM schema in Figure 3.38 adopts the first approach. The ORM partition (exclusion and totality) constraint is now implied by the combination of the subtype definitions and the three constraints on the fact type Patient is of Gender.

While the subtype definitions in Figure 3.38 are trivial, in practice more complicated subtype definitions are sometimes required. As a basic example, consider a schema with the fact types City is in Country and City has Population, and now define LargeUScity as follows: Each LargeUScity is a City that is in Country "US" and has Population > 1000000. There does not seem to be any convenient way of doing this in UML, at least not with discriminators. We could perhaps add a derived Boolean isLarge attribute, with an associated derivation rule in OCL, and then add a final subtype definition in OCL, but this would be less readable than the ORM definition just given.

3.7 OTHER CONSTRAINTS AND DERIVATION RULES

A *value constraint* restricts the population of a value type to a finite set of values specified either in full (*enumeration*), by start and end values (*range*), or some

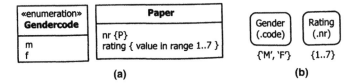

(a)   (b)

FIGURE 3.39

Data value restrictions declared as enumerations or textual constraints: (a) using any formal or informal language, and (b) in ORM.

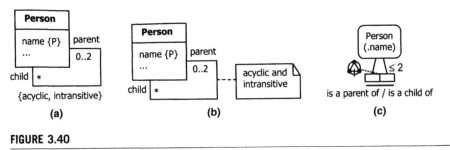

(a)   (b)   (c)

FIGURE 3.40

Ring constraints expressed in (a) UML, (b) UML, and (c) ORM.

combination of both (*mixture*). The values themselves are primitive data values, typically character strings or numbers.

In UML, enumeration types may be modeled as classes, stereotyped as enumerations, with their values listed (somewhat uninmitively) as attributes. Ranges and mixtures may be specified by declaring a textual constraint in braces, using any formal or informal language. For example, see Figure 3.39(a).

Figure 3.39(b) depicts the same value constraints in ORM. Value constraints other than enumeration, range, and mixture may be declared in UML or ORM as textual constraints—for example, {committeeSize must be an odd number}. For further UML examples, see Rumbaugh et al. (1999, pp. 236, 268).

A ring fact type has at least two roles played by the same object type (either directly or indirectly via a supertype). A *ring constraint* applies a logical restriction on the role pair. For example, the association Person is a parent of Person might be declared acyclic and intransitive.

UML does not provide ring constraints built in, so the modeler needs to specify these as a textual constraint in some chosen language or as a note. In UML, if a textual constraint applies to just one model element (e.g., an association), it may be added in braces next to that element, as in Figure 3.40(a). Here the {acyclic, intransitive} notation is nonstandard but is assumed to be user supported.

It is the responsibility of the modeling tool to ensure that the constraint is linked internally to the relevant model element and to interpret any textual constraint expressions. If the tool cannot interpret the constraint, it should be placed inside a note (dog-eared rectangle), without braces, showing that it is merely a comment, and explicitly linked to the relevant model element(s), as shown in Figure 3.40(b). Figure 3.40(c) displays the ring constraints graphically in ORM.

A *join constraint* applies to one or more role sequences, at least one of which is projected from a path from one predicate through an object type to another predicate. The act of passing from one role through an object type to another role invokes a conceptual join, since the same object instance is asserted to play both the roles. Although join constraints arise frequently in real applications, UML has no graphic symbol for them. To declare them on a UML diagram, write a constraint or comment in a note attached to the model elements involved.

For example, Figure 3.41 links a comment to three associations. This example is based on a room-scheduling application at a university with built-in facilities in various lecture and tutorial rooms. Example facility codes are PA = personal address system, DP = data projection facility, and INT = Internet access.

ORM provides deep support for join constraints. Role sequences featuring as arguments in set comparison constraints may arise from projections over a join path. For example, in Figure 3.42, the subset constraint runs from the Room-Facility role pair projected from the path: Room at an HourSlot is booked for an Activity that requires a Facility. This path includes a conceptual join on Activity. The constraint may be formally verbalized as: If a Room at an HourSlot is booked for an Activity that requires a Facility then that Room provides that Facility. Figure 3.42 includes a satisfying population for the three fact types. This again illustrates how ORM facilitates validation constraints via sample populations. The UML associations in Figure 3.41 are not so easily populated on the diagram.

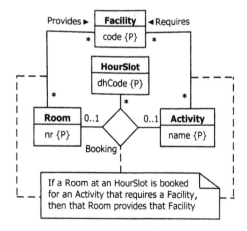

FIGURE 3.41

Join constraint specified as a comment in UML.

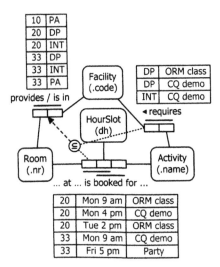

FIGURE 3.42

A join-subset constraint in ORM.

In UML, the term *aggregation* is used to describe a *whole/part relationship*. For example, a team of people is an aggregate of its members, so this membership may be modeled as an aggregation association between Team and Person. Several different forms of aggregation might be distinguished in real-world cases. For example, Odell and Bock (Odell 1998, pp. 137–165) discuss six varieties of aggregation (component-integral, material-object, portion-object, place-area, member-bunch, and member-partnership), and Henderson-Sellers (Barbier et al., 2003) also distinguishes several kinds of aggregation.

UML 2.0 associations are classified into one of three kinds: ordinary association (no aggregation), shared (or simple) aggregation, or composite (or strong) aggregation. Therefore, UML recognizes only two varieties of aggregation: shared and composite. Some versions of ER include an aggregation symbol (typically only one kind). ORM and popular ER approaches currently include no special symbols for aggregation.

These different stances with respect to aggregation are somewhat reminiscent of the different modeling positions with respect to null values. Although over 20 kinds of null have been distinguished in the literature, the relational model recognizes only 1 kind of null. Codd's version 2.0 of the relational model includes 2 kinds of null, and ORM argues that nulls have no place in base conceptual models (because all its asserted facts are atomic). But let's return to the topic at hand.

Shared aggregation is denoted in UML as a binary association, with a *hollow diamond* at the "whole" or "aggregate" end of the association. *Composition (composite aggregation)* is depicted with a *filled diamond*. For example, Figure

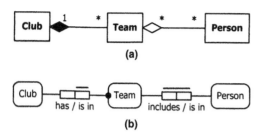

FIGURE 3.43

Composition (composite aggregation) and shared aggregation in (a) UML and (b) ORM.

3.43(a) depicts a composition association from Club to Team and a shared aggregation association from Team to Person.

In ORM, which currently has no special notation for aggregation, this situation would be modeled as shown in Figure 3.43(b). Does Figure 3.43(a) convey any extra semantics that are not captured in Figure 3.43(b)? At the conceptual level, it is doubtful whether there are any additional useful semantics. At the implementation level, however, there are additional semantics. Let's discuss this in more detail.

The UML specification declares that "both kinds of aggregation define a transitive . . . relationship." The use of "transitive" here is somewhat misleading, since it refers to indirect aggregation associations rather than base aggregation associations. For example, if Club is an aggregate of Team, and Team is an aggregate of Person, it follows that Club is an aggregate of Person.

However, if we wanted to discuss this result, it should be exposed as a *derived association.* In UML, derived associations are indicated by prefixing their names with a *slash* "/". The *derivation rule* can be expressed as a constraint, either connected to the association by a dependency arrow or simply placed beside the association as in Figure 3.44(a).

In ORM, derived fact types are marked with a trailing asterisk, with their derivation rules specified in an ORM textual language (see Figure 3.44(b)). In many cases, derivation rules may also be diagrammed as a join-subset or join-equality constraint. As this example illustrates, the derived transitivity of aggregations can be captured in ORM without needing a special notation for aggregation.

The UML specification declares that "both kinds of aggregation define a transitive, antisymmetric relationship (i.e., the instances form a directed, noncyclic graph)." Recall that a relation R is antisymmetric if and only if, for all x and y, if x is not equal to y, then xRy implies that not yRx. It would have been better to simply state that paths of aggregations must be acyclic.

At any rate, this rule is designed to stop errors such as the one shown in Figure 3.45. If a person is part of a team, and a team is part of a club, it doesn't make sense to say that a club is part of a person. Since ORM does not specify whether an association is an aggregation, illegal diagrams like this can't occur in ORM.

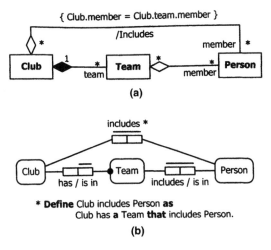

(a)

(b)

FIGURE 3.44

A derived aggregation in (a) UML and (b) ORM.

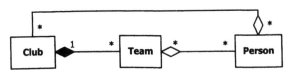

FIGURE 3.45

Illegal UML model. Aggregations should not form a cycle.

Of course, it is possible for an ORM modeler to make a silly mistake by adding an association such as Club is part of Person, where "is part of" is informally understood in the aggregation sense, and this would not be formally detectable. But avoidance of such a bizarre occurrence doesn't seem to be a compelling reason to add aggregation to ORM's formal notation. There are plenty of associations between Club and Person that do make sense, and plenty that don't. In some cases, however, it is important to assert constraints such as acyclicity, and this is handled in ORM by ring constraints. That said, there have been some recent proposals to add formal semantics for various forms of the part-of relationship to ORM. For example, Keet (2006) proposes adding several different mereological part-of predicates as well as four kinds of meronymic relations.

Composition does add some important semantics to shared aggregation. To begin with, it requires that each part belongs to at most one whole at a time. In ORM, this is captured by adding a uniqueness constraint to the role played by the part (e.g., see the role played by Team in Figure 3.43(b)). In UML, the multiplicity at the whole end of the association must be 1 or 0..1. If the multiplicity is 1, as

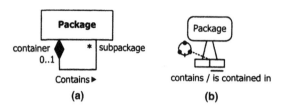

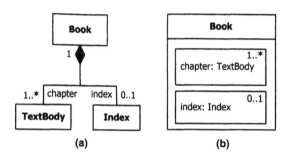

FIGURE 3.46

Direct containment modeled in (a) UML and (b) ORM.

FIGURE 3.47

Alternative UML notations for aggregation.

in Figure 3.43(a), the role played by the part is both unique and mandatory, as in Figure 3.43(b).

As an example where the multiplicity is 0..1 (i.e., where a part optionally belongs to a whole), consider the ring fact type of **Figure 3.46**, Package contains Package. Here "contains" is used in the sense of "directly contains." The UML specification notes that "composition instances form a strict tree (or rather a forest)." This strengthening from directed acyclic graph to tree is an immediate consequence of the functional nature of the association (each part belongs to at most one whole), and therefore ORM requires no additional notation for this. In this example, the ORM schema explicitly includes an acyclic constraint. This direct containment association is intransitive by implication (acyclicity implies irreflexivity, and any functional, irreflexive association is intransitive).

UML allows some alternative notations for aggregation. If a class is an aggregate of more than one class, the association lines may be shown joined to a single diamond, as in Figure 3.47(a). For composition, the part classes may be shown nested inside the whole by using role names, and multiplicities of components may be shown in the top right corners, as in Figure 3.47(b).

Some authors list kinds of associations that are easily confused with aggregation but should not be modeled as such (e.g., topological inclusion, classification inclusion, attribution, attachment, and ownership (see Martin & Odell, 1998; Odell, 1998).

For example, `Finger belongs to Hand` is an aggregation, but `Ring belongs to Finger` is not. There is some disagreement among authors about what should be included on this list. For example, some treat attribution as a special case of aggregation—namely, a composition between a class and the classes of its attributes (Rumbaugh et al., 1999).

For conceptual modeling purposes, agonizing over such distinctions might not be worth the trouble. Obviously there are different stances that you could take about how, if at all, aggregation should be included in the conceptual modeling phase. You can decide what is best for you. The literature summary at the end of the chapter provides further discussion on this issue.

Let's now look at the notion of *initial values*. The basic syntax of an attribute specification in UML includes six components as shown. Square and curly brackets are used literally here as delimiters (not as Backus–Naur Form [BNF] symbols to indicate optional components).

visibililty name [*multiplicity*]: *type-expression = initial-value* {*property string*}

If an attribute is displayed at all, its name is the only thing that must be shown. The visibility marker (+, #, −, and ~ denote public, protected, private, and package, respectively) is an implementation concern and will be ignored in our discussion. Multiplicity has been discussed earlier and is specified for attributes in square brackets (e.g., [1..*]).

For attributes, the default multiplicity is 1—that is, [1..1]. The type expression indicates the domain on which the attribute is based (e.g., `String`, `Date`). Initial value and property string declarations may be optionally declared. Property strings may be used to specify aspects such as changeability.

An attribute may be assigned an initial value by including the value in the attribute declaration after "=" (e.g., `diskSize` = 9; `country` = USA; `priority` = normal). The language in which the value is written is an implementation concern.

In Figure 3.48(a), the `nrColors` attribute is based on a simple domain (e.g., `PositiveInteger`) and has been given an initial value of 1. The resolution attribute is based on a composite domain (e.g., `PixelArea`) and has been assigned an initial value of (640,480).

Unless overridden by another initialization procedure (e.g., a constructor), declared initial values are assigned when an object of that class is created. This is similar to the database notion of *default values,* where during the insertion of a tuple an attribute may be assigned a predeclared default value if a value is not supplied by the user.

However, UML uses the term *default value* in other contexts only (e.g., template and operation parameters), and some authors claim that default values are not part of UML models (Rumbaugh et al., 1999, p. 249).

The SQL standard treats **null** as a special instance of a default value, and this is supported in UML, since the specification notes that "a multiplicity of 0..1 provides for the possibility of null values: the absence of a value." So an optional attribute in UML can be used to model a feature that will appear as a column with

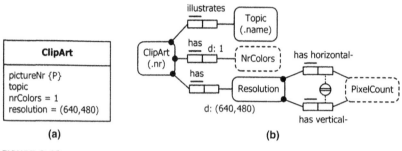

FIGURE 3.48

Attributes assigned initial values in (a) UML and (b) ORM extension.

the default value of null, when mapped to a relational database. Presumably a multiplicity of [0..*] or [0..*n*] for any *n* > 1 also allows nulls for multivalued attributes, even though an empty collection could be used instead.

Currently, ORM has no explicit support for initial/default values. However, UML initial values and relational default values could be supported by allowing default values to be specified for ORM roles. At the meta-level, we add the fact type `Role has default- Value`. At the external level, instances of this could be specified on a predicate properties sheet, or entered on the diagram (e.g., by attaching an annotation such as d: *value* to the role, and preferably allowing this display to be toggled on/off). For example, the role played by `NrColors` in Figure 3.48(b) is allocated a default value of 1. When mapped to SQL, this should add the declaration `default 1` to the column definition for `ClipArt.nrColors`.

To support the composite initial values allowed in UML, composite default values could be specified for ORM roles played by compositely identified object types (coreferenced or nested). When coreferencing involves at least two roles played by the same or compatible object types, an order is needed to disambiguate the meaning of the composite value. For example, in Figure 3.48(b) the role played by `Resolution` is assigned a default composite value of (640,480). To ensure that the 640 applies to the horizontal pixel count and the 480 applies to the vertical pixel count (rather than the other way around), this ordering needs to be applied to the defining roles of the external uniqueness constraint. ORM tools often determine this ordering from the order in which the roles are selected when entering this constraint.

If all or most roles played by an object type have the same default, it may be useful to allow a default value to be specified for the object type itself. This could be supported in ORM by adding the meta fact type `ObjectType has default- Value` and providing some notation for instantiating it (e.g., by an entry in an Object Type Properties sheet or by annotating the object type shape with d: *value*). This corresponds to the default clause permitted in a create domain statement in the SQL standard. Note that an object type default can always be expressed instead by role-based defaults, but not conversely (since the default may vary with the role).

Specification of default values does not cover all the cases that can arise with regard to default information in general. A proposal for providing greater support for default information in ORM is discussed in Halpin and Vermeir (1997), but this goes beyond the built-in support for defaults in either UML or SQL. Default information can be modeled informally by using a predicate to convey this intention to a human. For example, we might specify the default medium (e.g., CD, DVD) preferences for delivery of soft products (e.g., music, video, software) using the $1:n$ fact type `Medium is default preference for SoftProduct`.

In cases like this where default values overlap with actual values, we may also wish to classify instances of relevant fact types as actual or default (e.g., `Shipment used Medium`). For the typical case where the uniqueness constraint on the fact type spans $n - 1$ roles, this can be achieved by including fact types to indicate the default status (e.g., `Shipment was based on Choice {actual, default}`), resulting in extra columns in the database to record the status. While this approach is generic, it requires the modeler and user to take full responsibility for distinguishing between actual and default values.

In UML, restrictions may be placed on the *changeability* of attributes, as well as the roles (ends) of binary associations. It is unclear whether changeability may be applied to the ends of *n*-ary associations. UML 2.0 recognizes the following four values for changeability, only one of which can apply at a given time:

- unrestricted
- readOnly
- addOnly
- removeOnly

The default changeability is unrestricted (any change is permitted). The value unrestricted was formerly called "changeable," which itself was formerly called "none." The other settings may be explicitly declared in braces. For an attribute, the braces are placed at the end of the attribute declaration. For an association, the braces are placed at the opposite end of the association from the object instance to which the constraint applies.

Recall that in UML a "link" is an instance of an association. The value *readOnly* (formerly called "frozen") means that once an attribute value or link has been inserted, it cannot be updated or deleted, and no additional values/links may be added to the attribute/association (for the constrained object instance).

The value *addOnly* means that although the original value/link cannot be deleted or updated, other values/links may be added to the attribute/association (for the constrained object instance). Clearly, addOnly is only meaningful if the maximum multiplicity of the attribute/association role exceeds its minimum multiplicity. The value *removeOnly* means that the only change permitted for an existing attribute value or link is to delete it.

As a simple if unrealistic example, see Figure 3.49. Here employee number, birth date, and country of birth are readOnly for `Employee`, so they cannot be changed from their original value. For instance, if we assign an employee the

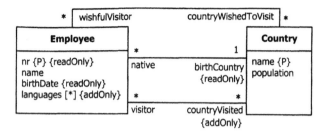

FIGURE 3.49

Changeability of attributes and association roles.

employee number "007," and enter his or her birth date as "02/15/1946" and birth country as "Australia," then we can never make any changes or additions to that.

Notice also that for a given employee, the set of languages and the set of countries visited are addOnly. Suppose that when facts about employee 007 are initially entered, we set his or her languages to {Latin, Japanese} and countries visited to {Japan}. As long as employee 007 is referenced in the database, these facts may never be deleted. However, we may add to these (e.g., later we might add the facts that employee 007 speaks German and visited India).

By default, the other properties are changeable. For example, employee 007 might legally change his name from Terry Hagar to Hari Seldon, and the countries he wants to visit might change over time from {Ireland, USA} to {Greece, Ireland}.

Some traditional data modeling approaches also note some restrictions on changeability. The Barker ER notation includes a diamond to mark a relationship as nontransferable (once an instance of an entity type plays a role with an object, it cannot ever play this role with another object). Although changeability restrictions can be useful, in practice their application in database settings is limited.

One reason for this is that we almost always want to allow facts entered into a database to be changed. With snapshot data, this is the norm, but even with historical data changes can occur. The most common occurrence of this is to allow for corrections of mistakes, which might be because we were told the wrong information originally or because we carelessly made a misspelling or typo when entering the data.

In exceptional cases, we might require that mistakes of a certain kind be retained in the database (e.g., for auditing purposes) but be corrected by entering later facts to compensate for the error. This kind of approach makes sense for bank transactions (see Figure 3.50). For example, if a deposit transaction for $100 was mistakenly entered as $1000, the record of this error is kept, but once the error is detected it can be compensated for by a bank withdrawal of $900. As a minor point, the balance is both derived and stored, and its readOnly status is

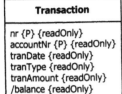

FIGURE 3.50

All attributes of Transaction are read only.

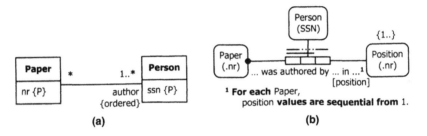

(a)   **(b)**

FIGURE 3.51

An ordered set modeled in (a) UML and (b) ORM.

typically implied by the readOnly settings on the base attributes, together with a rule for deriving balance.

Some authors allow changeability to be specified for a class, as an abbreviation for declaring this for all its attributes and opposite association ends (Booch et al., 1999, p. 184). For instance, all the {readOnly} constraints in Figure 3.50 might be replaced by a single {readOnly} constraint below the name Transaction. While this notation is neater, it would be rarely used. Even in this example, we would probably want to allow for the possibility of adding nonfrozen information later (e.g., a transaction might be audited by zero or more auditors).

Changeability settings are useful in the design of program code. Although changeability settings are not currently supported in ORM, which focuses on static constraints, they are being considered in extensions to support dynamic constraints. In the wider picture, being able to completely model security issues (e.g., who has the authority to change what) would provide extra value.

As discussed earlier, UML allows {ordered} and {unique} properties to be specified for multivalued attributes and association ends. Since {unique} is true by default, the use of {ordered} alone indicates an ordered set (a sequence with no duplicates). For example, Figure 3.51(a) shows one way of modeling authorship of papers in UML. Each paper has a list or sequence of authors, each of whom may appear at most once on the list.

This may be modeled in flat ORM by introducing a `Position` object type to store the sequential position of any author on the list, as shown in Figure 3.51(b). The uniqueness constraint on the first two roles declares that for each paper, an author occupies at most one position; the constraint covering the first and third roles indicates that for any paper, each position is occupied by at most one author. The textual constraint indicates that the list positions are numbered sequentially from 1.

Although this ternary representation may appear awkward, it is easy to populate and it facilitates any discussion involving position; for example, who is the second author for paper 21? From an implementation perspective, an ordered set structure could still be chosen.

An ordered set is an example of a collection type. Some versions of ORM allow collections to be specified as mapping annotations in a similar way to UML, and some ORM versions allow collections to be modeled directly as first-class objects.

UML 2.0 introduced the notion of *association redefinition*. This concept is complex and applies to generalizations as well as associations. One main use of it is to specify stronger constraints on an association role that specializes a role played by a supertype. For example, in Figure 3.52(a) the `executiveCar` role redefines the `assignedCar` role, applying a stronger multiplicity constraint on it that applies only to executives. Effectively, the association `Executive is assigned CompanyCar` is treated as a specialization of the `Employee is assigned Company-Car` association. Although some versions of ORM support a similar notion, most ORM versions require the stronger multiplicity to be asserted in a textual constraint, as shown in Figure 3.52(b).

Now let's consider *derived data*. In UML, derived elements (e.g., attributes, associations, or association roles) are indicated by prefixing their names with "/". Optionally, a *derivation rule* may be specified as well. The derivation rule can be expressed as a constraint or note, connected to the derived element by a dashed line. This line is actually shorthand for a dependency arrow, optionally annotated

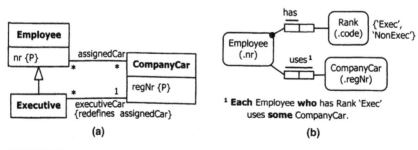

(a)   (b)

FIGURE 3.52

Association redefinition in (a) UML and (b) ORM.

with the stereotype name «derive». Since a constraint or note is involved, the arrow tip may be omitted (the constraint or note is assumed to be the source). For example, Figure 3.53(a) includes area as a derived attribute. Figure 3.53(b) shows the ORM schema.

The UML dependency line may also be omitted entirely, with the constraint shown in braces next to the derived element (in this case, it is the modeling tool's responsibility to maintain the graphical linkage implicitly). A club membership example of this was included earlier.

As another example, Figure 3.54(a) expresses uncle information as a derived association. For illustration purposes, role names are included for all association ends. The corresponding ORM schema is shown in Figure 3.54(b), where the derivation rule is specified in relational style.

Although precise role names are not always elegant, the use of role names in derivation rules involving a path projection can facilitate concise expression of rules, as shown here in the UML model. By adding role names to the ORM schema,

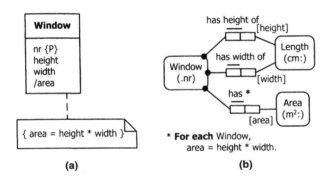

FIGURE 3.53

Derived area association in (a) UML and (b) ORM.

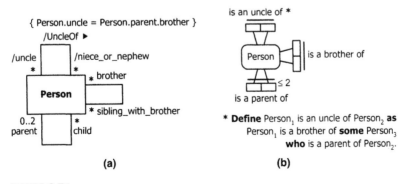

FIGURE 3.54

Derived uncle association in (a) UML and (b) ORM.

the derivation rule may be specified compactly in attribute style as follows: `* define uncle of Person as brother of parent of Person`. More complex derivation rules can be stated informally in English or formally in a language such as OCL.

One advantage of ORM's approach to derivation rules is that it is more stable, since it is not impacted by schema changes such as attributes being later remodeled as associations.

3.8 MAPPING FROM ORM TO UML

The *UMLmap procedure* in Table 3.3 provides basic guidelines for mapping ORM schemas to UML class diagrams. Selected entity types and value types map to object classes and data types, including attribute domains when associations are replaced by attributes. We now illustrate this procedure. As a preparatory move, step 1 binarizes any sets of exclusive binaries, as shown in Figure 3.55.

Table 3.3 UMLmap Procedure

Step	Action
1	Binarize any sets of exclusive unaries.
2	Model selected object types as classes, and map a selection of their $n:1$ and $1:1$ associations as attributes. To store facts about a value type, make it a class.
3	Map remaining unary fact types to Boolean attributes or subclasses.
4	Map $m:n$ and n-ary fact types to associations or association classes. Map objectified associations to association classes.
5	Map ORM constraints to UML graphic constraints, textual constraints, or notes.
6	Map subtypes to subclasses, and if needed, subtype definitions to textual constraints.
7	Map derived fact types to derived attributes/associations, and map semi-derived fact types to attributes/associations plus rules.

FIGURE 3.55

Step 1: replace any set of exclusive binaries by a binary fact type.

In step 2, we decide which object types to model as classes and which $n:1$ and $1:1$ ORM associations to remodel as attributes. Typically, entity types that play functional fact roles become classes. Functional binary ($n:1$ and $1:1$) associations from an entity type A to a value type B, or to an entity type B about which you never want to record details, usually map to an attribute of A. If you have specified role names, these can usually be used as attribute names, with the object type name becoming the attribute's domain name.

The mapping in Figure 3.56 illustrates several of these step 2 considerations, as well as step 6 (map ORM constraints to UML graphic constraints, textual constraints, or notes). The {P} and {UI} annotations for preferred identifier and uniqueness are not standard UML. The value constraint on gender codes is captured using an enumeration type.

In rare cases, value types that are independent, play an explicit mandatory role, or play a functional fact role in an $1:n$ fact type map to classes. The example in Figure 3.57(a) deals with cases where we store title–gender restrictions (e.g., the title "Mr." is restricted to the male gender). The example in Figure 3.57(b) uses a

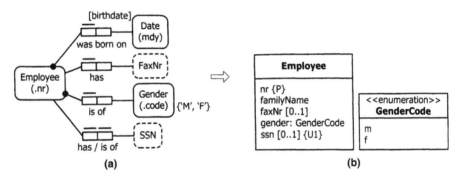

(a)   **(b)**

FIGURE 3.56

Step 2: map selected $n:1$ and $1:1$ associations to attributes.

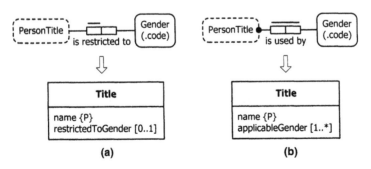

(a)   **(b)**

FIGURE 3.57

Step 2: rare cases of value types mapping to classes.

multivalued attribute to store all the genders applicable to a title (e.g., the title "Dr." applies to both male and female genders). The `Title` class gives fast access from title to applicable gender, but slow access from gender to title. As discussed earlier, multivalued attributes should be used sparingly.

In step 3 we map unaries to Boolean attributes or to subclasses. The example in Figure 3.58 assumes a closed-world interpretation for the unary. With an open-world approach, the `isSmoker` attribute is assigned a multiplicity of [0..1] and the `{complete}` constraint is removed from the subclassing.

In step 4, the remaining fact types are mapped to associations. Any $m:n$ associations should normally remain that way. In the example in Figure 3.59, the $n:1$ fact type is retained as an association because it relates two entity types that become classes in the mapping. Even if the $m:n$ association did not apply, we would normally retain `Country` as a class, since now or later we are likely to record details for it (e.g., country name).

If an $m:n$ association involves a value type (e.g., `Employee has PhoneNr`) instead of using a multivalued attribute, see if it is possible to transform the $m:n$ association into multiple $n:1$ associations (e.g. `Employee has PhoneNr1`; `Employee has PhoneNr2`; etc.).

If each object type in an n-ary fact type should map to a class (e.g., it plays other functional roles), then map the n-ary fact type to an n-ary association. Figure 3.60 provides an example.

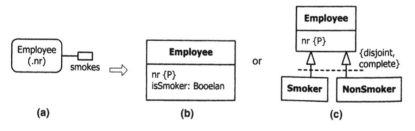

(a) **(b)** **(c)**

FIGURE 3.58

Step 3: map unaries to Boolean attributes or subclasses.

(a) **(b)**

FIGURE 3.59

Step 4: map remaining fact types to associations.

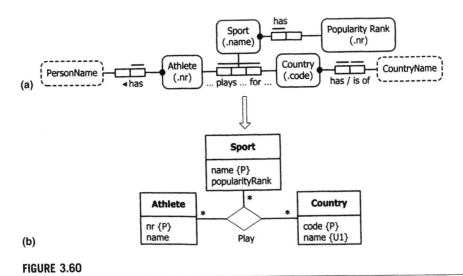

FIGURE 3.60

Step 4: map some *n*-ary fact types to *n*-ary associations.

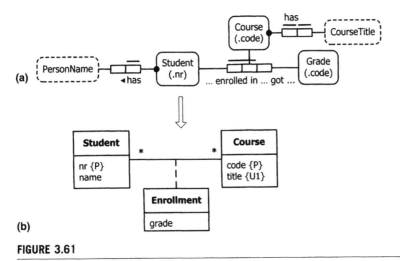

FIGURE 3.61

Step 4: map some *n*-ary fact types to association classes.

If an object type in a ternary fact type should not map to a class (typically an $m:n:1$ uniqueness pattern with it outside the uniqueness constraint), then objectify the rest of the association as an association class and map its role as an attribute. Figure 3.61 shows an example.

Objectified associations map to association classes, as shown earlier in Figure 3.18. Some cases of coreference could be mapped into qualified associations, but

Table 3.4 Mapping Main ORM Graphic Constraints to UML (for step 5)

ORM Constraint	UML
Internal UC	Maximum multiplicity of 1, or {Un}
External UC	Qualified association or textual constraint
Simple mandatory	Minimum multiplicity of 1, or textual constraint
Inclusive-OR	Textual constraint (unless within exclusive-OR)
Frequency	Multiplicity or textual constraint
Value	Enumeration or textual constraint
Subset and Equality	Subset(s) or textual constraint
Exclusion	Textual constraint (unless within exclusive-OR)
Ring constraints	Textual constraint
Join constraints	Textual constraint
Object cardinality	Class multiplicity

mapping to separate attributes or associations supplemented by a textual composite uniqueness constraint offers a more general solution.

In step 5, the simplest constraints in ORM usually map in an obvious way to multiplicity constraints, as illustrated earlier. The more complex ORM constraints have no graphic counterpart in UML, so you need to record these separately in textual form. Table 3.4 summarizes the main correspondences.

In step 6, subtypes are mapped to subclasses, adding relevant subclassing constraints. Subtype definitions are handled with discriminators and/or textual constraints. For example, the ORM schema considered earlier in Figure 3.38 maps to the UML schema in Figure 3.37.

In step 7, we map derived and semi-derived fact types. The schemas in Figures 3.53 and 3.54 provide simple examples.

With these hints, and the examples discussed earlier, you should now have enough background to do the mapping manually for yourself.

3.9 SUMMARY

UML has been adopted by the OMG as a method for object-oriented analysis and design. Although mainly focused on the design of object-oriented programming code, it can be used for modeling database applications by supplementing its predefined notations with user-defined constraints.

UML 2.0 includes 13 main diagram types, comprising 6 for structure (class, object, component, deployment, package, and composite) and 7 for behavior (use case, state machine, activity, sequence, collaboration, interaction overview, and timing). When stripped of implementation details, class diagrams are essentially an extended form of ER diagrams minus a standard notation for value-based identification.

The basic correspondence between data structures and instances in UML and ORM is summarized in Table 3.5. Classes are basically entity types and are depicted as named rectangles, with compartments for attributes and operations, and so forth. In UML, facts are stored either in attributes of classes or in associations among two or more classes. Binary associations are depicted as lines. Ternary and longer associations include a diamond. Role names may be placed at association ends, and an association may be given a name. An association may be objectified as an association class, corresponding to nesting in ORM. Associations may be qualified to provide a weak form of coreference.

Table 3.5   Correspondence between ORM and UML Data Instances and Structures

ORM	UML
Entity	Object
Value	Data value
Object	Object or Data value
Entity type	Class
Value type	Data type
Object type	Class or Data type
— (use relationship type)	Attribute
Unary relationship type	— (use Boolean attribute)
2+-ary relationship type	Association
2+-ary relationship instance	Link
Nested object type	Association class
Coreference	Qualified association §

§ = *incomplete coverage of corresponding concept.*

Attributes and association ends may be annotated with multiplicity constraints that indicate both optionality and cardinality (e.g., 0..1 = at most one, 1 = exactly one, * = zero or more, 1..* = one or more). Attributes have a default multiplicity of 1, and association ends have a default multiplicity of *. Refer to Table 3.4 for the main correspondences between constraints in UML and ORM.

Subset constraints are allowed only between whole associations and are denoted by {subset} next to a dashed arrow. An exclusive-OR constraint is depicted by {xor} next to a dashed line connecting the relevant associations.

Subclasses are connected to their superclasses by a line with an open arrow-head at the superclass end. Subclassing may be annotated using the keywords {complete}, {incomplete}, {disjoint}, {overlapping}, {root}, and {leaf}. A discriminator (e.g., gender) may be used to indicate the basis for a subclass graph.

Whole/part associations may be displayed as aggregations using a small diamond at the whole end. A hollow diamond denotes shared aggregation (a part may belong to more than one whole), and a filled diamond indicates composition or composite aggregation (a part may belong to at most one whole at a time).

Attributes may be assigned initial (default) values. Derived attributes and associations are indicated by prepending "/" to their name. Attributes and binary association roles may be assigned a changeability setting: unrestricted, readOnly, addOnly, or removeOnly. ReadOnly means that once an attribute value or link has been inserted, it cannot be updated or deleted, and no additional values/links may be added to the attribute/association (for the constrained object instance). AddOnly means that although the original value/link cannot be deleted or updated, other values/links may be added to the attribute/association (for the constrained object instance).

A multivalued attribute or multivalued association end may be adorned with {ordered} to indicate implementation as an ordered set. One way of modeling this in ORM is to explicitly introduce a Position object type to indicate the order.

An association may be redefined by declaring an association role to be a special case of a compatible role played by a superclass. One use of this is to strengthen the constraints on the specialized association roles.

UML models are best developed by mapping them from ORM models and noting any additional ORM constraints as comments.

3.10 LITERATURE SUMMARY

The UML specification is accessible online at *www.omg.org/uml/*. For a detailed discussion of UML by "the three amigos" (Booch, Rumbaugh, and Jacobson), see Booch et al. (1999) and Rumbaugh et al. (1999). Their suggested modeling process for using the language is discussed in Jacobson et al. (1999). Martin and Odell (1998) provide a general coverage of object-oriented modeling using the UML notation. Muller (1999) provides a detailed treatment of UML for the purposes of database modeling. A thorough discussion of OMT for database applications is given in Blaha and Premerlani (1998), although their notation for multiplicity constraints differs from the UML standard. The Object Constraint Language is covered in detail in Warmer and Kleppe (2003). Bennett, McRobb, and Farmer (2006) provide a detailed discussion of how to use UML 2.0 for object-oriented systems analysis and design.

On the topic of aggregation, Rumbaugh et al. (1999, p. 148) argue:

> Aggregation conveys the thought that the aggregate is inherently the sum of its parts. In fact, the only real semantics that it adds to association is the constraint that chains of aggregate links may not form cycles. . . . Some authors have distinguished several kinds of aggregation, but the distinctions are fairly subtle and probably unnecessary for general modeling.

There are plenty of other distinctions (apart from aggregation) we could make about associations, but don't feel compelled to do so. For a very detailed discussion arguing for an even more thorough treatment of aggregation in UML, see Barbier et al. (2000).

The view that security issues have priority over changeability settings is nicely captured by the following comment of John Harris, in a thread on the InConcept website:

> Rather than talk of "immutable" data I think it is better to talk of a privilege requirement. For instance, you can't change your recorded salary but your boss can, whether it's because you've had a pay rise or because there's been a typing error. Privileges can be as complicated or as simple as they need to be, whereas "immutable" can only be on or off. Also, privileges can be applied to the insertion of new data and removal of old data, not just to updates.

A collection of readings critiquing UML is contained in Siau and Halpin (2000). The Precise UML group, comprised largely of European academics, has published several papers mainly aimed at providing a more rigorous semantic basis for UML. A useful collection of their papers is accessible from their website at *www.puml.org*.

Requirements Analysis and Conceptual Data Modeling

4

This chapter shows how the entity–relationship (ER) and Unified Modeling Language (UML) approaches can be applied to the database life cycle, particularly in steps I through II(b) (as defined in Section 1.2), which include the requirements analysis and conceptual data modeling stages of logical database design.

4.1 INTRODUCTION

Logical database design is accomplished with a variety of approaches, including the top-down, bottom-up, and combined methodologies. The traditional approach, particularly for relational databases, has been a low-level, bottom-up activity, synthesizing individual data elements into normalized tables after carefully analyzing the data element interdependencies defined during the requirements analysis. Although the traditional process has been somewhat successful for small- to medium-size databases, when used for large databases its complexity can be overwhelming to the point where practicing designers do not bother to use it with any regularity. In practice, a combination of the top-down and bottom-up approaches is used; in most cases, tables can be defined directly from the requirements analysis.

The conceptual data model has been most successful as a tool for communication between the designer and the end user during the requirements analysis and logical design phases. Its success is due to the fact that the model, using either ER or UML, is easy to understand and convenient to represent. Another reason for its effectiveness is that it is a top-down approach using the concept of abstraction. The number of entities in a database is typically far fewer than the number of individual data elements, because data elements usually represent the attributes. Therefore, using entities as an abstraction for data elements and focusing on the relationships between entities greatly reduces the number of objects under consideration and simplifies the analysis. Though it is still necessary to represent data elements by attributes of entities at the conceptual level, their dependencies are normally confined to the other attributes within the entity or, in some cases, to attributes associated with other entities with a direct relationship to their entity.

The major interattribute dependencies that occur in data models are the dependencies between the *entity keys*, which are the unique identifiers of different entities that are captured in the conceptual data modeling process. Special cases, such as dependencies among data elements of unrelated entities, can be handled when they are identified in the ensuing data analysis.

The logical database design approach defined here uses both the conceptual data model and the relational model in successive stages. It benefits from the simplicity and ease of use of the conceptual data model and the structure and associated formalism of the relational model. To facilitate this approach, it is necessary to build a framework for transforming the variety of conceptual data model constructs into tables that are already normalized or that can be normalized with a minimum of transformation. The beauty of this type of transformation is that it results in normalized or nearly normalized SQL tables from the start; frequently, further normalization is not necessary.

Before we do this, however, we need to first define the major steps of the relational logical design methodology in the context of the database life cycle.

4.2 REQUIREMENTS ANALYSIS

Step I, requirements analysis, is an extremely important step in the database life cycle and is typically the most labor intensive. The database designer must interview the end user population and determine exactly what the database is to be used for and what it must contain. The basic objectives of requirements analysis are:

- To delineate the data requirements of the enterprise in terms of basic data elements.

- To describe the information about the data elements and the relationships among them needed to model these data requirements.

- To determine the types of transactions that are intended to be executed on the database and the interaction between the transactions and the data elements.

- To define any performance, integrity, security, or administrative constraints that must be imposed on the resulting database.

- To specify any design and implementation constraints, such as specific technologies, hardware and software, programming languages, policies, standards, or external interfaces.

- To thoroughly document all of the preceding in a detailed requirements specification. The data elements can also be defined in a data dictionary system, often provided as an integral part of the database management system.

The conceptual data model helps designers accurately capture the real data requirements because it requires them to focus on semantic detail in the data relationships, which is greater than the detail that would be provided by functional dependencies (FDs) alone. The semantics of the ER model, for instance, allow for direct transformations of entities and relationships to at least first normal form (1NF) tables. They also provide clear guidelines for integrity constraints. In addition, abstraction techniques such as generalization provide useful tools for integrating end user views to define a global conceptual schema.

4.3 CONCEPTUAL DATA MODELING

Let us now look more closely at the basic data elements and relationships that should be defined during requirements analysis and conceptual design. These two life cycle steps are often done simultaneously.

Consider the substeps in step II(a), conceptual data modeling, using the ER model:

- Classify entities and attributes (classify classes and attributes in UML).
- Identify the generalization hierarchies (for both the ER model and UML).
- Define relationships (define associations and association classes in UML).

The remainder of this section discusses the tasks involved in each substep.

4.3.1 Classify Entities and Attributes

Though it is easy to define entity, attribute, and relationship constructs, it is not as easy to distinguish their roles in modeling the database. What makes a data element an entity, an attribute, or even a relationship? For example, project headquarters are located in cities. Should city be an entity or an attribute? A vita is kept for each employee. Is vita an entity or a relationship?

The following guidelines for classifying entities and attributes will help the designer's thoughts converge to a normalized relational database design:

- Entities should contain descriptive information.
- Multivalued attributes should be classified as entities.
- Attributes should be attached to the entities they most directly describe.

Now we examine each guideline in turn.

Entity Contents

Entities should contain descriptive information. If there is descriptive information about a data element, the data element should be classified as an entity. If a data element requires only an identifier and does not have relationships, it should be classified as an attribute. With city, for example, if there is some descriptive information such as country and population for a city, then city should be classified as an entity. If only the city name is needed to identify a city, then `city` should be classified as an attribute associated with some entity, such as `Project`. The exception to this rule is that if the identity of the value needs to be constrained by set membership, you should create it as an entity. For example, `state` is much the same as `city`, but you probably want to have a `State` entity that contains all the valid state instances. Examples of other data elements in the real world that are typically classified as entities include `Employee`, `Task`, `Project`, `Department`, `Company`, `Customer`, and so on.

Multivalued Attributes

Classify multivalued attributes as entities. If more than one value of a descriptor attribute corresponds to one value of an identifier, the descriptor should be classified as an entity instead of an attribute, even though it does not have descriptors itself. A large company, for example, could have many divisions, some of them possibly in different cities. In that case, `division` could be classified as a multivalued attribute of `company`, but it would be better classified as an entity, with `division-address` as its identifier. If attributes are restricted to be single valued only, the later design and implementation decisions will be simplified.

Attribute Attachment

Attach attributes to the entities they most directly describe. For example, `office-building-name` should normally be an attribute of the entity `Department`, rather than the entity `Employee`. The procedure of identifying entities and attaching attributes to entities is iterative. Classify some data elements as entities and attach identifiers and descriptors to them. If you find some violation of the preceding guidelines, change some data elements from entity to attribute (or from attribute to entity), attach attributes to the new entities, and so forth.

4.3.2 Identify the Generalization Hierarchies

If there is a generalization hierarchy among entities, then put the identifier and generic descriptors in the supertype entity and put the same identifier and specific descriptors in the subtype entities.

For example, suppose the following five entities were identified in an ER model:

- `Employee`, with identifier `empno` and descriptors `empname`, `address`, and `date-of-birth`.
- `Manager`, with identifier `empno` and descriptors `empname` and `jobtitle`.
- `Engineer`, with identifier `empno` and descriptors `empname`, `highest-degree`, and `jobtitle`.
- `Technician`, with identifier `empno` and descriptors `empname` and `specialty`.
- `Secretary`, with identifier `empno` and descriptors `empname` and `best-skill`.

Let's say we determine, through our analysis, that the entity `Employee` could be created as a generalization of `Manager`, `Engineer`, `Technician`, and `Secretary`. Then we put identifier `empno` and generic descriptors `empname`, `address`, and `date-of-birth` in the supertype entity `Employee`; identifier `empno` and specific descriptor `jobtitle` in the subtype entity `Manager`; identifier `empno` and specific descriptor `highest-degree` and `jobtitle` in the subtype entity `Engineer`; and so on. Later, if we decide to eliminate `Employee` as a table, the original identifiers and generic attributes can be redistributed to all the subtype tables.

4.3.3 Define Relationships

We now deal with data elements that represent associations among entities, which we call *relationships*. Examples of typical relationships are `works-in`, `works-for`, `purchases`, `drives`, or any verb that connects entities. For every relationship, the following should be specified: degree (binary, ternary, etc.); connectivity (one-to-many, etc.); optional or mandatory existence; and any attributes associated with the relationship and not the entities. The following are some guidelines for defining the more difficult types of relationships.

Redundant Relationships

Analyze redundant relationships carefully. Two or more relationships that are used to represent the same concept are considered redundant. Redundant relationships are more likely to result in unnormalized tables when transforming the ER model into relational schemas. Note that two or more relationships are allowed between the same two entities, as long as those relationships have different meanings. In this case they are not considered redundant. One important case of nonredundancy is shown in Figure 4.1(a) for the ER model and Figure 4.1(c) for UML. If `belongs-to` is a one-to-many relationship between `Employee` and `Professional-association`, if `located-in` is a one-to-many relationship between `Professional-association` and `City`, and if `lives-in` is a one-to-many relationship between `Employee` and `City`, then `lives-in` is not redundant, because the relationships are unrelated. However, consider the situation shown in Figure 4.1(b) for the ER model and Figure 4.1(d) for UML. The employee works on a project located in a city, so the `works-in` relationship between `Employee` and `City` is redundant and can be eliminated.

Ternary Relationships

Define ternary relationships carefully. We define a ternary relationship among three entities only when the concept cannot be represented by several binary relationships among those entities. For example, let us assume there is some association among entities `Technician`, `Project`, and `Notebook`. If each technician can be working on any of several projects and using the same notebooks on each project, then three many-to-many binary relationships can be defined (see Figure 4.2(a) for the ER model and Figure 4.2(c) for UML). If, however, each technician

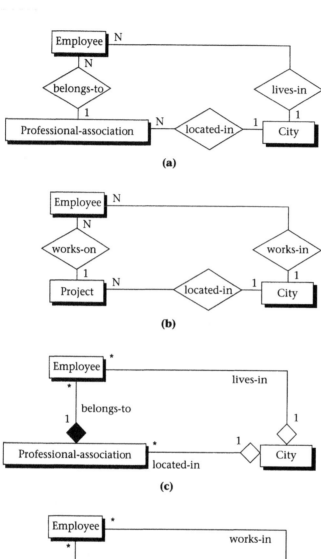

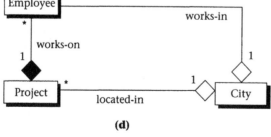

FIGURE 4.1

Redundant relationships: (a) nonredundant relationships, (b) redundant relationships using transitivity, (c) nonredundant associations, and (d) redundant associations using transitivity.

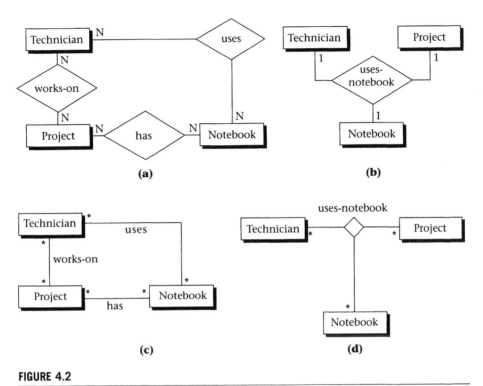

FIGURE 4.2

Ternary relationships: (a) binary relationships, (b) different meaning using a ternary relationship, (c) binary associations, and (d) different meaning using a ternary association.

is constrained to use exactly one notebook for each project and that notebook belongs to only one technician, then a one-to-one-to-one ternary relationship should be defined (see Figure 4.2(b) for the ER model and Figure 4.2(d) for UML). The approach to take in ER modeling is to first attempt to express the associations in terms of binary relationships; if this is impossible because of the constraints of the associations, try to express them in terms of a ternary.

The meaning of connectivity for ternary relationships is important. Figure 4.2(b) shows that for a given pair of instances of Technician and Project, there is only one corresponding instance of Notebook; for a given pair of instances of Technician and Notebook, there is only one corresponding instance of Project; and for a given pair of instances of Project and Notebook, there is only one instance of Technician. In general, we know by our definition of ternary relationships that if a relationship among three entities can only be expressed by a functional dependency involving the keys of all three entities, then it cannot be expressed using only binary relationships, which only apply to associations between two entities. Object-oriented design provides arguably a better way to model this situation (Muller, 1999).

4.3.4 **Example of Data Modeling: Company Personnel and Project Database**

Let us suppose it is desirable to build a company-wide database for a large engineering firm that keeps track of all full-time personnel, their skills and projects assigned, the departments (and divisions) they worked in, the engineering professional associations they belonged to, and the engineering desktop computers allocated. During the requirements collection process—that is, interviewing the end users—we obtain three views of the database.

ER Modeling of Individual Views Based on Requirements

The first view, a management view, defines each employee as working in a single department, and defines a division as the basic unit in the company, consisting of many departments. Each division and department has a manager, and we want to keep track of each manager. The ER model for this view is shown in Figure 4.3(a).

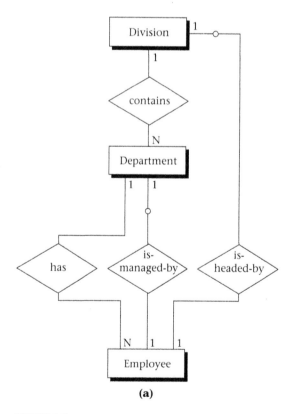

(a)

FIGURE 4.3

Example of data modeling: (a) management view.

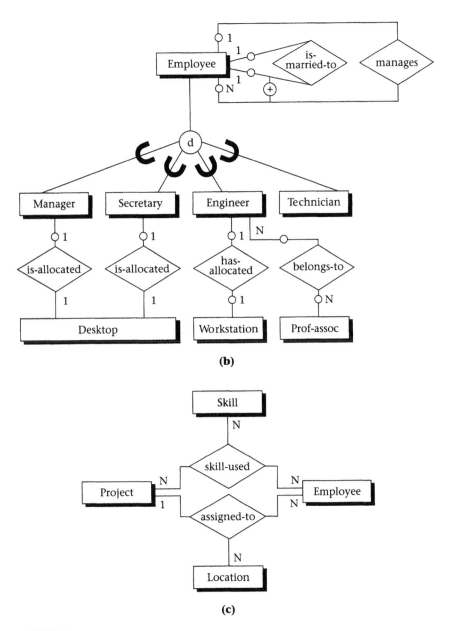

(b)

(c)

FIGURE 4.3

(b) employee view, (c) employee assignment view. (*Continued*)

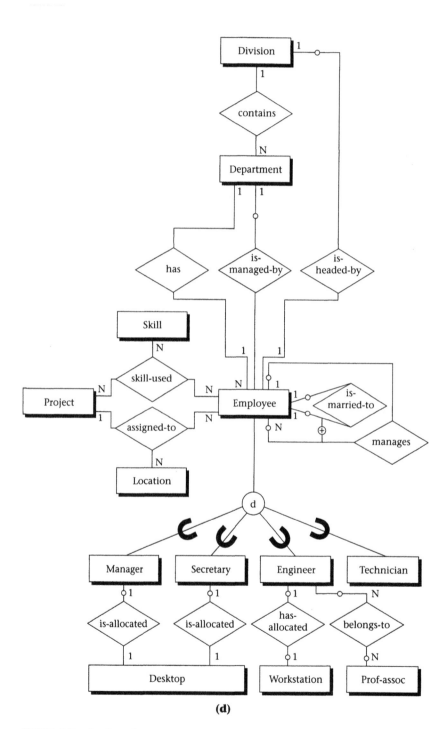

FIGURE 4.3 *Continued*

(d) the global ER schema.

The second view defines each employee as having a job title: engineer, technician, secretary, manager, and so on. Engineers typically belong to professional associations and might be allocated an engineering workstation (or computer). Secretaries and managers are each allocated a desktop computer. A pool of desktops and workstations is maintained for potential allocation to new employees and for loans while an employee's computer is being repaired. Any employee may be married to another employee, and we want to keep track of these relationships to avoid assigning an employee to be managed by his or her spouse. This view is illustrated in Figure 4.3(b).

The third view, shown in Figure 4.3(c), involves the assignment of employees, mainly engineers and technicians, to projects. Employees may work on several projects at one time, and each project could be headquartered at different locations (cities). However, each employee at a given location works on only one project at that location. Employee skills can be individually selected for a given project, but no individual has a monopoly on skills, projects, or locations.

Global ER Schema

A simple integration of the three views over the entity `Employee` defines results in the global ER schema (diagram) in Figure 4.3(d), which becomes the basis for developing the normalized tables. Each relationship in the global schema is based upon a verifiable assertion about the actual data in the enterprise, and analysis of those assertions leads to the transformation of these ER constructs into candidate SQL tables.

Note that equivalent views and integration could be done for a UML conceptual model over the class `Employee`. We will use the ER model for the examples in the rest of this chapter, however.

The diagram shows examples of binary, ternary, and binary recursive relationships; optional and mandatory existence in relationships; and generalization with the disjointness constraint. Ternary relationships `skill-used` and `assigned-to` are necessary, because binary relationships cannot be used for the equivalent notions. For example, one employee and one location determine exactly one project (a functional dependency). In the case of `skill-used`, selective use of skills to projects cannot be represented with binary relationships.

The use of optional existence, for instance, between `Employee` and `Division` or between `Employee` and `Department`, is derived from our general knowledge that most employees will not be managers of any division or department. In another example of optional existence, we show that the allocation of a workstation to an engineer may not always occur, nor will all desktops or workstations necessarily be allocated to someone at all times. In general, all relationships, optional existence constraints, and generalization constructs need to be verified with the end user before the ER model is transformed to SQL tables.

In summary, the application of the ER model to relational database design offers the following benefits:

- Use of an ER approach focuses end users' discussions on important relationships between entities. Some applications are characterized by counterexamples affecting a small number of instances, and lengthy consideration of these instances can divert attention from basic relationships.

- A diagrammatic syntax conveys a great deal of information in a compact, readily understandable form.

- Extensions to the original ER model, such as optional and mandatory membership classes, are important in many relationships. Generalization allows entities to be grouped for one functional role or to be seen as separate subtypes when other constraints are imposed.

- A complete set of rules transforms ER constructs into mostly normalized SQL tables, which follow easily from real-world requirements.

4.4 VIEW INTEGRATION

A critical part of the database design process is step II(b), the integration of different user views into a unified, nonredundant global schema. The individual end user views are represented by conceptual data models, and the integrated conceptual schema results from sufficient analysis of the end user views to resolve all differences in perspective and terminology. Experience has shown that nearly every situation can be resolved in a meaningful way through integration techniques.

Schema diversity occurs when different users or user groups develop their own unique perspectives of the world or, at least, of the enterprise to be represented in the database. For instance, the marketing division tends to have the whole product as a basic unit for sales, but the engineering division may concentrate on the individual parts of the whole product. In another case, one user may view a project in terms of its goals and progress toward meeting those goals over time, but another user may view a project in terms of the resources it needs and the personnel involved. Such differences cause the conceptual models to seem to have incompatible relationships and terminology. These differences show up in conceptual data models as different levels of abstraction; connectivity of relationships (one-to-many, many-to-many, and so on); or as the same concept being modeled as an entity, attribute, or relationship, depending on the user's perspective.

As an example of the latter case, in Figure 4.4 we see three different perspectives of the same real-life situation—the placement of an order for a certain product. The result is a variety of schemas. The first schema (Figure 4.4(a)) depicts Customer, Order, and Product as entities and places and for-a as relationships. The second schema (Figure 4.4(b)), however, defines orders as a relationship between Customer and Product and omits Order as an entity altogether. Finally, in the third case (Figure 4.4(c)), the relationship orders has been replaced by another relationship, purchases; order-no, the identifier (key) of an order, is

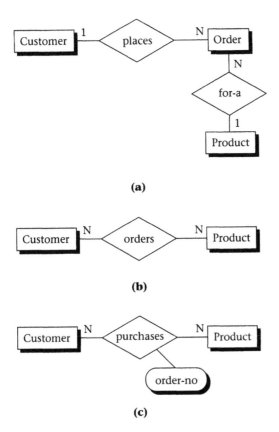

(a)

(b)

(c)

FIGURE 4.4

Schemas, placement of an order: the concept of (a) order as an entity, (b) order as a relationship, and (c) order as an attribute.

designated as an attribute of the relationship purchases. In other words, the concept of order has been variously represented as an entity, a relationship, and an attribute, depending on perspective.

There are four basic steps needed for conceptual schema integration:

1. Preintegration analysis.
2. Comparison of schemas.
3. Conformation of schemas.
4. Merging and restructuring of schemas.

4.4.1 **Preintegration Analysis**

The first step, preintegration analysis, involves choosing an integration strategy. Typically, the choice is between a binary approach with two schemas merged at one time and an *n*-ary approach with *n* schemas merged at one time, where *n* is between 2 and the total number of schemas developed in the conceptual design. The binary approach is attractive because each merge involves a small number of data model constructs and is easier to conceptualize. The *n*-ary approach may require only one grand merge, but the number of constructs may be so large that it is not humanly possible to organize the transformations properly.

4.4.2 Comparison of Schemas

In the second step, comparison of schemas, the designer looks at how entities correspond and detects conflicts arising from schema diversity—that is, from user groups adopting different viewpoints in their respective schemas. Naming conflicts include synonyms and homonyms. Synonyms occur when different names are given for the same concept; these can be detected by scanning the data dictionary, if one has been established for the database. Homonyms occur when the same name is used for different concepts. These can only be detected by scanning the different schemas and looking for common names.

Structural conflicts occur in the schema structure itself. Type conflicts involve using different constructs to model the same concept. In Figure 4.4, for example, an entity, a relationship, or an attribute can be used to model the concept of order in a business database. Dependency conflicts result when users specify different levels of connectivity (one-to-many, etc.) for similar or even the same concepts. One way to resolve such conflicts might be to use only the most general connectivity (e.g., many-to-many). If that is not semantically correct, change the names of entities so that each type of connectivity has a different set of entity names. Key conflicts occur when different keys are assigned to the same entity in different views. For example, a key conflict occurs if an employee's full name, employee ID number, and social security number are all assigned as keys.

4.4.3 Conformation of Schemas

The resolution of conflicts often requires user and designer interaction. The basic goal of the third step is to align or conform schemas to make them compatible for integration. The entities, as well as the key attributes, may need to be renamed. Conversion may be required so that concepts modeled as entities, attributes, or relationships are conformed to be only one of them. Relationships with equal degree, roles, and connectivity constraints are easy to merge. Those with differing characteristics are more difficult and, in some cases, impossible to merge. In addition, relationships that are not consistent—for example, a relationship using generalization in one place and the exclusive-OR in another—must be resolved. Finally, assertions may need to be modified so that integrity constraints remain consistent.

Techniques used for view integration include abstraction, such as generalization and aggregation to create new supertypes or subtypes, or even the introduction of new relationships. As an example, the generalization of Individual over different values of the descriptor attribute job-title could represent the consolidation of two views of the database—one based on an individual as the basic unit of personnel in the organization and another based on the classification of individuals by job titles and special characteristics within those classifications.

4.4.4 Merging and Restructuring of Schemas

The fourth step consists of the merging and restructuring of schemas. This step is driven by the goals of completeness, minimality, and understandability. Completeness requires all component concepts to appear semantically intact in the global schema. Minimality requires the designer to remove all redundant concepts in the global schema. Examples of redundant concepts are overlapping entities and truly semantically redundant relationships; for example, Ground-Vehicle and Automobile might be two overlapping entities. A redundant relationship might occur between Instructor and Student. The relationships direct-research and advise may or may not represent the same activity or relationship, so further investigation is required to determine whether they are redundant or not. Understandability requires that the global schema make sense to the user.

Component schemas are first merged by superimposing the same concepts and then restructuring the resulting integrated schema for understandability. For instance, if a supertype/subtype combination is defined as a result of the merging operation, the properties of the subtype can be dropped from the schema because they are automatically provided by the supertype entity.

4.4.5 Example of View Integration

Let us look at two different views of overlapping data. The views are based on two separate interviews of end users. We adapt the interesting example cited by Batini et al. (1986) to a hypothetical situation related to our example.

In Figure 4.5(a) we have a view that focuses on reports and includes data on departments that publish the reports, topic areas in reports, and contractors for whom the reports are written. Figure 4.5(b) shows another view, with publications as the central focus and keywords on publication as the secondary data. Our objective is to find meaningful ways to integrate the two views and maintain completeness, minimality, and understandability.

We first look for synonyms and homonyms, particularly among the entities. Note that a synonym exists between the entities Topic-area in schema 1 and Keyword in schema 2, even though the attributes do not match. However, we find that the attributes are compatible and can be consolidated. This is shown in Figure 4.6(a), which presents a revised schema, schema 2.1. In schema 2.1, Keyword has been replaced by Topic-area.

Next we look for structural conflicts between schemas. A type conflict is found to exist between the entity Department in schema 1 and the attribute dept-name in schema 2.1. The conflict is resolved by keeping the stronger entity type,

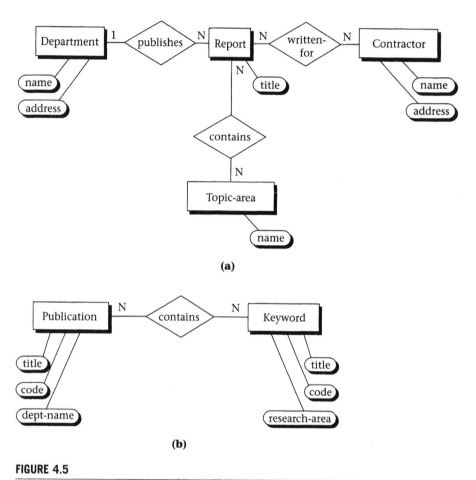

FIGURE 4.5

View integration, find meaningful ways to integrate: (a) original schema 1, focused on reports, and (b) original schema 2, focused on publications.

Department, **and moving the attribute type** dept-name **under** Publication **in schema 2 to the new entity,** Department, **in schema 2.2 (see Figure 4.6(b)).**

At this point we have sufficient commonality between schemas to attempt a merge. In schemas 1 and 2.2 we have two sets of common entities, Department and Topic-area. Other entities do not overlap and must appear intact in the superimposed, or merged, schema. The merged schema, schema 3, is shown in Figure 4.7(a). Because the common entities are truly equivalent, there are no bad side effects of the merge due to existing relationships involving those entities in one schema and not in the other. (Such a relationship that remains intact exists in schema 1 between Topic-area and Report, for example.) If true equivalence cannot be established, the merge may not be possible in the existing form.

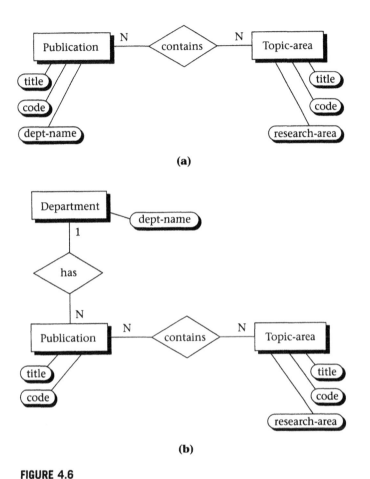

FIGURE 4.6

View integration, type conflict: (a) schema 2.1, in which Keyword has changed to Topic-area, and (b) schema 2.2, in which the attribute dept-name has changed to an attribute and an entity.

In Figure 4.7, there is some redundancy between Publication and Report in terms of the relationships with Department and Topic-area. Such a redundancy can be eliminated if there is a supertype/subtype relationship between Publication and Report, which does in fact occur in this case because Publication is a generalization of Report. In schema 3.1 (Figure 4.7(b)) we see the introduction of this generalization from Report to Publication. Then in schema 3.2 (Figure 4.7(c)) we see that the redundant relationships between Report and Department and Topic-area have been dropped. The attribute title has been eliminated as an attribute of Report in Figure 4.7(c) because title already appears as an attribute of Publication at a higher level of abstraction; title is inherited by the subtype Report.

The final schema, in Figure 4.7(c), expresses completeness because all the original concepts (Report, Publication, Topic-area, Department, and Contractor) are kept intact. It expresses minimality because of the transformation of dept-name from an attribute in schema 1 to an entity and attribute in schema 2.2, and the merger between schema 1 and schema 2.2 to form schema 3, and because of the elimination of title as an attribute of Report and of Report relationships with Topic-area and Department. Finally, it expresses understandability in that the final schema actually has more meaning than individual original schemas.

The view integration process is one of continual refinement and reevaluation. It should also be noted that minimality may not always be the most efficient way to proceed. If, for example, the elimination of the redundant relationships publishes and/or contains from schema 3.1 to schema 3.2 causes the time required to perform certain queries to be excessively long, it may be better from a performance viewpoint to leave them in. This decision could be made during the

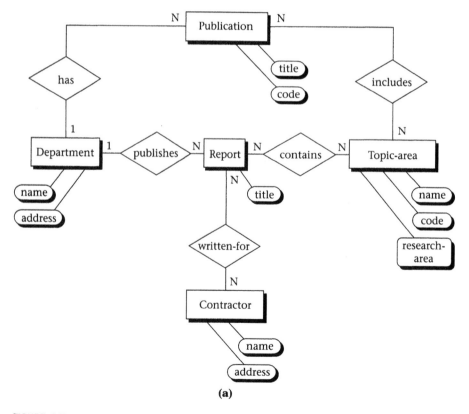

(a)

FIGURE 4.7

View integration, the merged schema: (a) schema 3, the result of merging schema 1 and schema 2.2.

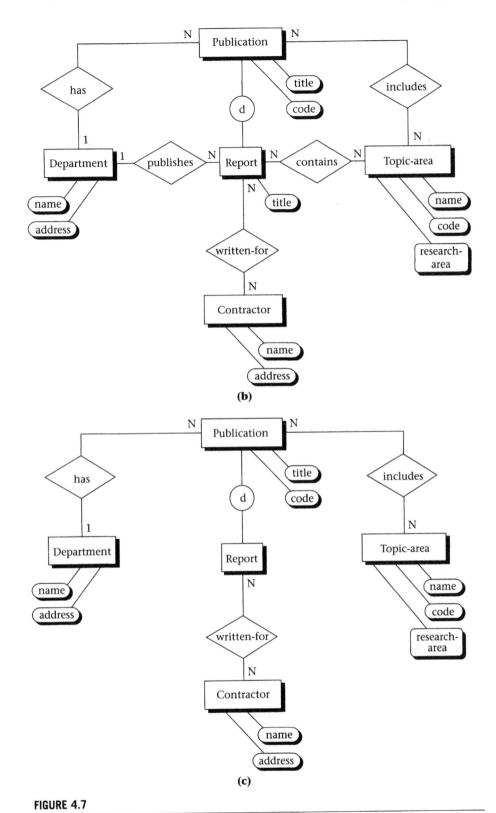

FIGURE 4.7

(b) schema 3.1, new generalization; and (c) schema 3.2, elimination of redundant relationships.

analysis of the transactions on the database or during the testing phase of the fully implemented database.

4.5 ENTITY CLUSTERING FOR ER MODELS

This section presents the concept of entity clustering, which abstracts the ER schema to such a degree that the entire schema can appear on a single sheet of paper or a single computer screen. This has happy consequences for the end user and database designer in terms of developing a mutual understanding of the database contents and formally documenting the conceptual model.

An entity cluster is the result of a grouping operation on a collection of entities and relationships. Entity clustering is potentially useful for designing large databases. When the scale of a database or information structure is large and includes a large number of interconnections among its different components, it may be very difficult to understand the semantics of such a structure and to manage it, especially for the end users or managers. In an ER diagram with 1000 entities, the overall structure will probably not be very clear, even to a well-trained database analyst. Clustering is therefore important because it provides a method to organize a conceptual database schema into layers of abstraction, and it supports the different views of a variety of end users.

4.5.1 Clustering Concepts

One should think of grouping as an operation that combines entities and their relationships to form a higher-level construct. The result of a grouping operation on simple entities is called an *entity cluster*. A grouping operation on entity clusters, or on combinations of elementary entities and entity clusters, results in a higher-level entity cluster. The highest-level entity cluster, representing the entire database conceptual schema, is called the *root entity cluster*.

Figure 4.8(a) illustrates the concept of entity clustering in a simple case where (elementary) entities R-sec (report section), R-abbr (report abbreviation), and Author are naturally bound to (dominated by) the entity Report; and entities Department, Contractor, and Project are not dominated. (Note that to avoid unnecessary detail, we do not include the attributes of entities in the diagrams.) In Figure 4.8(b), the dark-bordered box around the entity Report and the entities it dominates defines the entity cluster Report. The dark-bordered box is called the EC box to represent the idea of an entity cluster. In general, the name of the entity cluster need not be the same as the name of any internal entity; however, when there is a single dominant entity, the names are often the same. The EC box number in the lower-right corner is a clustering-level number used to keep track of the sequence in which clustering is done. The number 2.1 signifies that the entity cluster Report is the first entity cluster at level 2. Note that all the original entities are considered to be at level 1.

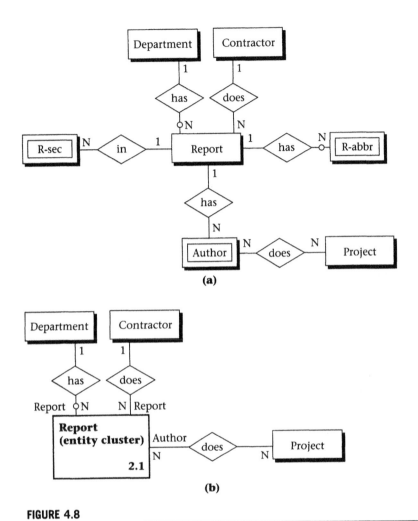

FIGURE 4.8

Entity clustering concepts: (a) ER model before clustering, and (b) ER model after clustering.

The higher-level abstraction, the entity cluster, must maintain the same relationships between entities inside and outside the entity cluster as those that occur between the same entities in the lower-level diagram. Thus, the entity names inside the entity cluster should appear just outside the EC box along the path of their direct relationship to the appropriately related entities outside the box, maintaining consistent interfaces (relationships) as shown in Figure 4.8(b). For simplicity, we modify this rule slightly: If the relationship is between an external entity and the dominant internal entity (for which the entity cluster is named), the entity cluster name need not be repeated outside the EC box. Thus, in

Figure 4.8(b), we could drop the name Report both places it occurs outside the Report box, but we must retain the name Author, which is not the name of the entity cluster.

4.5.2 Grouping Operations

Grouping operations are the fundamental components of the entity clustering technique. They define what collections of entities and relationships comprise higher-level objects, the entity clusters. The operations are heuristic in nature and (see Figure 4.9) include the following.

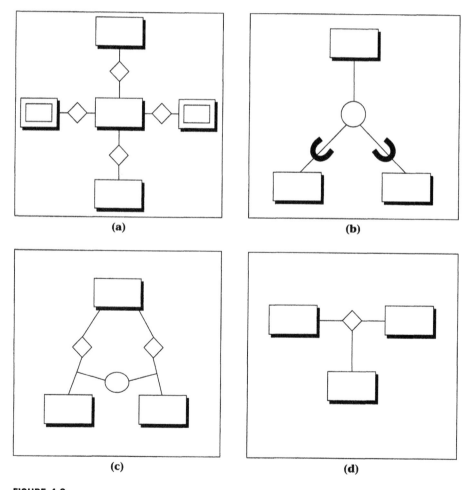

(a)   **(b)**

(c)   **(d)**

FIGURE 4.9

Grouping operations: (a) dominance grouping, (b) abstraction grouping, (c) constraint grouping, and (d) relationship grouping.

- Dominance grouping.
- Abstraction grouping.
- Constraint grouping.
- Relationship grouping.

These grouping operations can be applied recursively or used in a variety of combinations to produce higher-level entity clusters—that is, clusters at any level of abstraction. An entity or entity cluster may be an object that is subject to combinations with other objects to form the next higher level. That is, entity clusters have the properties of entities and can have relationships with any other objects at any equal or lower level. The original relationships among entities are preserved after all grouping operations, as illustrated in Figure 4.8.

Dominant objects or entities normally become obvious from the ER diagram or the relationship definitions. Each dominant object is grouped with all its related nondominant objects to form a cluster. Weak entities can be attached to an entity to make a cluster. Multilevel data objects using abstractions such as generalization and aggregation can be grouped into an entity cluster. The supertype or aggregate entity name is used as the entity cluster name. Constraint-related objects that extend the ER model to incorporate integrity constraints, such as the exclusive-OR, can be grouped into an entity cluster. Additionally, ternary or higher-degree relationships potentially can be grouped into an entity cluster. The cluster represents the relationship as a whole.

4.5.3 Clustering Technique

The grouping operations and their order of precedence determine the individual activities needed for clustering. We can now learn how to build a root entity cluster from the elementary entities and relationships defined in the ER modeling process. This technique assumes that a top-down analysis has been performed as part of the database requirement analysis and that the analysis has been documented so that the major functional areas and subareas are identified. Functional areas are often defined by an enterprise's important organizational units, business activities, or, possibly, by dominant applications for processing information. As an example, recall Figure 4.3 (reconstructed in Figure 4.10), which can be thought of as having three major functional areas: company organization (Division, Department), project management (Project, Skill, Location, Employee), and employee data (Manager, Secretary, Engineer, Technician, Prof-assoc, Workstation, and Desktop). Note that the functional areas are allowed to overlap. Figure 4.10 uses an ER diagram resulting from the database requirement analysis to show how clustering involves a series of bottom-up steps using the basic grouping operations. The following list explains these steps.

1. *Define points of grouping within functional areas.* Locate the dominant entities in a functional area through natural relationships, local *n*-ary relationships, integrity constraints, abstractions, or just the central focus of many simple

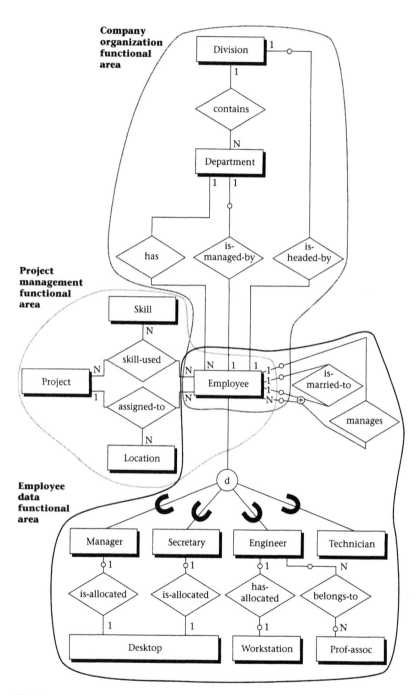

FIGURE 4.10

ER diagram: clustering technique.

relationships. If such points of grouping do not exist within an area, consider a functional grouping of a whole area.

2. *Form entity clusters.* Use the basic grouping operations on elementary entities and their relationships to form higher-level objects, or entity clusters. Because entities may belong to several potential clusters, we need to have a set of priorities for forming entity clusters. The following set of rules, listed in priority order, defines the set that is most likely to preserve the clarity of the conceptual model:

   a. Entities to be grouped into an entity cluster should exist within the same functional area; that is, the entire entity cluster should occur within the boundary of a functional area. For example, in Figure 4.10, the relationship between Department and Employee should not be clustered unless Employee is included in the company organization functional area with Department and Division. In another example, the relationship between the supertype Employee and its subtypes could be clustered within the employee data functional area.

   b. If a conflict in choice between two or more potential entity clusters cannot be resolved (e.g., between two constraint groupings at the same level of precedence), leave these entity clusters ungrouped within their functional area. If that functional area remains cluttered with unresolved choices, define functional subareas in which to group unresolved entities, entity clusters, and their relationships.

3. *Form higher-level entity clusters.* Apply the grouping operations recursively to any combination of elementary entities and entity clusters to form new levels of entity clusters (higher-level objects). Resolve conflicts using the same set of priority rules given in step 2. Continue the grouping operations until all the entity representations fit on a single page without undue complexity. The root entity cluster is then defined.

4. *Validate the cluster diagram.* Check for consistency of the interfaces (relationships) between objects at each level of the diagram. Verify the meaning of each level with the end users.

The result of one round of clustering is shown in Figure 4.11, where each of the clusters is shown at level 2.

4.6 SUMMARY

Conceptual data modeling, using either the ER or UML approach, is particularly useful in the early steps of the database life cycle, which involve requirements analysis and logical design. These two steps are often done simultaneously, particularly when requirements are determined from interviews with end users and modeled in terms of data-to-data relationships and process-to-data relationships. The conceptual data modeling step (ER approach) involves the classification of

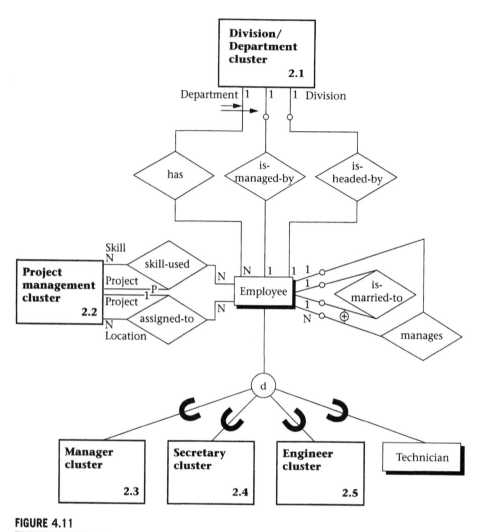

FIGURE 4.11

Clustering results.

entities and attributes first, then the identification of generalization hierarchies and other abstractions, and finally the definition of all relationships among entities. Relationships may be binary (the most common), ternary, and higher-level *n*-ary. Data modeling of individual requirements typically involves creating a different view for each end user's requirements. Then the designer must integrate those views into a global schema, so that the entire database is pictured as an integrated whole. This helps to eliminate needless redundancy—such elimination is particularly important in logical design. Controlled redundancy can be created later, at the physical design level, to enhance database performance. Finally, an entity cluster is a grouping of entities and their corresponding relationships into a higher-level abstract object. Clustering promotes the simplicity that is vital for fast end user comprehension.

4.7 LITERATURE SUMMARY

Conceptual data modeling is defined in Tsichritzis and Lochovsky (1982); Brodie, Mylopoulos, and Schmidt (1984); Nijssen and Halpin (1989); and Batini, Ceri, and Navathe (1992). Discussion of the requirements data collection process can be found in Martin (1982), Teorey and Fry (1982), and Yao (1985).

View integration has progressed from a representation tool (Smith & Smith, 1977) to heuristic algorithms (Batini, Lenzerini, & Navathe, 1986; Elmasri & Navathe, 2003). These algorithms are typically interactive, allowing the database designer to make decisions based on suggested alternative integration actions.

A variety of entity clustering models have been defined that provide a useful foundation for the clustering technique (Feldman & Miller, 1986; Dittrich, Gotthard, & Lockemann, 1986; Teorey et al., 1989).

Logical Database Design

5

5.1 INTRODUCTION

If we produced a conceptual data model and had it effectively reviewed and verified, the next step would be to translate it into a logical data model suitable for implementation using the target database management system (DBMS).

In this chapter we look at the most common situation (in which the DBMS is relational) and describe the transformations and design decisions that we need to apply to the conceptual model to produce a logical model suitable for direct implementation as a relational database. Later it may be necessary to make some changes to this initial relational model to achieve performance goals; for this purpose we will produce a physical data model.

The advantages of producing a logical data model as an intermediate deliverable rather than proceeding directly to the physical data model are:

1. Since it has been produced by a set of well-defined transformations from the conceptual data model, the logical data model reflects business information requirements without being obscured by any changes required for performance; in particular, it embodies rules about the properties of the data (such as functional dependencies). These rules cannot always be deduced from a physical data model, which may have been denormalized or otherwise compromised.

2. If the database is ported to another DBMS supporting similar structures (e.g., another relational DBMS or a new version of the same DBMS having different performance properties), the logical data model can be used as a baseline for the new physical data model.

The task of transforming the conceptual data model to a relational logical model is quite straightforward—certainly more so than the conceptual modeling stage—and is, even for large models, unlikely to take more than a few days. In fact, many computer-aided software engineering (CASE) tools provide facilities for the logical data model to be generated automatically from the conceptual model.

(They generally achieve this by bringing forward some decisions to the conceptual modeling stage, and/or applying some default transformation rules, which may not always provide the optimum result.)

We need to make a number of transformations; some of these lend themselves to alternatives and therefore require decisions to be made, while others are essentially mechanical. We describe both types in detail in this chapter. Generally, the decisions do not require business input, which is why we defer them until this time.

If you are using a DBMS that is not based on a simple relational model, you will need to adapt the principles and techniques described here to suit the particular product. However, the basic relational model currently represents the closest thing to a universal, simple view of structured data for computer implementation, and there is a good case for producing a relational data model as an interim deliverable, even if the target DBMS is not relational. From here on, unless otherwise qualified, the term *logical model* should be taken as referring to a relational model.

Similarly, if you are using a CASE tool that enforces particular transformation rules, or perhaps does not even allow for separate conceptual and logical models, you will need to adapt your approach accordingly.

In any event, even though this chapter describes what is probably the most mechanical stage in the data modeling life cycle, your attitude should not be mechanistic. Alert modelers will frequently uncover problems and challenges that have slipped through earlier stages, and will need to revisit requirements or the conceptual model.

The next section provides an overview of the transformations and design decisions in the sequence in which they would usually be performed. The following sections cover each of the transformations and decisions in more detail. A substantial amount of space is devoted to subtype implementation, a central decision in the logical design phase. The other critical decision in this phase is the definition of primary keys: Poor choice of primary keys is one of the most common and expensive errors in data modeling. We conclude the chapter by looking at how to document the resulting logical model.

5.2 OVERVIEW OF THE TRANSFORMATIONS REQUIRED

The transformations required to convert a conceptual data model to a logical model can be summarized as follows.

1. Table specification:
   a. Exclusion of entity classes not required in the database.
   b. Implementation of classification entity classes, for which there are two options.

    c. Removal of derivable many-to-many relationships (if our conceptual modeling conventions support these).[1]

    d. Implementation of many-to-many relationships as intersection tables.

    e. Implementation of *n*-ary relationships (if our conceptual modeling conventions support these)[2] as intersection tables.

    f. Implementation of supertype/subtypes: mapping one or more levels of each subtype hierarchy to tables.

    g. Implementation of other entity classes: each becomes a table.

2. Basic column specification:

    a. Removal of derivable attributes (if our conceptual modeling conventions support these).[3]

    b. Implementation of category attributes, for which there are two options.

    c. Implementation of multivalued attributes (if our conceptual modeling conventions support these),[4] for which there are multiple options.

    d. Implementation of complex attributes (if our conceptual modeling conventions support these),[5] for which there are two options.

    e. Implementation of other attributes as columns.

    f. Possible introduction of additional columns.

    g. Determination of column data types and lengths.

    h. Determination of column nullability.

At this point, the process becomes iterative rather than linear, as we have to deal with some interdependency between two tasks. We cannot specify foreign keys until we know the primary keys of the tables to which they point; on the other hand, some primary keys may include foreign key columns (which can make up part or all of a table's primary key).

What this means is that we cannot first specify all the primary keys across our model, then specify all the foreign keys in our model—or the reverse. Rather, we need to work back and forth.

First, we identify primary keys for tables derived from independent entity classes (these are entity classes that are not at the "many" end of any nontransferable mandatory many-to-one relationship;[6] loosely speaking, they are the "stand-alone" entity classes). Now we can implement all of the foreign keys pointing back to those tables. Doing this will enable us to define the primary keys for the tables representing any entity classes dependent on those independent entity

---

[1]UML supports derived relationships; entity–relationship (ER) conventions generally do not.

[2]UML and Chen conventions support *n*-ary relationships; ER conventions generally do not.

[3]UML supports derived attributes; ER conventions generally do not.

[4]UML supports multivalued attributes.

[5]Although not every CASE tool currently supports complex attributes, there is nothing in the UML or ER conventions to preclude the inclusion of complex attributes in a conceptual model.

[6]An entity class that is at the "many" end of a nontransferable mandatory many-to-one relationship may be assigned a primary key, which includes the foreign key implementing that relationship.

classes and then implement the foreign keys pointing back to them. This is described, with an example, in Section 5.5.

So, the next step is as follows.

3. Primary key specification (for tables representing independent entity classes):
   a. Assessment of existing columns for suitability.
   b. Introduction of new columns as surrogate keys.

Then, the next two steps are repeated until all of the relationships have been implemented.

4. Foreign key specification (to those tables with primary keys that already have been identified):
   a. Removal of derivable one-to-many relationships (if our conceptual modeling conventions support these).[7]
   b. Implementation of one-to-many relationships as foreign key columns.
   c. Implementation of one-to-one relationships as foreign keys or through common primary keys.

5. Primary key specification (for those tables representing entity classes dependent on other entity classes for which primary keys have already been identified):
   a. Inclusion of foreign key columns representing mandatory relationships.
   b. Assessment of other columns representing mandatory attributes for suitability.
   c. Possible introduction of additional columns as "tie-breakers."

We counsel you to follow this sequence, tempting though it can be to jump ahead to "obvious" implementation decisions. There are a number of dependencies between the steps, and unnecessary mistakes are easily made if some discipline is not observed.

5.3 TABLE SPECIFICATION

In general, each entity class in the conceptual data model becomes a table in the logical data model and is given a name that corresponds to that of the source entity class (see Section 5.7).

5.3.1 The Standard Transformation

There are, however, exceptions to this "one table per entity" picture:

- Some entity classes may be excluded from the database.
- Classification entity classes (if included in the conceptual model) may not be implemented as tables.

---

[7]UML supports derived relationships; ER conventions generally do not.

- Tables are created to implement many-to-many and *n*-ary relationships (those involving more than two entity classes).
- A supertype and its subtypes may not all be implemented as tables.

We discuss these exceptions and additions later in the sequence in which we recommend you tackle them. In practice, the implementation of subtypes and supertypes is usually the most challenging of them.

Finally, note that we may also generate some classification tables during the next phase of logical design (see Section 5.4.2), when we select our method(s) of implementing category attributes.

5.3.2 Exclusion of Entity Classes from the Database

In some circumstances an entity class may have been included in the conceptual data model to provide context, and there is no actual requirement for that application to maintain data corresponding to that entity class. It is also possible that the data are to be held in some medium other than the relational database, such as nondatabase files, XML streams, and so on.

5.3.3 Classification Entity Classes

We do not recommend that you specify classification entity classes purely to support category attributes during the conceptual modeling phase. If, however, you are working with a conceptual model that contains such entity classes, you should not implement them as tables at this stage but defer action until the next phase of logical design (column specification, as described in Section 5.4.2) to enable all category attributes to be looked at together and consistent decisions made.

5.3.4 Many-to-Many Relationship Implementation

A many-to-many relationship can be represented as an additional entity class linked to the two original entity classes by one-to-many relationships.

The Usual Case
In the same way, each many-to-many relationship in the conceptual data model can be converted to an intersection table with two foreign keys (the primary keys of the tables implementing the entity classes involved in that relationship).

Derivable Many-to-Many Relationships
Occasionally, you may discover that a many-to-many relationship that you have documented can be derived from attributes of the participating entity classes. Perhaps we have proposed `Applicant` and `Welfare Benefit` entity classes and a many-to-many relationship between them (Figure 5.1).

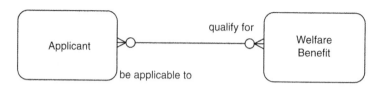

APPLICANT (Applicant ID, Name, Birth Date, . . .)
WELFARE BENEFIT (Benefit ID, Minimum Eligible Age, Maximum Eligible Age . . .)

FIGURE 5.1

A derivable many-to-many relationship.

On further analysis, we discover that eligibility for benefits can be determined by comparing attributes of the applicant with qualifying criteria for the benefit (e.g., `birth date` compared with `eligible age` attributes).

In such cases, if our chosen CASE tool does not allow us to show many-to-many relationships in the conceptual data model without creating a corresponding intersection table in the logical data model, we should delete the relationship on the basis that it is derivable (and therefore redundant); we do not want to generate an intersection table that contains nothing but derivable data.

If you are using Unified Modeling Language (UML), you can specifically identify a relationship as being derivable, in which case the CASE tool should not generate an intersection table. If you look at any model closely, you will find opportunities to document numerous such many-to-many relationships derivable from inequalities (i.e., greater than, less than) or more complex formulas and rules. For example:

- Each `Employee Absence` may occur during one or more `Strikes` and each `Strike` may occur during one or more `Employee Absences` (derivable from comparison of dates).
- Each `Aircraft Type` may be able to land at one or more `Airfields` and each `Airfield` may be able to support landing of one or more `Aircraft Types` (derivable from airport services and runway facilities and aircraft type specifications).

If our chosen CASE tool does not allow us to show many-to-many relationships in the conceptual data model without including a corresponding intersection table in the logical data model, what do we say to the business reviewers? Having presented them with a diagram, which they have approved, we now remove one or more relationships.

It is certainly not appropriate to surreptitiously amend the model on the basis that "we know better." Nor is it appropriate to create two conceptual data models, a business stakeholder model and an implementation model. Our opposition to these approaches is that the first involves important decisions being taken without business stakeholder participation, and the second complicates the modeling process for little gain. We have found that the simplest and most effective approach in this situation is to remove the relationship(s) from the conceptual data model but inform business stakeholders that we have done so and explain why. We show how the relationship is derivable from other data, and demonstrate, using sample transactions, that including the derivable relationship will add redundancy and complexity to the system.

Alternative Implementations

A DBMS that supports the SQL99 Set Type Constructor feature enables implementation of a many-to-many relationship without creating an additional table. However, we do not recommend that you include such a structure in your logical data model. The decision as to whether to use such a structure should be taken at the physical database design stage.

5.3.5 Relationships Involving More Than Two Entity Classes

The entity–relationship conventions that we use here do not support the direct representation of relationships involving three or more entity classes (*n*-ary relationships). If we encounter such relationships at the conceptual modeling stage, we will be forced to represent them using intersection entity classes, anticipating the implementation. There is nothing more to do at this stage, since the standard transformation from entity class to table will have included such entity classes. However, you should check for normalization; such structures provide the most common situations of data that are in third normal form but not in fourth or fifth normal form.

If you are using UML (or other conventions that support *n*-ary relationships), you will need to resolve the relationships (i.e., represent each *n*-ary relationship as an intersection table).

5.3.6 Supertype/Subtype Implementation

The relational model and relational DBMSs do not provide direct support for subtypes or supertypes. Therefore, any subtypes that were included in the conceptual data model are normally replaced by standard relational structures in the logical data model. Since we are retaining the documentation of the conceptual data model, we do not lose the business rules and other requirements represented by the subtypes we created in that model. This is important, since there is more than one way to represent a supertype/subtype set in a logical data model and the decisions we make to represent each such set may need to be revisited in the light of new information (such as changes to transaction profiles, other changes to business processes, or new facilities provided by the DBMS) or if the system is ported to a different DBMS. Indeed if the new DBMS supports subtypes directly, supertypes and subtypes can be retained in the logical data model; the SQL99

(ANSI/ISO/IEC 9075) standard provides for direct support of subtypes and at least one object-relational DBMS provides such support.

Implementation at a Single Level of Generalization

One way of leveling a hierarchy of subtypes is to select a single level of generalization. In the example in Figure 5.2, we can do this by discarding Party, in which case we implement only its subtypes, Individual and Organization, or by discarding Individual and Organization and implementing only their supertype, Party. Actually, "discard" is far too strong a word, since all the business rules and other requirements represented by the subtypes have been retained in the conceptual data model.

We certainly will not discard any attributes or relationships. Tables representing subtypes *inherit* the attributes and relationships of any "discarded" supertypes, and tables representing supertypes *roll up* the attributes and relationships of any "discarded" subtypes. So if we implement Individual and Organization as tables, but not Party, each will inherit all the attributes and relationships of Party. Conversely, if we implement Party as a table but not Individual or Organization, we need to include in the Party table any attributes and relationships specific to Individual or Organization. These attributes and relationships would become *optional* attributes and relationships of Party. In some cases, we might choose to combine attributes or relationships from different subtypes to form a single attribute or relationship. For example, in rolling up purchase and sale into financial transaction, we might combine price and sale value into amount. This is generalization at the attribute level.

If we implement at the supertype level, we also need to add a Type column to allow us to preserve any distinctions that the discarded subtypes represented and that cannot be derived from existing attributes of the supertype. In this example we would introduce a Party Type column to allow us to distinguish those parties that are organizations from those who are individuals.

If we are rolling up two or more levels of subtypes, we have some choice as to how many Type columns to introduce. For a generally workable solution, we suggest you simply introduce a single Type column based on the lowest level of subtyping. In Figure 5.3, if you decide to implement at the Party level, add a single Party Type column, which will hold values of Adult, Minor, Private

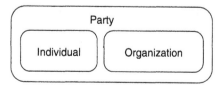

FIGURE 5.2

A simple supertype/subtype set.

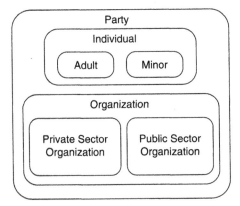

FIGURE 5.3

A more complex supertype/subtype structure.

Party Type	Organization/Individual Indicator
Private Sector Organization	Organization
Public Sector Organization	Organization
Adult	Individual
Minor	Individual

FIGURE 5.4

Reference table of `Party` types.

`Sector Organization,` **and** `Public Sector Organization.` **If you want to distinguish which of these are persons and which are organizations, you will need to introduce an additional reference table with four rows as in Figure 5.4.**

Implementation at Multiple Levels of Generalization

Returning to the example in Figure 5.2, a third option is to implement all three entity classes in the `Party` hierarchy as tables. We link the tables by carrying the foreign key of `Party` in the `Individual` and `Organization` tables. The appeal of this option is that we do not need to discard any of our concepts and rules. On the other hand, we can easily end up with a proliferation of tables, violating our aim of simplicity. And these tables usually will not correspond on a one-to-one basis with familiar concepts; the `Individual` table in this model does not hold all the attributes of individuals, only those that are not common to all parties. The concept of an individual is represented by the `Party` and `Individual` tables in combination.

Figure 5.6 illustrates all three options for implementing the supertype/subtype structure in Figure 5.5. (The exclusivity arc drawn across the set of relationships indicates that they are mutually exclusive.)

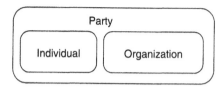

PARTY (Party ID, First Contact Date)
INDIVIDUAL (Family Name, Given Name, Gender, Birth Date)
ORGANIZATION (Registered Name, Incorporation Date, Employee Count)

FIGURE 5.5

A conceptual data model with a supertype/subtype set.

Other Options

There may be other options in some situations. First, we may create a table for the supertype and tables for only *some* of the subtypes. This is quite common when some subtypes do not have any attributes or relationships in addition to those of the supertype, in which case those subtypes do not need separate tables.

Second, if a supertype has three or more subtypes and some of those subtypes have similar attributes and relationships, we may create single tables for similar subtypes and separate tables for any other subtypes, with or without a table for the supertype. In this case, we are effectively recognizing an intermediate level of subtyping and should consider whether it is worth including it in the conceptual model. For example, in a financial services conceptual data model the Party Role entity class may have Customer, Broker, Financial Advisor, Employee, Service Provider, and Supplier subtypes. If we record similar facts about brokers and financial advisors, it may make sense to create a single table in which to record both these roles; similarly, if we record similar facts about service providers and suppliers, it may make sense to create a single table in which to record both these roles.

Which Option?

Which option should we choose for each supertype hierarchy? An important consideration is the enforcement of referential integrity. Consider this situation:

1. The database administrator (DBA) intends to implement referential integrity using the DBMS referential integrity facilities.
2. The target DBMS only supports standard referential integrity between foreign keys and primary keys.[8]

---

[8]That is without any selection of rows from the referenced table (i.e., only the rows of a subtype) or multiple referenced tables (i.e., all the rows of a supertype). The authors are not aware of any DBMSs that provide such facilities.

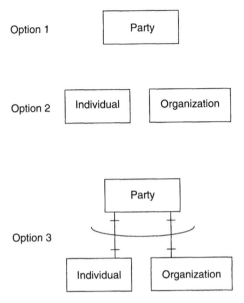

Option 1:
PARTY (Party ID, First Contact Date, Family Name, Given Name, Gender, Birth Date, Registered Name, Incorporation Date, Employee Count)
Option 2:
INDIVIDUAL (Party ID, First Contact Date, Family Name, Given Name, Gender, Birth Date)
ORGANIZATION (Party ID, First Contact Date, Registered Name, Incorporation Date, Employee Count)
Option 3:
PARTY (Party ID, First Contact Date)
INDIVIDUAL (Party ID, Family Name, Given Name, Gender, Birth Date)
ORGANIZATION (Party ID, Registered Name, Incorporation Date, Employee Count)

FIGURE 5.6

Implementing a supertype/subtype set in a logical data model.

In this case, each entity that is at the "one" end of a one-to-many relationship must be implemented as a table, whether it is a supertype or a subtype, so that the DBMS can support referential integrity of those relationships.

This is because standard DBMS referential integrity support allows a foreign key value to be any primary key value from the one associated table. If a subtype is represented by a subset of the rows in a table implementing the supertype rather than as its own separate table, any foreign keys implementing relationships to that subtype can have any primary key value including those of the other subtypes. Referential integrity on a relationship to that subtype can therefore only be managed by either program logic or a combination of DBMS referential integrity support and program logic.

By contrast, if the supertype is represented by multiple subtype tables rather than its own table, any foreign key implementing relationships to that supertype can have any value from any of the subtype tables. Referential integrity on a relationship to that supertype can therefore only be managed in program logic.

Another factor is the ability to present data in alternative ways. We do not always access the tables of a relational database directly. Usually we access them through *views*, which consist of data from one or more tables combined or selected in various ways. We can use the standard facilities available for constructing views to present data at the subtype or supertype level, regardless of whether we have chosen to implement subtypes, supertypes, or both. However, there are some limitations. Not all views allow the data presented to be updated. This is sometimes due to restrictions imposed by the particular DBMS, but there are also some logical constraints on what types of views can be updated. In particular, these arise where data have been combined from more than one table, and it is not possible to unambiguously interpret a command in terms of which underlying tables are to be updated. It is beyond the scope of this chapter to discuss view construction and its limitations in any detail. Broadly, the implications for the three implementation options are:

1. *Implementation at the supertype level:* If we implement a `Party` table, a simple selection operation will allow us to construct `Individual` and `Organization` views. These views will be logically updateable.

2. *Implementation at the subtype level:* If we implement separate `Individual` and `Organization` tables, a `Party` view can be constructed using the "union" operator. Views constructed using this operator are not updateable.

3. *Implementation of both supertype and subtype levels:* If we implement `Individual`, `Organization`, and `Party` tables, full views of `Individual` and `Organization` can be constructed using the "join" operator. Some views using this operator are not updateable, and DBMSs differ on precisely what restrictions they impose on join view updateability. They can be combined using the union operator to produce a `Party` view, which again will not be updateable.

Nonrelational DBMSs offer different facilities and may make one or other of the options more attractive. The ability to construct useful, updateable views becomes another factor in selecting the implementation option that is most appropriate.

What is important, however, is to recognize that views are not a substitute for careful modeling of subtypes and supertypes, and to consider the appropriate level for implementation. Identification of useful data classifications is part of the data modeling process, not something that should be left to some later task of view definition. If subtypes and supertypes are not recognized in the conceptual modeling stage, we cannot expect the process model to take advantage of them. There is little point in constructing views unless we have planned to use them in our programs.

Implications for Process Design

If a supertype is implemented as a table and at least one of its subtypes is implemented as a table as well, any process creating an instance of that subtype (or one of *its* subtypes) must create a row in the corresponding supertype table as well as the row in the appropriate subtype table(s). To ensure that this occurs, those responsible for writing detailed specifications of programs (which we assume are written in terms of table-level transactions) from business-level process specifications (which we assume are written in terms of entity-level transactions) must be informed of this rule.

5.4 BASIC COLUMN DEFINITION

5.4.1 Attribute Implementation: The Standard Transformation

With some exceptions, each attribute in the conceptual data model becomes a column in the logical data model and should be given a name that corresponds to that of the corresponding attribute (see Section 5.7). The principal exceptions to this are:

- Category attributes.
- Derivable attributes.
- Attributes of relationships.
- Complex attributes.
- Multivalued attributes.

The following subsections describe each of these exceptions.

We may also add further columns for various reasons. The most common of these are surrogate primary keys and foreign keys (covered in Sections 5.5 and 5.6, respectively), but there are some additional situations, discussed in Section 5.4.7. The remainder of Section 5.4 looks at some issues applicable to columns in general.

Note that in this phase we may end up specifying additional tables to support category attributes.

5.4.2 Category Attribute Implementation

In general, DBMSs provide the following two distinct methods of implementing a category attribute:

1. As a foreign key to a classification table.
2. As a column on which a constraint is defined limiting the values that the column may hold.

The principal advantage of the classification table method is that the ability to change codes or descriptions can be granted to users of the database rather than them having to rely on the database administrator to make such changes. However, if any procedural logic depends on the value assigned to the category attribute, such changes should only be made in controlled circumstances in which synchronized changes are made to procedural code.

If you have adopted our recommendation of showing category attributes in the conceptual data model as attributes rather than relationships to classification entity classes, and you select the "constraint on column" method of implementation, your category attributes become columns like any other, and there is no more work to be done. If, however, you select the "classification table" method of implementation, you must:

1. Create a table for each domain that you have defined for category attributes, with `Code` and `Meaning` columns.
2. Create a foreign key column that references the appropriate domain table to represent each category attribute.[9]

For example, if you have two category attributes in your conceptual data model, each named `customer type` (one in the `Customer` entity class and the other in an `Allowed Discount` business rule entity class recording the maximum discount allowed for each customer type), then each of these should belong to the same domain, also named `Customer Type`. In this case, you must create a `Customer Type` table with `Customer Type Code` and `Customer Type Meaning` columns and include foreign keys to that table in your `Customer` and `Allowed Discount` tables to represent the `customer type` attributes.

By contrast, if you have modeled category attributes in the conceptual data model as relationships to classification entity classes, and you select the classification table option, your classification entity classes become tables like any other and the relationships to them become foreign key columns like any other. If, however, you select the "constraint on column" option, you must not create tables for those classification entity classes, but you must represent each relationship to a classification entity class as a simple column, not as a foreign key column.

5.4.3 Derivable Attributes

Since the logical data model should not specify redundant data, derivable attributes in the conceptual data model should not become columns in the logical

---

[9]Strictly speaking, we should not be specifying primary or foreign keys at this stage, but the situation here is so straightforward that most of us skip the step of initially documenting only a relationship.

Table: **ORDER LINE** (<u>Order No</u>, <u>Product No</u>, Order Quantity, Applicable Discount Rate, Quoted Price, Promised Delivery Date, Actual Delivery Date)

View: **ORDER LINE** (<u>Order No</u>, <u>Product No</u>, Order Quantity, Applicable Discount Rate, Quoted Price, Promised Delivery Date, Actual Delivery Date,
Total Item Cost = Order Quantity * Quoted Price * (1- Applicable Discount Rate/100.0))

FIGURE 5.7

A table and a view defining a derivable attribute.

data model. However, the designer of the physical data model needs to be advised of derivable attributes so as to decide whether they should be stored as columns in the database or calculated "on the fly." We therefore recommend that, for each entity class with derivable attributes, you create a view based on the corresponding table, which includes (as well as the columns of that table) a column for each derived attribute, specifying how that attribute is calculated. Figure 5.7 illustrates this principle.

5.4.4 Attributes of Relationships

If the relationship is many-to-many or *n*-ary, its attributes should be implemented as columns in the table implementing the relationship. If the relationship is one-to-many, its attributes should be implemented as columns in the table implementing the entity class at the "many" end. If the relationship is one-to-one, its attributes can be implemented as columns in either of the tables used to implement one of the entity classes involved in that relationship.

5.4.5 Complex Attributes

In general, unless the target DBMS provides some form of *row data type* facility (such as Oracle™'s Nested Tables), built-in complex data types (such as foreign currencies or timestamps with associated time zones), or *constructors* with which to create such data types, each component of a complex attribute will require a separate column. For example, a currency amount in an application dealing with multiple currencies will require a column for the amount and another column in which the currency unit for each amount can be recorded. Similarly, a time attribute in an application dealing with multiple time zones may require a column in which the time zone is recorded as well as the column for the time itself. Addresses are another example of complex attributes. Each address component will require a separate column.

An alternative approach where a complex attribute type has many components (e.g., addresses) is to:

1. Create a separate table in which to hold the complex attribute.
2. Hold only a foreign key to that table in the original table.

5.4.6 Multivalued Attribute Implementation

Consider the conceptual data model of a multi-airline timetable database in Figure 5.8. A flight (e.g., AA123, UA345) may operate over multiple flight legs, each of which is from one port to another. Actually a flight has no real independent existence but is merely an identifier for a series of flight legs. Although some flights operate year-round, others are seasonal and may therefore have one or more operational periods (in fact, two legs of a flight may have different operational periods: the Chicago–Denver flight may only continue to Los Angeles in the summer). And of course not all flights are daily, so we need to record the days of the week on which a flight (or rather its legs) operates. In the conceptual

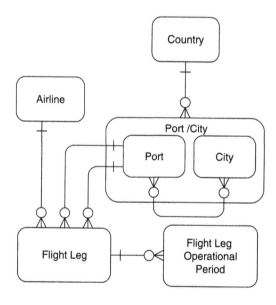

PORT/CITY (Code, Name, Time Zone)
COUNTRY (Code, Name)
AIRLINE (Code, Name)
FLIGHT LEG (Flight Number, Leg Number, Departure Local TimeOfDay, Arrival Local Time TimeOfDay, Arrival Additional Day Count, Aircraft Type, {Meal Types})
FLIGHT LEG OPERATIONAL PERIOD (Start Date, End Date, {Week Days})

FIGURE 5.8

Implementing a multivalued attribute.

data model we can do this using the multivalued attribute {week days}. At the same time we should record for the convenience of passengers on long-distance flights what meals are served (on a trans-Pacific flight there could be as many as three). The {meal types} multivalued attribute supports this requirement.

In general, unless the target DBMS supports the SQL99 Set Type Constructor feature, which enables direct implementation of multivalued attributes, normal practice is to represent each such attribute in the logical data model using a separate table. Thus, the {meal types} attribute of the Flight Leg entity class could be implemented using a table (with the name Flight Leg Meal Type, that is, the singular form of the attribute name prefixed by the name of its owning entity class) with the following columns:

1. A foreign key to the Flight Leg table (representing the entity class owning the multivalued attribute).
2. A column in which a single meal type can be held (with the name Meal Type, that is, the singular form of the attribute name).

The primary key of this table can simply be all of these columns.

Similarly normal practice would be to represent the {week days} attribute in the logical data model using a Flight Leg Operational Period Week Day table with a foreign key to Flight Leg Operational Period and a Week Day column. However, the case may be that:

1. The maximum number of values that may be held is finite and small.
2. There is no requirement to sort using the values of that attribute.

Then, the designer of the physical data model may well create, rather than add an additional table, a set of columns (one for each value) in the original table (the one implementing the entity class with the multivalued attribute). For example, {week days} can be implemented using seven columns in the Flight Leg Operational Period table, one for each day of the week, each holding a flag to indicate whether that flight leg operates on that day during that operational period.

If the multivalued attribute is textual, the modeler may even implement it in a single column in which all the values are concatenated, or separated if necessary by a separator character. This is generally only appropriate if queries searching for a single value in that column are not rendered unduly complex or slow. If this is likely to occur, it may be better from a pragmatic point of view to model such attributes this way in the logical data model as well, to avoid the models diverging so much. For example, {meal types} can be implemented using a single Meal Types column in the Flight Leg table, since there is a maximum of three meals that can be served on one flight leg.

By way of another example, an Employee entity class may have the attribute dependent names, which could be represented by a single column in the Employee table, which would hold values such as "Peter" or "Paul, Mary."

5.4.7 Additional Columns

In some circumstances additional columns may be required. We have already seen the addition of a column or columns to identify subtypes in a supertype table. Other columns are typically required to hold data needed to support system administration, operation, and maintenance. The following examples will give you a flavor.

A very common situation is when a record is required of who inserted each row and when, and of who last updated each row and when. In this case, you can create a pair of DateTime columns, usually named along the lines of Insert DateTime and Last Update DateTime, and a pair of text columns, usually named along the lines of Insert User ID and Last Update User ID. Of course, if a full audit trail of all changes to a particular table is required, you will need to create an additional table with the following columns:

- Those making up a foreign key to the table to be audited.
- An Update DateTime column, which together with the foreign key columns makes up the primary key of this table.
- An Update User ID column.
- The old and/or new values of the remaining columns of the table to be audited.

The meaning attribute in a classification entity class in the conceptual data model is usually a relatively short text that appears as the interpretation of the code in screens and reports. If the differences between some meanings require explanation that would not fit in the Meaning column, then an additional, longer Explanation column may need to be added.

By contrast, additional columns holding abbreviated versions of textual data may be needed for any screens, other displays (such as networked equipment displays), reports, and other printouts (such as printed tickets) in which there may be space limitations. A typical example is location names: Given the fact that these may have the same initial characters (e.g., "Carlton" and "Carlton North"), simple truncation of such names may produce indistinguishable abbreviations.

Another situation in which additional columns may be required is when a numeric or date/time attribute may hold approximate or partly defined values such as "at least $10,000," "approximately $20,000," "some time in 1968," "July 25, but I can't remember which year." To support values like the first two examples, you might create an additional text column in which a qualifier of the amount in the numeric column can be recorded. To support values like the other two examples, you might store the year and month/day components of the date in separate columns.

5.4.8 Column Data Types

If the target DBMS and the data types available in that DBMS are known, the appropriate DBMS data type for each domain can be identified and documented.

Each column representing an attribute should be assigned the appropriate data type based on the domain of the corresponding attribute. Each column in a foreign key should be given the same data type as the corresponding column in the corresponding primary key.

5.4.9 Column Nullability

If an attribute has been recorded as mandatory in the business rule documentation accompanying the conceptual data model, the corresponding column should be marked as mandatory in the logical data model; the standard method for doing this is to follow the column name and its data type with the annotation NOT NULL. By contrast, if an attribute has been recorded as optional, the corresponding column should be marked as optional using the annotation NULL.

Any row in which no value has been assigned to that attribute for the entity instance represented by that row will have a null marker rather than a value assigned to that column. Nulls can cause a variety of problems in queries, as Chris Date has pointed out.[10]

Ranges provide a good example of a situation in which it is better to use an actual value than a null marker in a column representing an optional attribute. The range end attribute is often optional because there is no maximum value in the last range in a set. For example, the End Date of the current record in a table that records current and past situations is generally considered to be optional as we have no idea when the current situation will change. Unfortunately, to use a null marker in End Date complicates any queries that determine the date range to which a transaction belongs, like the first query in Figure 5.9. Loading a "high value" date (a date that is later than the latest date that the application could still be active) into the End Date column of the current record enables us to use the second, simpler, query in Figure 5.9.

5.5 PRIMARY KEY SPECIFICATION

There is the possibility that the primary key of a table may include foreign keys to other tables. However, at this point in the translation to a logical model, we haven't defined the foreign keys, and cannot do so until we have defined the primary keys of the tables being referenced. We resolve this "chicken and egg" situation with an iterative approach.

At the start of this step of the process, you can only determine primary keys for those tables that correspond to independent entity classes, since, as we have seen, the primary keys of such tables will not include foreign keys. You therefore first select an appropriate primary key for each of these tables, if necessary adding

---

[10]Date, C. J. *Relational Database Writings, 1989-1991*. Pearson Education POD, 1992.

```
select TRANSACTION.*, HISTORIC_PRICE.PRICE
from TRANSACTION, HISTORIC_PRICE
where TRANSACTION.TRANSACTION_DATE between
HISTORIC_PRICE.START_DATE and HISTORIC_PRICE.END_DATE
or TRANSACTION.TRANSACTION_DATE >
HISTORIC_PRICE.START_DATE and HISTORIC_PRICE.END_DATE is null;


select TRANSACTION.*, HISTORIC_PRICE.PRICE
from TRANSACTION, HISTORIC_PRICE
where TRANSACTION.TRANSACTION_DATE between
HISTORIC_PRICE.START_DATE and HISTORIC_PRICE.END_DATE;
```

FIGURE 5.9

Queries involving date ranges.

a surrogate key column as a key in its own right or to supplement existing attributes.

Having specified primary keys for at least some tables, you are now in a position to duplicate these as foreign keys in the tables corresponding to related entity classes. Doing that is the subject of the next section.

You are now able to determine the primary keys of those tables representing entity classes dependent on the entity classes for which you have already identified primary keys (since you now have a full list of columns for these tables, including foreign keys). You can then duplicate these in turn as foreign keys in the tables corresponding to related entity classes. You then repeat this step, "looping" until the model is complete.

This may sound complicated, but, in practice, this iterative process moves quickly and naturally, and the discipline will help to ensure that you select sound primary keys and implement relationships faithfully. The process is illustrated in Figure 5.10:

- Policy Type and Person are obviously independent, and Organization Unit is at the "many" end of a transferable relationship, so we can identify primary keys for them immediately.
- Policy is at the "many" end of a nontransferable relationship, so it depends on Policy Type having a defined primary key.
- Policy Event and Person Role in Policy are at the "many" ends of nontransferable relationships, so they depend on Policy and Person having defined primary keys.

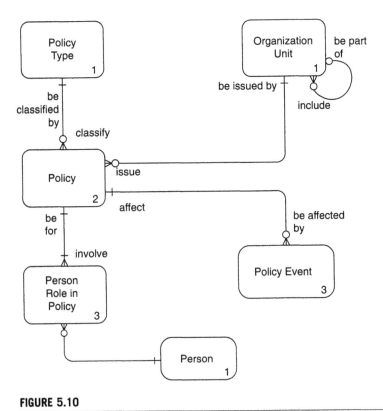

FIGURE 5.10

Primary and foreign key specification.

5.6 FOREIGN KEY SPECIFICATION

Foreign keys are our means of implementing one-to-many (and occasionally one-to-one) relationships. This phase of logical design requires that we know the primary key of the entity class at the "one" end of the relationship, and, as discussed in Section 5.2, the definition of primary keys is, in turn, dependent on the definition of foreign keys. So, we implement the relationships that meet this criterion, and then we return to define more primary keys.

This section commences with the basic rule for implementing one-to-many relationships. This rule will cover the overwhelming majority of situations. The remainder of the section looks at a variety of unusual situations. It is worth being familiar with them because they do show up from time to time, and, as a professional modeler, you need to be able to recognize and deal with them.

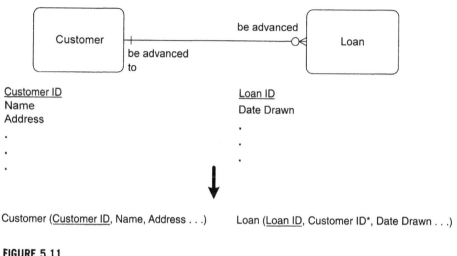

Customer (<u>Customer ID</u>, Name, Address . . .)   Loan (<u>Loan ID</u>, Customer ID*, Date Drawn . . .)

FIGURE 5.11

Deriving foreign keys from relationships.

5.6.1 One-to-Many Relationship Implementation

Translating the links implied by primary and foreign keys in a relational model into lines representing one-to-many relationships on an ER diagram is a useful technique when we have an existing database that has not been properly documented in diagrammatic form.

The Basic Rule

The process of recovering the design in this all-too-frequent situation is an example of the broader discipline of "reverse engineering" and is one of the less glamorous tasks of the data modeler.

When moving from a conceptual to a logical data model, however, we work from a diagram to tables and apply the following rule (shown in Figure 5.11):

> A one-to-many relationship is supported in a relational database by holding the primary key of the table representing the entity class at the "one" end of the relationship as a foreign key in the table representing the entity class at the "many" end of the relationship.

In the logical data model, therefore, we create, in the table representing the entity class at the "many" end of the relationship, a copy of the primary key of the entity class at the "one" end of the relationship. (Remember that the primary key may consist of more than one column, and we will, of course, need to copy all of its columns to form the foreign key.) Each foreign key column should be given the same name as the primary key column from which it was derived, possibly with the addition of a prefix. Prefixes are necessary in two situations:

1. If there is more than one relationship between the same two entity classes, in which case prefixes are necessary to distinguish the two different foreign keys—for example, `Preparation Employee ID` and `Approval Employee ID`.

2. A self-referencing relationship will be represented by a foreign key that contains the same column(s) as the primary key of the same table, so a prefix will be required for the column names of the foreign key; typical prefixes are `Parent`, `Owner`, and `Manager` (in a organizational reporting hierarchy).

Note the use of the asterisk in Figure 5.11. This is a convention sometimes used to indicate that a column of a table is all or part of a foreign key. Different CASE tools use different conventions.

A column forming part of a foreign key should be marked as `NOT NULL` if the relationship it represents is mandatory at the "one" end; conversely, if the relationship is optional at the "one" end, it should be marked as `NULL`.

Alternative Implementations

A DBMS that supports the SQL99 Set Type Constructor feature enables implementation of a one-to-many relationship within one table. However, we do not recommend that you include such a structure in your logical data model; the decision as to whether to use such a structure should be made at the physical database design stage.

Some DBMSs (including DB2) allow a one-to-many relationship to be implemented by holding a copy of *any* candidate key of the referenced table, not just the primary key. (The candidate key must have been defined to the DBMS as unique.) This prompts two questions:

1. How useful is this?
2. Does the implementation of a relationship in this way cause problems in system development?

The majority of database designs cannot benefit from this option. However, consider the tables in Figure 5.12 from a public transport management system. The two alternative candidate keys for `Actual Vehicle Trip` (in addition to the one chosen) follow.

SCHEDULED VEHICLE TRIP (Route No, Trip No, Direction Code, Scheduled Departure TimeOfDay)

ACTUAL VEHICLE TRIP (Vehicle No, Trip Date, Actual Departure TimeOfDay, Route No, Direction Code, Trip No)

PASSENGER TRIP (Ticket No, Trip Date, Trip Start Time, Route No, Direction Code)

FIGURE 5.12

Tables with candidate keys.

```
Route No + Trip No + Trip Date
```

and

```
Route No + Direction Code + Trip Date + Actual Departure TimeOfDay
```

However, in the system as built, these were longer than the key actually chosen (by one and three bytes, respectively). Since a very large number of records would be stored, the shortest key was chosen to minimize the data storage costs of tables, indexes, and so on. There was a requirement to identify which `Actual Vehicle Trip` each `Passenger Trip` took place on.

In a DBMS that constrains a foreign key to be a copy of the primary key of the other table, `Vehicle No` and `Actual Departure TimeOfDay` would have had to be added to the `Passenger Trip` table at a cost of an extra four bytes in each of a very large number of rows. The ability to maintain a foreign key that refers to any candidate key of the other table meant that only `Trip No` needed to be added at a cost of only one extra byte.

Of course, exploitation of this option might be difficult if the CASE tool being used to build the application did not support it. Beyond the issue of tool support, there do not appear to be any technical problems associated with this option. However, it is always sensible to be as simple and consistent as possible; the less fancy stuff that programmers, users, and DBAs have to come to grips with, the more time they can devote to using the data model properly!

5.6.2 One-to-One Relationship Implementation

A one-to-one relationship can be supported in a relational database by implementing both entity classes as tables, then using the same primary key for both. This strategy ensures that the relationship is indeed one-to-one and is the preferred option.

In fact, this is the way we retain the (one-to-one) association between a supertype and its subtypes when both are to be implemented as tables (see "Implementation at Multiple Levels of Generalization" section).

However, we cannot use the same primary key when dealing with a *transferable* one-to-one relationship. If we used `Part No` to identify both `Part Type` and `Bin` in our earlier example (reproduced in Figure 5.13), it would not be stable as a key of `Bin` (whenever a new part was moved to a bin, that key's bin would change).

FIGURE 5.13

A one-to-one relationship.

In this situation we would identify Bin by Bin No and Part Type by Part No, and we would support the relationship with a foreign key: either Bin No in the Part Type table or Part No in the Bin table. Of course, what we are really supporting here is not a one-to-one relationship anymore, but a one-to-many relationship. We have flexibility whether we like it or not! We will need to include the one-to-one rule in the business rule documentation. A relational DBMS will support such a rule by way of a unique index on the foreign key, providing a simple practical solution. Since we have a choice as to the direction of the one-to-many relationship, we will need to consider other factors, such as performance and flexibility. Will we be more likely to relax the "one part per bin" or the "one bin per part" rule?

Incidentally, we once struck exactly this situation in practice. The database designer had implemented a single table, with a key of Bin No. Parts were thus effectively identified by their bin number, causing real problems when parts were allocated to a new bin. In the end, they "solved" the problem by relabeling the bins each time parts were moved!

5.6.3 Derivable Relationships

Occasionally a one-to-many relationship can be derived from other data in one or more of the tables involved. (We discussed derivable many-to-many relationships in the "Derivable Many-to-Many Relationships" section.) The following example is typical. In Figure 5.14, we are modeling information about diseases and their groups (or categories), as might be required in a database for medical research.

During our analysis of attributes we discover that disease groups are identified by a range of numbers (Low No through High No) and that each disease in that group is assigned a number in the range. For example, 301 through 305 might represent "Depressive Illnesses," and "Postnatal Depression" might be allocated the number 304. Decimals can be used to avoid running out of numbers. We see exactly this sort of structure in many classification schemes, including the Dewey decimal classification used in libraries. We can use either High No or Low No as the primary key; we have arbitrarily selected Low No.

If we were to implement this relationship using a foreign key, we would arrive at the tables in Figure 5.15. However, the foreign key Disease Group Low No in the Disease table is derivable; we can determine which disease group a given

FIGURE 5.14

Initial ER model of diseases and groups.

DISEASE (<u>Disease No</u>, Disease Group Low No*, Disease Name, . . .)
DISEASE GROUP (<u>Disease Group Low No</u>, Disease Group High No, . . .)

FIGURE 5.15

Relational model of diseases and groups.

disease belongs to by finding the disease group with the range containing its disease number. It therefore violates our requirement for nonredundancy.

In UML we can mark the relationship as derivable, in which case no foreign key is created, but many CASE tools will generate a foreign key to represent each relationship in an ER diagram (whether you want it or not). In this case, the best option is probably to retain the relationship in the diagram and the associated foreign key in the logical data model and to accept some redundancy in the latter as the price of automatic logical data model generation.

Including a derivable foreign key may be worthwhile if we are generating program logic based on navigation using foreign keys. But carrying redundant data complicates updates and introduces the risk of data inconsistency. In this example, we would need to ensure that if a disease moved from one group to another, the foreign key would be updated. In fact, this can happen only if the disease number changes (in which case we should regard it as a new disease—if we were unhappy with this rule, we would need to allocate a surrogate key) or if we change the boundaries of existing groups. We may well determine that the business does not require the ability to make such changes; in this case, the derivable foreign key option becomes more appealing.

Whether or not the business requires the ability to make such changes, the fact that Disease No must be no less than Disease Group Low No and no greater than the corresponding Disease Group High No should be included in the business rule documentation.

The preceding situation occurs commonly with dates and date ranges. For example, a bank statement might include all transactions for a given account between two dates. If the two dates were attributes of the Statement entity class, the relationship between Transaction and Statement would be derivable by comparing these dates with the transaction dates. In this case, the boundaries of a future statement might well change, perhaps at the request of the customer or because we wished to notify him or her that the account was overdrawn. If we choose the redundant foreign key approach, we will need to ensure that the foreign key is updated in such cases.

5.6.4 Optional Relationships

In a relational database, a one-to-many relationship that is optional at the "many" end (as most are) requires no special handling. However, if a one-to-many relationship is optional at the "one" end, the foreign key representing that relationship must be able to indicate in some way that there is no associated row in the refer-

FIGURE 5.16

Optional relationship.

enced table. The most common way of achieving this is to make the foreign key column(s) "nullable" (able to be null or empty in some rows). However, this adds complexity to queries. A simple join of the two tables (an "inner join") will only return rows with non-null foreign keys. For example, if nullable foreign keys are used, a simple join of the Agent and Policy tables illustrated in Figure 5.16 will only return those policies actually sold by an agent. One of the major selling points of relational databases is the ease with which end users can query the database. The novice user querying these data to obtain a figure for the total value of policies is likely to get a value significantly less than the true total. To obtain the true total, it is necessary to construct an outer join or use a union query, which the novice user may not know about.

A way around this problem is to add a Not Applicable row to the referenced table and include a reference to that row in each foreign key that would otherwise be null. The true total can then be obtained with only a simple query. The drawback is that other processing becomes more complex because we need to allow for the "dummy" agent.

Alternatives to Nulls

Section 5.4.9 discusses some problems with nulls in nonkey columns. We now discuss two foreign key situations in which alternatives to nulls can make life simpler.

Optional Foreign Keys in Hierarchies

In a hierarchy represented by a recursive relationship, that relationship must be optional at both ends. However, we have found that making top-level foreign keys self-referencing rather than null (see the first two rows in Figure 5.17) can simplify the programming of queries that traverse a varying number of levels. For example, a query to return the HR Department and all its subordinate departments does not need to be a union query, as it can be written as a single query that traverses the maximum depth of the hierarchy.

Other Optional Foreign Keys

If a one-to-many relationship is optional at the "one" end, a query that joins the tables representing the entity classes involved in that relationship may need to

ORG UNIT (Org Unit ID, Org Unit Name, Parent Org Unit ID*)

Org Unit ID	Org Unit Name	Parent Org Unit ID
1	Production	1
2	H/R	2
21	Recruitment	2
22	Training	2
221	IT Training	22
222	Other Training	22

FIGURE 5.17

An alternative simple hierarchy table.

Surname	Initial	Union Code
Chekhov	P	APF
Kirk	J	null
McCoy	L	null
Scotty	M	ETU
Spock	M	null
Sulu	H	APF
Uhura	N	TCU

Union Code	Union Name
APF	Airline Pilots' Federation
ETU	Electrical Trades Union
TCU	Telecommunications Union

```
select    SURNAME, INITIAL, UNION_NAME
from      EMPLOYEE join UNION on
EMPLOYEE.UNION_CODE = UNION.UNION_CODE;

select    SURNAME, INITIAL, UNION_NAME
from      EMPLOYEE left join UNION on
EMPLOYEE.UNION_CODE = UNION.UNION_CODE;
```

FIGURE 5.18

Tables at each end of an optional one-to-many relationship.

take account of that fact if it is not to return unexpected results. For example, consider the tables in Figure 5.18. If we wish to list all employees and the unions to which they belong, the first query in Figure 5.18 will only return four employees (those who belong to unions) rather than all of them. By contrast, an outer join, indicated by the keyword "left,"[11] as in the second query in Figure 5.18, will return all employees.

If users are able to access the database directly through a query interface, it is unreasonable to expect all users to understand this subtlety. In this case, it may be better to create a dummy row in the table representing the entity class at the

---

[11]The keyword "right" may also be used if all rows from the second table are required rather than all rows from the first table.

Surname	Initial	Union Code
Chekhov	P	APF
Kirk	J	N/A
McCoy	L	N/A
Scotty	M	ETU
Spock	M	N/A
Sulu	H	APF
Uhura	N	TCU

Union Code	Union Name
APF	Airline Pilots' Federation
ETU	Electrical Trades Union
TCU	Telecommunications Union
N/A	Not applicable

FIGURE 5.19

A dummy row at the "one" end of an optional one-to-many relationship.

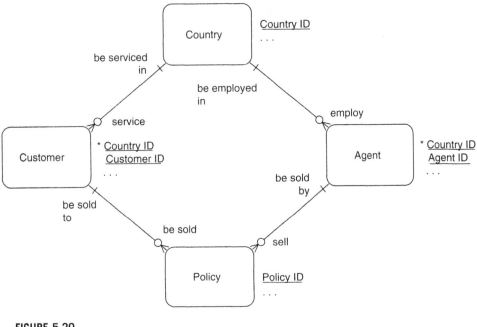

FIGURE 5.20

ER model leading to overlapping foreign keys.

"one" end of the relationship and replace the null foreign key in all rows in the other table by the key of that dummy row, as illustrated in Figure 5.19. The first, simpler query in Figure 5.18 will now return all employees.

5.6.5 Overlapping Foreign Keys

Figure 5.20 is a model for an insurance company that operates in several countries. Each agent works in a particular country, *and sells only to customers in that country*. Note that the ER diagram *allows* for this situation but does not enforce the rule.

If we apply the rule for representing relationships by foreign keys, we find that the Country ID column appears twice in the Policy table—once to support the link to Agent and once to support the link to Customer. We can distinguish the columns by naming one Customer Country ID and the other Agent Country ID. But because of our rule that agents sell only to customers in their own country, both columns will always hold the same value. This seems a clear case of data redundancy, easily solved by combining the two columns into one. Yet, there are arguments for keeping two separate columns.

The two-column approach is more flexible; if we change the rule about selling only to customers in the same country, the two-column model will easily support the new situation. But here we have the familiar trade-off between flexibility and constraints; we can equally argue that the one-column model does a better job of enforcing an important business rule, if we are convinced that the rule will apply for the life of the database.

There is a more subtle flexibility issue: What if one or both of the relationships from Policy became optional? Perhaps it is possible for a policy to be issued without involving an agent. In such cases, we would need to hold a null value for the foreign key to Agent, but this involves "nulling out" the value for Country ID, part of the foreign key to Customer. We would end up losing our link to Customer. We have been involved in some long arguments about this one, the most common suggestion being that we only need to set the value of Agent ID to null and leave Country ID untouched.

But this involves an inconsistency in the way we handle foreign keys. It might not be so bad if we only had to tell *programmers* to handle the situation as a special case ("Don't set the whole of the foreign key to null in this instance"), but these days program logic may be generated automatically by a CASE tool that is not so flexible about handling nonstandard situations. The DBMS itself may recognize foreign keys and rely on them not overlapping in order to support referential integrity.

Our advice is to include both columns and also to include the rule that agents and customers must be from the same country in the business rule documentation.

Of course, we can alternatively use stand-alone keys for Customer and Agent. In this case, the issue of overlapping foreign keys will not arise, but again the rule that agents and customers must be from the same country should be included in the business rule documentation.

5.6.6 Split Foreign Keys

The next structure has a similar flavor but is a little more complex. You are likely to encounter it more often than the overlapping foreign key problem, once you know how to recognize it!

Figure 5.21 shows a model for an organization that takes orders from customers and dispatches them to the customers' branches. Note that the primary key of `Branch` is a combination of `Customer No` and `Branch No`, a choice that would be appropriate if we wanted to use the customers' own branch numbers rather than define new ones ourselves. In translating this model into relational tables, we need to carry two foreign keys in the `Ordered Item` table. The foreign key to `Order` is `Order No`, and the foreign key to `Branch` is `Customer No + Branch No`. Our `Ordered Item` table, including foreign keys (marked with asterisks), is shown in Figure 5.22.

But let us assume the reasonable business rule that the customer who places the order is also the customer who receives the order. Then, since each order is placed and received by one customer, `Order No` is a determinant of `Customer No`. The `Ordered Item` table is therefore not fully normalized, as `Order No` is a determinant but is not a candidate key of the table.

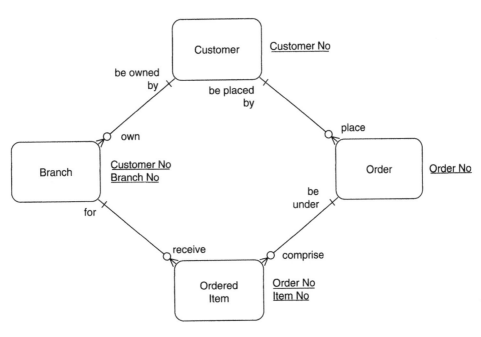

FIGURE 5.21

ER model leading to split foreign key.

ORDERED ITEM (Order No*, Item No, Product, Customer No*, Branch No*)

FIGURE 5.22

Ordered item table.

We already have a table with `Order No` as the key and `Customer No` as a nonkey item. Holding `Customer No` in the `Ordered Item` table tells us nothing new and involves us in the usual problems of unnormalized structures. For example, if the `Customer No` for an order was entered incorrectly, it would need to be corrected for every item in that order. The obvious solution seems to be to remove `Customer No` from the `Ordered Item` table. But this causes its own problems.

First, we have broken our rule for generating a foreign key for each one-to-many relationship. Looked at another way, if we were to draw a diagram from the tables, would we include a relationship line from `Ordered Item` to `Branch`? Not according to our rules, but we started off by saying there *was* a relationship between the two; `Branch No` is in the `Ordered Item` table to support a relationship to `Branch`.

But there is more to the problem than a diagramming nicety. Any CASE tool that generates foreign keys automatically from relationships is going to include `Customer No` in the `Ordered Item` table. A program generator that makes the usual assumption that it can find the full primary key of `Branch` in the `Ordered Item` table will be in trouble if `Customer No` is excluded. Again, standard facilities for enforcing referential integrity are most unlikely to support the special situation that arises if `Customer No` is excluded.

Whether we include or exclude `Customer No`, we face serious problems. When you encounter this situation, which you should pick up through a normalization check after generating the foreign keys, we strongly suggest you go back and select different primary keys. In this case, a stand-alone `Branch No` as the primary key of `Branch` will do the job. (The original `Branch No` and `Customer No` will become nonkey items, forming a second candidate key.) You will lose the constraint that the customer who places the order receives the order. This will need to be included in the business rule documentation.

5.7 TABLE AND COLUMN NAMES

There are two factors affecting table and column names:

1. The target DBMS (if known) may impose a limit on the length of names, may require that there are no spaces or special characters other than underlines in a name, and may require names to be in all uppercase or all lowercase.
2. There may be a standard in force within the organization as to how tables and columns are named.

If there is no name length limit and no table/column naming standard, the best approach to table and column naming is to use the corresponding entity class or attribute name, with spaces and special characters replaced by underlines if necessary (e.g., the entity class `Organization Unit` would be represented by the table `organization_unit`). An alternative, provided the target DBMS supports mixed-case names, is to delete all spaces and special characters and capitalize the first letter of each word in the name (e.g., `OrganizationUnit`; the so-called "CamelCase").

In our experience, installation table/column naming standards often require that table names all start with a particular prefix, typically "t_" or "Tbl." Our example table name would then be `t_organization_unit` or `TblOrganization-Unit`, respectively.

If the target DBMS imposes a name length limit, it is usually necessary to abbreviate the words that make up table and column names. If so, two principles should be observed:

1. Use abbreviations consistently.
2. Do not also abbreviate entity class and attribute names, as these are for use by the business, not the database.

5.8 LOGICAL DATA MODEL NOTATIONS

How should a logical data model be presented to users and reviewers? There is a choice of diagrammatic and textual notations.

An ER diagram can be used to present a logical data model using the following conventions:

- Each table is represented by a box as if it were an entity class.
- Each foreign key in a table is represented by a line from that table to the referenced table, marked as "optional many" at the foreign key end and either "mandatory one" or "optional one" at the primary key end, depending on whether the column is mandatory (`NOT NULL`) or optional (`NULL`), which will have been derived from the optionality of the relationship that the particular foreign key represents.
- All columns (including foreign keys) should be listed either on the diagram (inside the box representing the table) or in a separate list depending on the facilities provided by the chosen CASE tool and the need to produce an uncluttered diagram that fits the page.

If this notation is chosen, it is important to be able to distinguish the logical data model diagram from the conceptual data model diagram. Your chosen CASE tool may provide different diagram templates for the two types of model with different notations, but if it does not, be sure to label clearly each diagram as to whether it is conceptual or logical.

Some UML CASE tools (e.g., Rational Rose) provide a quite different diagram type for the logical data model; although it consists of boxes and lines, the boxes look quite different from those used in a class model.

The textual notations available also depend on the CASE tool chosen but generally conform to one of the following three formats:

1. "Relational" notation, as in Figure 5.23, in which each table name is listed and followed on the same line by the names of each of its columns and the entire set of column names enclosed in parentheses or braces.

2. "List" notation, as in Figure 5.24, in which each table name and column name appear in a line on its own, and the data type and length (and possibly the definition) of each column is shown.

3. DDL (data description language), as in Figure 5.25, in which the instructions to the DBMS to create each table and its columns are couched.

EMPLOYEE (Employee Number, Employee Name, Department Number)
DEPARTMENT (Department Number, Department Name, Department Location)
QUALIFICATION (Employee Number, Qualification Description, Qualification Year)

FIGURE 5.23

Employee model using relational notation.

EMPLOYEE

Employee Number: 5 Numeric—The number allocated to this employee by the Human Resources Department
Employee Name: 60 Characters—The name of this employee: the surname, a comma and space, the first given name plus a space and the middle initial if any
Department Number: The number used by the organization to identify the Department that pays this employee's salary

DEPARTMENT

Department Number: 2 Numeric—The number used by the organization to identify this Department
Department Name: 30 Characters—The name of this Department as it appears in company documentation
Department Location: 30 Characters—The name of the city where this Department is located

QUALIFICATION

Employee Number: 5 Numeric—The number allocated to the employee holding this qualification by the Human Resources Department
Qualification Description: 30 Characters—The name of this qualification
Qualification Year: Date Optional—The year in which this employee obtained this qualification

FIGURE 5.24

Employee model using list notation.

```
create table EMPLOYEE (
EMPLOYEE_NUMBER integer not null,
EMPLOYEE_NAME char(60) not null,
DEPARTMENT_NUMBER integer not null);
alter table EMPLOYEE add constraint PK1 primary key (EMPLOYEE_NUMBER);

create table DEPARTMENT (
DEPARTMENT_NUMBER: integer not null,
DEPARTMENT_NAME char(30) not null,
DEPARTMENT_LOCATION: char(30) not null);
alter table DEPARTMENT add constraint PK2 primary key (DEPARTMENT_NUMBER);

create table QUALIFICATION (
EMPLOYEE_NUMBER integer not null,
QUALIFICATION_DESCRIPTION char(30) not null,
QUALIFICATION_YEAR date null);
alter table QUALIFICATION add constraint PK3 primary key (EMPLOYEE_NUMBER,
QUALIFICATION_DESCRIPTION);
alter table EMPLOYEE add constraint FK1 foreign key (DEPARTMENT_NUMBER)
references DEPARTMENT;
alter table QUALIFICATION add constraint FK2 foreign key (EMPLOYEE_NUMBER)
references EMPLOYEE;
```

FIGURE 5.25

Employee model using DDL notation.

5.9 SUMMARY

The transformation from conceptual model to logical model is largely mechanical, but there are a few important decisions to be made by the modeler. Subtypes and supertypes need to be "leveled." Tables can represent a selected single level of generalization or multiple levels of generalization.

The allowed values of category attributes need to be specified either by a constraint on the relevant column or by the addition of a new table to hold them. Care needs to be taken in the interdependent tasks of primary key specification and implementation of relationships using foreign keys. At all stages of this phase, there are exceptions and unusual situations that the professional modeler needs to be able to recognize and deal with.

Normalization

Given any pool of entities and attributes, there are a number of ways you can group them into relations. In this chapter, you will be introduced to the process of *normalization*, through which you create relations that avoid most of the problems that arise from bad relational design.

There are at least two ways to approach normalization. The first is to work from an entity–relationship (ER) diagram. If the diagram is drawn correctly, then there are some simple rules you can use to translate it into relations that will avoid most relational design problems. The drawback to this approach is that it can be difficult to determine whether your design is correct. The second approach is to use the theoretical concepts behind good design to create your relations. This is a bit more difficult than working from an ER diagram, but often results in a better design.

In practice, you may find it useful to use a combination of both approaches. First, create an ER diagram and use it to design your relations. Then, check those relations against the theoretical rules for good design.

6.1 TRANSLATING AN ER DIAGRAM INTO RELATIONS

An ER diagram in which all many-to-many relationships have been transformed into one-to-many relationships through the introduction of composite entities can be translated directly into a set of relations. To do so:

- Create one table for each entity.
- For each entity that is only at the "one" end of one or more relationships, and not at the "many" end of any relationship, create a single-column primary key, using an arbitrary unique number if no natural primary key is available.
- For each entity that is at the "many" end of one or more relationships, include the primary key of each parent entity (those at the "one" end of the relationships) in the table as foreign keys.
- If an entity at the "many" end of one or more relationships has a natural primary key (e.g., an order or invoice number), use that single column as the primary

key. Otherwise, concatenate the primary key of its parent or parents with any other column or columns needed for uniqueness to form the table's primary key.

Following these guidelines, we end up with the following tables for the Lasers Only database:

```
customer (customer_numb, customer_first_name, customer_last_name,
    customer_street, customer_city, customer_state, customer_zip,
    customer_phone, credit_card_numb, card_exp_date)
item (item_numb, title, distributor_numb, retail_price,
    release_date, genre)
order (order_numb, customer_numb, order_date, order_filled)
order_lines (order_numb, item_numb, quantity, discount_applied,
    selling_price, line_cost, shipped)
distributor (distributor_numb, distributor_name, distributor_
    street, distributor_city, distributor_city, distributor_state,
    distributor_zip, distributor_phone, distributor_contact_person,
    contact_person_ext)
actor (actor_numb, actor_name)
performance (actor_numb, item_numb, role)
producer (producer_name, studio)
production (producer_name, item_numb)
```

Note: You will see some of these relations reworked a bit throughout this chapter to help illustrate various aspects of database design. However, the preceding is the design that results from a direct translation of the ER diagram.

6.2 NORMAL FORMS

The theoretical rules that the design of a relation meet are known as *normal forms*. Each normal form represents an increasingly stringent set of rules. Theoretically, the higher the normal form, the better the design of the relation.

As you can see in Figure 6.1, there are six nested normal forms, indicating that if a relation is in one of the higher, inner normal forms, it is also in all of the normal forms below it.

In most cases, if you can place your relations in third normal form (3NF), then you will have avoided most of the problems common to bad relational designs. Boyce-Codd (BCNF) and fourth normal form (4NF) handle special situations that arise only occasionally. However, they are conceptually easy to understand and can be used in practice if the need arises.

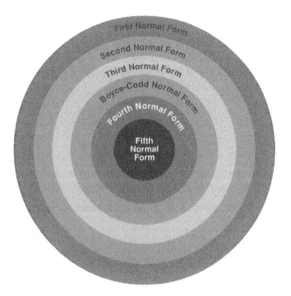

FIGURE 6.1

Nested normal forms.

Fifth normal form (5NF), however, is a complex set of criteria that is extremely difficult to work with. It is, for example, very difficult to verify that a relation is in 5NF. Most practitioners do not bother with 5NF, knowing that if their relations are in 3NF (or 4NF if the situation warrants), then their designs are generally problem free.

Note: In addition to the six normal forms in Figure 6.1, there is another normal form—domain/key normal form—that is of purely theoretical importance and, to this date, has not been used as a practical design objective.

6.3 FIRST NORMAL FORM

A table is in first normal form (1NF) if it meets the following criteria: *The data are stored in a two-dimensional table with no repeating groups.* The key to understanding 1NF is therefore understanding the nature of a repeating group of data.

6.3.1 Understanding Repeating Groups

A *repeating group* is an attribute that has more than one value in each row. For example, assume that you were working with an employee's relation and needed

Emp. ID	First	Last	Children's Names	Children's Birthdates
1001	Jane	Doe	Mary, Sam	1/1/92, 5/15/94
1002	John	Doe	Mary, Sam	1/1/92, 5/15/94
1003	Jane	Smith	John, Pat, Lee, Mary	10/5/94, 10/12/90, 6/6/96, 8/21/94
1004	John	Smith	Michael	7/4/96
1005	Jane	Jones	Edward, Martha	10/21/95, 10/15/89

FIGURE 6.2

A relation with repeating groups.

to store the names and birth dates of the employee's children. Because each employee can have more than one child, the names of children and the children's birth dates each form a repeating group.

Note: A repeating group is directly analogous to a multivalued attribute in an ER diagram.

There is actually a very good reason why repeating groups are disallowed. To see what might happen if they were present, take a look at Figure 6.2, an instance of the employee's relation we were just discussing.

Notice that there are multiple values in a single row in both of the columns, children's names and children's birthdates. This presents two major problems:

- There is no way to know exactly which birth date belongs to which child. It is tempting to say that we can associate the birth dates with the children by their positions in the list, but there is nothing to ensure that the relative positions will always be maintained.

- Searching the table is very difficult. If, for example, we want to know which employees have children born before 1995, the database management system (DBMS) will need to perform data manipulations to extract the individual dates from the children's birth dates column before it can evaluate the dates themselves. Given that there is no way to know how many birth dates there are in the column for any specific row, the processing overload for searching becomes even greater.

The solution to these problems is, of course, to get rid of the repeating groups altogether.

6.3.2 Handling Repeating Groups

There are two ways to get rid of repeating groups to bring a relation into conformance with the rules for 1NF—a correct way and an incorrect way. We will look first at the incorrect way so you will know what *not* to do.

Emp. ID	First	Last	Child Name 1	Child B_date 1	Child Name 2	Child B_date 2	Child Name 3	Child B_date 3
1001	Jane	Doe	Mary	1/1/92	Sam	5/15/94		
1002	John	Doe	Mary	1/1/92	Sam	5/15/94		
1003	Jane	Smith	John	10/5/94	Pat	10/12/90	Lee	6/6/96
1004	John	Smith	Michael	7/4/96				
1005	Jane	Jones	Edward	10/21/95	Martha	10/15/89		

FIGURE 6.3

A relation handling repeating groups in the incorrect way.

In Figure 6.3 you can see a relation that handles repeating groups by creating multiple columns for the multiple values. This particular example includes three pairs of columns for a child's name and birth date.

The relation in Figure 6.3 does meet the criteria for 1NF: The repeating groups are gone and there is no problem identifying which birth date belongs to which child. However, the design has introduced several problems of its own:

- The relation is limited to three children for any given employee. This means that there is no room to store Jane Smith's fourth child. Should you put another row for Jane Smith into the table? If so, then the primary key of this relation can no longer be just `employee ID`. The primary key must include at least one child's name as well.

- The relation wastes space for people who have less than three children. Given that disk space is one of the least expensive elements of a database system, this is probably the least of the problems with this relation.

- Searching for a specific child becomes very clumsy. To answer the question "Does anyone have a child named Lee?" the DBMS must construct a query that includes a search of all three child name columns because there is no way to know in which column the name might be found.

The right way to handle repeating groups is to create another table (another entity) to handle multiple instances of the repeating group. In the example we have been using, we would create a second table for the children, producing something like Figure 6.4.

Neither of the two new tables contains any repeating groups, and this form of the design avoids all the problems of the preceding solution:

- There is no limit to the number of children who can be stored for a given employee. To add another child, you simply add another row to the table.
- There is no wasted space. The `children` table uses space only for data that are present.
- Searching for a specific child is much easier because the child's name is found in only one column.

Employees

Emp. ID	First	Last
1001	Jane	Doe
1002	John	Doe
1003	Jane	Smith
1004	John	Smith
1005	Jane	Jones

Children

Emp. ID	Child Name	Birthdate
1001	Mary	1/1/92
1001	Sam	5/15/94
1002	Mary	1/1/92
1002	Sam	5/15/94
1003	John	10/5/94
1003	Pat	10/12/90
1003	Lee	6/6/96
1003	Mary	8/21/94
1004	Michael	7/4/96
1005	Edward	10/21/95
1005	Martha	10/15/89

FIGURE 6.4

The correct way to handle the repeating group.

6.3.3 **Problems with 1NF**

Although 1NF relations have no repeating groups, they are full of other problems. To see what those problems are, we will look at the following table. (This table comes from Lasers Only's original data management system rather than the new-and-improved design you saw earlier in this chapter.) Expressed in the notation for relations that we have been using, the relation is:

```
orders (customer number, first name, last name, street, city,
    state, zip, phone, order date, item number, title, price, has
    shipped)
```

The first thing we need to do is determine the primary key for this table. The customer number alone will not be sufficient because it repeats for every item ordered by the customer. The item number will also not suffice, because it is repeated for every order on which it appears. We cannot use the order number because it is repeated for every item on the order. The only solution is a concatenated key; in this example, this is the combination of the order number and the item number.

Given that the primary key is made up of the order number and the item number, there are two important things we cannot do with this relation:

- We cannot add data about a customer until the customer places at least one order because without an order and an item on that order, we do not have a complete primary key.

- We cannot add data about a merchandise item we are carrying without that item being ordered. There must be an order number to complete the primary key.

The preceding are *insertion anomalies*, a situation that arises when you are prevented from inserting data into a relation because a complete primary key is not available. (Remember that no part of a primary key can be null.)

Note: To be strictly correct, there is a third insertion anomaly in the orders relation: You cannot insert an order until you know one item on the order. In a practical sense, however, no one would enter an order without there being an item ordered.

Insertion anomalies are common in 1NF relations that are not also in any of the higher normal forms. In practical terms, they occur because there are data about more than one entity in the relation. The anomaly forces you to insert data about an unrelated entity (e.g., a merchandise item) when you want to insert data about another entity (such as a customer).

First normal form relations can also give us problems when we delete data. Consider, for example, what happens if a customer cancels the order of a single item:

- In cases where the deleted item was the only item on the order, you lose all data about the order.
- In cases where the order was the only order on which the item appeared, you lose data about the item.
- In cases where the deleted item was the only item ordered by a customer, you lose all data about the customer.

These *deletion anomalies* occur because part of the primary key of a row becomes null when the merchandise item data are deleted, forcing you to remove the entire row. The result of a deletion anomaly is the loss of data that you would like to keep. In practical terms, you are forced to remove data about an unrelated entity when you delete data about another entity in the same table.

Note: Moral to the story: More than one entity in a table is a very bad thing.

There is a final type of anomaly in the orders relation that is not related to the primary key: a *modification*, or *update*, anomaly. The orders relation has a great deal of unnecessary duplicated data, in particular information about customers. When a customer moves, then the customer's data must be changed in every row, for every item, on every order ever placed by the customer. If every row is not changed correctly, then data that should be the same are no longer the same. The potential for these inconsistent data is the modification anomaly.

6.4 SECOND NORMAL FORM

The solution to anomalies in a 1NF relation is to break down the relation so that there is one relation for each entity in the 1NF relation. The `orders` relation, for example, will break down into four relations (customers, merchandise items, orders, and line items). Such relations are in at least second normal form (2NF).

In theoretical terms, 2NF is defined as follows: *The relation is in 1NF and all nonkey attributes are functionally dependent on the entire primary key.*

The new term in the preceding is *functionally dependent*, a special relationship between attributes.

6.4.1 Understanding Functional Dependencies

A functional dependency is a one-way relationship between two attributes such that at any given time, for each unique value of attribute A, only one value of attribute B is associated with it through the relation. For example, assume that A is the customer number from the `orders` relation. Each customer number is associated with one customer first name, one last name, one street address, one city, one state, one zip code, and one phone number. Although the values for those attributes may change, at any moment, there is only one.

We therefore can say that `first name`, `last name`, `street`, `city`, `state`, `zip`, and `phone` attributes are functionally dependent on the `customer number`. This relationship is often written as

```
customer number -> first name, last name, street, city, state,
   zip, phone
```

and read "customer number determines first name, last name, street, city, state, zip, and phone." In this relationship, `customer number` is known as the *determinant* (an attribute that determines the value of other attributes).

Notice that the functional dependency does not necessarily hold in the reverse direction. For example, any given first or last name may be associated with more than one customer number. (It would be unusual to have a `customer` table of any size without some repetition of names.)

The functional dependencies in the `orders` table are:

```
customer number -> first name, last name, street, city, state,
   zip, phone
```

```
item number -> title, price
order number -> customer number, order date
item number + order number -> has shipped
```

Notice first that there is one determinant for each entity in the relation and that the determinant is what we have chosen as the entity identifier. Notice also that when an entity has a concatenated identifier, the determinant is also concatenated. In this example, whether an item has shipped depends on the combination of the item and the order.

6.4.2 Using Functional Dependencies to Reach 2NF

If you have correctly identified the functional dependencies among the attributes in a database environment, then you can use them to create 2NF relations. Each determinant becomes the primary key of a relation. All the attributes that are functionally dependent on it become nonkey attributes in the relation.

The four relations into which the original orders relation should be broken are:

```
customers (customer number, first name, last name, street, city,
    state, zip, phone)
items (item number, title, price)
orders (order number, customer number, order date)
line items (order number, item number, has shipped)
```

Each of these should in turn correspond to a single entity in your ER diagram.

Note: When it comes to deciding what is driving database design—functional dependencies or entities—it is really a "chicken and egg" situation. What is most important is that there is consistency between the ER diagram and the functional dependencies you identify in your relations. It makes no difference whether you design by looking for functional dependencies or for entities. In most cases, database design is an iterative process in which you create an initial design, check it, modify it, and check it again. You can look at either functional dependencies and/or entities at any stage in the process, checking one against the other for consistency.

The relations we have created from the original orders relation have eliminated the anomalies present in the original:

- It is now possible to insert data about a customer before the customer places an order.
- It is now possible to insert data about an order before we know an item on the order.
- It is now possible to store data about merchandise items before they are ordered.

- Line items can be deleted from an order without affecting data describing that item, the order itself, or the merchandise item.
- Data describing the customer are stored only once, and therefore any change to those data need to be made only once. A modification anomaly cannot occur.

6.4.3 Problems with 2NF Relations

Although 2NF eliminates problems from many relations, you will occasionally run into relations that are in 2NF yet still exhibit anomalies. Assume, for example, that each laser disc title that Lasers Only carries comes from one distributor and that each distributor has only one warehouse, which has only one phone number. The following relation is therefore in 2NF:

```
items (item number, title, distributor, warehouse phone number)
```

For each `item number`, there is only one value for the `title`, `distributor`, and `warehouse phone number` items. However, there is one insertion anomaly—you cannot insert data about a distributor until you have an item from that distributor—and a deletion anomaly—if you delete the only item from a distributor, you lose data about the distributor. There is also a modification anomaly—the distributor's warehouse phone number is duplicated for every item the company gets from that distributor. The relation is in 2NF, but not 3NF.

6.5 THIRD NORMAL FORM

Third normal form is designed to handle situations like the one you just read about in the preceding section. In terms of entities, the `items` relation does contain two entities: the `Merchandise Item` and the `Distributor`. That alone should convince you that the relation needs to broken down into two smaller relations, both of which are now in 3NF:

```
items (item number, distributor)
distributors (distributor, warehouse phone number)
```

The theoretical definition of 3NF says: *The relation is in 2NF and there are no transitive dependencies.* The functional dependencies found in the original relation are an example of a *transitive dependency*.

6.5.1 Transitive Dependencies

A transitive dependency exists when you have the following functional dependency pattern:

```
A -> B and B -> C therefore A -> C
```

This is precisely the case with the original `items` relation. The only reason that the `warehouse phone number` is functionally dependent on the `item number` is because the `distributor` is functionally dependent on the `item number` and the `phone number` is functionally dependent on the `distributor`. The functional dependencies are really:

```
item number -> distributor
distributor -> warehouse phone number
```

Note: Transitive dependencies take their name from the transitive property in mathematics, which states that if a > b and b > c, then a > c.

There are two determinants in the original `items` relation, each of which should be the primary key of its own relation. However, it is not merely the presence of the second determinant that creates the transitive dependency. What really matters is that the second determinant is not a candidate key for the relation.

Consider, for example, this relation:

```
items (item number, UPC code, distributor, price)
```

The `item number` is an arbitrary value that Lasers Only assigns to each merchandise item. The `UPC code` is an industry-wide code that is unique to each item as well. The functional dependencies in this relation are:

```
item number -> UPC code, distributor, price
UPC code -> item number, distributor, price
```

Is there a transitive dependency here? No, because the second determinant is a candidate key. (Lasers Only could just as easily have used the UPC code as the primary key.) There are no insertion, deletion, or modification anomalies in this relation; it describes only one entity—the `Merchandise Item`.

A transitive dependency therefore exists only when the determinant that is not the primary key is not a candidate key for the relation. For example, in the `items` table we have been using as an example, the distributor is a determinant but not a candidate key for the table. (There can be more than one item coming from a single distributor.)

When you have a transitive dependency in a 2NF relation, you should break the relation into two smaller relations, each of which has one of the determinants in the transitive dependency as its primary key. The attributes determined by the determinants become the nonkey attributes in each relation. This removes the transitive dependency—and its associated anomalies—and places the relations in 3NF.

Note: A 2NF relation that has no transitive dependencies is, of course, automatically in 3NF.

6.6 BOYCE-CODD NORMAL FORM

For most relations, 3NF is a good design objective. Relations in that state are free of most anomalies. However, occasionally you run across relations that exhibit special characteristics where anomalies still occur. BCNF and 4NF were created to handle such special situations.

> *Note:* If your relations are in 3NF and do not exhibit the special characteristics that BCNF and 4NF were designed to handle, then they are automatically in 4NF. As mentioned earlier in this chapter, it is extremely difficult to determine if a relation is in 5NF without the aid of a computer to do the analyses, and therefore we rarely use 5NF in practice.

The easiest way to understand BCNF is to start with an example. Assume that Lasers Only decides to add a relation to its database to handle employee work scheduling. Each employee works one or two four-hour shifts a day at the store. During each shift, an employee is assigned to one station (a place in the store, such as the front desk or the stockroom). Only one employee works a station during a given shift.

A relation to handle the schedule might be designed as follows:

```
schedule (employee ID, date, shift, station, worked shift?)
```

Given the rules for the scheduling (one person per station per shift), there are two possible primary keys for this relation: `employee ID + date + shift` or `date + shift + station`. The functional dependencies in the relation are:

```
employee ID + date + shift -> station, worked shift?
date + shift + station -> employee ID, worked shift?
```

Keep in mind that this holds true only because there is only one person working each station during each shift.

> *Note:* There is very little difference between the two candidate keys as far as the choice of a primary key is concerned. In cases like this, you can choose either one.

This `schedule` relation exhibits overlapping concatenated candidate keys. (Both candidate keys have date and shift in common.) BCNF was designed to deal with relations that exhibit this characteristic.

To be in BCNF, a relation must meet the following rule: *The relation is in 3NF and all determinants are candidate keys.* BCNF is considered to be a more general way of looking at 3NF because it includes those relations with the overlapping candidate keys. The sample `schedule` relation we have been considering does meet the criteria for BCNF because the two determinants are indeed candidate keys.

6.7 FOURTH NORMAL FORM

Like BCNF, 4NF was designed to handle relations that exhibit a special characteristic that does not arise too often. In this case, the special characteristic is something known as a *multivalued dependency*.

As an example, consider the following relation:

```
movie info (title, star, producer)
```

A given movie can have more than one star; it can also have more than one producer. The same star can appear in more than one movie; the producer can also work on more than one movie (e.g., see Figure 6.5). The relation must therefore include all columns in its key.

Because there are no nonkey attributes, this relation is in BCNF. Nonetheless, the relation exhibits anomalies:

- You cannot insert the stars of a movie without knowing at least one producer.
- You cannot insert the movie's producer without knowing at least one star.
- If you delete the only producer from a movie, you lose information about its stars.
- If you delete the only star from a movie, you lose information about its producers.
- Each producer's name is duplicated for every star in the movie. By the same token, each star's name is duplicated for each movie producer. This unnecessary duplication forms the basis of a modification anomaly.

There are at least two unrelated entities in this relation, one that handles the relationship between a movie and its stars and another that handles the relation-

Title	Star	Producer
Great Film	Lovely Lady	Money Bags
Great Film	Handsome Man	Money Bags
Great Film	Lovely Lady	Helen Pursestrings
Great Film	Handsome Man	Helen Pursestrings
Boring Movie	Lovely Lady	Helen Pursestrings
Boring Movie	Precocious Child	Helen Pursestrings

FIGURE 6.5

A relation with a multivalued dependency.

ship between a movie and its producers. In a practical sense, that is the cause of the anomalies. (Arguably, there are also `Movie`, `Star`, and `Producer` entities involved.)

However, in theoretical terms, the anomalies are caused by the presence of a multivalued dependency in the same relation, which must be eliminated to go to 4NF. The rule for 4NF is: *The relation is in BCNF and there are no multivalued dependencies.*

6.7.1 Multivalued Dependencies

A multivalued dependency exists when for each value of attribute A, there exists a finite set of values of attribute B that are associated with it and a finite set of values of attribute C that are also associated with it. Attributes B and C are independent of each other.

In the example we have been using, there is just such a dependency. First, for each movie title, there is a group of actors (the stars) who are associated with the movie. For each title, there is also a group of producers who are associated with it. However, the actors and the producers are independent of one another.

> *Note:* At this point, do not let semantics get in the way of database theory. Yes, it is true that producers fund the movies that the actors are starring in, but in terms of database relationships, there is no direct connection between the two.

The multivalued dependency can be written as:

```
title ->> star
title ->> producer
```

and read "title multidetermines star and title multidetermines producer."

> *Note:* To be strictly accurate, a functional dependency is a special case of a multivalued dependency where what is being determined is one value rather than a group of values.

To eliminate the multivalued dependency and bring this relation into 4NF, you split the relation, placing each part of the dependency in its own relation:

```
movie stars (title, star)
movie producers (title, producer)
```

With this design, you can independently insert and remove stars and producers without affecting the other. Star and producer names also appear only once for each movie with which they are involved.

6.8 NORMALIZED RELATIONS AND DATABASE PERFORMANCE

Normalizing the relations in a database separates entities into their own relations and makes it possible for you to enter, modify, and delete data without disturbing entities other than the one directly being modified. However, normalization is not without its downside.

When you split relations so that relationships are represented by matching primary and foreign keys, you force the DBMS to perform matching operations between relations whenever a query requires data from more than one table. For example, in a normalized database you store data about an order in one relation, data about a customer in a second relation, and data about the order lines in yet a third relation. The operation typically used to bring the data into a single table so you can prepare an output such as an invoice is known as a *join*.

In theory, a join looks for rows with matching values between two tables and creates a new row in a result table every time it finds a match. In practice, however, performing a join involves manipulating more data than the simple combination of the two tables being joined would suggest. Joins of large tables (those of more than a few hundred rows) can significantly slow down the performance of a DBMS.

To understand what can happen, you need to know something about the relational algebra join operation. As with all relational algebra operations, the result of a join is a new table.

Note: Relational algebra is a set of operations used to manipulate and extract data from relations. Each operation performs a single manipulation of one or two tables. To complete a query, a DBMS uses a sequence of relational algebra operations; relational algebra is therefore procedural. SQL, on the other hand, is based on the relational calculus, which is nonprocedural, allowing you to specify what you want rather than how to get it. A single SQL Retrieval command can require a DBMS to perform any or all of the operations in the relational algebra.

6.8.1 Equi-Joins

In its most common form, a join forms new rows when data in the two source tables match. Because we are looking for rows with equal values, this type of join is known as an *equi-join* (or a *natural equi-join*). As an example, consider the two tables in Figure 6.6.

Notice that the ID number column is the primary key of the customers table and that the same column is a foreign key in the orders table. The ID number column in orders therefore serves to relate orders to the customers to which they belong.

```
customers

ID number first name    last name

001        Jane         Doe
002        John         Doe
003        Jane         Smith
004        John         Smith
005        Jane         Jones
006        John         Jones

orders

order number  ID number  order date   order total

001           002        10/10/99        250.65
002           002         2/21/00        125.89
003           003        11/15/99       1567.99
004           004        11/22/99        180.92
005           004        12/15/99        565.00
006           006        10/8/99          25.00
007           006        11/12/99         85.00
008           006        12/29/99        109.12
```

FIGURE 6.6

Two tables with a primary key–foreign key relationship.

```
result_table

ID number first_name   last_name   order_numb   order_date   order_total

002       John         Doe         001          10/10/99        250.65
002       John         Doe         002           2/21/00        125.89
003       Jane         Smith       003          11/15/99       1597.99
004       John         Smith       004          11/22/99        180.92
004       John         Smith       005          12/15/99        565.00
006       John         Jones       006          10/8/99          25.00
006       John         Jones       007          11/12/99         85.00
006       John         Jones       008          12/29/99        109.12
```

FIGURE 6.7

The joined result table.

Assume that you want to see the names of the customers who placed each order. To do so, you must join the two tables, creating combined rows wherever there is a matching ID number. In database terminology, we are joining the two tables *over* ID number. The result table can be found in Figure 6.7.

An equi-join can begin with either source table. (The result should be the same regardless of the direction in which the join is performed.) The join compares each row in one source table with the rows in the second. For each row in the first that matches data in the second source table in the column or columns over which the join is being performed, a new row is placed in the result table.

Assuming that we are using the `customers` table as the first source table, producing the result table in Figure 6.7 might therefore proceed conceptually as follows:

1. Search `orders` for rows with an ID number of 001. Because there are no matching rows in `orders`, do not place a row in the result table.
2. Search `orders` for rows with an ID number of 002. There are two matching rows in `orders`. Create two new rows in the result table, placing the same customer information at the end of each row in `orders`.
3. Search `orders` for rows with an ID number of 003. There is one matching row in `orders`. Place one new row in the result table.
4. Search `orders` for rows with an ID number of 004. There are two matching rows in `orders`. Place two rows in the result table.
5. Search `orders` for rows with an ID number of 005. There are no matching rows in `orders`. Therefore, do not place a row in the result table.
6. Search `orders` for rows with an ID number of 006. There are three matching rows in `orders`. Place three rows in the result table.

Notice that if an ID number does not appear in both tables, then no row is placed in the result table. This behavior categorizes this type of join as an *inner join*.

6.8.2 What Is Really Going On: Product and Restrict

From a relational algebra point of view, a join can be implemented using two other operations: product and restrict. As you will see, this sequence of operations requires the manipulation of a great deal of data and, if implemented by a DBMS, can result in very slow query performance.

The *restrict* operation retrieves rows from a table by matching each row against logical criteria (a *predicate*). Those rows that meet the criteria are placed in the result table; those that do not meet the criteria are omitted.

The product operation (the mathematical Cartesian product) makes every possible pairing of rows from two source tables. In Figure 6.8, for example, the product of the `customers` and `orders` tables produces a result table with 48 rows (the six customers times the eight orders). The `ID number` column appears twice because it is a part of both source tables.

> *Note:* Although 48 rows may not seem like a lot, consider the size of a product table created from tables with 100 and 1000 rows! The manipulation of a table of this size can tie up a lot of disk input/output and computer processing unit time.

In some rows, the ID number is the same. These are the rows that would have been included in a join. We can therefore apply a restrict predicate to the product

product_table

ID number (Customers)	first name	last name	ID number (Orders)	order number	order date	order total
001	Jane	Doe	002	001	10/10/99	250.65
001	Jane	Doe	002	002	2/21/00	125.89
001	Jane	Doe	003	003	11/15/99	1597.99
001	Jane	Doe	004	004	11/22/99	180.92
001	Jane	Doe	004	005	12/15/99	565.00
001	Jane	Doe	006	006	10/8/99	25.00
001	Jane	Doe	006	007	11/12/99	85.00
001	Jane	Doe	006	008	12/29/99	109.12
002	John	Doe	002	001	10/10/99	250.65
002	John	Doe	002	002	2/21/00	125.89
002	John	Doe	003	003	11/15/99	1597.99
002	John	Doe	004	004	11/22/99	180.92
002	John	Doe	004	005	12/15/99	565.00
002	John	Doe	006	006	10/8/99	25.00
002	John	Doe	006	007	11/12/99	85.00
002	John	Doe	006	008	12/29/99	109.12
003	Jane	Smith	002	001	10/10/99	250.65
003	Jane	Smith	002	002	2/21/00	125.89
003	Jane	Smith	003	003	11/15/99	1597.99
003	Jane	Smith	004	004	11/22/99	180.92
003	Jane	Smith	004	005	12/15/99	565.00
003	Jane	Smith	006	006	10/8/99	25.00
003	Jane	Smith	006	007	11/12/99	85.00
003	Jane	Smith	006	008	12/29/99	109.12
004	John	Smith	002	001	10/10/99	250.65
004	John	Smith	002	002	2/21/00	125.89
004	John	Smith	003	003	11/15/99	1597.99
004	John	Smith	004	004	11/22/99	180.92
004	John	Smith	004	005	12/15/99	565.00
004	John	Smith	006	006	10/8/99	25.00
004	John	Smith	006	006	10/8/99	25.00
004	John	Smith	006	008	12/29/99	109.12
006	John	Jones	002	001	10/10/99	250.65
006	John	Jones	002	002	2/21/00	125.89
006	John	Jones	003	003	11/15/99	1597.99
006	John	Jones	004	004	11/22/99	180.92
006	John	Jones	004	005	12/15/99	565.00
006	John	Jones	006	006	10/8/99	25.00
006	John	Jones	006	006	10/8/99	25.00
006	John	Jones	006	008	12/29/99	109.12

FIGURE 6.8

The product of the customers and orders tables.

table to end up with the same table provided by the join you saw earlier. The predicate's logical condition can be written as:

```
customers.id_numb = orders.id_numb
```

The rows that are selected by this predicate appear in black in Figure 6.9; those eliminated by the predicate are in gray. Notice that the black rows are exactly the same as those in the result table of the join (Figure 6.7).

joined_table

ID number (Customers)	first name	last name	ID number (Orders)	order number	order date	order total
001	Jane	Doe	002	001	10/10/99	250.65
001	Jane	Doe	002	002	2/21/00	125.89
001	Jane	Doe	003	003	11/15/99	1597.99
001	Jane	Doe	004	004	11/22/99	180.92
001	Jane	Doe	004	005	12/15/99	565.00
001	Jane	Doe	006	006	10/8/99	25.00
001	Jane	Doe	006	007	11/12/99	85.00
001	Jane	Doe	006	008	12/29/99	109.12
002	**John**	**Doe**	**002**	**001**	**10/10/99**	**250.65**
002	**John**	**Doe**	**002**	**002**	**2/21/00**	**125.89**
002	John	Doe	003	003	11/15/99	1597.99
002	John	Doe	004	004	11/22/99	180.92
002	John	Doe	004	005	12/15/99	565.00
002	John	Doe	006	006	10/8/99	25.00
002	John	Doe	006	007	11/12/99	85.00
002	John	Doe	006	008	12/29/99	109.12
003	Jane	Smith	002	001	10/10/99	250.65
003	Jane	Smith	002	002	2/21/00	125.89
003	**Jane**	**Smith**	**003**	**003**	**11/15/99**	**1597.99**
003	Jane	Smith	004	004	11/22/99	180.92
003	Jane	Smith	004	005	12/15/99	565.00
003	Jane	Smith	006	006	10/8/99	25.00
003	Jane	Smith	006	007	11/12/99	85.00
003	Jane	Smith	006	008	12/29/99	109.12
004	John	Smith	002	001	10/10/99	250.65
004	John	Smith	002	002	2/21/00	125.89
004	John	Smith	003	003	11/15/99	1597.99
004	**John**	**Smith**	**004**	**004**	**11/22/99**	**180.92**
004	**John**	**Smith**	**004**	**005**	**12/15/99**	**565.00**
004	John	Smith	006	006	10/8/99	25.00
004	John	Smith	006	006	10/8/99	25.00
004	John	Smith	006	008	12/29/99	109.12
006	John	Jones	002	001	10/10/99	250.65
006	John	Jones	002	002	2/21/00	125.89
006	John	Jones	003	003	11/15/99	1597.99
006	John	Jones	004	004	11/22/99	180.92
006	John	Jones	004	005	12/15/99	565.00
006	**John**	**Jones**	**006**	**006**	**10/8/99**	**25.00**
006	**John**	**Jones**	**006**	**006**	**10/8/99**	**25.00**
006	**John**	**Jones**	**006**	**008**	**12/29/99**	**109.12**

FIGURE 6.9

The product of the customers and orders tables after applying a restrict predicate.

Note: Although this may seem like a highly inefficient way to implement a join, it is actually quite flexible, in particular because the relationship between the columns over which the join is being performed doesn't have to be equal. A user could just as easily request a join where the value in table A was greater than the value in table B, and so on.

6.8.3 **The Bottom Line**

Because of the processing overhead created when performing a join, some database designers make a conscious decision to leave tables unnormalized. For example, if Lasers Only always accessed the line items at the same time it accessed order information, then a designer might choose to combine the line item and order data into one table, knowing full well that the unnormalized relation exhibits anomalies. The benefit is that retrieval of order information will be faster than if it were split into two tables.

Should you leave unnormalized relations in your database to achieve better retrieval performance? In this author's opinion, there is rarely any need to do so. Assuming that you are working with a relatively standard DBMS that supports SQL as its query language, there are SQL syntaxes that you can use when writing queries that avoid joins. That being the case, it does not seem worth the problems that unnormalized relations present to leave them in the database. Careful writing of retrieval queries can provide performance that is nearly as good as that of retrieval from unnormalized relations.

Note: For a complete discussion of writing SQL queries to avoid joins, see Harrington's book, *SQL Clearly Explained*, Second Edition, also published by Morgan Kaufmann.

6.9 FURTHER READING

There are many books available that deal with the theory of relational databases. You can find useful supplementary information in S. Stanczyk, B. Champion, and R. Leton. *Theory and Practice of Relational Databases*. Taylor & Rances, 2001.

Physical Database Design

7.1 INTRODUCTION

The transition from logical to physical database design marks a change in focus and in the skills required. In this chapter, we are going to develop a set of data structures, making those structures perform on a particular hardware platform using the facilities of our selected database management system (DBMS). Instead of business and generic data structuring skills, we require a detailed knowledge of general performance-tuning techniques and of the facilities provided by the DBMS. Frequently this means that a different, more technical person will take on the role of database design. In this case, the data modeler's role will be essentially to advise on the impact of changes to tables and columns, which may be required as a last resort to achieve performance goals.

An enduring myth about database design is that the response time for data retrieval from a normalized set of tables and columns will be longer than acceptable. As with all myths there is a grain of truth in the assertion. Certainly, if a large amount of data are to be retrieved or if the database itself is very large and either the query is unduly complex or the data have not been appropriately indexed, a slow response time may result. However, there is a lot that can be done in tuning the database and in careful crafting of queries, before denormalization or other modification of the tables and columns defined in a logical data model becomes necessary. This has become increasingly true as overall computer performance has improved and DBMS designers have continued to develop the capabilities of their optimizers (the built-in software within a DBMS that selects the most efficient means of executing each query).

Before we go any further, we need to clarify some terminology. The data modeler's focus will be on the tables and columns (and the views based on them). He or she will typically refer to the tables and columns delivered by the physical database design process as the *physical data model* to distinguish it from the logical data model. As we saw in Chapter 5, the logical data model is an ideal structure, which reflects business information requirements and makes assertions about data properties, such as functional dependency, without being obscured by any changes required for performance.

The database designer will be interested not only in the tables and columns but also in the infrastructure components—indexes and physical storage mechanisms—that support data management and performance requirements. Since program logic depends only on tables and columns (and views based on them), that set of components is often referred to as the *logical schema*,[1] while the remainder may be referred to as the *physical schema*.[2] These alternative uses of the terms "logical" and "physical" can easily lead to confusion!

This chapter reviews the inputs that the physical database designer needs in addition to the logical data model. Then it looks at a number of options available for achieving performance goals. The options fall into three broad categories:

1. Design decisions that do not affect program logic (i.e., that preserve the structure of the logical data model).
2. Approaches to redesigning queries themselves to run faster (rather than changing the database structure).
3. Design decisions that entail changes to the structures specified in the logical data model.

Finally, we look at the definition of views.

If you are a specialist data modeler, you may be tempted to skip this chapter, since much of it relates to the tools and work of the physical database designer. We encourage you not to do so. One of the key factors in getting good outcomes in physical database design is the level of communication and respect between the database designer and the data modeler. That means understanding what the other party does and how they do it. Good architects maintain an up-to-date knowledge of building materials.

On the other hand, if you are responsible for physical database design, you need to recognize that this chapter merely scratches the surface of the many features and facilities available to you in a modern DBMS. Many of these are DBMS specific, and accordingly better covered in vendor manuals or guides for the specific product. Specialist physical database designers generally focus on one (or a limited number) of DBMSs, in contrast to modelers whose specialization is more likely to be in a specific business domain.

7.2 INPUTS TO DATABASE DESIGN

As well as the logical data model, the database designer will require other information to be able to make sound design decisions.

---

[1]Equivalent to the ANSI/SPARC conceptual schema and external schemas.
[2]Equivalent to the ANSI/SPARC internal schema.

1. *The process model*, detailing input processes (creation and updating of rows in tables) and output requirements (retrieval of data from the database), enabling the database designer to establish:

   a. The circumstances in which rows are added to each table—how frequently on average and at peak times (e.g., 1 per day or 100 per second), and how many at a time; plus such details as whether the primary key of an added row depends on the time that it is added, so that rows added at about the same time have similar primary keys, which can impact performance both through contention and the need to rebalance the primary key index.

   b. The circumstances in which rows are updated in each table—how frequently on average and at peak times plus the likelihood that rows with similar primary keys are updated at about the same time, which may affect locking (see Section 7.5.1).

   c. The circumstances in which rows are deleted from each table—how frequently and how many at a time (deletes, like inserts, affect all indexes on the table).

   d. The circumstances in which rows are retrieved from each table—what columns in the table are used for selecting rows, how many rows are retrieved, what other tables are referenced, and what columns in the referring and referenced tables are correlated or joined.

2. *The process/entity matrix* (often referred to as a CRUD—create, read, update, delete—matrix) or mapping that shows which processes access each entity class and how (create, update, retrieve), providing the database designer with a list of the processes that create, update, and retrieve each entity class.

3. *Nonstructural data requirements:*

   a. *Retention:* how long data in each table is to be retained before deletion or archiving, whether there is a requirement for data to be removed from a table within a certain time frame.

   b. *Volumes:* how many rows are likely to be included in each table at system rollout, how many additional rows are likely to be created within a given time period (retention and volumes enable the database designer to establish how big each table will be at various times during the life of the application).

   c. *Availability:* whether data are required on a full-time basis, and if not, for how long and how frequently the database can be inaccessible by users, enabling the database designer to plan for:

      i. Any batch processes specified in the process model.

      ii. Downtime during which the database can be reorganized (i.e., data and indexes redistributed more evenly across the storage medium).

      iii. Whether data need to be replicated at multiple sites to provide fallback in the event of network failure.

   d. *Freshness:* how up to date the data available to those retrieving it have to be, enabling the database designer to decide whether it is feasible to have separate update and retrieval copies of data (see Section 7.6.4).

e. *Security requirements:* driving access permissions and possibly prompting table partitioning and creation of views reflecting different subsets of data available to different classes of users.

4. *Performance requirements:* usually expressed in terms of the response time, the time taken by each defined exchange in each application/user dialog (i.e., the time between the user pressing the Enter key and the application displaying the confirmation of the creation or updating of the data in the database or the results of the query). These enable the database designer to focus on those creates, updates, and retrieval queries that have the most critical performance requirements. (Beware of statements such as "all queries must exhibit subsecond response time"; this is rarely true and indicates that the writer has not bothered to identify the critical user operations. We once encountered this statement in a contract that also contained the statement "The application must support retrieval queries of arbitrary complexity.")

5. *The target DBMS:* not only the "brand" (e.g., DB2, Informix, Oracle, SQL Server, Access, and so on), but the version, enabling the database designer to establish what facilities, features, and options are provided by that DBMS.

6. *Any current or likely limitations on disk space:* these will be a factor in choosing one or the other option where options differ in their use of disk space (e.g., see Section 7.6.8).

7. *Any likely difficulties in obtaining skilled programming resources:* these may prompt the avoidance of more complex data structures where these impact programming complexity (e.g., see Sections 7.6.4 and 7.6.5).

7.3 OPTIONS AVAILABLE TO THE DATABASE DESIGNER

The main challenge facing the database designer is to speed up those transactions with critical performance requirements. The slowest activities in a database are almost always the reading of data from the storage medium into main memory and the writing of data from main memory back to the storage medium, and it is on this data access (also known as I/O, input/output) that we now focus.

Commercial relational DBMSs differ in the facilities and features they offer, the ways in which those facilities and features are implemented, and the options available within each facility and feature. It is beyond the scope and intention of this chapter to detail each of these; in any case, given the frequency with which new versions of the major commercial DBMSs are released, our information would soon be out of date. Instead, we offer a list of the most important facilities and features offered by relational DBMSs and some principles for their use. This can be used by:

1. The database designer, as a checklist of what facilities and features to read up on in the DBMS documentation.

2. The data modeler who is handing over to a database designer, as a checklist of issues to examine during any negotiations over changes to tables and columns.

We first look at those design decisions that do not affect program logic. We then look at ways in which queries can be crafted to run faster. We finally look at various types of changes that can be made to the logical schema to support faster queries when all other techniques have been tried and some queries still do not run fast enough. This is also the sequence in which these techniques should be tried by the database designer.

Note that those design decisions that do not affect program logic can be revisited and altered after a database has been rolled out with minimal, if any, impact on the availability of the database and, of course, none on program logic. Changes to the logical schema, however, require changes to program logic. They must therefore be made in a test environment (along with those program changes), tested, packaged, and released in a controlled manner like any other application upgrade.

7.4 DESIGN DECISIONS THAT DO NOT AFFECT PROGRAM LOGIC

The discussion in this section makes frequent reference to the term *block*. This is the term used in the Oracle DBMS product to refer to the smallest amount of data that can be transferred between the storage medium and main memory. The corresponding term in IBM's DB2 database management system is *page*.

7.4.1 Indexes

Indexes provide one of the most commonly used methods for rapidly retrieving specified rows from a table without having to search the entire table.

Each table can have one or more indexes specified. Each index applies to a particular column or set of columns. For each value of the column(s), the index lists the location(s) of the row(s) in which that value can be found. For example, an index on `Customer Location` would enable us to readily locate all of the rows that had a value for `Customer Location` of (say) New York.

The specification of each index includes:

- The column(s).
- Whether it is unique (i.e., whether there can be no more than one row for any given value; see "Index Properties" section).
- Whether it is the sorting index (see "Index Properties" section).
- The structure of the index (for some DBMSs; see "Balanced Tree Indexes" and "Bit-Mapped Indexes" sections).

The advantages of an index are that:

- It can improve data access performance for a retrieval or update.
- Retrievals that only refer to indexed columns do not need to read any data blocks (access to indexes is often faster than direct access to data blocks bypassing any index).

The disadvantages are that each index:

- Adds to the data access cost of a create transaction or an update transaction in which an indexed column is updated.
- Takes up disk space.
- May increase lock contention (see Section 7.5.1).
- Adds to the processing and data access cost of reorganize and table load utilities.

Whether an index will actually improve the performance of an individual query depends on two factors:

1. Whether the index is actually used by the query.
2. Whether the index confers any performance advantage on the query.

Index Usage by Queries

DML (Data Manipulation Language)[3] only specifies what you want, not how to get it. The optimizer built into the DBMS selects the best available access method based on its knowledge of indexes, column contents, and so on. Thus, index usage cannot be explicitly specified but is determined by the optimizer during DML compilation. How it implements the DML will depend on:

- The DML clauses used, in particular the predicate(s) in the where clause (see Figure 7.1 for examples).
- The tables accessed, their size, and content.
- What indexes there are on those tables.

```
select    EMP_NO, EMP_NAME, SALARY
from      EMPLOYEE
where     SALARY > 80000;

update    EMPLOYEE
set       SALARY = SALARY* 1.1
where     SALARY > 80000;
```

FIGURE 7.1

Retrieval and update queries.

---

[3]This is the SQL query language, often itself called "SQL," and most commonly used to retrieve data from a relational database.

```
select      EMP_NO, EMP_NAME, SALARY
from        EMPLOYEE
where       SALARY > all
 (select    SALARY
 from       EMPLOYEE
 where      DEPT_NO = '123');
```

FIGURE 7.2

An ALL subquery.

```
select      EMP_NO, EMP_NAME
from        EMPLOYEE as E1
where       exists
 (select*
 from       EMPLOYEE as E2
 where      E2.EMP_NAME = E1.EMP_NAME
 and        E2.EMP_NO <> E1.EMP_NO);
```

FIGURE 7.3

A correlated subquery.

Some predicates will preclude the use of indexes; these include:

- Negative conditions (e.g., "not equals" and those involving NOT).
- LIKE predicates in which the comparison string starts with a wildcard.
- Comparisons including scalar operators (e.g., +) or functions (e.g., data type conversion functions).
- ANY/ALL subqueries, as in Figure 7.2.
- Correlated subqueries, as in Figure 7.3.

Certain update operations may also be unable to use indexes. For example, while the retrieval query in Figure 7.1 can use an index on the Salary column if there is one, the update query in the same figure cannot.

Note that the DBMS may require that, after an index is added, a utility is run to examine table contents and indexes and recompile each SQL query. Failure to do this would prevent any query from using the new index.

Performance Advantages of Indexes

Even if an index is available and the query is formulated in such a way that it can use that index, the index may not improve performance if more than a certain proportion of rows are retrieved. That proportion depends on the DBMS.

Index Properties

If an index is defined as *unique*, each row in the associated table must have a different value in the column or columns covered by the index. Thus, this is a means of implementing a uniqueness constraint, and a unique index should therefore be created on each table's primary key as well as on any other sets of columns having a uniqueness constraint. However, since the database administrator can always drop any index (except perhaps that on a primary key) at any time, a unique index cannot be relied on to be present whenever rows are inserted. As a result, most programming standards require that a uniqueness constraint is explicitly tested for whenever inserting a row into the relevant table or updating any column participating in that constraint.

The sorting *index* (called the *clustering index* in DB2) of each table is the one that controls the sequence in which rows are stored during a bulk load or reorganization that occurs during the existence of that index. Clearly there can be only one such index for each table. Which column(s) should the sorting index cover? In some DBMSs there is no choice; the index on the primary key will also control row sequence. Where there is a choice, any of the following may be worthy candidates, depending on the DBMS:

- Those columns most frequently involved in inequalities (e.g., where > or >= appears in the predicate).
- Those columns most frequently specified as the sorting sequence.
- The columns of the most frequently specified foreign key in joins.
- The columns of the primary key.

The performance advantages of a sorting index are:

- Multiple rows relevant to a query can be retrieved in a single I/O operation.
- Sorting is much faster if the rows are already more or less in sequence (note that rows can get out of sequence between reorganizations).

By contrast, creating a sorting index on one or more columns may confer no advantage over a nonsorting index if those columns are mostly involved in index-only processing (i.e., if those columns are mostly accessed only in combination with each other or are mostly involved in = predicates).

Consider creating other (nonunique, nonsorting) indexes on:

- Columns searched or joined with a low hit rate.
- Foreign keys.
- Columns frequently involved in aggregate functions, existence checks, or DISTINCT selection.
- Sets of columns frequently linked by AND in predicates.
- Code and meaning columns for a classification table if there are other less-frequently accessed columns.
- Columns frequently retrieved.

Indexes on any of the following may not yield any performance benefit:

- Columns with low cardinality (the number of different values is significantly less than the number of rows) unless a bit-mapped index is used (see "Bit-Mapped Indexes" section).

- Columns with skewed distribution (many occurrences of one or two particular values and few occurrences of each of a number of other values).
- Columns with low population (NULL in many rows).
- Columns that are frequently updated.
- Columns that take up a significant proportion of the row length.
- Tables occupying a small number of blocks, unless the index is to be used for joins, a uniqueness constraint, or referential integrity, or if index-only processing is to be used.
- Columns with the varchar (variable length) data type.

Balanced Tree Indexes

Figure 7.4 illustrates the structure of a *balanced tree index* (often referred to as a *B-tree index*) used in most relational DBMSs. Note that the depth of the tree may be only one (in which case the index entries in the root block point directly to data blocks); two (in which case the index entries in the root block point to leaf blocks in which index entries point to data blocks); three (as shown in the figure); or more than three (in which the index entries in nonleaf blocks point to other nonleaf blocks). The term *balanced* refers to the fact that the tree structure is symmetrical. If insertion of a new record causes a particular leaf block to fill up, the index entries must be redistributed evenly across the index with additional index blocks created as necessary, leading eventually to a deeper index.

Particular problems may arise with a balanced tree index on a column or columns on which inserts are sequenced (i.e., each additional row has a

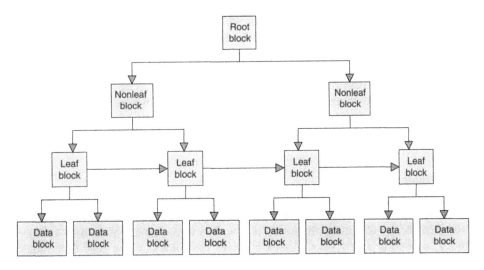

FIGURE 7.4

Balanced tree index structure.

higher value in those column(s) than the previous row added). In this case, the insertion of new index entries is focused on the rightmost (highest value) leaf block, rather than evenly across the index, resulting in more frequent redistribution of index entries that may be quite slow if the entire index is not in main memory. This makes a strong case for random, rather than sequential, primary keys.

Bit-Mapped Indexes

Another index structure provided by some DBMSs is the *bit-mapped index*. This has an index entry for each value that appears in the indexed column. Each index entry includes a column value followed by a series of bits, one for each row in the table. Each bit is set to one if the corresponding row has that value in the indexed column and zero if it has some other value. This type of index confers the most advantage where the indexed column is of low cardinality (the number of different values is significantly less than the number of rows). By contrast, such an index may impact negatively on the performance of an insert operation into a large table as every bit in every index entry that represents a row after the inserted row must be moved one place to the right. This is less of a problem if the index can be held permanently in main memory (see Section 7.4.3).

Indexed Sequential Tables

A few DBMSs support an alternative form of index referred to as *ISAM* (indexed sequential access method). This may provide better performance for some types of data population and access patterns.

Hash Tables

Some DBMSs provide an alternative to an index to support random access in the form of a hashing algorithm to calculate block numbers from key values. Tables managed in this fashion are referred to as *hashed random* (or "hash" for short). Again, this may provide better performance for some types of data population and access patterns. Note that this technique is of no value if partial keys are used in searches (e.g., "Show me the customers whose names start with 'Smi'") or a range of key values is required (e.g., "Show me all customers with a birth date between 1/1/1948 and 12/31/1948"), whereas indexes do support these types of query.

Heap Tables

Some DBMSs provide for tables to be created without indexes. Such tables are sometimes referred to as *heaps*. If the table is small (only a few blocks) an index may provide no advantage. Indeed if all the data in the table will fit into a single block, accessing a row via an index requires two blocks to be read (the index block and the data block) compared with reading in and scanning (in main memory) the one block; in this case, an index degrades performance. Even if the data in the table require two blocks, the average number of blocks read to access a single row is still less than the two necessary for access via an index. Many reference (or classification) tables fall into this category.

Note, however, that the DBMS may require that an index be created for the primary key of each table that has one, and a classification table will certainly require a primary key. If so, performance may be improved by one of the following:

- Creating an additional index that includes both code (the primary key) and meaning columns; any access to the classification table that requires both columns will use that index rather than the data table itself (which is now in effect redundant but only takes up space rather than slowing down access).

- Assigning the table to main memory in such a way that ensures the classification table remains in main memory for the duration of each load of the application (see Section 7.4.3).

7.4.2 **Data Storage**

A relational DBMS provides the database designer with a variety of options (depending on the DBMS) for the storage of data.

Table Space Usage

Many DBMSs enable the database designer to create multiple *table spaces* to which tables can be assigned. Since these table spaces can each be given different block sizes and other parameters, tables with similar access patterns can be stored in the same table space and each table space then tuned to optimize the performance for the tables therein. The DBMS may even allow you to interleave rows from different tables, in which case you may be able to arrange, for example, for the Order Item rows for a given order to follow the Order row for that order, if they are frequently retrieved together. This reduces the average number of blocks that need to be read to retrieve an entire order. The facility is sometimes referred to as *clustering*, which may lead to confusion with the term *clustering index* (see "Index Properties" section).

Free Space

When a table is loaded or reorganized, each block may be loaded with as many rows as can fit (unless rows are particularly short and there is a limit imposed by the DBMS on how many rows a block can hold). If a new row is inserted and the sorting sequence implied by the primary index dictates that the row should be placed in an already full block, that row must be placed in another block. If no provision has been made for additional rows, that will be the last block (or if that block is full, a new block following the last block). Clearly this "overflow" situation will cause a degradation over time of the sorting sequence implied by the primary index and will reduce any advantages conferred by the sorting sequence of that index.

This is where *free space* enters the picture. A specified proportion of the space in each block can be reserved at load or reorganization time for rows subsequently inserted. A fallback can also be provided by leaving every *n*th block empty at load or reorganization time. If a block fills up, additional rows that belong in that block will be placed in the next available empty block. Note that once this happens, any attempt to retrieve data in sequence will incur extra block reads. This caters, of course, not only for insertions but for increases in the length of existing rows, such as those that have columns with the `varchar` data type.

The more free space you specify, the more rows can be fitted in or increased in length before performance degrades and reorganization is necessary. At the same time, more free space means that any retrieval of multiple consecutive rows will need to read more blocks. Obviously for those tables that are read-only, you should specify zero free space. In tables that have a low frequency of create transactions (and update transactions that increase row length), zero free space is also reasonable, since additional data can be added after the last row. Free space can and should be allocated for indexes as well as data.

Table Partitioning

Some DBMSs allow you to divide a table into separate *partitions* based on one of the indexes. For example, if the first column of an index is the state code, a separate partition can be created for each state. Each partition can be independently loaded or reorganized and can have different free space and other settings.

Drive Usage

Choosing where a table or index is on disk enables you to use faster drives for more frequently accessed data or to avoid channel contention by distributing across multiple disk channels tables that are accessed in the same query.

Compression

One option that many DBMSs provide is the compression of data in the stored table (e.g., shortening of null columns or text columns with trailing space). While this may save disk space and increase the number of rows per block, it can add to the processing cost.

Distribution and Replication

Modern DBMSs provide many facilities for distributing data across multiple networked servers. Among other things, distributing data in this manner can confer performance and availability advantages. However, this is a specialist topic and is outside the scope of this brief overview of physical database design.

7.4.3 Memory Usage

Some DBMSs support multiple *input/output buffers* in main memory and enable you to specify the size of each buffer and allocate tables and indexes to particular buffers. This can reduce or even eliminate the need to swap frequently accessed tables or indexes out of main memory to make room for other data. For example, a buffer could be set up that is large enough to accommodate all the classification tables in their entirety. Once they are all in main memory, any query requiring data from a classification table does not have to read any blocks for that purpose.

7.5 CRAFTING QUERIES TO RUN FASTER

We have seen in the "Index Usage by Queries" section that some queries cannot make use of indexes. If a query of this kind can be rewritten to make use of an index, it is likely to run faster. As a simple example, consider a retrieval of employee records in which there is a GENDER column that holds either "M" or "F." A query to retrieve only male employees could be written with the predicate GENDER <> "F" (in which case it cannot use an index on the GENDER column) or with the predicate GENDER = "M" (in which case it can use that index). The optimizer (capable of recasting queries into logically equivalent forms that will perform better) is of no help here even if it "knows" that there are currently only "M" and "F" values in the GENDER column, since it has no way of knowing that some other value might eventually be loaded into that column. Thus, GENDER = "M" is not logically equivalent to GENDER <> "F".

There are also various ways in which subqueries can be expressed differently. Most noncorrelated subqueries can be alternatively expressed as a join. An IN subquery can always be alternatively expressed as an EXISTS subquery, although the converse is not true. A query including > ALL (SELECT ...) can be alternatively expressed by substituting > (SELECT MAX(...)) in place of > ALL (SELECT...).

Sorting can be very time consuming. Note that any query including GROUP BY or ORDER BY will sort the retrieved data. These clauses may, of course, be unavoidable in meeting the information requirement. (ORDER BY is essential for the query result to be sorted in a required order, since there is otherwise no guarantee of the sequencing of result data, which will reflect the sorting index only so long as no inserts or updates have occurred since the last table reorganization.) However, there are two other situations in which unnecessary sorts can be avoided.

One is DISTINCT, which is used to ensure that there are no duplicate rows in the retrieved data, which it does by sorting the result set. For example, if the query is retrieving only addresses of employees, and more than one employee lives at the same address, that address will appear more than once unless the DISTINCT clause is used. We have observed that the DISTINCT clause is sometimes used when duplicate rows are impossible; in this situation it can be removed without affecting the query result but with significant impact on query performance.

Similarly, a UNION query without the ALL qualifier after UNION ensures that there are no duplicate rows in the result set, again by sorting it (unless there is a usable index). If you know that there is no possibility of the same row resulting from more than one of the individual queries making up a UNION query, add the ALL qualifier.

7.5.1 Locking

DBMSs employ various *locks* to ensure, for example, that only one user can update a particular row at a time, or that, if a row is being updated, users who wish to use that row are either prevented from doing so or see the preupdate row consistently until the update is completed. Many business requirements imply the use of locks. For example, in an airline reservation system, if a customer has reserved a seat on one leg of a multileg journey, that seat must not be available to any other user, but if the original customer decides not to proceed when he or she discovers that there is no seat available on a connecting flight, the reserved seat must be released.

The lowest level of lock is *row level* where an individual row is locked but other rows in the same block are still accessible. The next level is *block level*, which requires less data storage for management but locks all rows in the same block as the one being updated. *Table* and *table space locks* are also possible. Locks may be *escalated,* whereby a lock at one level is converted to a lock at the next level to improve performance. The designer may also specify *lock acquisition* and *lock release* strategies for transactions accessing multiple tables. A transaction can either acquire all locks before starting or acquire each lock as required, and it can either release all locks after committing (completing the update transaction) or release each lock once no longer required.

7.6 LOGICAL SCHEMA DECISIONS

We now look at various types of changes that can be made to the logical schema to support faster queries when the techniques we have discussed have been tried and some queries still do not run fast enough.

7.6.1 Alternative Implementation of Relationships

If the target DBMS supports the SQL99 Set Type Constructor feature:

1. A one-to-many relationship can be implemented within one table.
2. A many-to-many relationship can be implemented without creating an additional table.

Figure 7.5 illustrates such implementations.

Department No	Department Code	Department Name	Employee Group	
			Employee No	Employee Name
123	ACCT	Accounts	37289	J Smith
			41260	A Chang
			50227	B Malik
135	PRCH	Purchasing	16354	D Sanchez
			26732	T Nguyen

Employee No	Employee Name	Assignment Group	
		Project No	Assignment Date
50227	B Malik	1234	27/2/95
		2345	2/3/95
37289	J Smith	1234	28/2/95

FIGURE 7.5

Alternative implementations of relationships in an SQL99 DBMS.

7.6.2 Table Splitting

Two implications of increasing the size of a table are:

1. Any balanced tree index on that table will be deeper (i.e., there will be more nonleaf blocks between the root block and each leaf block and, thus, more blocks to be read to access a row using that index).
2. Any query unable to use any indexes will read more blocks in scanning the entire table.

Thus, all queries—those that use indexes and those that do not—will take more time. Conversely, if a table can be made smaller, most, if not all, queries on that table will take less time.

Horizontal Splitting

One technique for reducing the size of a table accessed by a query is to split it into two or more tables with the same columns and to allocate the rows to different tables according to some criteria. In effect we are defining and implementing subtypes. For example, although it might make sense to include historical data in the same table as the corresponding current data, it is likely that different queries access current and historical data. Placing current and historical data in different tables with the same structure will certainly improve the performance of queries on current data. You may prefer to include a copy of the current data in the historical data table to enable queries on all data to be written without the UNION operator. This is duplication rather than splitting; we deal with that separately in Section 7.6.4 due to the different implications duplication has for processing.

Vertical Splitting

The more data there are in each row of a table, the fewer rows there are per block. Queries that need to read multiple consecutive rows will therefore need to read more blocks to do so. Such queries might take less time if the rows could be made shorter. At the same time, shortening the rows reduces the size of the table and (if it is not particularly large) increases the likelihood that it can be retained in main memory. If some columns of a table constitute a significant proportion of the row length and are accessed significantly less frequently than the remainder of the columns of that table, there may be a case for holding those columns in a separate table using the same primary key.

For example, if a classification table has Code, Meaning, and Explanation columns, but the Explanation column is infrequently accessed, holding that column in a separate table on the same primary key will mean that the classification table itself occupies fewer blocks, increasing the likelihood of it remaining in main memory. This may improve the performance of queries that access only the Code and Meaning columns. Of course, a query that accesses all columns must join the two tables; this may take more time than the corresponding query on the original table. Note also that if the DBMS provides a long text data type with the property that columns using that data type are not stored in the same block as the other columns of the same table, and the Explanation column is given that data type, no advantage accrues from splitting that column into a separate table.

Another situation in which vertical splitting may yield performance benefits is where different processes use different columns, such as when an Employee table holds both personnel information and payroll information.

7.6.3 Table Merging

We have encountered proposals by database designers to merge tables that are regularly joined in queries.

An example of such a proposal is the merging of the Order and Order Line tables shown in Figure 7.6. Since the merged table can only have one set of columns making up the primary key, this would need to be Order No and Line No, which means that order rows in the merged table would need a dummy Line No value (since all primary key columns must be non-null); if that value were zero, this would have the effect of all Order Line rows following their associated Order row if the index on the primary key were also the primary index. Since all rows in a table have the same columns, Order rows would have dummy (possibly null) Product Code, Unit Count, and Required By Date columns, while Order Line rows would have dummy (again possibly null) Customer No and Order Date

Separate: **ORDER** (<u>Order No</u>, Customer No, Order Date)

  ORDER LINE (<u>Order No</u>, <u>Line No</u>, Product Code, Unit Count, Required By Date)

Merged: **ORDER/ORDER LINE** (<u>Order No</u>, <u>Line No</u>, Customer No, Order Date, Product Code, Unit Count, Required By Date)

FIGURE 7.6

Separate and merged `Order` and `Order Line` tables.

columns. Alternatively, a single column might be created to hold the `Required By Date` value in an `Order` row and the `Order Date` value in an `Order Line` row.

The rationale for this approach is to reduce the average number of blocks that need to be read to retrieve an entire order. However, the result is achieved at the expense of a significant change from the logical data model. If a similar effect can be achieved by interleaving rows from different tables in the same table space, this should be done instead.

7.6.4 Duplication

We saw in the "Horizontal Splitting" section how we might separate current data from historical data to improve the performance of queries accessing only current data by reducing the size of the table read by those queries. As we indicated then, an alternative is to duplicate the current data in another table, retaining all current data as well as the historical data in the original table. However, whenever we duplicate data, there is the potential for errors to arise unless there is strict control over the use of the two copies of the data. The following are among the things that can go wrong:

- Only one copy is being updated, but some users read the other copy thinking it is up to date.
- A transaction causes the addition of a quantity to a numeric column in one copy, but the next transaction adds to the same column in the other copy. Ultimately, the effect of one or other of those transactions will be lost.
- One copy is updated, but the data from the other copy are used to overwrite the updated copy, in effect wiping out all updates since the second copy was taken.

To avoid these problems, a policy must be enforced whereby only one copy can be updated by transactions initiated by users or batch processes (the current data table in the preceding example). The corresponding data in the other copy (the complete table in the preceding example) are either automatically updated simultaneously (e.g., via a DBMS trigger) or, if it is acceptable for users accessing that copy to see out-of-date data, replaced at regular intervals (e.g., daily).

Another example of an "active subset" of data that might be copied into another table are data on insurance policies, contracts, or any other agreements or arrangements that are reviewed, renewed, and possibly changed on a cyclical basis, such as yearly. Toward the end of a calendar month the data for those policies that are due for renewal during the next calendar month could become a "hot spot" in the table holding information about all policies. It may therefore improve performance to copy the policy data for the next renewal month into a separate table. The change over from one month to the other must, of course, be carefully managed, and it may make sense to have "last month," "this month," and "next month" tables as well as the complete table.

Another way in which duplication can confer advantages is in optimization for different processes. We shall see in Section 7.6.7 how hierarchies in particular can benefit from duplication.

7.6.5 Denormalization

Technically, denormalization is any change to the logical schema that results in it not being fully normalized. In the context of physical database design, the term is often used more broadly to include the addition of derivable data of any kind, including that derived from multiple rows.

Four examples of strict violations of normalization are shown in the model of Figure 7.7:

1. It can be assumed that `Customer Name` and `Customer Address` have been copied from a `Customer` table with primary key `Customer No`.
2. `Customer No` has been copied from the `Order` table to the `Order Line` table.
3. It can be assumed that `Unit Price` has been copied from a `Product` table with primary key `Product Code`.
4. `Total Price` can be calculated by multiplying `Unit Price` by `Unit Count`.

Changes such as this are intended to offer performance benefits for some transactions. For example, a query on the `Order Line` table that also requires the `Customer No` does not have to also access the `Order` table. However, there is a down side: each such additional column must be carefully controlled.

ORDER (<u>Order No</u>, Customer No, Customer Name, Customer Address, Order Date)
ORDER LINE (<u>Order No</u>, <u>Line No</u>, Customer No, Customer Name, Customer Address, Product Code, Unit Count, Unit Price, Total Price, Required By Date)

FIGURE 7.7

Denormalized `Order` and `Order Line` tables.

1. It should not be able to be updated directly by users.
2. It must be updated automatically by the application (e.g., via a DBMS trigger) whenever there is a change to the original data on which the copied or derived data are based.

The second requirement may slow down transactions other than those that benefit from the additional data. For example, an update of Unit Price in the Product table will trigger an update of Unit Price and Total Price in every row of the Order Line table with the same value of Product Code. This is a familiar performance trade-off; enquiries are made faster at the expense of more complex (and slower) updating.

There are some cases where the addition of redundant data is generally accepted without qualms and they may indeed be included in the logical data model or even the conceptual data model. If a supertype and its subtypes are all implemented as tables, we are generally happy to include a column in the supertype table that indicates the subtype to which each row belongs.

Another type of redundant data frequently included in a database is the aggregate, particularly where data in many rows would have to be summed to calculate the aggregate "on the fly." Indeed, one would never think of not including an Account Balance column in an Account table (to the extent that there will most likely have been an attribute of that name in the Account entity class in the conceptual data model), yet an account balance is the sum of all transactions on the account since it was opened. Even if transactions of more than a certain age are deleted, the account balance will be the sum of the opening balance on a statement plus all transactions on that statement.

Two other structures in which redundant data often feature are ranges and hierarchies. We discuss these in the next two sections.

7.6.6 Ranges

There are many examples of ranges in business data. Among the most common are date ranges. An organization's financial year is usually divided into a series of financial or accounting periods. These are contiguous, in that the first day of one accounting period is one day later than the last day of the previous one. Yet we usually include both first and last day columns in an accounting period table (not only in the physical data model, but probably in the logical and conceptual data models as well), even though one of these is redundant in that it can be derived from other data. Other examples of date ranges can be found in historical data:

1. We might record the range of dates for which a particular price of some item or service applied.
2. We might record the range of dates for which an employee reported to a particular manager or belonged to a particular organization unit.

Time ranges (often called "time slots") can also occur, such as in scheduling or timetabling applications. Classifications based on quantities are often created by dividing the values that the quantity can take into "bands" (e.g., age bands, price ranges). Such ranges often appear in business rule data, such as the duration bands that determine the premiums of short-term insurance policies.

Our arguments against redundant data might have convinced you that we should not include range ends as well as starts (e.g., Last Date as well as First Date, Maximum Age as well as Minimum Age, Maximum Price as well as Minimum Price). However, a query that accesses a range table that does not include both end and start columns will look like this:

```
select      PREMIUM_AMOUNT
from        PREMIUM_RULE as PR1
where       POLICY_DURATION >= MINIMUM_DURATION
and         POLICY_DURATION < MIN
  (select   PR2.MINIMUM_DURATION
  from      PREMIUM_RULE as PR2
  where     PR2.MINIMUM_DURATION > PR1.MINIMUM_DURATION);
```

However, if we include the range end Maximum Duration as well as the range start Minimum Duration the query can be written like this:

```
select      PREMIUM_AMOUNT
from        PREMIUM_RULE
where       POLICY_DURATION between MINIMUM_DURATION
and         MAXIMUM_DURATION;
```

The second query is not only easier to write but will take less time to run (provided there is an index on Policy Duration) unless the Premium Rule table is already in main memory.

7.6.7 Hierarchies

Hierarchies may be specific, as in the left diagram in Figure 7.8, or generic, as in the right diagram. Figure 7.9 shows a relational implementation of the generic version.

Generic hierarchies can support queries involving traversal of a fixed number of levels relatively simply (e.g., to retrieve each top-level organization unit together with the second-level organization units that belong to it).

Often, however, it is necessary to traverse a varying number of levels (e.g., retrieve each top-level organization unit together with the bottom-level organization units that belong to it). Queries of this kind are often written as a collection of UNION queries in which each individual query traverses a different number of levels.

There are various alternatives to this inelegant approach, including some nonstandard extensions provided by some DBMSs. In the absence of these, the simplest thing to try is the population of the recursive foreign key, as shown in Figure 7.10.

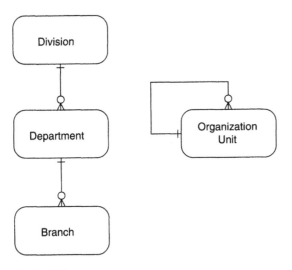

FIGURE 7.8

Specific and generic hierarchies.

ORG UNIT (Org Unit ID, Org Unit Name, Parent Org Unit ID)

Org Unit ID	Org Unit Name	Parent Org Unit ID
1	Production	null
2	H/R	null
21	Recruitment	2
22	Training	2
221	IT Training	22
222	Other Training	22

FIGURE 7.9

A simple hierarchy table.

ORG UNIT (Org Unit ID, Org Unit Name, Parent Org Unit ID)

Org Unit ID	Org Unit Name	Parent Org Unit ID
1	Production	1
2	H/R	2
21	Recruitment	2
22	Training	2
221	IT Training	22
222	Other Training	22

FIGURE 7.10

An alternative way of implementing a hierarchy.

If that does not meet all needs, one of the following alternative ways of representing a hierarchy in a relational table, each of which is illustrated in Figure 7.11, may be of value:

1. Include not only a foreign key to the parent organization unit but foreign keys to the "grandparent," "great-grandparent," and so on, organization units (the number of foreign keys should be one less than the maximum number of levels in the hierarchy).

2. As a variation of the previous suggestion, include a foreign key to each "ancestor" at each level.

ORG UNIT (Org Unit ID, Org Unit Name, Parent Org Unit ID, Grandparent Org Unit ID)

Org Unit ID	Org Unit Name	Parent Org Unit ID	Grandparent Org Unit ID
1	Production	null	null
2	H/R	null	null
21	Recruitment	2	null
22	Training	2	null
221	IT Training	22	2
222	Other Training	22	2

ORG UNIT (Org Unit ID, Org Unit Name, Level 1 Org Unit ID, Level 2 Org Unit ID)

Org Unit ID	Org Unit Name	Level 1 Org Unit ID	Level 2 Org Unit ID
1	Production	1	null
2	H/R	2	null
21	Recruitment	2	21
22	Training	2	22
221	IT Training	2	22
222	Other Training	2	22

ORG UNIT (Org Unit ID, Level Difference, Org Unit Name, Ancestor Org Unit ID)

Org Unit ID	Level Difference	Org Unit Name	Ancestor Org Unit ID
1	1	Production	null
2	1	H/R	null
21	1	Recruitment	2
22	1	Training	2
221	1	IT Training	22
221	2	IT Training	2
222	1	Other Training	22
222	2	Other Training	2

FIGURE 7.11

Further alternative ways of implementing a hierarchy.

3. Store all "ancestor"/"descendant" pairs (not just "parents" and "children") together with the difference in levels. In this case, the primary key must include the level difference as well as the ID of the "descendant" organization unit.

As each of these alternatives involves redundancy, they should not be directly updated by users; instead, the original simple hierarchy table shown in Figure 7.9 should be retained for update purposes and the additional table updated automatically by the application (e.g., via a DBMS trigger). More alternatives can be found in Celko's excellent book on this subject.[4]

7.6.8 Integer Storage of Dates and Times

Most DBMSs have the "date" data type, offering the advantages of automatic display of dates in a user-friendly format and a wide range of date and time arithmetic. The main disadvantage of storing dates and times using the "date" rather than the "integer" data type is the greater storage requirement, which in one project we worked on, increased the total data storage requirement by 15 percent. In this case, we decided to store dates in the critical large tables in "integer" columns in which were loaded the number of days since some base date. Similarly, times of day could be stored as the number of minutes (or seconds) since midnight. We then created views of those tables (see Section 7.7) in which data type conversion functions were used to derive dates in "dd/mm/yyyy" format.

7.6.9 Additional Tables

The processing requirements of an application may well lead to the creation of additional tables that were not foreseen during business information analysis and so do not appear in the conceptual or logical data models. These can include:

- Summaries for reporting purposes.
- Archive retrieval.
- User access and security control data.
- Data capture control, logging, and audit data.
- Data distribution control, logging, and audit data.
- Translation tables.
- Other migration/interface support data.
- Metadata.

7.7 VIEWS

The definition of *views* is one of the final stages in database design, since it relies on the logical schema being finalized. Views are "virtual tables" that are a selection

---

[4] Celko, J., *Joe Celko's Trees and Hierarchies in SQL for Smarties*. Morgan Kaufmann, 2004.

of rows and columns from one or more real tables and can include calculated values in additional virtual columns. They confer various advantages, among them support for users accessing the database directly through a query interface. This support can include:

- The provision of simpler structures.
- Inclusion of calculated values such as totals.
- Inclusion of alternative representations of data items (e.g., formatting dates as integers as described in Section 7.6.8).
- Exclusion of data for which such users do not have access permission.

Another function that views can serve is to isolate not only users but programmers from changes to table structures. For example, if the decision is taken to split a table as described in Section 7.6.2 but access to that table was previously through a view that selected all columns of all rows (a so-called "base view"), the view can be recoded as a union or join of the two new tables. For this reason, installation standards often require a base view for every table. Life, however, is not as simple as that, since there are two problems with this approach:

- Union views and most join views are not updateable, so program code for update facilities usually must refer to base tables rather than to views.
- As we show in Section 7.7.3, normalized views of denormalized tables lose any performance advantages conferred by that denormalization.

Some standards that we do recommend, however, are presented and discussed in the next four sections.

7.7.1 Views of Supertypes and Subtypes

However a supertype and its subtypes have been implemented, each of them should be represented by a view. This enables at least "read" access by users to all entity classes that have been defined in the conceptual data model rather than just those that have ended up as tables.

If we implement only the supertype as a table, views of each subtype can be constructed by selecting in the WHERE clause only those rows that belong to that subtype and including only those columns that correspond to the attributes and relationships of that subtype.

If we implement only the subtypes as tables, a view of the supertype can be constructed by a UNION of each subtype's base view.

If we implement both the supertype and the subtypes as tables, a view of each subtype can be constructed by joining the supertype table and the appropriate subtype table, and a view of the supertype can be constructed by a UNION of each of those subtype views.

7.7.2 Inclusion of Derived Attributes in Views

If a derived attribute has been defined as a business information requirement in the conceptual data model, it should be included as a calculated value in a view representing the owning entity class. This again enables user access to all attributes that have been defined in the conceptual data model.

7.7.3 Denormalization and Views

If we have denormalized a table by including redundant data in it, it may be tempting to retain a view that reflects the normalized form of that table, as in Figure 7.12.

However, a query of such a view that includes a join to another view so as to retrieve an additional column will perform that join even though the additional column is already in the underlying table. For example, a query to return the name and address of each customer who has ordered product "A123" will look like what is shown in Figure 7.13 and will end up reading the Customer and Order tables as well as the Order Line table to obtain Customer Name and Customer Address, even though those columns have been copied into the Order Line table. Any

Tables:

CUSTOMER (<u>Customer No</u>, Customer Name, Customer Address)

ORDER (<u>Order No</u>, Customer No, Customer Name, Customer Address, Order Date)

ORDER LINE (<u>Order No</u>, <u>Line No</u>, Customer No, Customer Name, Customer Address, Product Code, Unit Count, Required By Date)

Views:

CUSTOMER (<u>Customer No</u>, Customer Name, Customer Address)

ORDER (<u>Order No</u>, Customer No, Order Date)

ORDER LINE (<u>Order No</u>, <u>Line No</u>, Product Code, Unit Count, Required By Date)

FIGURE 7.12

Normalized views of denormalized tables.

```
select CUSTOMER_NAME, CUSTOMER_ADDRESS
from ORDER LINE join ORDER on
ORDER LINE. ORDER_NO = ORDER.ORDER_NO join CUSTOMER on
ORDER.CUSTOMER_NO = CUSTOMER.CUSTOMER_NO
where PRODUCT_CODE = 'A123';
```

FIGURE 7.13

Querying normalized views.

performance advantage that may have accrued from the denormalization is therefore lost.

7.7.4 Views of Split and Merged Tables

If tables have been split or merged, as described in Sections 7.6.2 and 7.6.3, views of the original tables should be provided to enable at least "read" access by users to all entity classes that have been defined in the conceptual data model.

7.8 SUMMARY

Physical database design should focus on achieving performance goals while implementing a logical schema that is as faithful as possible to the ideal design specified by the logical data model. The physical designer will need to take into account (among other things) stated performance requirements, transaction and data volumes, available hardware, and the facilities provided by the DBMS.

Most DBMSs support a wide range of tools for achieving performance without compromising the logical schema, including indexing, clustering, partitioning, control of data placement, data compression, and memory management. In the event that adequate performance across all transactions cannot be achieved with these tools, individual queries can be reviewed and sometimes rewritten to improve performance.

The final resort is to use tactics that require modification of the logical schema. Table splitting, denormalization, and various forms of data duplication can provide improved performance but usually at a cost in other areas. In some cases, such as hierarchies of indefinite depth and specification of ranges, data duplication may provide a substantial payoff in easier programming as well as performance. Views can be utilized to effectively reconstruct the conceptual model but are limited in their ability to accommodate update transactions.

Denormalization

The phrase "smaller, faster, cheaper" has long been the credo of the builders of computer chips, personal digital assistants (PDAs), quantum computers, and even printers. It is well known to be a difficult task to optimize all three at the same time, and most of the time there are important trade-offs that need to be addressed. A similar phrase, "faster, better, cheaper," was used in NASA, but came into serious question after several critical losses in the past decade, including the infamous *Mars Climate Orbiter* with its disastrous mix of English and metric units in the same system. In database design we would very much like to optimize performance (fast queries), maintainability (fast updates), and integrity (avoiding unwanted deletes) if we can, but the reality is that there are often serious trade-offs in these objectives that need to be addressed.

First, it is important to distinguish the difference between normalization and denormalization. *Normalization* is the process of breaking up a table into smaller tables to eliminate unwanted side effects of deletion of certain critical rows and to reduce the inefficiencies of updating redundant data often found in large universal tables. Sometimes, however, normalization is taken too far and some queries become extremely inefficient due to the extra joins required for the smaller tables. *Denormalization* is the process of adding columns to some tables to reduce the joins and is done if the integrity of the data is not seriously compromised. This chapter explains these trade-offs with some simple examples.

8.1 BASICS OF NORMALIZATION

Database designers sometimes use processing requirements to refine the database schema definition during the physical design phase or as a method for tuning the database if there are real performance bottlenecks. Schema refinement, or denormalization, is often used in online transaction processing (OLTP) if meaningful efficiency gains can be made without loss of data integrity, and if it is relatively easy to implement. Denormalization is also very common in online analytical processing (OLAP) through the use of the star schema.

Relational database tables sometimes suffer from some rather serious problems in terms of performance, integrity, and maintainability. For example, when the entire database is defined as a single large table, it can result in a large amount of redundant data and lengthy searches for just a small number of target rows. It can also result in long and expensive updates, and deletions in particular can result in the elimination of useful data as an unwanted side effect.

Such a situation is shown in Figure 8.1, where products, salespersons, customers, and orders are all stored in a single table, `sales`. In this table we see that certain product and customer information is stored redundantly, wasting storage space. Certain queries such as "Which customers (by customer number) ordered vacuum cleaners last month?" would require a search of the entire table. Also, updates, such as changing the address of the customer Galler, would require changing multiple rows. Finally, deleting an order by a valued customer, such as Fry (who bought an expensive computer), if that is his or her only outstanding order, deletes the only copy of his or her name, address, and credit rating as a side effect. Such information may be difficult (or sometimes impossible) to recover.

If we had a method of breaking up such a large table into smaller tables so that these types of problems would be eliminated, the database would be much more efficient and reliable. Classes of relational database schemes or table definitions, called *normal forms*, are commonly used to accomplish this goal. The creation of a normal form database table is called *normalization*. It is accomplished by

sales

productName	orderNo	custNo	custName	custAddress	creditRat	date
vacuum cleaner	1300	45	Galler	Chicago	6	1-3-06
computer	2735	13	Fry	Plymouth	10	4-15-05
refrigerator	2460	27	Remley	Ann Arbor	8	9-12-04
DVD player	1509	34	Honeyman	Detroit	3	12-5-04
iPod	2298	55	Jagadish	Ann Arbor	9	6-2-06
radio	1986	91	Antonelli	Chicago	7	5-10-05
CD player	1817	43	Arden	Dexter	8	8-3-02
vacuum cleaner	2902	91	Antonelli	Chicago	7	10-1-04
vacuum cleaner	1885	63	Karmeisool	Mt. Clemens	5	10-31-98
refrigerator	1943	45	Galler	Chicago	6	1-4-04
television	2315	39	Patel	Chelsea	8	7-31-06

FIGURE 8.1

Single table database for `sales`.

analyzing the interdependencies among individual attributes associated with those tables and taking projections (subsets of columns) of larger tables to form smaller ones.

Let's look at an alternative way of representing the same data of the `sales` table in two smaller tables—`productSales` and `customer`—as shown in Figure 8.2. These two tables can be derived (displayed) from the `sales` table by the following two SQL queries:

productSales

orderNo	productName	custNo	date
1300	vacuum cleaner	45	1-3-06
2735	computer	13	4-15-05
2460	refrigerator	27	9-12-04
1509	DVD player	34	12-5-04
2298	iPod	55	6-2-06
1986	radio	91	5-10-05
1817	CD player	43	8-3-02
2902	vacuum cleaner	91	10-1-04
1885	vacuum cleaner	63	10-31-98
1943	refrigerator	45	1-4-04
2315	television	39	7-31-06

customer

custNo	custName	custAddress	creditRat
45	Galler	Chicago	6
13	Fry	Plymouth	10
27	Remley	Ann Arbor	8
34	Honeyman	Detroit	3
55	Jagadish	Ann Arbor	9
91	Antonelli	Chicago	7
43	Arden	Dexter	8
63	Karmeisool	Mt. Clemens	5
39	Patel	Chelsea	8

FIGURE 8.2

Two table databases, `productSales` and `customer`.

```
SELECT orderNo, productName, custNo, date AS productSales
    FROM sales;
SELECT custNo, custName, custAddress, creditRat AS customer
    FROM sales;
```

These queries show that they are nothing more than projections of the `sales` table over two different sets of columns. If we join the two tables, `productSales` and `customer`, over the common attribute `custNo`, they will produce the original table, `sales`. This is called a *lossless join* and shows that the two tables are equivalent to the single table in terms of meaningful content.

The two smaller tables, `productSales` and `customer`, have nice performance and storage properties that the `sales` table doesn't. Let's revisit the problems in the `sales` table.

1. We see that certain product and customer information is stored redundantly, wasting storage space. The redundant data are `custNo`, `custName`, `cust Address`, and `creditRat`. In the two-table equivalent, there is only redundancy in `custNo`. Attribute values for `custName`, `custAddress`, and `creditRat` are only stored once. In most cases, as is the case here, this separation of data results in smaller tables.

    Certain queries such as "Which customers (by customer number) ordered vacuum cleaners last month?" would require a search of the entire `sales` table. In the two-table case, this query still requires a search of the entire `product-Sales` table, but this table is now much smaller than the `sales` table and will take a lot less time to scan.

2. Updates, such as changing the address of the customer Galler, would require changing multiple rows. In the two-table equivalent, the customer address appears only once in the `customer` table, and any update to that address is confined to a single row in the `customer` table.

3. Deleting an order by a valued customer—for example, in the case of Fry (who bought an expensive computer), if that is his or her only outstanding order, it deletes the only copy of his or her name, address, and credit rating as a side effect. In the two-table equivalent, Fry's order can still be deleted, but his or her name, address, and credit rating are all still maintained in the `customer` table.

In fact, the two-table equivalent is in third normal form (3NF)—actually a stronger form of 3NF, called Boyce-Codd normal form (BCNF). It has the property that only the key of the table uniquely defines the values of all the other attributes of the table. For example, the key value for 45 for `custNo` in the `customer` table determines that the customer name, Galler, is the only value that can occur in the same row as the customer number 45. The `custNo` value also uniquely determines the customer address and the credit rating. This property of uniqueness is useful in keeping tables small and nonredundant. These unique properties can be expressed in terms of functional dependencies (FDs), as follows.

```
sales table
orderNo -> productName, custNo, custName, custAddress,
creditRat, date
custNo -> custName, custAddress, creditRat

productSales table
orderNo -> productName, custNo, date

customer table
custNo -> custName, custAddress, creditRat
```

In the `customer` and `productSales` tables, only the key uniquely determines the values of all the nonkeys in each table, which is the condition necessary for 3NF. In the `sales` table, you have a nonkey, `custNo`, which uniquely determines several attributes in addition to the key, `orderNo`. Thus, the `sales` table does not satisfy 3NF, and this dependency on nonkeys is the source of the loss of integrity and multiple updates in a nonnormalized database.

8.2 COMMON TYPES OF DENORMALIZATION

Denormalization is often used to suggest alternative logical structures (schemas) during physical design and thus provides the designers with other feasible solutions to choose from. More efficient databases are the likely outcome of evaluating alternative structures. This process is referred to as denormalization, because the schema transformation can cause the degree of normalization in the resulting table to be less than the degree of at least one of the original tables. The two most common types of denormalization are two entities in a one-to-one relationship and two entities in a one-to-many relationship.

8.2.1 Two Entities in a One-to-One Relationship

The tables for these entities could be implemented as a single table, thus avoiding frequent joins required by certain applications. As an example, consider the following two tables in 3NF and BCNF.

```
CREATE TABLE   report
   (reportNum      INTEGER,
    reportName     VARCHAR(64),
    reportText     VARCHAR(256),
    PRIMARY KEY(reportNum));

CREATE TABLE   reportAbbreviation
   (abbreviation   CHAR(6),
    reportNum      INTEGER NOT NULL UNIQUE,
    PRIMARY KEY (abbreviation),
    FOREIGN KEY (reportNum) REFERENCES report);
```

The functional dependencies for these tables are:

- *Table report:* reportNum -> reportName, reportText
- *Table reportAbbreviation:* abbreviation -> reportNum
- reportNum -> abbreviation

EXAMPLE QUERY 8.1

```
SELECT r.reportName, ra.abbreviation
  FROM report AS r, reportAbbreviation AS ra
  WHERE r.reportNum = ra.reportNum;
```

In this relationship we denormalize report by defining report2 to include abbreviation and thus eliminate the abbreviation table completely. The new entry in report2 is shown in bold.

```
CREATE TABLE report2
(reportNum      INTEGER,
 reportName     VARCHAR(30),
 reportText     VARCHAR(256),
 abbreviation CHAR(6),
 PRIMARY KEY (reportNum));
```

The functional dependencies for the new report table are:

Table report2: reportNum -> reportName, reportText, abbreviation, abbreviation -> reportNum

The revised table, report2, is also in 3NF and BCNF, so there can be no loss of data integrity due to deletes involving reportNum or abbreviation. If a report is deleted, then both its report number and abbreviation are deleted, so neither one is left orphaned in the database.

8.2.2 Two Entities in a One-to-Many Relationship

Sometimes logical design results in very simple tables with very few attributes, where the primary key is a foreign key in another table you want to join with. In such cases, when a query wants data from both tables, it may be more efficient to implement them as individually named columns as an extension of the parent entity (table).

Let's look at the following example. The department table is the "parent" table and emp is the "child" table since one department can have potentially many employees and each employee (emp) is in only one department.

```
CREATE TABLE department
    (deptNum   INTEGER,
     deptName  VARCHAR(30),
     PRIMARY KEY (deptNum));
```

```
CREATE TABLE emp
    (empNum    INTEGER,
    empName    VARCHAR(30),
    manager    VARCHAR(30),
    deptNum    INTEGER,
    PRIMARY KEY (empNum),
    FOREIGN KEY (deptNum) REFERENCES department);
```

The functional dependencies for these two tables are:

- *Table department:* deptNum -> deptName
- *Table emp:* empNum -> empName, manager, deptNum

EXAMPLE QUERY 8.2

```
SELECT e.empName, d.deptName
    FROM emp AS e, department AS d
    WHERE d.deptNum = e.deptNum;
```

In this relationship we denormalize emp by defining emp2 to include deptName from the department table. The new attribute deptName in emp2 is shown in bold.

```
CREATE TABLE department
    (deptNum    INTEGER,
    deptName    VARCHAR(30),
    PRIMARY KEY (deptNum));
```

```
CREATE TABLE emp2
    (empNum    INTEGER,
    empName    VARCHAR(30),
    manager    VARCHAR(30),
    deptNum    INTEGER,
    deptName   VARCHAR(30),
    PRIMARY KEY (empNum),
    FOREIGN KEY (deptNum) REFERENCES department);
```

The functional dependencies for these two tables are:

> Table department: deptNum -> deptName
> Table emp2: empNum -> empName, manager, deptNum
> deptNum -> deptName

The department table is still in 3NF, but the emp2 table has lost normalization to below 3NF. To compensate for the lost normalization in emp2, we could keep department as a redundant table. The cost of this redundancy is in storage space and increased update time, since updates involving deptName will have to be made to both tables. A third option is to leave the two original tables unchanged. Let's

Table 8.1 Comparison of Denormalization Options for Example Query 8.2

Option	Normalization	Query Time	Update Time	Storage Space
1—emp2 only	Less than 3NF, delete anomaly possible	Low, no joins needed	Low, no redundancy	Potentially higher
2—emp2 and department	3NF	Low, no joins needed	Lower due to redundancy	Highest
3—emp and department	3NF	Higher, join required	High, only hurt if deptNum is changed	Original

summarize the trade-offs for these three options based on Example Query 8.2 (see Table 8.1):

- *Option 1:* Consolidate into one table, emp2.
- *Option 2:* Consolidate into one table, emp2, and retain the department table as redundant.
- *Option 3:* No change to emp and department tables.

The analysis of these three options goes as follows:

Option 1 (emp2). This is pure denormalization. It optimizes the query time and usually improves the update times. Storage space can be higher or lower, depending on the relative sizes of the department and emp tables. The normalization definitely is less, leaving a potential delete anomaly and loss of integrity if the last record containing a particular deptNum and deptName combination is deleted. If this is not an issue, then denormalization is definitely a winning strategy. Query and update times are usually more important than storage space.

Option 2 (emp2 and department). This is denormalization with redundancy to prevent the delete anomaly between deptNum and deptName. This strategy should only be used if the loss of integrity is a real issue here. Like pure denormalization, it greatly improves query time at the expense of update time and storage space.

Option 3 (emp and department). This is the original database schema, which should be kept if the query and update times are acceptable. To denormalize would require a reorganization of the database schema and repopulation of emp2, a potentially significant overhead.

In summary, the key effects of denormalization are:

1. A definite improvement (decrease) in query time.
2. A potential increase in update time.

3. A potential increase in storage space.
4. A potential loss of data integrity due to certain deletions.
5. The necessity for program transformations for all relevant queries.
6. The overhead needed to reorganize one or more tables (e.g., emp to emp2).

These effects require careful consideration. The example in Section 8.3 goes into more details of this analysis.

Many database systems have software that provides data synchronization between redundant data and base data, and thus supports the concept of denormalization using redundancy. For instance, software such as DB2 Everyplace, Oracle Data Hubs, Oracle Streams, SQL Server Compare (Red-Gate Software), and SQL Server Everywhere Edition all provide such critical data synchronization services.

8.3 TABLE DENORMALIZATION STRATEGY

A practical strategy for table denormalization is to select only the most dominant processes to determine those modifications that will most likely improve performance. The basic modification is to add attributes to existing tables to reduce join operations. The steps of this strategy for relational databases follow.

1. Minimize the need for denormalization by developing a clear and concise logical database design, including tables that are at least 3NF or BCNF. This establishes the requirement of an accurate representation of reality and flexibility of the design for future processing requirements. If the original database does not meet performance requirements, consider denormalization as one of the options for improving performance.

2. Select the dominant queries and updates based on such criteria as high frequency of execution, high volume of data accessed, response time constraints, or explicit high priority. Remember this rule of thumb: Any process whose frequency of execution or data volume accessed is 10 times that of another process is considered to be dominant.

3. Define extended tables with extra columns, when appropriate, to reduce the number of joins required for dominant queries.

4. Evaluate total cost for storage, query, and update for the database schema, with and without the extended table, and determine which configuration minimizes total cost.

5. Consider also the data integrity due to denormalization. If an extended table appears to have lower storage and processing (query and update) costs and insignificant data integrity problems, then use that schema for physical design in addition to the original candidate table schema. Otherwise use only the

original schema. Also, try very hard to use database management system (DBMS) features to keep the redundant data in sync with the base data.

8.4 EXAMPLE OF DENORMALIZATION

The following example illustrates how to proceed through the database life cycle, in a practical way, for a simple relational database. We will see how denormalization extends a logical design methodology to attain significant improvements in performance, given that the available access methods are known.

8.4.1 Requirements Specification

The management of a large retail store would like a database to keep track of sales activities. The requirements for this database lead to six entities and their unique identifiers, as shown in Table 8.2.

The following assertions describe the data relationships:

- Each customer has one job title, but different customers may have the same job title. (*Note:* Consider this a special database where customer job titles are important.)
- Each customer may place many orders, but only one customer may place a particular order.
- Each department has many salespeople, but each salesperson must work in only one department. (*Note:* This may not be a realistic constraint for some retail businesses.)
- Each department has many items for sale, but each item is sold in only one department (item means item type, like IBM PC).

Table 8.2 Sales Activities Requirements

Entity	Entity ID	ID Length (average, in bytes)	Cardinality
Customer	custNum	6	80,000
Job	jobTitle	24	80
Order	orderNum	9	200,000
Salesperson	salesName	20	150
Department	deptNum	2	10
Item	itemNum	6	5,000

■ For each order, items ordered in different departments must involve different salespeople, but all items ordered within one department must be handled by exactly one salesperson. In other words, for each order, each item has exactly one salesperson, and for each order, each department has exactly one salesperson.

8.4.2 **Logical Design**

An entity-relationship (ER) diagram and a set of FDs to correspond to each of the assertions are given in Table 8.3. Figure 8.3 presents the ER diagram. Normally the ER diagram is developed without knowing all the FDs, but in this example the nonkey attributes are omitted so that the entire database can be represented with only a few statements and FDs. The result of this analysis, relative to each of the assertions given, is shown in the table.

The tables needed to represent the semantics of this problem can be easily derived from the constructs for entities and relationships. Primary keys and foreign keys are explicitly defined.

```
CREATE TABLE customer (custNum CHAR(6),
    jobTitle   VARCHAR(256),
    PRIMARY KEY (custNum),
    FOREIGN KEY (jobTitle) REFERENCES job);

CREATE TABLE job (jobTitle  VARCHAR(256),
    PRIMARY KEY (jobTitle));

CREATE TABLE order (orderNum CHAR(9),
    custNum    CHAR(6) not null,
    PRIMARY KEY (orderNum),
    FOREIGN KEY (custNum) REFERENCES customer);
```

Table 8.3 ER Diagram FDs Assertions

ER Construct	FDs
Customer(many): Job(one)	custNum -> jobTitle
Order(many): Customer(one)	orderNum -> custNum
Salesperson(many): Department(one)	salesName -> deptNum
Item(many): Department(one)	itemNum -> deptNum
Order(many): Item(many): Salesperson(one)	orderNum,itemNum -> salesName
Order(many): Department(many): Salesperson (one)	orderNum,deptNum -> salesName

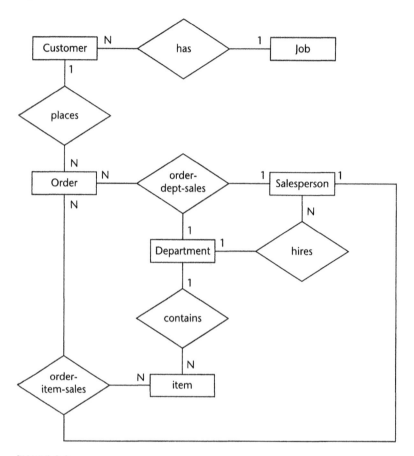

FIGURE 8.3

ER diagram for a simple database.

```
CREATE TABLE salesperson (salesName VARCHAR(256),
    deptNum    CHAR(2),
    PRIMARY KEY (salesName),
    FOREIGN KEY (deptNum) REFERENCES department);
CREATE TABLE department (deptNum CHAR(2),
    PRIMARY KEY (deptNum));
CREATE TABLE item (itemNum CHAR(6),
    deptNum CHAR(2),
    PRIMARY KEY (itemNum),
    FOREIGN KEY (deptNum) REFERENCES department);
CREATE TABLE orderItemSales (orderNum CHAR(9),
    itemNum    CHAR(6),
    salesName  varCHAR(256) not null,
```

```
      PRIMARY KEY (orderNum, itemNum),
      FOREIGN KEY (orderNum) REFERENCES order,
      FOREIGN KEY (itemNum) REFERENCES item,
      FOREIGN KEY (salesName) REFERENCES salesperson);
   CREATE TABLE orderDeptSales (orderNum CHAR(9),
      deptNum    CHAR(2),
      salesName  VARCHAR(256) not null,
      PRIMARY KEY (orderNum, deptNum),
      FOREIGN KEY (orderNum) REFERENCES order,
      FOREIGN KEY (deptNum) REFERENCES department,
      FOREIGN KEY (salesName) REFERENCES salesperson);
```

Further logical design can be done to minimize the number of 3NF tables (Teorey, Lightstone, and Nadeau, 2006). However, we will assume the tables defined here are complete and focus on the database refinement using denormalization to increase the efficiency for executing queries and updates.

8.4.3 Schema Refinement Using Denormalizaton

We now look at the quantitative trade-offs of the refinement of tables to improve processing efficiency. Assume that each of the following transactions are to be executed once per fixed time unit.

EXAMPLE QUERY 8.3

Select all order numbers assigned to customers who are computer engineers.

```
SELECT o.orderNum, c.custNum, c.jobTitle
   FROM   order AS o, customer AS c
   WHERE  c.custNum = o.custNum
   AND    c.jobTitle = 'computer engineer';
```

EXAMPLE UPDATE 8.4

Add a new customer, a painter, with number 423378 and the customer's order number, 763521601, to the database.

```
INSERT INTO customer (custNum, jobTitle) VALUES
('423378','painter');
INSERT INTO order (orderNum, custNum) VALUES
('763521601','423378');
```

Analysis of Example Query 8.3 The system query optimizer can choose from a number of different ways to execute the transaction Example Query 8.3. Let us first assume that the tables are all ordered physically by their primary keys. We use the sort-merge join strategy for the first transaction: Sort the order table by `custNum`, then join tables `order` and `customer` with a single scan of each, and select only rows that have `jobTitle` of computer engineer. We then project on `orderNum` to answer the query. To simplify the analysis we assume that a sort of *nb* blocks takes $2 \times nb \log_3 nb$ block accesses and that computer engineers make up 5 percent of the customers and orders in the database. ∎

All row accesses are sequential in this strategy. For simplicity we have a block size of 4 KB (4096 bytes) and a prefetch buffer size of 64 KB, as done in DB2. We can estimate the input/ouput (I/O) service time by first computing the effective prefetch blocking factors for the `order`, `customer`, `orderCust`, and `compEngr` tables: 4369 (64 KB/15 bytes per row), 2176, 1680, and 1680, respectively. We assume an IBM U320 146-GB hard drive with an average seek of 3.6 ms, an average rotational delay of 2 ms (for 15,000 RPM), and a transfer rate of 320 MB/sec.

I/O time for a block access in a table scan = rotational delay +
transfer of a prefetch buffer
= 2 ms + 64 KB/320 MB/sec
= 2.2 ms

Block accesses = sort `order` table + scan `order` table +
scan `customer` table + create `orderCust` table +
scan `orderCust` table + create `compEngr` table +
project `compEngr` table
= $(2 \times 4369 \log_3 4369) + 4369 + 37 + 120 + 120 + 6 + 6$
= $2 \times 4369 \times 7.63 + 4658$
= 71,329

I/O time = 71,329 block accesses × 2.2 ms
= 156.9 seconds

Analysis of Example Update 8.4 The strategy to execute the second transaction, Example Update 8.4, using the same schema, is to scan each table (`order` and `customer`) and rewrite both tables in the new `order` table.

Block accesses = scan `order` table + scan `customer` table +
rewrite `order` table + rewrite `customer` table
= 4369 + 37 + 4369 + 37
= 8812

I/O time = 8812 block accesses × 2.2 ms
= 19.4 seconds

Defining the Denormalized Table orderCust If we combine the `customer` and `order` tables to avoid the join in Example Query 8.3, the resulting schema will have a single table `orderCust`, with primary key `orderNum` and nonkey attributes `custNum` and `jobTitle`, instead of separate tables `order` and `customer`. This not only avoids the join, but also the sort needed to get both tables ordered by `custNum`.

```
CREATE TABLE orderCust (orderNum CHAR(9),
    custNum   CHAR(6) not null,
    jobTitle  VARCHAR(256),
    PRIMARY KEY (orderNum);
```

The strategy for Example Query 8.3 is now to scan `orderCust` once to find the computer engineers, write the resulting data on disk, and then read back from disk to project the resulting temporary table, `compEngr`, to answer the query.

$$\begin{aligned} \text{Block accesses} = &\text{ scan } orderCust + \text{ write 5 percent of } orderCust \text{ on disk } + \\ &\text{ project 5 percent of } orderCust \\ = &\ 120 + 6 + 6 \\ = &\ 132 \end{aligned}$$

$$\begin{aligned} \text{I/O time} = &\ 132 \text{ block accesses} \times 2.2 \text{ ms} \\ = &\ 0.3 \text{ second} \end{aligned}$$

The strategy for Example Update 8.4, using this refined schema, is to scan `orderCust` once to find the point of insertion and then to scan again to reorder the table.

$$\begin{aligned} \text{Block accesses} = &\text{ scan } orderCust + \text{ scan } orderCust \\ = &\ 120 + 120 \\ = &\ 240 \end{aligned}$$

$$\begin{aligned} \text{I/O time} = &\ 240 \text{ block accesses} \times 2.2 \text{ ms} \\ = &\ 0.5 \text{ second} \end{aligned}$$

Common to both strategies is the addition of an order record to the `orderItemSales` and `orderDeptSales` tables. For the sake of simplicity, we will assume these tables to be unsorted, so the addition of a new order will require only one record access at the end of the table and, thus, negligible I/O time.

The basic performance and normalization data for these two schemas and the two transactions given previously are summarized in Table 8.4. The refined schema dramatically reduces the I/O time for the query transaction and the update, but the cost is storage space and significant reduction in the degree of normalization. The normalization is reduced because we now have a transitive FD: `orderNum -> custNum -> jobTitle` in the `orderCust` table. The implication of this, of course, is that there is a delete anomaly for `jobTitle` when a customer deletes an order or the order is filled (in particular, when the `jobTitle` value deleted is the last instance of that `jobTitle` in the database).

The significance of these performance and data integrity differences depends on the overall objectives as well as the computing environment for the database,

Table 8.4 Comparison of Performance and Integrity of Original Tables and Join Table

	Original Schema (order and customer tables)	Denormalized Schema (orderCust table)
Query time	156.9 sec	0.3 sec
Update time	19.4 sec	0.5 sec
Storage space (relevant tables)	5.4 MB	7.8 MB
Normalization	3NF	Less than 3NF

and it must be analyzed in that context. For instance, the performance differences must be evaluated for all relevant transactions, present and projected. Storage space differences may or may not be significant in the computing environment. Integrity problems with the deletion commands need to be evaluated on a case-by-case basis to determine whether the side effects of certain record deletions are destructive to the objectives of the database. In summary, the database designer now has the ability to evaluate the trade-offs among query and update requirements, storage space, and integrity associated with normalization. This knowledge can be applied to a variety of database design problems.

TIPS AND INSIGHTS FOR DATABASE PROFESSIONALS

- **Tip 1: Normalize first, then consider denormalizing if performance is poor.** You can maximize the probability of a good logical design by carefully creating a conceptual model using the ER approach or UML. These modeling methods tend to result in relational databases that are close to being or are already normalized. Normalization tends to reduce redundancy and provides a high level of integrity to the database. When the actual tables are not conducive to good performance (e.g., when they are so small that dominant queries must do extra joins on them each time they are executed), then consider merging two tables to avoid the join and reduce I/O time. If the benefit of this merge (and possible denormalization) in I/O time saved is greater than the cost in I/O time for the redundancy of data needed to avoid a delete anomaly, in terms of updates, then go ahead with the merge.

- **Tip 2: Denormalize addresses whenever possible.** Addresses can be very long and cumbersome to access, so it is often useful to store addresses separately and access them through joins only when explicitly needed. Furthermore, addresses are often stored redundantly across the database, so if one copy gets deleted, it can be recovered elsewhere. Usually the performance gains of avoiding joins most of the time and avoiding extra bytes in a query are worth the redundancy and the extra updates needed. Addresses are usually fairly static and don't change often.

- ■ **Tip 3: Make use of existing DBMS-provided software to synchronize data between redundant data to support denormalization and the base data.** Examples of data synchronization software include DB2 Everyplace, Oracle Data Hubs, Oracle Streams, SQL Server Compare (Red-Gate Software), and SQL Server Everywhere Edition.

8.5 SUMMARY

In this chapter we explored an in-depth definition and example for the use of denormalization to enhance performance of a relational database. The example reviews the life cycle steps of logical design before the denormalization step of schema refinement to increase efficiency for query processing.

8.6 FURTHER READING

The idea for extending a table for usage efficiency came from Schkolnick and Sorenson (1980), and practical advice on denormalization is given in Rodgers (1989).

Ramakrishnan, R., and Gehrke, J. *Database Management Systems.* 3rd ed. McGraw-Hill, 2004.

Rodgers, U. Denormalization: Why, What, and How? *Database Programming and Design* 2(12): 46–53, 1989.

Schkolnick, M., and Sorenson, P. Denormalization: A Performance-Oriented Database Design Technique. In *Proceedings from the AICA 1980 Congress*, Bologna, Italy. Brussels: AICA, 1980, pp. 363–377.

Shasha, D., and Bonnet, P. *Database Tuning.* Morgan Kaufmann, 2003.

Silberschatz, A., Korth, H. F., and Sudarshan, S. *Database System Concepts.* 5th ed. McGraw-Hill, 2006.

Teorey, T., Lightstone, S., and Nadeau, T. *Database Modeling and Design: Logical Design.* 4th ed. Morgan Kaufmann, 2006.

Business Metadata Infrastructure

9.1 INTRODUCTION

Numerous things need to be kept in mind when planning an infrastructure to support metadata, especially business metadata. This chapter addresses these considerations and will serve as a guide as you determine what kind of infrastructure best fits your current environment.

The chapter discusses what kinds of business metadata you may want to track and provides a data model as a guide. The metadata environment is shown to be like a data warehouse in many respects, requiring much of the same infrastructure components. Special tools are often required for both the capture and display of business metadata. Special integration and delivery mechanisms are discussed—namely, data federation and service orientation. Administrative sources of records and historical issues should also be considered in terms of structural and storage considerations. Lastly, the chapter covers the issues of buy versus build, with a third alternative in the mix: extend an existing product.

9.2 TYPES OF BUSINESS METADATA

One of the first decisions concerning infrastructure that you must make is what type of business metadata is important to the enterprise, as well as important enough to merit storage and management. Some of the major areas you will want to consider are:

- Business terms
- Business term definitions (Does a term have more than one definition? What about history?)
- Business rules
- Authority/governance/stewardship
- Origin: where things came from (may be different from authority!)

- Scope: What is the scope or boundaries of authority?
- Organizations (both internal and external)

These are just a few of many different types of business metadata you may want to collect and manage. Remember, however, that data have costs; you can't just throw in everything. The "kitchen sink" metadata management strategy will be very costly, and we guarantee that it won't all apply to your specific business needs.

Figure 9.1 shows a high-level, conceptual metamodel that you can use as a guide to decide which kinds of metadata to manage. It shows some of each type of metadata: business and technical. It is not intended to be an exhaustive model; in your environment you may come up with things unique to your business.

Entities may have a lot of detail behind them, and when made into a logical model, it will be larger. Each entity has a prefix indicating whether it is business (BMD) or technical (TMD) metadata. The model uses the Barker notation; you read each relationship as two sentences. For the purpose of aesthetics, we have left the relationship names off of the diagram, so read each with a generic verb phrase such as "is associated with." A dotted line represents optional, solid is mandatory,

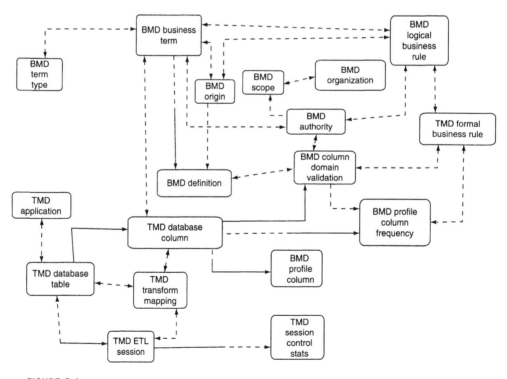

FIGURE 9.1

Business and technical metamodel.

and a crow's foot is one or more. So the relationship between business term and definition would be read as follows:

- Each BMD business term may be associated with one or more definitions.
- Each BMD definition must be associated with one and only one BMD business term.

Just as you may create other entities that are not shown in this model (or omit some!), you may not agree with the relationships shown. For example, you may want to enforce a rule that mandates only one definition for every term. That is your choice. The model is included as a guideline only and is not to be interpreted as the only way to model metadata.

Note that the model includes technical metadata; this is for the purpose of integration, which we will explain in more detail later in the chapter. It is highly recommended that you be able to relate business and technical metadata together, to serve all sorts of purposes.

The data profiling metadata are indicated in the model as business metadata. They are actually both business and technical, but we refer to them as business because they enable the business to validate its definitions and data. Realize that the data profiling metadata may have to be presented to the business user in a special format so that they can be understood more easily. However, many businesspeople are direct users of some profiling tools, especially Data Flux, because it is so easy to use and it creates wonderful charts and graphs. Businesspeople like charts and graphs! A picture is better than a thousand words, the old proverb says.

The model doesn't show some interesting areas that you might want to consider:

- Business context, including background information such as departmental history and corporate reorganizations
- History and life cycle of the business metadata itself
- Modification history (who modified the data, when, and why)
- Aggregations, summaries, and formulas
- Business process models
- Business motivation
- Images, including pictures of personnel
- Geography
- Weather
- News feeds

9.3 THE METADATA WAREHOUSE

Business metadata are collected in various ways. The infrastructure therefore needs to support a variety of collection mechanisms including Web 2.0 technologies. Business metadata are also created through a transformation of technical metadata. The conclusion is that a good solution resembles a data warehouse architecture, but one designed specifically to handle metadata (see Figure 9.2).

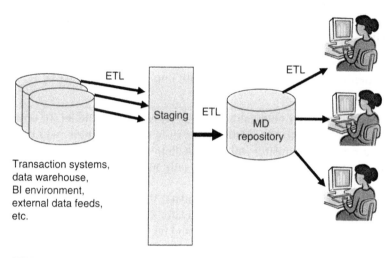

FIGURE 9.2

Metadata infrastructure, metadata data warehouse.

This means that you must have all of the necessary components that you would need if you were building a data warehouse; the only difference would be the lack of a specialized delivery structure like you normally see in the BI environment (e.g., star schema or cube physical structure). You will still probably have to use ETL or common metadata bridges, as shown in Figure 9.2, because the metadata will have to be moved to the appropriate repository in the BI environment. Fortunately, many software and open systems firms provide metadata bridges or integration software that will help you accomplish the metadata ETL task. A quick search on the Internet for "metadata integration" will yield hundreds of responses for you to select from.

A special structure like a star scheme is not required because metadata in general and business metadata in particular do not require analytics. One possible exception are data-quality statistics. Most business metadata are semistructured textual content; some are unstructured comment text or even images. Business metadata add context to the data, and they usually do so with textual descriptions. Obviously, textual descriptions cannot be "sliced and diced" like numbers can. Therefore, the data delivery side of the equation, though fraught with its own challenges, is usually easier than data warehousing and does not require a specialized physical data structure. We will, however, discuss a few exceptions.

9.3.1 Business Metadata Differences

The main difference between the infrastructure required for a data warehouse and that required for business metadata is the type of content. Business metadata usually consist of text. Now, however, we are beginning to see images as business metadata, and even really simple syndication (RSS) feeds, maps, and weather data.

Some of these new data sources become links and do not go through ETL at all. A traditional ETL strategy and software may not be able to handle some of these types of objects, and even if they could, special hardware requirements would need to be considered, owing to their large size. The same can be said for the staging area, which in data warehouse architectures is usually a dedicated set of tables or separate database. The staging area that houses business metadata may end up being a combination of structures, including both flat files and a database. The enterprise metadata repository may also end up being a combination, consisting of a content management system and database. Databases are not the best technology to manage large documents and images/multimedia. Just as in data warehousing, the overall data architecture strategy for your metadata repository environment may be centralized or federated. The choice for the architecture will be largely dependent on the capabilities of the technology tools selected and the organization's funding capabilities.

9.4 DELIVERY CONSIDERATIONS

From an infrastructure perspective, it is important to note the general requirements for the possible delivery strategies.

9.4.1 Delivery in the Legacy Environment

You may want to deliver contextual information to legacy applications, like business term and/or form field definitions. Legacy environments were generally not created using open technology, so you may have to get very creative. First, are your applications homegrown (developed in-house), or are they commercial off-the-shelf software (COTS)? Obviously, you have a better chance of modifying the applications directly to display business metadata like term definitions if the application was internally developed in-house. You may even be lucky enough to have someone still around who understands how this might be done!

Commercial products, on the other hand, are usually very closed systems. Some may provide extension options, but watch out! Sometimes commercial products will void their warranty or service agreement if you tinker with their internals.

Getting Creative

There may be a way to creatively deliver descriptive metadata in the transaction environment by not having to interface with the legacy applications—by using a portal.

We created a corporate dictionary/glossary for a client, which was using the AquaLogic portal set of tools. We created a very simple glossary search portlet that looks like Google's one fill-in-the-blank text box with a "Go!" button to the right. We placed the portlet on the intranet home page so that it was available anywhere. An even better mechanism that we looked into (but did not implement because it required too much work) was to have an icon on the tray for the dictionary search mini-application. The problem with either method is that they are not context sensitive; they do not recognize where the mouse or insertion point is at any given point in time.

If your homegrown application was developed fairly recently (in the last five to ten years), then it may have a context-sensitive help mechanism built in. This mechanism can be hijacked for the purpose of business metadata. However, the downside to this arrangement is that someone has to write it, and this process sounds like "documentation." Neither users nor programmers get excited about this! There is a better way, as will be described later. First, however, we need to describe business metadata in the conventional BI environment.

9.4.2 Infrastructure Required for BI Environments

BI tools like the Cognos suite of products usually come with a means of delivering some descriptions to the user. For example, when browsing the tree of the business element names, hover text is available. In other words, when your mouse hovers over the business element name, it can display a definition or description that you provide. Cognos, however, has its own metadata repository and requires that this hover text be referenced from its repository. This means that if you have an enterprise metadata repository, you will have to build ETL to move the definitions from the enterprise repository into the tool's specialized repository.

9.4.3 Graphical Affinity

Special infrastructure may be required for certain delivery mechanisms—for example, graphical affinity and visual analytic tools. Some of these tools can enhance the display of both data and metadata to add clarity that only pictures can provide. "Heat maps" show the concentration of documents clustered around specific topics using colors like degrees of red and blue. Affinity diagrams can show how one person is tied to various cases or events in the system, and different roles can be indicated with different symbols.

In these cases, special tools such as IDS Visualization, Seepower by Compudigm, and VisuaLinks by Visual Analytics, Inc. may be needed, and expertise in these tools may also be required. Consultants, such as Jordan Rose, who have expert knowledge in a specific tool, can jumpstart your project and get it up and running faster, because you don't need to factor in the learning curve. Companies like PPC specialize in development of the visual analytic application and also mentoring your personnel, so when new views of the data are required, your staff can create them.

9.4.4 Web 2.0 Technology: Mashups!

A very exciting method is now available that can capture and deliver business metadata at the same time: mashups. *Mashups* are integrated Web applications that usually consist of a collection of different types of components and data, all displayed together on the same Web page. The really cool feature of these new tools that have recently been released is their ability to allow ordinary users—not just programmers—to create their own mashup, with no programming.

For example, BEA has released AquaLogic Pages, a product that provides all the infrastructure, toolkits, and plumbing needed to allow users to design and create their own conglomeration of components—from fetching rows directly from a database to calling a Web service, accessing an RSS feed, or even creating their own data table or publishing a preexisting Excel spreadsheet. On the same Web page, the user can link objects together so that they feed data to one another, also with no programming.[1] For example, the user who while analyzing a BI report discovers declining sales in January can access a weather report for the dates in question and place a comment on the page stating the reason for the decline in sales: There was a series of major snowstorms in that geographical area. In a similar manner, the same technique can be used to dynamically adjust inventory: A snowstorm is predicted for a certain geographic area, and a hardware retailer can stock up on sand, rock salt, and shovels to accommodate an influx of sales in the affected stores—all within the mashup.

9.5 INTEGRATION

To manage the entire metadata environment, business and technical metadata must sometimes be integrated.

9.5.1 Business and Technical Metadata Integration

Business changes will affect the technical environment, and the faster IT can respond to change, the more effectively the business can compete in the ever-changing marketplace. One of the first places that changes can be spotted proactively and managed is in the metadata environment.

A hypothetical flow of events in the metadata environment is as follows:

- In a wiki on marketing's portal, someone makes a comment that a new field is needed in one of marketing's key applications. Marketing has determined that a new measure of ad campaign performance is needed that will help the department determine the effectiveness of campaigns, move efficiently, and respond faster.

---

[1]For this system to work, a developer is required in the beginning to develop templates that the users can plug and play. The template will have the built-in "hooks" that allow it to connect to other components to get/receive data. Once these templates are built, the users can link them together with other components, allowing them to send and receive data from these other components.

- The marketing representative proposing the change creates a new business term in the glossary and provides the formula required in the definition to compute the measure.

- IT determines where the data currently reside through analysis of technical metadata, using the formula entered in the glossary as a reference; the metadata repository is used to find the data elements that are tied to the business terms used in the definition's formula. IT creates a new mashup, displaying a database query showing examples of the actual data and posing questions on the wiki, seeking verification that the data are correct.

- Meanwhile, marketing itself has created a mashup, accessing data from the marketing application and creating the required field. This not only answers the immediate need, but also helps IT further understand the requirements of the field, as well as be able to pose more sophisticated questions regarding the source data used as input for the computation.

- IT is then able to gather requirements in an asynchronous way. The requirements are recorded in the conversation back and forth, and clarity can be reached more rapidly. Meanwhile, marketing is not held hostage while IT develops the field, because marketing uses its own field on the mashup.

The integration described here is quite complex:

- It requires that users understand what the data in their source systems mean, which dictates that definitions exist for data elements (the data dictionary, which defines system data elements, is not the same thing as a business glossary, which defines business terms).

- It requires that impact analysis be performed from a business metadata description.

- It requires software that helps businesspeople to create their own mashups.

- It may even be possible, providing the right integrated infrastructure exists, to generate a data model from well-placed business terms in the glossary.

Example of an Integrated Metadata Repository Tool

Tools are now starting to become available that provide the integration necessary between business and technical metadata, and also promote a reasonable way to store some business metadata. IBM, like many companies, has embarked on an acquisition frenzy in order to be the first on the block with a truly integrated metadata repository across many tools. The following pieces are now integrated in their metadata repository, out of the box:

- Business glossary
- Data profile data
- ETL
- Data-quality data

- Data models (and data element definitions)
- Physical schema

A data analyst can look at the glossary and display a list of data elements that represent that business term in the systems throughout the enterprise. Data profiling results for a given data element can be shown side by side with the business definition in order to determine whether the data accurately reflect what the definition indicates. In the same way, a data warehouse field can be compared with the business term definition, and if they are not synchronized, ETL jobs can be examined to determine what the problem might be. Although most of this analysis will be done by technical people, the business is the ultimate beneficiary of this integration, because it will be able to directly benefit from more accurate data and more transparent analysis with better traceability.

9.5.2 Integration and Administrative Source of Record: Conflict Resolution

Metadata reside all over the enterprise. Just as in a data warehouse, conflicts may arise when metadata are extracted from multiple sources. One type of metadata may have different values, but it is supposed to be the same piece of metadata. This happens in the context of master data management (MDM) projects all the time, when customer data is located in five different systems. Which is the best? Which is the "gold copy"? In the case of metadata, would all values go in the metadata repository or only in the "gold copy"?

Data elements are an example of this situation. Suppose you have a data element called `Recognized Revenue`, which shows up in three different systems, each time with a different definition. Which definition is correct? As you can imagine, these three data elements may actually represent entirely different concepts, which is another issue that your metadata repository must be able to handle. But suppose they really are the same thing. Which definition is the best one? Which do you use? The usual solution to that problem is for you to include each definition along with each data element, but the universal data concept will need its own definition.

But what about stuff that is supposed to be the same metadata, which shows up in different places, and one gets updated and all the other locations are not kept in synch? Definitions maintained in an Excel spreadsheet are one example. The definitions are supposed to be created in the spreadsheet and copied to the database design tool, but then a new data modeler, who doesn't know anything about the spreadsheet, joins the staff. He or she maintains the definitions in the database design tool. The same situation often happens across tools; the definition may be created and maintained in both Cognos and the database design tool. Which takes precedence?

One way to help resolve this problem is to create a CRUD (create, read, update, delete) matrix illustrating tools and files that maintain metadata objects. See Table 9.1 for an example.

Table 9.1 Metadata System of Record Matrix

Meta Object	Strategic Modeling Tool	Tactical Modeling Tool	DBMS Tool	Data Integration Tool	Reporting Tool
Entity name	C				
Entity type	C				
Entity definition	C	U			R
Entity scope	C				
Entity active ind	C	U			
Entity logical business rule	C	U		U	R

9.5.3 Integration Technologies

We have compared the metadata environment to a data warehouse and discussed the use of a physical metadata repository. This approach, like the data warehouse, has many advantages, such as the existence of a single physical source of record that can be always counted on to be up to date.

Federated Metadata

Another approach to integrated metadata management is virtual integration, known as *federated*. In this approach, a user requests metadata and an integration engine, using conflict-resolution rules and source information, goes out in real time, sources the requested data, and reconciles the data "on the fly." Federated tools (e.g., MetaMatrix) have the ability to interface with tools in both directions: get and receive metadata. For example, these tools would be able to get data definitions from the database design tool and feed them to the Cognos repository for display when viewing a data mart, all virtually with no need for a physical repository.

Business Metadata as a Service

Software services, or services-oriented architectures, are becoming a popular way to obtain integrated data. A data service—in this case a metadata service—is invoked, data are obtained, and all the mechanics are done by the service, independent of hardware or software platform. Services can be invoked by software programs internally or by businesspeople if an interface is provided to them.

Business metadata service delivery can be used either with or without a metadata repository; it is a data delivery mechanism. If services are desired, the appropriate infrastructure, centralized or federated, must be in place to support the delivery of the service.

9.6 ADMINISTRATIVE ISSUES

This section addresses a few of the administration issues that will have infrastructure ramifications.

9.6.1 Administration Functionality Requirements

The metadata infrastructure must account for how the metadata environment will be managed and administered. These issues include:

- How security will be managed both for the access of metadata and the access to the reporting environment.
- How the operational activities of metadata governance, acquisition, configuration, versioning, change management, and the like will be administered.
- How workflow and metadata quality checks, audits, and errors will be administered.
- How the program code will be managed and upgrades or new releases will be managed.
- How the metadata will be duplicated/replicated, how it will be backed up, and the processes to support disaster recovery.
- How the programs will be operationally scheduled, monitored, and debugged if necessary.

Use cases are an effective means of documenting the requirements and the actions that will need monitoring to administer the metadata environment. These issues may result in additional hardware, software, or resource requirements.

9.6.2 Do You Keep History?

Should you maintain history on each metadata object? The answer will probably vary, depending on the type of business metadata. For example, you may want to keep history of business term definitions. The most obvious type of business metadata that you definitely want to keep are data profiling statistics, because they show how data quality is showing improvement or degradation over time.

Those familiar with data warehouse development will recognize that the same set of issues that are used to address slowly changing dimensions apply here as well. Those issues include:

- Is the requirement to only keep and report the latest value for the metadata object? In this case, we overwrite the value of the metadata, and thus only the most recent value can be communicated.
- Is the requirement to keep a limited number of values for the metadata? This may be the case where the need is to keep the current version and one previous version of the metadata value. In this case, we must copy the current value

and overwrite the previous value, and then we must also overwrite the current value with the new value of the metadata.

■ Is the requirement to keep all values for the metadata? In this case, we must keep all the history of the values for the metadata object, which is often critical to business processes and communications. However, the ability to achieve this requirement will be directly dependent on the capabilities of the hardware and software infrastructure.

9.7 METADATA REPOSITORY: BUY OR BUILD?

The first question a chief information officer of a business asks very early in the planning process is "Do we buy or build it ourselves?" Acquiring the licenses to achieve many of the things we have discussed in this chapter is easily a mid-six-figure endeavor. However, the software licensing price for some products can be less than five figures, less than $10,000. So how do we make the decision and arrive at an answer to the question? Some of the issues that impact the decision can be funding availability and organizational/cultural related. Organizations that normally purchase software solutions will have a natural tendency to consider the "buy" alternative. Conversely, organizations that tend to develop software internally will tend to consider the "build" alternative. In either case, we recommend that the organization fully define its metadata integration requirements prior to making the decision. For example, in the beginning of the chapter, we provided a data model to help you hone in on the specific business metadata you are interested in tracking.

9.7.1 Considerations in Making the Decision

Some organizations know they don't have the capital funds available, and they also know that the metadata project must begin. In that case, the decision should be easy; having no capital allocation of funds means they must build it. Funding and time-frame pressures often force the buy or build decision to be easier.

The following is by no means an all-inclusive list, but the decision to buy or build can include these considerations:

■ Are the capital funds available for a purchase?
■ Does the organization prefer to purchase solutions, or does it prefer to build solutions to fit their specific needs?
■ Does the organization have the skills and resources to complete a build solution? This can be a challenge for most organizations attempting metadata at an enterprise level.
■ Can a compromise be achieved that limits the project scope so that the resources of the organization can achieve a successful build solution?
■ Does a solution have to be implemented in a time frame that can only be achieved with a buy solution?

- Are there buy solutions available that are within our funding capabilities and closely match our functional requirements?

Note that even if the decision is to buy, a model of the desired metadata is essential to evaluate each particular package.

9.7.2 Special Challenges of Business Metadata

Business metadata is primarily unstructured and has complex relationships that are far closer to a network model rather than a relational model. When you evaluate commercially available products, you will need to realize that most, if not all, of these products do not support all business metadata out of the box. Thus, these products may not even have structures to contain and maintain business metadata. Even IBM, which is farther along in terms of an integrated business and technical metadata repository, doesn't support business rules (to our knowledge at this time). Therefore, when you purchase a product, you will most likely have to extend the repository to support business metadata objects and life cycle. However, in order to technically integrate business metadata with your technical metadata, a common integration structure must exist. Again, having a data model of your requirements is crucial to this process.

9.8 THE BUILD CONSIDERATIONS

Building an integrated metadata solution is a significant and complex custom software development project. These efforts can be the equivalent of a significant data warehousing project (addressing data rather than metadata). However, business dictionary, ontology, or taxonomy build projects can have considerably less complexity and risk.

9.9 THE THIRD ALTERNATIVE: USE A PREEXISTING REPOSITORY

There is a third alternative in addition to buy versus build: Use a repository from an existing tool. For example, many data warehouse tools use their own repository to get their jobs done:

- ETL tools (Informatica, IBM, Ab Initio, etc.)
- BI tools (Cognos, Business Objects, etc.)
- Data profiling tools (Informatica IDE, SAS Data Flux, etc.)
- Enterprise Information Integration (EII) tools (Metamatrix, Composite, etc.)
- Enterprise Application Integration (EAI) tools and service-oriented architecture (SOA) tools (BEA, IBM WebSphere, Tibco, etc.)

This solution can be a workable one, because since a repository already exists, you don't have to build it from scratch. However, you must remember that when you build any extension to a preexisting product, you must be careful because the product is subject to change. It is always recommended that you use the APIs (such as database views) provided by the vendor and not link your structures directly with the underlying structures of the product's database. In addition, it is advisable that you isolate your structures in some way from the product's structures in order to minimize the impact of upgrades and prevent your structures from being destroyed. For example, if you are using Oracle, put your structures in another schema and use a database link to link your structures to the product's structures.

9.10 SUMMARY

There is no "one size fits all" infrastructure for metadata, especially business metadata. You must pay close attention to your specific requirements and focal areas, and select an infrastructure that supports your needs. Requirements gathering is always a best practice, regardless of which option you choose.

We have discussed different issues that an overarching metadata infrastructure must address. These issues include delivery methods and specialized delivery requirements. We have also laid out some guidelines for evaluating and selecting an approach to the metadata repository, outlining three alternatives: (1) buy a commercially available product; (2) build your own repository; or (3) retrofit an existing product.

At this writing, commercially available product support for business metadata has started to emerge. In this chapter, we have pointed out some of the special considerations that business metadata presents, and we have highlighted the fact that even if you choose to buy a product, you will still most likely have to end up extending it in some way to support your business metadata.

Storing: XML and Databases

10.1 INTRODUCTION

The act of querying XML obviously requires that there is XML to be queried. What most standards related to querying XML do not address is the question of where that XML is found.

In this chapter, we discuss several ways in which XML documents can be made available for querying. Among these are ordinary computer file systems, websites, relational database systems, extensible markup language database systems, and other persistent storage systems. Such persistence facilities may present a single XML document at a time, or they might provide the ability to query a collection of documents at once. Another source of XML, however, does not require persistent storage but involves XML that is presented to a client (such as a querying facility) as it is generated. The capability of generating XML (usually dynamically) and transmitting it to one or more clients in real time is often called *streaming*. Querying XML that is persistently stored offers several advantages and challenges, while querying streaming XML presents other advantages and challenges.

As you read this chapter, you'll learn about the different ways that XML can be stored (persistent XML) along with the advantages and challenges involved in querying that persistent XML. The mechanisms for storing persistent XML data range up to enterprise-level database systems, with all of the robustness, scalability, transaction control, and security that such systems offer.

You'll also learn about the advantages and challenges associated with queries evaluated against XML streams. Such data might be broadcast for consumption by many clients (e.g., stock ticker data) or might be streamed to a single client (e.g., real-time communication systems, such as instant messaging). The common thread is that data, once transmitted, cannot be retrieved a second time.

There is also a middle ground in which XML is often used: message queuing systems. Such systems often require that data be stored in some temporary location until they can be transmitted to the consumer, but the systems rarely involve long-term persistence of the data. Such data are sometimes queried while residing in temporary storage locations and sometimes when they have been released from storage and are being transmitted to a receiving agent, and thus behave more like streamed data.

10.2 THE NEED FOR PERSISTENCE

A great deal of the XML data most people encounter today are stored somewhere; that is, they are *persistent*. Storing XML data persistently makes a great deal of sense for data that may be used many times, especially when that data have a high value and may have been expensive, even difficult, to create.

Examples of such XML abound: Our movie collection is documented in an XML document; corporations are increasingly likely to store business data like purchase orders in an XML form; many technical books are being produced from XML sources; the W3C's specifications themselves are all coded in XML; even computer applications' initialization and scripting information are increasingly represented in XML. Of course, different types of information present different requirements for persistent storage. Some sorts, such as the books owned by a publisher, probably need to be retained for lengthy periods of time, while others (e.g., messaging data) might have a lifetime measured in seconds or minutes. The various mechanisms discussed in the remainder of this section easily support the wide variety of requirements for storing XML.

10.2.1 Databases

A *database*, according to Wikipedia,[1] is "an information set with a regular structure." A database system, or database management system (DBMS), is thus (for our purposes, at least) a computer system that manages a computerized database. While it's not unknown for some people to apply the term *database management system* to extremely primitive data management products, the term is most often used to describe systems that provide a number of important characteristics for data integrity. Among these characteristics are:

- Query tools, such as a query language like SQL or XQuery.

- Transaction capabilities that include the so-called ACID properties: *a*tomicity of operations, *c*onsistency of the database as a whole, *i*solation from other concurrent users' operations, and *d*urability of operations even across system crashes.

- Scalability and robustness.

- Management of security and performance, including registration and management of users and their privileges, creation of indices on the data, and provision hints for the optimization of operations.

---

[1]Wikipedia, The Free Encyclopedia; available at *www.en.wikipedia.org*.

Several types of database management systems are in wide use by enterprises of all sorts, but we believe that only three are commonly employed to store and manage XML data: relational, object-oriented, and "pure XML." All of these types of database inherently provide the ability not only to store and retrieve XML documents but also to search that data through the use of query languages of some sort. Querying XML data in a DBMS is probably more effective than querying XML data stored in other media, if for no other reason than the existence of various performance-enhancing features of a DBMS, such as indices.

It is worth noting one important consideration when storing XML in a database system: XML, by definition, is based on the Unicode character set.[2] Not all database systems support Unicode, and some support Unicode only when that character set was chosen when the database system was installed or when the specific database was created. Increasingly, however, we see that all of the major relational database systems are being updated to employ Unicode internally, implying that this may no longer be a serious issue in a few years. We have not investigated the status of Unicode in object-oriented DBMSs, but the fact that many of them have Java interfaces suggests that they may use Unicode internally. Naturally, pure-XML databases will always use Unicode internally.

Relational Databases

You won't be surprised to hear that a very large fraction of persistent XML is found in relational databases, right along with other data vital to an enterprise's business. Most large businesses today—and an increasing percentage of smaller businesses—depend on relational databases to store and protect their data.

Relational database management systems (RDBMSs) have been on the scene since the early 1980s and have arguably become the most widely used form of DBMS. The billions of dollars that have been invested into commercial relational database systems (such as Oracle's Oracle database, IBM's DB2, and Microsoft's SQL Server) have given them formidable strengths in the data management environment. Such systems are tremendously scalable, often able to handle thousands of concurrent users accessing many terabytes—even petabytes—of data.

Some say that the relational database systems—because of the two decades and billions of dollars invested in their infrastructure and code, their proven ability to adapt to new types of data, and their entrenchment in so many organizations—might never be superseded in the marketplace by other, more specialized database products. Whether this is mere hubris or a realistic view of the world, we see that the vendors of RDBMS products are adapting very quickly to a world in which XML support is a major requirement.

Starting in roughly 2001, most commercial relational database vendors began adding support for XML data into their products. Initially, the focus was on merely storing XML documents and retrieving them in whole, without the ability to

---

[2]*The Unicode Standard, Version 4.1.0* (Mountain View, CA: The Unicode Consortium, 2005). Available at *www.unicode.org/versions/Unicode4.1.0/*.

perform any significant operations on the content of those documents. Some systems merely stored serialized XML data in character string columns or CLOB (character large object) columns, while others explored ways of breaking the XML data down into component elements, attributes, and other nodes for storage into columns in various tables. (This latter mechanism, commonly called *shredding* the XML, is discussed in Section 10.2.3.)

As the vendors' experience with—and customers' requirements for—XML grew, the products gained more direct support for XML as a true data type of its own. A native XML type (see Section 10.3) was defined for the use of database designers and application authors. New built-in functions were developed to transform ordinary relational data into XML structures of the users' choice. And a variety of ways were invented to query within XML stored in that native XML type, including the ability to invoke XPath and XQuery on that XML. In addition, these products have been given the ability to support XML metadata, largely in the form of XML schema.

Of course, we may be biased by our years of participation in the relational database world, but we believe that RDBMS products are rapidly becoming as fully capable of managing XML data as they are of managing ordinary business data.

Object-Oriented Databases

In the late 1980s and early 1990s, a new form of DBMS was introduced to the data management marketplace, the object-oriented database management system (OODBMS). Unlike the RDBMS products, OODBMS products suffered from not having a formal data model on which their design was based. As a result, the meaning of the term OODBMS varied widely between implementations. What they all had in common, of course, was that they managed *objects* instead of *tuples* of *attributes* or *rows* of *columns*.

Arguably, the real world is better represented as a collection of objects, each having a state (data about the individual object) and behaviors (functions that implement common semantics of classes of objects). Object-oriented programming languages (OOPLs) were coming into prominence (and have since tended to dominate some application domains), and it was natural to want to persistently store the objects being manipulated in OOPL programs. Some OODBMSs took the approach of allowing individual objects (or classes of objects) handled by a particular OOPL program to be "marked" with a flag that indicated whether or not the object (or members of the class) were to be automatically placed into persistent storage, without any specific action (e.g., a `store` command) taken by the program. Others made the OODBMS an integral part of the OOPL so that storing and retrieving objects was done completely seamlessly without any application code involved. Still others required that the OOPL programs explicitly store and retrieve objects when the program made the decision to do so.

What was generally missing from all of these OODBMS products was a common query language that allowed applications to locate objects based on their states and to retrieve information about specific objects. The RDBMS world had standard-ized on the database language SQL, so the OODBMS community[3] decided to adapt SQL for use as a query language in their world; the result of that adaptation is a language called OQL, which is a search and retrieval–only language without built-in update capabilities.

A significant portion of the XML community views XML as naturally object-oriented; for example, every node in an XML document has a unique identity, as do objects in all object-oriented systems. Consequently, when XML became a significant market force, we expected that Object Data Management Group (ODMG) would quickly move to incorporate this new type of data, if only by adapting an XML data model like the Document Object Model (DOM)[4] for use in the context of ODMG. While the owners of the ODMG standard have not yet published a new version with explicit XML support, a group of academics did just that in a system they called Ozone.[5] Subsequently, an open-source effort providing an Ozone database system[6] was established. The documentation of this effort states that "ozone [*sic*] includes a fully W3C-compliant DOM implementation that allows you to store XML data."

We are unaware of any significant presence in the marketplace of OODBMS products that incorporate explicit support of XML as a data type (in the sense that the Ozone system does, at least). This may be due to the fact that OODBMSs in general have found secure niches in the data management community and that those niches have little need for XML except as a data interchange format. It may also be due to the fact that many (but not all) RDBMSs have embraced object technology and are popularly known as object-relational database management systems (ORDBMSs). In any case, we do not perceive a near-term movement toward the use of OODBMS products for large-scale management of XML data.

Native XML Databases

We were not surprised that a number of start-up companies as well as some estab-lished data management companies determined that XML data would be best managed by a DBMS that was designed specifically to deal with semistructured data—that is, a native XML database.

But what, exactly, is a native XML database? One resource we found[7] defines it in terms of the following three principle characteristics.

---

[3]R.G.G. Cattell, et al. (eds.). *The Object Data Standard (ODBM 3.0)*. Morgan Kaufmann, 2000.

[4]*Document Object Model (DOM) Level 3 Core Specification Version 1.0.* Cambridge, MA: World Wide Web Consortium, 2004. Available at *www.w3.org/TR/DOM-Level-3-Core*.

[5]Serge Abiteboul, Jennifer Widom, and Tirthankar Lahiri. *A Unified Approach for Querying Struc-tured Data and XML*, 1998. Available at *www.w3.org/TandS/QL/QL98/pp/serge.html*.

[6]The Ozone Database Project. Available at *www.ozone-db.org*.

[7]Kimbro Staken. *Introduction to Native XML Databases*, 2001. Available at *www.xml.com/pub/a/2001/10/31/nativexmldb.html*.

- Defines a (logical) model for an XML document.
- Has an XML document as its fundamental unit of (logical) storage.
- Is not required to have any particular underlying physical storage model.

Undoubtedly, the most important of those three criteria is the first one: the definition of a model for XML documents. A number of data models for XML are in current use. The specific model chosen for a native XML database system is less important than the requirement that it support arbitrarily deep levels of nesting and complexity, document order, unique identity of nodes, mixed content, semi-structured data, and so on.

Unfortunately for companies that invested heavily in the development of what we call pure-XML database systems, the widely accepted definition of "native XML" database systems doesn't exclude other existing technologies. The definition cited earlier makes it clear that relational database systems can provide all of the required characteristics of a native XML database. This can be done either by building an XML-centric layer atop a relational system or by incorporating new XML-specific facilities directly into relational engines. Of course, that doesn't mean that there is no marketplace for pure-XML DBMSs. However, we suspect that, like OODBMSs before them, pure-XML DBMSs will find small but secure niches for themselves where they satisfy very specific needs that are not targeted by RDBMS (or ORDBMS) products.

10.2.2 Other Persistent Media

While a great proportion of enterprise XML data is managed by explicit DBMSs, we believe that a large majority of XML in the world today does not get stored in DBMSs at all. Instead, XML documents are found in ordinary operating system files and on Web pages. A quick search of just one of our computers found several thousand XML documents, most of which we didn't even realize were there, since they were created as part of the installation of several software products.

The advantage of storing XML documents in ordinary files on your own computer is, of course, that everybody with a computer has a file system, while most of us don't (yet) have formal DBMSs installed on our computers or even unrestricted access to our organizations' DBMSs. Better yet, those files are completely under your control and not governed by some database administrator somewhere in your organization. Of course, there are disadvantages as well: You're usually responsible for backing up your own files, lack of transactional control makes data loss more likely, and the problems of keeping track of perhaps thousands of XML files are quite tedious. Perhaps more importantly, there is usually no way to enforce any consistent relationships among those thousands of XML files—those documents that specify configuration information for software products might define the same operating system environment variable in multiple, incompatible ways.

Some people argue that a single XML document can be a sort of "database in a file." If you take this type of approach, you would just mark up your data "on the fly," making up tag names as you go. Unfortunately, unless you write a good XML schema to validate that document, it's awfully difficult to keep that data internally consistent, because you might use different "spellings" of tags to represent the same conceptual entity; for example, `<SerialNumber>` one time, `<SerNum>` another time, `<Serial-num>` a third time, all to represent the serial numbers of the products that you own. We recommend strongly against such an approach to storing your data, although the concept might be very useful for transporting data from one environment to another—that is, as a data exchange representation.

XML documents that are found across the World Wide Web (WWW) probably don't outnumber those found in ordinary file systems, but you are personally likely to find more Web-available XML documents than there are XML documents on your personal file system. The problem with those Web documents is that a given website may or may not be "reachable" at any given time, making access to those documents somewhat less dependable at any moment than access to your own documents.

That, of course, has implications on querying those XML documents. A query facility that accesses files stored in your local file system always has access to those files (subject only to the availability of your file system), whereas a query facility that searches data on the WWW may sometimes find a given document and other times not find it because of websites going offline temporarily (or permanently).

Nonetheless, we believe there is a market for XML querying tools that don't depend on the existence of a DBMS but that search XML documents in local file systems and across the WWW. Many of these tools will implement XQuery, while others may provide some other query language.

10.2.3 Shredding Your Data

In the "Relational Databases" section we mention that some relational database vendors provided a way for XML documents to be broken down into their component elements, attributes, and other nodes for storage into columns in one or more tables. It can be argued that such *shredding* of XML documents does not preserve the integrity—the "XML-ness"—of those documents. While that argument is probably valid for some shredding implementations, others manage to preserve the documents' XML-ness. In fact, such implementations usually provide options that allow the user to control what level of XML-ness must be preserved. Vendors of those products typically provide a variety of ways of reconstructing the XML documents from the shredded fragments. What many of the shredding implementations do not do particularly well is to allow queries to be written that depend heavily on complex structures in some XML documents or that search for data located at arbitrarily deep levels of nesting.

The purpose of shredding is to improve (relative to character string or CLOB representations, that is) the efficiency of access to the data found in XML documents. When XML serves the same purposes as its ancestor SGML—that is, representation of *documents*, such as books and technical reports—the data represented in the XML are semistructured by nature. However, XML is also used to represent much more regular, or structured, data, such as purchase orders and personnel records. Most people would not consider shredding an appropriate way of handling books or magazine articles marked up in XML. Instead, it is much more likely to be used for dealing with data-oriented XML.

Shredding can be done in a very naive manner, such as defining an SQL table for each element type (at least those that are allowed to have mixed content) in a document, with columns for each attribute, the nonelement content of those elements, and the content of child elements that are not allowed to have element content themselves. For simple documents, the naive approach might not be completely inappropriate, as illustrated in Example 10.1 and Table 10.1.

EXAMPLE 10.1

Shredding an XML Document into a Relational Database

First, the XML to be shredded:

```
<movies>
  <movie runtime="99">
    <title>What About Bob?</title>
    <MPAArating>PG</MPAArating>
    <yearReleased>1991</yearReleased>
    <director>
      <givenName>Frank</givenName>
      <familyName>Oz</familyName>
    </director>
  </movie>
  <movie runtime="108">
    <title>A Fish Called Wanda</title>
    <MPAArating>R</MPAArating>
    <yearReleased>1988</yearReleased>
    <director>
      <givenName>Charles</givenName>
      <familyName>Chrichton</familyName>
    </director>
  </movie>
  <movie runtime="90">
    <title>Best in Show</title>
    <MPAArating>PG-13</MPAArating>
    <yearReleased>2000</yearReleased>
    <director>
      <givenName>Christopher</givenName>
      <familyName>Guest</familyName>
```

Table 10.1 Result of Shredding Movies Document

movies_table				movies_table	
movie_id				movie_id	
124				124	
391				391	
227P				227P	

movie_table

movie_id	runtime	title	MPAArating	yearReleased	director_id
124	99	*What About Bob?*	PG	1991	12
227	90	*Best in Show*	PG-13	2000	418
391	108	*A Fish Called Wanda*	R	1988	693

director_table

director_id	givenName	familyName
693	Charles	Chrichton
12	Frank	Oz
418	Christopher	Guest

```
    </director>
   </movie>
</movies>
```

Now, the definitions of (reasonable) SQL tables into which the shredded XML data will be placed:

```
CREATE TABLE movies_table (
  movie_id      INTEGER PRIMARY KEY,
  FOREIGN KEY (movie_id) REFERENCES movie_table(movie_id) )

CREATE TABLE movie_table (
  movie_id      INTEGER PRIMARY KEY,
  runtime       INTEGER,
  title         CHARACTER VARYING(100),
  MPAArating    CHARACTER VARYING(10),
  yearReleased  INTEGER,
  director_id   INTEGER )
```

```
CREATE TABLE director_table (
  director_id    INTEGER PRIMARY KEY,
  givenName      CHARACTER VARYING(50),
  familyName     CHARACTER VARYING(50) )
```

The data shown in Table 10.1 contain something that the input document did not contain: an id code for each movie and each director. Since the input didn't contain those id codes, where did they come from? Well, the application that performed the shredding simply had to make them up.

Now that the data have been shredded, applications are dealing with purely relational data and can write ordinary SQL statements to query and otherwise manipulate that data. At this point, it's trivially easy to write SQL queries to find out the longest movie in our collection:

```
SELECT MAX(runtime) FROM movie_table;
```

Similarly, to know the name of the director of the longest movie, we could join data from two tables:

```
SELECT givenName || ' ' || familyName
FROM movie_table AS m, director_table as d
WHERE m.director_id = d.director_id
  AND m.runtime = (SELECT MAX(runtime) FROM movie_table)
```

It is a bit harder to reconstruct the original structure of the input. In order to restore the original XML document from the shredded data, a somewhat complicated SQL query would have to be written to discover the names of the tables and columns (using the standardized SQL schema views such as the tables and columns views, unless the table names are known a priori by the application), then join the various tables together on their respective primary key and foreign key relationships, and finally construct the resulting XML document. We leave the writing of such a sequence of SQL statements as an exercise for the reader; after all, most vendors of shredding-capable relational systems provide tools that reproduce the original XML document automatically.[8] We note, however, that such relational systems normally aim to preserve a data model representation of the XML documents and not the actual sequence of characters that may have been provided in the serialized XML input. The ordering of XML elements (remember that elements in an XML document have a defined and stable order) is preserved in those systems by a variety of techniques that may involve the assignment of some sort of sequence numbering scheme to sibling elements of a given parent.

More complex XML documents, like those you'll undoubtedly find throughout your organization's business documents, don't lend themselves to naive shredding

---

[8]In fact, such tools often do not produce a new XML document that is identical in every respect to the initial document. Differences often include changes in nonsignificant white space and the exact representation of literals (canonical form for such literals may be used instead).

techniques. The tools doing the shredding often permit users knowledgeable about the data to give clues about how the shredding should be performed (sometimes using a graphical interface) or to "tweak" the table and column definitions before the XML-to-relational mapping is finished.

There will always be a use for shredding, particularly in applications that merely receive structured data in an XML format and always need to store it as ordinary relational data.[9] However, with the increased emphasis in all major relational database implementations on true native XML support, we believe that shredding is going to diminish in popularity for most applications. It's only fair to note, however, that implementers continue to come up with more and more sophisticated shredding techniques targeted at a variety of usage scenarios.

10.3 SQL/XML'S XML TYPE

There is a relatively new part of the SQL standard[10] designed to allow applications to integrate their XML data and their ordinary business data in their SQL statements. The centerpiece of SQL/XML is the creation of a new built-in SQL type: the XML type. Logically enough, the name of the type is "XML," just as the type intended for storing integers is named "Integer."

The design of SQL/XML's eXtensible Markup Language type makes it a true native XML database type. Therefore, if you were to create a SQL table with a column of type XML, the values stored in that type must be XML values, and those values retain all of their XML-ness. In SQL/XML:2003, the XML type was based on the XML Information Set. The next edition of SQL/XML[11] replaced its use of the Infoset with the adoption of the XQuery 1.0 and XPath 2.0 data model. Along with the adoption of the XQuery data model, the basic definition of the XML type has been updated accordingly.

Of course, that does not mean that SQL/XML implementations are required to store values of the XML type in a collection of data structures that are isomorphic to the XQuery data model descriptions. Implementations might choose to store serialized XML documents and dynamically parse them into data model instances whenever they are referenced, or they might store some other already-parsed representation that can be mapped onto the data model definitions when required.

---

[9]For those who need to do shredding (or, in a more generalized sense, mapping of XML to relational data), a number of XML mapping products make that task easier. Some with which we are familiar are Altova's MapForce (*www.altova.com*), Oracle's XDB schema processor and the schema annotations it supports (*www.oracle.com*), and IBM's Document Access Definition (DAD) component of DB2's XML Extender (*www.ibm.com*).
[10]ISO/IEC 9075-14:2003(E), *Information Technology—Database Languages—SQL—Part 14: XML-Related Specifications (SQL/XML)*. Geneva: International Organization for Standardization, 2003.
[11]Final Draft International Standard (FDIS) 9075-14:2005, *Information Technology—Database Languages—SQL—Part 14: XML-Related Specifications (SQL/XML)*. Geneva: International Organization for Standardization, 2005.

In fact, implementations could even choose to shred (fully or partially) those XML values, as long as the process is transparent to applications. The internal storage details of XML type values are left up to the implementation, in the same way as the corresponding details of `date` and `float` values are the concern of only the implementation.

With the advent of the XML type in SQL, concerns such as CLOB versus shredding will, for the most part, become even less visible to the application developer. XML will be stored in XML columns, and native SQL facilities (augmented, when desired, by XQuery) will be used to manipulate those XML values.

10.4 ACCESSING PERSISTENT XML DATA

Neither XQuery nor SQL (nor, for that matter, any query language) exists in a vacuum—in spite of the fact that they are generally specified as though nothing else existed. Instead, applications are typically written in one or more other programming languages, such as C/C++, Java, and even COBOL. When those applications require access to a query language, they must use some sort of application programming interface (API) to cause their queries to be executed and the results to be materialized in the host language environment.

Most of the more conventional programming languages (such as C and COBOL) access SQL database systems by invoking a call-level interface such as SQL/CLI[12] or one of the various proprietary APIs that correspond to SQL/CLI. SQL/XML:2003 did not provide SQL/CLI extensions to deal with the XML type, but that was a deliberate choice. Because languages like C and COBOL do not have built-in data types for XML, all results of SQL statements that return a value of the XML type are implicitly cast to character string (that is, serialized) before the result is given to the invoking program.

Java programs typically access SQL database systems through the JDBC API.[13] JDBC, version 3.0, contains no provisions for exchanging XML values between a Java program and an SQL database management system. The spec does say that it "does not preclude interacting with other technologies, including XML, CORBA, or nonrelational data," but it offers no additional information about how such interaction should be done (other Java-related specifications provide those capabilities). It's not inconceivable that JDBC, version 4.0, offers more direct support for access to XML data handled by SQL database systems; for details of any such capability, see JDBC 4.0.

There are, however, proprietary JDBC API extensions offered by a number of vendors of SQL database engines and by vendors of middle-tier ("middleware")

---

[12]ISO/IEC 9075-3:2003(E), *Information Technology—Database Languages—SQL—Part 3: Call-Level Interface (SQL/CLI)*. Geneva: International Organization for Standardization, 2003.
[13]*JDBC 3.0 API*. Santa Clara, CA: Sun Microsystems, Inc., 2002. Available at *www.java.sun.com/products/jdbc/download.html#corespec30*.

facilities. Nonetheless, the "most standard" way for Java programs to access the XML data stored in SQL databases is for them to retrieve XML data using JDBC's `getObject()` method and then to cast the retrieved object to an XML class defined in another Java-related specification, such as JAXP.[14] At that point, the interfaces defined in that other specification can be employed to handle the XML data.

Another API will assist Java programs in accessing persistent XML data, whether they are stored in a relational database system, an object-oriented database system, a true native XML database system, or flat files. This API, called XQJ,[15] "defines a set of interfaces and classes that enable an application to submit XQuery queries to an XML data source and process the results of these queries." In other words, it will provide a direct interface from Java programs to XML data sources without those programs having to intermix multiple APIs, such as JDBC and JAXP.

An Early Draft Review version of the XQJ specification is available at *www.jcp.org/en/jsr/detail?id=225*. While that document is decidedly incomplete, it allows interested parties to gain an idea of what the final API will provide. We encourage readers to become familiar with XQJ because we believe that it will be one of the dominant APIs for querying and updating XML data from Java applications.

10.5 XML "ON THE FLY": NONPERSISTENT XML DATA

Throughout this chapter, we have focused on XML data that are persistently stored on various media. There are significant advantages to be had when the XML data to be queried are persistently stored. For example, query processors might be able to access specialized data structures (such as indices) to improve a query's performance.

But not all applications find it suitable to store XML data persistently before querying them. For example, XML data containing stock market quotations might be broadcast to WAP-enabled cell phones that are programmed to alert their owners whenever particular stocks achieve a particular price. Not only are the phones generally incapable of storing very large quantities of data, but the nature of the data stream is unsuitable for storage before querying.

In particular, such data streams are literally neverending; they may continue uninterrupted for months on end, perhaps with each stock quotation represented as a separate XML document. In addition, the queries are supposed to detect the specified conditions immediately and not after periodic store-and-query episodes.

---

[14] *Java API for XML Processing (JAXP) 1.3*. Santa Clara, CA: Sun Microsystems, Inc., 2002. Available at *www.jcp.org/aboutJava/communityprocess/pfd/jsr206/index2.html*.

[15] *XQuery API for Java™*. Available at *www.jcp.org/en/jsr/detail?id=225* (currently in development).

Consequently, XML querying systems must be able to process XML documents that never exist on any persistent medium but that are only temporarily stored (perhaps in RAM) while the query is evaluated against them. There are several reasons why querying streaming XML is problematic. Consider the XML document shown in Example 10.2, in which we've incorporated a large number of stock ticker elements into a single document for illustrative purposes.

EXAMPLE 10.2

Streamed XML Document

```
<?xml version="1.0"?>
<stockTrades>
  <stockTicker symbol="XMPL">
    <tradeTime>2005-06-02T14:53:13.055</tradeTime>
    <tradeUnits>2000</tradeUnits>
    <tradePrice>193.21</tradePrice>
  </stockTicker>
  ...
  <stockTicker symbol="XDOCS">
    <tradeTime>2005-06-02T14:56:41.683</tradeTime>
    <tradeUnits>100</tradeUnits>
    <tradePrice>12.45</tradePrice>
  </stockTicker>
  ...
  <stockTicker symbol="XMPL">
    <tradeTime>2005-06-02T14:58:34.002</tradeTime>
    <tradeUnits>400</tradeUnits>
    <tradePrice>194.65</tradePrice>
  </stockTicker>
</stockTrades>
```

Now imagine a query that must retrieve the current price of XMPL if and only if the preceding ten trades all increased in price. Further, imagine that there are hundreds, even thousands, of stock-Ticker elements represented by ellipses (...). A query that examines this XML document—as it streams past—is forced to evaluate information without having access to all the information in the document. In this case, the query would retrieve information from this stockTicker element's tradePrice child element, if and only if this stockTicker element's preceding sibling stock-Ticker element's tradePrice child element had a lesser value, and that stockTicker element's preceding sibling stockTicker element's tradePrice child element had a lesser value than *that*, and so on until the tenth preceding sibling stockTicker element's tradePrice child element matched the required criterion.

In general, access to an element's ancestors and preceding siblings (and other "reverse-axis" nodes) requires the ability to traverse backward in the document.

But how can that be done when the document is too large for available storage? In general, it cannot. Because the stream relentlessly flows past, there is no way to go back "upstream" to capture data that have already gone by. And there lies the principal difficulty in querying streaming XML. There are (again, in general) only two ways to resolve this problem:

1. Queries can be prohibited (syntactically or by means of execution-time checks) from accessing nodes reachable only through the use of one of those reverse axes.
2. Queries are permitted to access such nodes only in documents (or document fragments) sufficiently small to be handled using limited resources.

Most streaming XML query processors choose one of these two alternatives.

Queries against streaming XML are best suited for small XML documents and relatively simple queries, perhaps involving a transformation of source XML into a more desirable form of XML or directly into HTML or even plain text. Another form of query eminently suitable for streaming applications is the sort that depends solely on "very local" data. For example, if we wanted to know the trade price of XMPL every time a trade was recorded, it's quite easy to detect those elements as they stream past and to supply the value of the `tradePrice` child element whenever a `stockTicker` element whose `symbol` attribute having the value `XMPL` is seen.

10.6 SUMMARY

This chapter explored the various facilities through which XML data can be stored persistently and the implications on querying such persistent XML. We've explored the pros and cons of using database technology versus ordinary file systems for storing and querying XML documents, and we've looked at shredding as a mechanism for storing XML documents into ordinary relational (or, indeed, other sorts of) databases. We've also examined the SQL standard's new built-in XML type, its relationship to shredding, and the implications on the APIs that application programs use to access SQL database management systems. Finally, we reviewed the nature of streaming XML, its uses, and the difficulties raised when querying such nonpersistent XML data.

Our conclusion, which we hope is clear from the text, is that we believe that most applications are better served by storing XML in some persistent medium and then querying those persistent XML data. Only when the XML data are inherently unsuitable for storing, we believe, are queries against streaming XML desirable.

Modeling and Querying Current Movement

11

In this chapter, we consider moving objects databases from the location management perspective. Suppose we need to manage in a database the locations of a set of mobile units (e.g., cars, trucks, helicopters, people carrying mobile phones) that are moving around *right now*. We wish to be able to retrieve their current positions. In fact, if it is known in the database not only where they are but also how they are moving right now, we should also be able to ask queries about the future.

After discussing some basic assumptions and issues in Section 11.1, we introduce a data model called MOST (moving objects spatiotemporal model) to describe current and expected future movement (Section 11.2). Associated with it is a query language called Future Temporal Logic (FTL), which allows us to express queries about future development (Section 11.3). We also study the problem of how often and when mobile objects should transmit updates of their current position, and speed, to the database in order to keep the inherent imprecision in the database management system (DBMS) knowledge about their locations bounded (Section 11.4). Finally, in Section 11.5 we consider *uncertain trajectories*—that is, motion plans with an associated bound on the uncertainty of the time-dependent position.

11.1 LOCATION MANAGEMENT

There are various applications that need to keep track of the locations of moving objects. For example, a query to a database representing the locations of taxicabs in a city might be: Retrieve the three free cabs closest to Königsallee 48 (a customer request position). For a trucking company database, queries might be: Which trucks are within 10 kilometers of truck T68 (which needs assistance)? Will truck T70 reach its destination within the next half hour? In a military application, a query might be: Retrieve the friendly helicopters that will arrive in the valley within the next 15 minutes.

Managing continuously changing positions in a database obviously is a problem, since normally data in a database are assumed to be constant until these data are explicitly updated. Sending very frequent updates would allow one to approximate the continuous movement by stepwise constant locations, but this incurs a very high update load and is not feasible for a large number of objects.

The basic idea developed in this chapter is to store a moving object not by its position directly but instead by its motion vector (i.e., its position as a function of time). In this way, the position represented in the database will change continuously, even without any explicit update to the database. It is still necessary to update the motion vector occasionally, but much less frequently than would be the case with stored positions.

It is important to note that within the DBMS data model, motion vectors are not visible explicitly (e.g., by a special data type). Instead, a concept of a *dynamic attribute* is introduced: an attribute that changes its value with time without explicit updates. The stored motion vector serves as an implementation for this more abstract view of dynamic attribute. Therefore, the data type of a dynamic attribute is the same as the corresponding static data type (e.g., `point`), and queries are formulated as if they refer to static positions. However, since the value of a dynamic attribute changes over time, so does the result of a query: The same query posed at different times will in general yield different results, even if the database contents are the same.

Clearly, if dynamic attributes are available, then the database represents knowledge not only about current but also about expected future positions. Therefore, we should be able to ask about the state of the database ten minutes from now, or even about a sequence of relationships between moving objects in the future. The FTL language is designed for this purpose.

Answers to queries referring to the future are always tentative, since it is possible that the database is changed by an explicit update to a dynamic attribute (i.e., its underlying motion vector is changed). For example, suppose, according to its motion vector, a truck is expected to arrive in a city within the next ten minutes. After this result has been given to a user, the truck stops (and sends a corresponding update of its motion vector). So, in fact, it does not arrive within ten minutes. Nevertheless, the answer given previously has to be regarded as correct, according to what was known in the database at that time.

When answers to queries can change over time even without updates to the database, the issue of *continuous queries* needs to be considered in a new light. For example, suppose a car is traveling along a highway and the driver issues a query: Retrieve cheap motels within five miles from the current position. It makes sense to ask for this query to be continuously reevaluated, since the answer changes while the car moves. While in classical databases continuous queries (such as triggers) need to be reevaluated on each relevant update, here it is not obvious how they can be executed. In the following text, a strategy is described to evaluate a continuous query only once; reevaluation is only needed on explicit updates.

Another important issue is the problem of inherent imprecision and uncertainty that is related to the frequency of updates. Clearly, the motion of an object as represented by its motion vector will normally not represent the real motion exactly. The distance between the database position and the real position is called the *deviation*. Assuming that with an update the real position and speed are transmitted, the deviation at the update time[1] is zero, and then it generally grows with time. The database should be aware not only of the expected position but also of the range of possible deviations at a given time.

To keep the deviation and therefore the uncertainty about an object's position bounded, we will assume a kind of "contract" between a moving object and the database managing its position: Whenever the deviation reaches a certain threshold, the moving object sends an update to inform the database about its current position and speed. Various policies exist for doing this; these are discussed in Section 11.4.

11.2 MOST—A DATA MODEL FOR CURRENT AND FUTURE MOVEMENT

We now introduce the moving objects spatiotemporal (MOST) data model used in the remainder of the chapter.

11.2.1 Basic Assumptions

First, let us recall some standard assumptions. A database is a set of object classes. Each object class is given by its set of attributes. It is also assumed that spatial data types, such as point, line, and polygon with suitable operations, are available.

Some object classes are designated as *spatial*, which means they have an attribute representing a spatial value, such as a point or a polygon. The object itself is then called a *point object* or a *polygon object*. Also, the operations on the spatial values are applied to the objects directly. So, for example, if we have two point objects p_1 and p_2 and a polygon object pol, we can apply spatial operations such as DIST(p_1, p_2), returning the distance between the point attribute values of p_1 and p_2, or INSIDE(p_1, pol), testing whether the point attribute value of p_1 lies inside the polygon attribute value of pol. For all of this to work, it is necessary that each object has *exactly one* spatial attribute. More specifically, we assume that each spatial object class is either a point class, a line class, or a polygon class.

Of particular interest in this model are point objects. A first way of modeling point objects lets them have a special attribute called pos, which, in turn, has two

---

[1]We assume that updates are executed instantaneously (i.e., there is no time difference between sending the update and performing the update in the database). In other words, valid time and transaction time are equal.

components, called *subattributes*, denoted `pos.x` and `pos.y` (in case of a two-dimensional coordinate system). The data types of the subattributes may be `int` or `real`.

Besides object classes, a database contains a special object called `Time`, which yields the current time at every instant. Time is discrete (i.e., the time domain is the natural numbers, represented as `int`), and the value of the `Time` object increases by one at each clock tick.

11.2.2 Dynamic Attributes

The fundamental new idea in the MOST model is the so-called *dynamic attributes*. Each attribute of an object class is classified to be either *static* or *dynamic*. A static attribute is as usual. A dynamic attribute changes its value with time automatically. For example, the schema for an object class describing cars moving freely in the *xy*-plane might be given as:

```
car (license_plate: string,
  pos: (x: dynamic real, y: dynamic real))
```

Not all attribute types are eligible to be dynamic. It is assumed that such a type has a value 0 and an addition operation. This holds for numeric types such as `int` or `real` but could be extended to types such as `point`.

Formally, a dynamic attribute A of type T (denoted $A{:}T$) is represented by three subattributes, `A.value`, `A.updatetime`, and `A.function`, where `A.value` is of type T, `A.updatetime` is a time value, and `A.function` is a function $f{:}$ int $\rightarrow T$ such that at time $t = 0, f(t) = 0$. The semantics of this representation are called the *value* of A at time t and defined as:

$$value(A, t) = \text{A. value} + \text{A. function}(t - \text{A. updatetime}) \text{ for } t \geq \text{A. updatetime}$$

An update sets `A.updatetime` to the current time value and changes `A.value`, `A.function`, or both.

If a query refers to the attribute A, its dynamic value is meant and used in the evaluation. Therefore, the result depends on the time when the query is issued. It is also possible to refer to the subattributes directly and so access the representation of a dynamic attribute. For example, a user can ask for objects for which `pos.x.function = 5` (meaning $f(t) = 5\,t$) to find objects whose speed in *x*-direction is 5. While dynamic attributes are intended to support description of movement, they may be used to describe other time-dependent values (e.g., temperature).

11.2.3 Representing Object Positions

We have already seen the first method to describe moving point objects by dynamic *x* and *y* subattributes of the position attribute `pos`. This is appropriate for objects moving freely in the *xy*-plane.

For vehicles, a more realistic assumption is that they move along road networks. The second method of modeling uses an attribute `loc` with six subattributes, called `loc.route`, `loc.startlocation`, `loc.starttime`, `loc.direction`, `loc.speed`, and `loc.uncertainty`. Here, `loc.route` is (a pointer to) a line spatial object, which describes the geometry of a path over the traffic network (i.e., the route along which the object is moving). `Loc.startlocation` is a point on `loc.route`, the location of the moving object at time `loc.starttime`. `Loc.direction` is a Boolean indicating the direction along the route (relative to east–west, north–south, or the end points of the route). `Loc.speed` is a function f giving the distance (along the route) from the `loc.startlocation` as a function of the time elapsed since the last location update—that is, since `loc.starttime`. It is assumed that every update sets `loc.starttime` and `loc.startlocation` to the position at that time. Again, we require $f(0) = 0$. In the most simple form, `loc.speed` stores a constant v, therefore, the distance from `loc.startlocation` at time `loc.starttime` $+ t$ is $v \times t$. `Loc.uncertainty` is either a constant or a function of the number of time units elapsed since the last location update. It represents a threshold on the deviation of the object; whenever the threshold is reached, the object will send a location update. `Loc.uncertainty` is used and further discussed later in Section 11.4.

The semantics of the `loc` attribute are again a time-dependent position (x, y) in the plane, which also happens to lie on the network. At time `loc.starttime`, it is `loc.startlocation`; at time `loc.starttime` $+ t$, it is the position on `loc.route` at distance `loc.speed` $\times t$ from `loc.startlocation` in the direction `loc.direction`. Query evaluation may take the uncertainty into account. That is, the answer to a query for the location of object m at time t may be: The object is on the route `loc.route` at most `loc.uncertainty` before or behind position (x, y).

The *uncertainty* subattribute is, of course, not specific to the network modeling; it might be added to the `pos` attribute as well. In this case, the answer to the query would be: The object is within a circle of radius *uncertainty* around position (x, y).

11.2.4 Database Histories

Queries in traditional database systems refer to the current state of the database. Queries in the MOST model may also refer to future states that are given implicitly by the dynamic attributes. First, we need to be more precise about what is meant by a database state.

A *database state* is a mapping that associates each object class with a set of objects of the appropriate type and associates the `Time` object with a time value. For any object o in a database, we denote its attribute A as $o.A$; if A has a subattribute B it is denoted as $o.A.B$. The value of $o.A$ in the database state s is denoted by $s(o.A)$, and $s(\text{Time})$ gives the time value of database state s. For each dynamic attribute A, its value in state s is $value(A, s(\text{Time}))$.

A *database history* is an infinite sequence of database states, one for each clock tick. It starts at some time u and extends infinitely into the future—therefore, it is s_u, s_{u+1}, s_{u+2}, and so on. We denote the history starting at time u by H_u. The value of an attribute A in two consecutive database states s_i, s_{i+1} can be different, either due to an explicit update of A or because A is a dynamic attribute whose value has changed implicitly. At any time t the database states with a lower timestamp than t are called *past database history*; the infinite remainder of the sequence with higher timestamps is called *future database history*.

Note that an explicit update at a time $t > u$ affects all states from t on of a given history H_u. Suppose until $t - 1$, the history H_u is:

$$s_u, s_{u+1}, s_{u+2}, \ldots, s_{t-1}, s_t, s_{t+1}, s_{t+2}, \ldots$$

Then, from time t on, the history is:

$$s_u, s_{u+1}, s_{u+2}, \ldots, s_{t-1}, s'_t, s'_{t+1}, s'_{t+2}, \ldots$$

Therefore, with each clock tick, we get a new database state, and with each update, we get a new history. We denote a history starting at time u and as of time $u + k$ (i.e., updates have been performed until and including time $u + k$) by $H_{u,k}$. Therefore, $H_{u,0} = H_u$, and with $t = u + k$ the history before the update is $H_{u,k-1}$, and after the update it is $H_{u,k}$.

Note that database histories are just a concept to define the semantics of queries; they are not stored or manipulated explicitly, which obviously would be impossible.

11.2.5 Three Types of Queries

Queries are predicates over database histories rather than just a single state. This leads to a distinction between three different types of queries, called *instantaneous, continuous*, and *persistent*. The same query can be posed in each of the three modes, with different results; these are explained next.

As we will see in Section 11.3, a query has an implicit concept of the current time. For example, there will be language constructs to express a condition "within the next ten time units," which means within ten time units from the current time. If nothing is said about time, the database state at the current time is meant. The current time is normally the time when the query is issued. We denote by $Q(H, t)$ a query Q evaluated on a database history H assuming a current time t.

A query Q posed at time t as an *instantaneous query* is evaluated as:

$$Q(H_t, t) \quad \text{(instantaneous query)}$$

That is, it is evaluated on the history starting at t, assuming t as the current time. For example, a query issued at time t by a car driver—"Find all motels within five miles from my position"—will return all the motels within five miles from the car's position at time t.

It is important to observe that the concept of an instantaneous query does not imply that only the current database state is used. For example, the driver might also pose the query "find all motels that I will reach within ten minutes," and this query refers to all database states having a timestamp between the current time and ten minutes later.

The second type of query is the continuous query. Query Q posed at time t as a *continuous query* is evaluated as a sequence of queries:

$$Q(H_t, t), Q(H_{t+1}, t+1), Q(H_{t+2}, t+2), \ldots \quad \text{(continuous query)}$$

In other words, it is reevaluated on each clock tick as a new instantaneous query. The answer to the query also changes over time; at instant u the result of the instantaneous query $Q(H_u, u)$ is valid. If the result of the continuous query is displayed to the user, the contents of the display may change without user interaction. For example, the car driver may decide to run the query, "Find all motels within five miles from my position," as a continuous query in order to be informed when suitable motels become available.

Of course, reevaluating the query on each clock tick is not feasible. Instead, an evaluation algorithm is given that computes the answer to a continuous query just once, in the form of a set of tuples annotated with timestamps. For each tuple, its timestamp indicates the period of time during which it belongs to the result. When time progresses, tuples whose time period is entered are added to the answer set, and tuples whose time period has expired are removed from the answer set.

As already discussed in this chapter as introduction, the answer to a future query is tentative. For a continuous query, this means that the result set (tuples with timestamps) may become invalid due to an explicit update. Therefore, a continuous query needs to be reevaluated on an update that may change its result set.

The third type of query, persistent query, is motivated by the fact that so far with continuous queries it is impossible to recognize certain kinds of developments over time. As an example, consider the query, "Q = Find all cars whose speed has doubled within five minutes." Suppose this is posed as a continuous query at time $t = 20$ (and let time units be minutes). Let o be a car with `o.loc.speed` = 40. Further, let the speed of o be explicitly updated to 60 at time 22 and to 80 at time 24.

When the continuous query is evaluated as $Q(H_{20}, 20)$, in all future states the speed of o is 40; therefore, it is not in the result. When it is evaluated as $Q(H_{22}, 22)$, in all future states the speed is 60. Similarly, when evaluated as an instantaneous query at time 24, in all future states the speed is 80. So o is never in the result.

Query Q posed at time t as a *persistent query* is evaluated as a sequence of queries:

$$Q(H_t, 0, t), Q(H_t, 1, t), Q(H_t, 2, t), \ldots \quad \text{(persistent query)}$$

Therefore, a persistent query is continuously evaluated on the history starting at time t and its answer changes when that history changes due to explicit updates.

Considering our example, when the fifth query in the previous sequence, $Q(H_{24}, 20)$, is evaluated, the fact that the speed of o has doubled from time 20 to time 24 is recognized, and o is returned as a result. Again, reevaluation does not really occur on each clock tick; instead, it is done on each update that might affect its result, as is done for continuous queries.

We have included persistent queries in the discussion in order to show the different kinds of continuous queries that are possible from a semantic point of view. However, to evaluate persistent queries, it is necessary to keep information about past contents of the database (i.e., to use a kind of temporal version of the MOST data model). So far, the MOST model is nontemporal, in the sense that values of subattributes are rewritten on updates and the previous values are lost. Extending the MOST model in this way is beyond the scope of this chapter, and we will not consider the evaluation of persistent queries further.

11.3 FTL—A QUERY LANGUAGE BASED ON FUTURE TEMPORAL LOGIC

In this section, we describe FTL, a query language that allows us to express conditions about the future. We first introduce the language by some examples (Section 11.3.1), then define the syntax (Section 11.3.2) and semantics (Section 11.3.3) of the language precisely. Finally, in Section 11.3.4, an algorithm for evaluating FTL queries is presented.

11.3.1 Some Example Queries

Several example queries for moving objects applications have already been mentioned; let us see how some of them would be expressed in FTL.

EXAMPLE 11.1

Which trucks are within ten miles of truck T68?

```
RETRIEVE t
FROM trucks t, trucks s
WHERE s.id = 'T68' ∧ dist(s, t) ≤ 10
```

The general form of a query is:[2]

```
RETRIEVE <target-list> FROM <object-classes>
WHERE <FTL-formula>
```

---

[2]In the original literature describing FTL, the FROM clause is omitted; a single implicit class of moving objects is assumed.

The FTL formula is the interesting part. In the first example, nothing special happens yet. The syntax used is a theoretical one; in practice, we would replace the logical connective ∧ by a keyword and and type <= instead of ≤. Observe that the distance operator dist is applied to the objects directly rather than to point attributes, as discussed in Section 11.2.1.

The FTL language as such only deals with instantaneous queries. How we can get from instantaneous to continuous queries has been explained in the previous section. But to require a query to be evaluated as a continuous query is not within the scope of the language; it has to be specified externally (e.g., at the user interface).

Therefore, the previous query is evaluated instantaneously at the time when it is issued. We assume trucks have a dynamic location (loc) attribute, and the distance is evaluated on the current positions of trucks *s* (T68) and *t*. The distance function dist is also assumed to operate over the network; therefore, it involves a shortest-path computation.

Observe that the query is beautifully (and perhaps deceivingly) simple; nothing needs to be said about time, yet the query refers to the current situation and its result will change when posed at different times.

EXAMPLE 11.2

Will truck T70 reach its destination within the next half hour?
As formulated, the query would require a Boolean (yes or no) result, which is not directly possible. Instead, we will retrieve truck T70 if it reaches its destination in time; otherwise, the result will be empty.

We assume destinations to be modeled as a point object class destinations, where points lie on the traffic network. The trucks object class has an attribute dest giving its destination in the form of a reference to such a destination object.

```
RETRIEVE t
FROM trucks t
WHERE t.id = 'T70' ∧ eventually_within_30 (dist(t, t.dest) = 0)
```

Here, we assume again that time units are minutes. New is the temporal operator eventually_within_c, where *c* is a numeric constant referring to time units. It can be applied to a predicate *p*. The meaning of eventually_within_c(*p*) is: Within the next *c* time units, *p* will become true.

EXAMPLE 11.3

To make the next example more interesting, we modify our helicopter query a bit: Retrieve the friendly helicopters that will arrive in the valley within the next 15 minutes and then stay in the valley for at least 5 minutes.

```
RETRIEVE h
FROM helicopters h
WHERE eventually_within_15 (inside(h, Valley) ∧
  always_for_5 (inside(h, Valley)))
```

Here, Valley is a polygon object and inside an operation comparing a point object with a polygon object. We assume that helicopters represented in this object class are all friendly; therefore, there is no explicit condition for that.

Note that the condition says that within 15 minutes a database state will be reached such that helicopter *h* is inside the valley, and for the next 5 time units, this will always be true.

We can see that it is possible in the language to specify sequences of conditions that must become true in a certain order and to specify bounds on the periods of time involved. In the next section, we define the structure of the language precisely.

11.3.2 Syntax

The interesting part of the FTL language is the FTL formulas. FTL is similar to first-order logic; therefore, the language consists of constants, variables, function symbols, predicate symbols, and so forth.

Definition. The FTL language consists of the following symbols:

1. *Constants*. These may be of the atomic data types (e.g., 54, "T68") or named objects in the database (e.g., Valley). The special database object Time is also a constant.
2. For each $n > 0$, a set of *n*-ary *function symbols*. Each function symbol denotes a function taking *n* arguments of particular types and returning a value of some type. Examples are +, * on type int, or the "." operator, which takes an object of some object class and an attribute name and returns a value of the attribute type.
3. For each $n \geq 0$, a set of *n*-ary *predicate symbols*. Each predicate symbol denotes a relation with *n* arguments of specified types. For example, ≤ and ≥ denote the usual arithmetic comparison operators.
4. *Variables*. These are typed and can range over object classes or atomic types. For example, h_{truck} is a variable ranging over the truck class, and j_{int} an integer variable. Usually the index denoting the domain of the variable is omitted.
5. Logical connectives ∧ and ¬.
6. The *assignment quantifier* ←.
7. Temporal modal operators until and nexttime.
8. Brackets and punctuation symbols (,), [,], and ,.

The MOST model and FTL language are designed to be implemented on top of a DBMS providing its own nontemporal query language (e.g., OQL). FTL allows us to embed so-called *atomic queries* from that underlying language. These are queries returning single values from atomic types (e.g., an integer). For example, the query

```
RETRIEVE d.name FROM destinations d WHERE d.id = 'd12'
```

is such an atomic query returning a `string` value. Within FTL, this atomic query is viewed as a *constant* symbol. It is also possible that such a query contains a variable. For example, the query

```
RETRIEVE d.name FROM destinations d WHERE d.id = y
```

has a free variable y. This is viewed as a function symbol denoting a unary function that returns for a given argument a `string` value.

Definition. A term is one of the following:

1. A constant c.
2. A variable v.
3. An attribute access $v.A$.
4. An application of a function to terms of appropriate types $f(t_1, \ldots, t_n)$.

For example, 10, $x + 3$, `dist`(x, y), and `d.name` are terms, and "retrieve `d.name` from destinations d where `d.id` $= y$" is also a term.

Definition. A well-formed formula is defined as follows:

1. If R is an n-ary predicate symbol and $t_1, \ldots, t_n$ are terms of appropriate types, then $R(t_1, \ldots, t_n)$ is a well-formed formula.
2. If f and g are well-formed formulas, then $f \wedge g$ and $\neg f$ are well-formed formulas.
3. If f and g are well-formed formulas, then f `until` g and `nexttime` f are well-formed formulas.
4. If f is a well-formed formula, x is a variable, and t is a term of the same type as x, then $([x \leftarrow t] \, f)$ is a well-formed formula. A variable in a formula is *free* if it is not in the scope of an assignment quantifier of the form $[x \leftarrow t]$.

The semantics of all this are defined in the next section. Observe that FTL does not have the existential and universal quantifiers of first-order logic;[3] instead, the assignment quantifier is offered that allows us to bind a variable to the result of a query in one of the states of a database history. In particular, it is possible to

---

[3]It is argued that this is to avoid problems of safety, which are more severe in the context of database histories. See standard database textbooks for a discussion of safety of the relational calculus, for example.

capture an atomic value at some point in time and relate it to other values at later points in time.

We have not yet discussed some constructs, such as `eventually_within_c`, occurring in the previous examples. These will be shown to be derivable from the primitives of the language and will be discussed in the following section.

11.3.3 Semantics

Let s_u be the state of the database when the query "retrieve `<target-list>` from `<object-classes>` where f" is entered. The semantics of formula f are defined with respect to the history starting with s_u—that is, history H_u.

First, we need to define the meaning of the symbols of the language:

1. *Constants* represent corresponding values from their domain. For example, 54 represents an integer, "T68" a character string, and `Valley` and `Time` represent database objects.

2. *Function symbols* have their standard interpretation or denote functions defined in the text. For example, the symbols + and * represent the standard addition and multiplication functions. The `dist` symbol represents the distance function described in Section 11.3.1.

3. *Predicate symbols* also have their standard interpretation. For example, $\leq$ denotes the standard less than or equal relation.

In the sequel, we do not distinguish in notation between such symbols and their interpretation. For example, for a constant symbol c, the value represented is also denoted as c.

Definition. A variable assignment for formula f is a mapping μ that assigns to each free variable in f a value from its domain. We denote by $\mu[x/u]$ the mapping obtained from μ by assigning the value u to variable x and leaving all other variables unchanged.

EXAMPLE 11.4

Let us assume that in the `truck` object class in Example 11.1, there are truck objects with object identifiers T_1 through T_{100}. Consider the formula

```
s.id = 'T68' ^ dist(s, t) ≤ 10
```

A possible variable assignment is $\mu = \{(s, T_{10}), (t, T_{20})\}$.

Definition. For a term t, its evaluation in a state s with respect to a variable assignment $\varphi_{s,\mu}$, denoted $\varphi_{s,\mu}[t]$, is defined as follows:

1. If t is a constant c, then $\varphi_{s,\mu}[c] = s(c)$.
2. If t is a variable v, then $\varphi_{s,\mu}[v] = \mu(v)$.

3. If t is an attribute access $v.A$, then $\varphi_{s,\mu}[v.A] = s(\mu[v].A)$.
4. If t is an application of function f to arguments $t_1, \ldots, t_n$, then $\varphi_{s,\mu}[f(t_1, \ldots, t_n)] = f(\varphi_{s,\mu}[t_1], \ldots, \varphi_{s,\mu}[t_n])$.

Observe that constants are evaluated in a database state; this is needed in particular for the constant Time. Also dynamic attributes are evaluated with respect to the current state. We now define the satisfaction of a formula at a state s on a history H with respect to a variable assignment μ. Satisfaction is defined inductively on the structure of formulas.

Definition. Formula f is *satisfied* at state s on history H with respect to variable assignment μ (satisfied at (s, μ), for short):

1. $R(t_1, \ldots, t_n)$ is satisfied $:\Leftrightarrow R(\varphi_{s,\mu}[t_1], \ldots, \varphi_{s,\mu}[t_n])$ holds.
2. $f \wedge g$ is satisfied $:\Leftrightarrow$ both f and g are satisfied at (s, μ).
3. $\neg f$ is satisfied $:\Leftrightarrow f$ is not satisfied at (s, μ).
4. f until g is satisfied $:\Leftrightarrow$ either g is satisfied at (s, μ), or there exists a future state s' on history H such that (g is satisfied at $(s', \mu) \wedge$ for all states s_i on history H before state s', f is satisfied at (s_i, μ)).
5. nexttime f is satisfied $:\Leftrightarrow f$ is satisfied at (s', μ), where s' is the state immediately following s in H.
6. $([x \leftarrow f] \, f)$ is satisfied $:\Leftrightarrow f$ is satisfied at $(s, \mu[x/\varphi_{s,\mu}[f]])$.

The assignment quantifier can be used in combination with the nexttime operator to detect change.

EXAMPLE 11.5

The formula $([x \leftarrow \mathrm{dist}(a, b)] \, (\mathrm{nexttime} \; \mathrm{dist}(a, b) > x))$ is evaluated as follows. Let us assume it is evaluated in a state s, for which s' is the next state.

$([x \leftarrow \mathrm{dist}(a, b)] \, (\mathrm{nexttime} \; \mathrm{dist}(a, b) > x))$ is satisfied at state s
$\Leftrightarrow (\mathrm{nexttime} \; \mathrm{dist}(a, b) > \beta\alpha)$ is satisfied at state s, where α is the distance between objects a and b, evaluated in state s
$\Leftrightarrow (\mathrm{dist}(a, b) > \alpha)$ is satisfied at state s'
$\Leftrightarrow (\beta > \alpha)$ where β is the distance between objects a and b, evaluated in state s'

So the formula is satisfied if the distance between objects a and b increases from the current state to the next state.

Based on the given syntactical primitives for constructing formulas whose meanings are now well defined, some derived notations can be defined as follows.

First, in addition to the logical connectors $\wedge$ and $\neg$, we can also use $\vee$ and $\Rightarrow$, which can be defined in terms of the first two. Second, temporal operators eventually and always can be defined as follows:

- `eventually` *g* means that *g* will be fulfilled at some future state. It can be defined as *true* `until` *g*.
- `always` *g* means that *g* is satisfied at all future states, including the present state. It is defined as ¬ (`eventually` (¬ *g*)).

In addition, it is useful to have related operators that have bounded, rather than infinite, periods of time. First, we define bounded versions of the `until` operator:

- *g* `until_within_c` *h* asserts that there exists a future time within at most *c* time units from now such that *h* holds, and until then *g* will be continuously satisfied.
- *g* `until_after_c` *h* asserts that there exists a future time after at least *c* time units from now such that *h* holds, and until then *g* will be continuously satisfied.

Based on these, we can define other bounded temporal operators:

- `eventually_within_c` *g* asserts that the formula *g* will be fulfilled within *c* time units from the current state, defined as *true* `until_within_c` *g*.
- `eventually_after_c` *g* means that *g* holds after at least *c* units of time, defined as *true* `until_after_c` *g*.
- `always_for_c` *g* asserts that the formula *g* holds continuously for the next *c* units of time, defined as *g* `until_after_c` *true*.

11.3.4 Evaluating FTL Queries

An interesting issue now is how FTL queries are processed and evaluated by an algorithm. From the set of FTL queries that can be formed according to Section 11.3.2, we here only consider the subset of so-called *conjunctive* formulas. Such a formula is constructed

- Without negations.
- Without the `nexttime` operator.
- Without any reference to the `Time` object (Section 11.2.1).

The reason for excluding negations is safety (i.e., finiteness of the result), since negations may introduce infinite answers. The condition of excluding the time variable in queries implies that for every query *q* that is on the right side of an assignment in *f* (i.e., as in [*x* ← θ]), the value returned by *q* at any time is independent of the time when it is evaluated; it is only the result of a *function* application assigning values to the free variables in *q*; and it depends only on the current positions of the objects. This condition also ensures that satisfaction of a nontemporal predicate when an object is at a particular position depends only on the position of the object but not on the time when the object reached the position.

The bounded temporal operators such as `eventually_within_c` are admitted, however. Since the `Time` object must not be used, the evaluation algorithm will handle the two basic operators `until_within_c` and `until_after_c` explicitly. As an additional constraint, only instantaneous and continuous, but not persistent, queries are allowed.

The basic idea for evaluating an FTL formula is to compute for each formula f with free variables $x_1, \ldots, x_k$ a relation $R_f(x_1, \ldots, x_k, t_{start}, t_{end})$. That relation has one attribute for each of the free variables in f and two additional attributes, t_{start} and t_{end}, describing a time interval. Each tuple $(o_1, \ldots, o_k, t_1, t_2)$ of R_f represents one instantiation $\rho = <o_1, \ldots, o_k>$ of the variables $x_1, \ldots, x_k$ such that the formula is true for this instantiation during the time interval $[t_1, t_2]$. Furthermore, for two tuples with the same *instantiation* $\rho = <o_1, \ldots, o_k>$ of the variables $x_1, \ldots, x_k$, the time intervals are disjoint and nonadjacent.

A set of tuples T with the same instantiation ρ and set of time intervals I represents a combination of objects $<o_1, \ldots, o_k>$ that fulfills f during times I. An FTL formula is structured into subformulas. The idea for evaluation is to compute relations for the atomic formulas first and then to evaluate formulas bottom-up, translating connectives into relation operations.

At the beginning of this section, we said that we consider a restricted class of formulas where negation and `nexttime` are missing and `until_within_c` and `until_after_c` are treated explicitly. Here is an updated definition for this case.

Definition. A *well-formed formula* (in the restricted case) is defined as follows:

1. If R is an n-ary predicate symbol and $t_1, \ldots, t_n$ are terms of appropriate types, then $R(t_1, \ldots, t_n)$ is a well-formed formula.
2. If f and g are well-formed formulas, then $f \wedge g$ is a well-formed formula.
3. If f and g are well-formed formulas, then f `until` g is a well-formed formula.
4. If f and g are well-formed formulas, then f `until_within_c` g is a well-formed formula.
5. If f and g are well-formed formulas, then f `until_after_c` g is a well-formed formula.
6. If f is a well-formed formula, x is a variable, and t is a term of the same type as x, then $([x \leftarrow t] f)$ is a well formed formula. A variable in a formula is *free* if it is not in the scope of an assignment quantifier of the form $[x \leftarrow t]$.

We now consider each of these cases in turn. Let h be a subformula with free variables $x_1, \ldots, x_l$.

Case 1: $h \equiv R (x_1, \ldots, x_l)$

Example: $h \equiv \mathtt{dist}(x_1, x_2) < 8$

We assume that for each such atomic predicate an algorithm exists returning for each possible instantiation $<o_i, o_j>$ the time intervals when the predicate holds.

Compute a relation R_h with all such tuples $<o_1, \ldots, o_p>$ and associated time intervals.

Case 2: $h \equiv f \wedge g$

Let R_f and R_g be the relations computed for the subformulas; for example:

$R_f(x_1, x_2, x_5, t_s, t_e)$
$R_g(x_1, x_4, x_5, x_7, t_s, t_e)$

Then the result relation will have the schema

$R_h(x_1, x_2, x_4, x_5, x_7, t_s, t_e)$

Suppose for an instantiation $<o_1, o_2, o_4, o_5, o_7>$, f is satisfied during I_1 and g is satisfied during I_2. Then $f \wedge g$ is satisfied during $I_1 \cap I_2$. Therefore, compute the result relation R_h as follows. Compute a join of R_f and R_g; common variables must be equal, and time intervals must intersect. For each result tuple its time interval is the intersection of the time intervals of the two joining tuples.

Case 3: $h \equiv f$ until g

Let R_f and R_g be the relations computed for the subformulas, with $p + 2$ and $q + 2$ attributes, respectively.

Consider tuple t_1 in R_f. Let T_1 be the set of all tuples with the same values in the first p attributes (same instantiation). Let I_1 be the set of time intervals in T_1. Similarly, consider t_2 in R_g, T_2, and I_2. Figure 11.1 shows tuples t_1 and t_2 with overlapping time intervals. Clearly, if f holds for the instantiation of t_1 during its time interval, and if g holds for the instantiation of t_2 during its time interval, then f until g holds for the union of their time intervals.

Now consider the complete sets of time intervals I_1 and I_2 for these two instantiations (Figure 11.2). When does f until g hold? Remember the semantics of f until g: f until g is satisfied :⇔ either g is satisfied at (s, μ), or there exists a future state s' on history H such that (g is satisfied at $(s', \mu) \wedge$ for all states s_i on history H before state s', f is satisfied at (s_i, μ)).

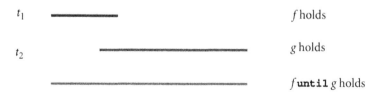

t_1 ——————— f holds

t_2 ————————— g holds

       ——————————— f **until** g holds

FIGURE 11.1

Overlapping time intervals for two instantiations of formulas f and g.

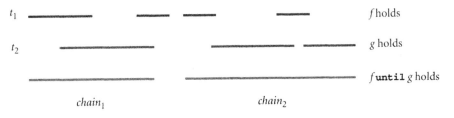

FIGURE 11.2

Time intervals for f until g.

Therefore, f until g holds for periods of time when there are chains of intervals alternating between t_1 and t_2 up to the end of a t_2 interval, as illustrated in Figure 11.2.

Hence, compute R_b as follows: Compute a join of R_f and R_g matching pairs of (sets of) tuples with relation to their variable instantiations. For the two resulting sets of intervals I_1 and I_2, compute their *maximal chains*. For each maximal chain, construct one result tuple, with time interval corresponding to the extent of the chain.

An alternative formulation is: Compute solution intervals for any suitable pair of intervals of t_1 and t_2. Merge all sequences of overlapping solution intervals into one, and return this in a result tuple.

Case 4: h ≡ f until_within_c g

Recall the semantics of this case: f until_within_c g asserts that there is a future time within at most c time units from now such that g holds, and until then f will be continuously satisfied. This case is illustrated in Figure 11.3.

Let t_1, t_2 be matching pairs of tuples from R_f and R_g with overlapping time intervals. Let $d = \max\{t_1.l, t_2.l - c\}$.[4] Then, f until_within_c g holds in the interval $[d, t_2.u]$. Extend to chains as before—that is, merge any overlapping solution intervals so they are displayed as one. The result relation is computed in a join, similar to Case 3.

Case 5: h ≡ [y ← q] f

Here, q is a query yielding an atomic result; for example:

$$y \leftarrow \text{height}(o)$$

Let R_f be the result relation for f. The term q is in general a query and has to yield an atomic result so that it can be assigned to y. It usually contains some free variables. The result relation R_q for $[y \leftarrow q]$ is assumed to have $p + 3$ attributes, where the first p attributes relate to the free variables in q; the number $(p + 1)$

---

[4]We denote by $t.l$ the left end of the time interval for tuple t, and by $t.u$ the right end.

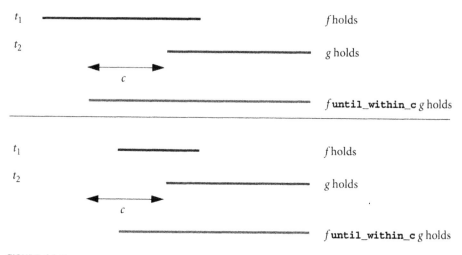

FIGURE 11.3

Time intervals for f until_within_c g.

attribute stores the value of q; and the remaining two attributes represent a time interval. Each instantiation of the free variables in q leads to a result value stored as the number $(p + 1)$ attribute value, and if this value holds during n disjoint time intervals, n corresponding tuples are stored in R_q.

In our example, R_q has four attributes. The first attribute keeps the object id, the third and fourth attributes describe a time interval, and the second attribute gives the height of the object during this interval.

The result relation R_b for b is computed by joining R_q and R_f with the join condition that for any two tuples t_1 from R_q and t_2 from R_f the attribute values corresponding to common variables are equal; the attribute value corresponding to the y value in R_f is equal to the query result value in t_1; and the time intervals of both tuples intersect. The output tuple consists of all variable attribute values stemming from t_1 and t_2, except for the attributes corresponding to variable y and the intersection of the intervals in t_1 and t_2.

This is what is described in the literature for Case 5. We believe there is a problem with this description—namely, the predicate f contains y as a free variable. The relation R_f has to be computed for all possible bindings of y but without any knowledge of the possible values for y. Note that in the other cases variables were ranging over object classes, so they could be bound to all existing object identifiers. It does not seem feasible to let y range over all integers if *height* would return an integer result, not to mention reals, if *height* returned a real number.

It seems that some additional trick is needed. For example, we might compute the relation R_q first. We could then project on the attribute corresponding to y and use the resulting set of values as a domain for the possible bindings of y in formula f.

This concludes the description of the algorithm for evaluating FTL formulas. The result relation *Answer(Q)* can be used in the following way to answer continuous and instantaneous queries. For a continuous query Q at each clock tick t, the instantiations of the tuples having an interval that contains t are shown to the user. Let us assume, for example, that *Answer(Q)* includes the tuples (2, 10, 15) and (5, 12, 14). Then, the object with id = 2 is shown between the clock ticks 10 and 15, and between the clock ticks 12 and 14 the object with id = 5 is displayed. In the case of an instantaneous query Q, the instantiations of all tuples having an interval that contains the current clock tick are presented.

11.4 LOCATION UPDATES—BALANCING UPDATE COST AND IMPRECISION

11.4.1 Background

The motion of spatial objects over time necessitates the transmission of updates of their current position and speed to the database in order to provide the database with up-to-date information for retrieval and query tasks and to keep the inherent imprecision in the database bounded. The main issue here is when and how often these position updates should be made. Frequent updating may be expensive in terms of cost and performance overhead; infrequent updates result in outdated answers to position queries. Consequently, the location of a moving object is inherently imprecise, since the object location stored in the database, which we will call *database location*, cannot always be identical to the actual location of the object. This holds regardless of the policy employed to update the database location of an object. Several *location update policies* may be applicable (e.g., the database location is updated every n clock tick). In this section, we introduce so-called *dead-reckoning* policies. These update the database whenever the distance between the actual location of a moving object and its database location exceeds a given *threshold th*—say, 100 meters. Thus, this threshold determines and bounds the location imprecision. For a moving object m, a query "What is the current location of m?" will then be answered by the DBMS with "The current location of m is (x, y) with a deviation of at most 100 meters." Here, the issue is how to determine the update threshold th in dead-reckoning policies.

The feature of imprecision leads us to two related but different concepts: deviation and uncertainty. The *deviation* of a moving object m at a specific instant t is the distance between m's actual location at time t and its database location at time t. In our example, the deviation is the distance between the actual location of m and (x, y). The *uncertainty* of m at an instant t is the size of the area comprising all possible, current positions of m. In our example, the uncertainty is the size of the area of a circle with a radius of 100 meters. Both deviation and uncertainty are afflicted with a cost in terms of incorrect decision making. The deviation (uncertainty) cost is proportional to the size of the deviation (uncertainty). We will see that the ratio between the costs of an uncertainty unit and a deviation unit depends on the interpretation of an answer.

To be able to update the database location of a moving object, we need an appropriate localization mechanism. In moving objects applications, each moving object is usually equipped with a *global positioning system* (GPS) and can thus generate and transmit the updates by using a wireless network. This introduces a third cost factor: communication or transmission cost. Furthermore, we can recognize an obvious trade-off between communication and imprecision in the sense that the higher the communication cost, the lower the imprecision, and vice versa. This leads to the issue of an information cost model in moving objects databases that balances imprecision and update cost. The model should also be able to cope with the situation where a moving object becomes disconnected and cannot send location updates.

11.4.2 The Information Cost of a Trip

The first issue we deal with relates to an information cost model for a trip taken by a moving object. We have seen that during a trip a moving object causes a deviation cost and an uncertainty cost, which both can be regarded as a penalty due to incorrect decision making. Moreover, a moving object causes update cost, since location update messages have to be sent to the database.

For a moving object the *deviation cost* depends both on the size of the deviation and the duration for which it lasts. The size of the deviation affects the decision-making process. The higher the deviation, the more difficult and imprecise it is to make a reliable decision based on the moving object's current position. To see that the duration for which the deviation persists plays a role for calculating the cost, we assume that there is one query per time unit that retrieves the location of a moving object. If the deviation lasts for n time units, its cost will be n times the cost of the deviation lasting for a single time unit, because all queries instead of only one have to pay the deviation penalty. Formally, for a given moving object, the cost of the deviation between a starting time t_1 and an ending time t_2 can be described by the *deviation cost function* $COST_d(t_1, t_2)$ yielding a nonnegative number. Assuming that the penalty for each unit of deviation during a time unit is weighted by the constant 1, the deviation cost function can be defined as:

$$COST_d(t_1, t_2) = \int_{t_1}^{t_2} d(t)\, dt$$

where $d(t)$ describes the deviation as a function of time. We also denote this function as a *uniform* deviation cost function. It is the basis for all later descriptions of update policies. Of course, other deviation cost functions are conceivable. An example is the step deviation cost function. This function yields a penalty of 0 for each time unit in which the deviation falls below a given threshold th, and it yields a penalty of 1 otherwise.

The *update cost* C_1 covers the effort for transmitting a single location update message from a moving object to the database. It is difficult to determine it precisely, because it can be different from one moving object to another, or even vary for a single moving object during a trip (e.g., due to changing availability of resources such as bandwidth or computation). Of course, we have to measure the update cost by using the same kind of unit as for the deviation cost. With respect to the ratio between the update cost and the cost of a deviation unit per time unit, we can state that it is equal to C_1, since the latter cost factor is assumed to be 1. We can also conclude that in order to reduce the deviation by 1 during a time unit, the moving object will need $1/C_1$ messages.

The *uncertainty cost* depends on the size of uncertainty and on the duration for which it lasts. A higher degree of uncertainty conveys less reliable information for answering a query. Formally, for a given moving object, the cost of the uncertainty between a starting time t_1 and an ending time t_2 can be described by the *uncertainty cost function* $COST_u(t_1, t_2)$ yielding a nonnegative number. Let the *uncertainty unit cost* C_2 be the penalty for each uncertainty unit during a time unit. This implies that C_2 is defined as the ratio between the cost of an uncertainty unit and the cost of a deviation unit, since the latter cost is assumed to be equal to 1. Then, the *uncer*tainty cost function $COST_u(t_1, t_2)$ can be defined as:

$$COST_u(t_1, t_2) = \int_{t_1}^{t_2} C_2 u(t)\, dt$$

where $u(t)$ is the value of the `loc.uncertainty` attribute (see Section 11.2.3) of the moving object as a function of time. We can now exert influence on the weighting and thus the importance of the uncertainty factor and the deviation factor. If for answering the query, "The current location of the moving object m is (x, y) with a deviation of at most u units," the uncertainty aspect is to be stressed, C_2 should be set higher than 1, and lower than 1 otherwise. In a dead-reckoning update policy, each update message to the database determines a new uncertainty, which is not necessarily lower than the previous one. Therefore, an increase of communication reduces the deviation but not necessarily the uncertainty.

We are now in the position to define the information cost of a trip taken by a moving object. Let t_1 and t_2 be the times of two consecutive location update messages. Then, the *information cost* in the half open interval $[t_1, t_2[$ is:

$$COST_I([t_1, t_2[) = C_1 + COST_d([t_1, t_2[) + COST_u([t_1, t_2[)$$

The result contains the message cost at time t_1 but not at time t_2. Since each location update message writes the actual current position of the moving object in the database, the deviation is reduced to 0. The total information cost is calculated by summing up all $COST_I([t_1, t_2[)$ values for every pair of consecutive update instants t_1 and t_2. Formally, let $t_1, t_2, \ldots, t_n$ be the instants of all update messages sent from a moving object. Let 0 be the time point when the trip started and t_{n+1} be the time point when the trip ended. Then, the *total information cost* of a trip is:

$$COST_I(0, t_{n+1}[) = COST_d([0, t_1[) + COST_u([0, t_1[) + \sum_{i=1}^{n} COST_I(t_i, t_{i+1}[)$$

11.4.3 Cost-Based Optimization for Dead-Reckoning Policies

Next, we consider the issue of information cost optimality. We know that the essential feature of all dead-reckoning update policies consists of the existence of a threshold *th* at any instant. This threshold is checked against the distance between the location of a moving object *m* and its database location. Therefore, both the DBMS and the moving object must have knowledge of *th*. When the deviation of *m* exceeds *th*, *m* sends a location update message to the database. This message contains the current location, the predicted speed, and the new deviation threshold *K*. The goal of dead-reckoning policies is to set *K*, which is stored by the DBMS in the `loc.uncertainty` subattribute, such that the total information cost is minimized.

The general strategy is the following: First, *m* predicts the future behavior and direction of the deviation. This prediction is used as a basis for computing the average cost per time unit between now and the next update as a function *f* of the new threshold *K*. Then, *K* is set to minimize *f*. The proposed method of optimizing *K* is not unique. The optimization is related to the average cost *per time unit* and not to the total cost between the two instants t_1 and t_2, because the total cost increases as the time interval until the next update increases. For the case that the deviation between two consecutive updates is described by a linear function of time, we can determine the optimal value *K* for `loc.uncertainty`.

Let C_1 denote the update cost and C_2 denote the uncertainty cost. We assume that t_1 and t_2 are the instants of two consecutive location updates, that the deviation $d(t)$ between t_1 and t_2 is given by the linear function $a(t - t_1)$ with $t_1 \leq t \leq t_2$ and a positive constant *a*, and that `loc.uncertainty` is fixed at *K* between t_1 and t_2. The statement is then that the total information cost per time unit between t_1 and t_2 is minimal if $K = \sqrt{(2aC_1)/(2C_2 + 1)}$ This can be shown as follows: We take the formula for computing the information cost in an interval $[t_1, t_2[$ and insert our assumptions. We obtain:

$$COST_I([t_1, t_2[) = C_1 + \int_{t_1}^{t_2} a(t - t_1)\,dt + \int_{t_1}^{t_2} C_2 K\,dt$$

$$= C_1 + 0.5a(t_2 - t_1)^2 + C_2 K(t_2 - t_1)$$

Let $f(t_2) = COST_I([t_1, t_2[)/(t_2 - t_1)$ denote the average information cost per time unit between t_1 and t_2 for update time t_2. We know that t_1 and t_2 are two consecutive update times. Therefore, at t_2 the deviation exceeds the threshold `loc.uncertainty` so that $K = a(t_2 - t_1)$. We can now replace t_2 in $f(t_2)$ by $K/a + t_1$ and obtain $f(K) = aC_1/K + (0.5 + C_2)K$. Using the derivative the minimum of $f(K)$ is at $K = \sqrt{(2aC_1)/(2C_2 + 1)}$.

What is the interpretation of this result? Assume that m is currently at instant t_1. This means that its deviation has exceeded the `loc.uncertainty` uncertainty threshold. Therefore, m needs to compute a new value for `loc.uncertainty` and transmit it to the database. Further assume that m predicts a linear behavior of the deviation. Then, `loc.uncertainty` has to be assigned a value that will remain fixed until the next update. To minimize the information cost, the recommendation then is that m should set the threshold to $K = \sqrt{(2aC_1)/(2C_2 + 1)}$.

Finally, we try to detect disconnection of a moving object from the database. Then, the moving object cannot send location updates. In this case, we are interested in a dead-reckoning policy in which the `loc.uncertainty` uncertainty threshold continuously decreases between updates. As an example of decrease, we consider a threshold `loc.uncertainty` *decreasing fractionally* and starting with a constant K. This means that during the first time unit after the location update u, the value of the threshold is K; during the second time unit after u the value is $K/2$; and during the ith time unit after u the value is K/i, until the next update, which determines a new K. Assuming a linear behavior of the deviation, the total information cost per time unit between t_1 and t_2 is given by the function

$$f(K) = \left(C_1 + 0.5K + C_2K\left(1 + 1/2 + 1/3 + \ldots + 1/\sqrt{K/a}\right)\right)/\sqrt{K/a}.$$

11.4.4 Dead-Reckoning Location Update Policies

A *location update policy* is a position update prescription or strategy for a moving object that determines when the moving object propagates its actual position to the database and what the update values are. We discuss here a few *dead-reckoning* location update policies that set the deviation bound (i.e., the threshold *th*) stored in the subattribute `loc.uncertainty` in a way so that the total information cost is minimized.

The first strategy is called the *speed dead-reckoning (sdr) policy*. At the beginning of a trip, the moving object m fixes an uncertainty threshold in an ad hoc manner and transmits it to the database into the `loc.uncertainty` subattribute. The threshold remains unchanged for the duration of the whole trip, and m updates the database whenever the deviation exceeds `loc.uncertainty`. The update information includes the current location and the current speed. A slight, more flexible variation or extension of this concept is to take another kind of speed (e.g., the average speed since the last update, the average speed since the beginning of the trip, or a speed that is predicted based on terrain knowledge).

The *adaptive dead-reckoning (adr) policy* starts like the *sdr* policy, with an initial deviation threshold th_1 selected arbitrarily and sent to the database by m at the beginning of the trip. Then, m tracks the deviation and sends an update message to the database when the deviation exceeds th_1. The update consists of the current speed, the current location, and a new threshold th_2 stored in the loc.uncertainty attribute. The threshold th_2 is computed as follows: Let us assume that t_1 denotes the number of time units from the beginning of the trip until the deviation exceeds th_1 for the first time and that I_1 is the deviation cost (according to the formula in Section 11.4.2) during that interval. Let us assume further $a_1 = 2I_1/t_{12}$. Then, $th_2 = \sqrt{(2a_2C_1)/(2C_2+1)}$. where C_1 is the update cost and C_2 is the uncertainty unit cost. When the deviation reaches th_2, a similar update is sent. This time the threshold is $th_3 = \sqrt{(2a_2C_1)/(2C_2+1)}$, where $a_2 = 2I_2/t_{22}$, I_2 is the deviation cost from the first update to the second update, and t_2 is the number of time units elapsed since the first location update. That is, a difference between a_1 and a_2 results in a difference between th_2 and th_3. Further thresholds th_i are computed in a similar way.

The main difference between the *sdr* policy and the *adr* policy is that the first policy pursues an ad hoc strategy for determining a threshold, while the latter policy is cost based. At each update instant p_i, the *adr* policy optimizes the information cost per time unit and assumes that the deviation following instant p_i will behave according to the linear function $d(t) = 2tI_i/t_{i2}$, where t is the number of time units after p_i, t_i is the number of time units between the preceding update and the current one at time p_i, and I_i is the deviation cost during the same time interval. This prediction of the future deviation can be explained as follows: *adr* approximates the current deviation from the time of the preceding update to time p_i by a linear function with slope $2I_i/t_{i2}$. At time p_i this linear function has the same deviation cost (i.e., I_i) as the actual current deviation. Due to the locality principle, the prediction of *adr* after the update at time p_i leads to a behavior of the deviation according to the same approximation function.

The last strategy we discuss is the *disconnection detection dead-reckoning (dtdr) policy*. This policy is an answer to the problem that updates are not generated because the deviation does not exceed the uncertainty threshold, but because the moving object m is disconnected. At the beginning of the trip, m sends an initial, arbitrary deviation threshold th_1 to the database. The uncertainty threshold loc.uncertainty is set to a fractionally decreasing value starting with th_1 for the first time unit. During the second time unit, the uncertainty threshold is $th_1/2$ and so on. Then, m starts tracking the deviation. At time t_1, when the deviation reaches the current uncertainty threshold (i.e., th_1/t_1), m sends a location update message to the database. The update comprises the current speed, the current location, and a new threshold th_2 to be stored in the loc.uncertainty subattribute.

For computing th_2, we use the function $f(K) = \left(C_1 + 0.5K + C_2K\left(1 + 1/2 + 1/3 + \ldots + \sqrt{k/a_1}\right)\right)/\sqrt{K/a_1}$ (see Section 11.4.3). Since $f(K)$ uses the slope factor a of the future deviation, we first estimate this deviation. Let I_1 be the cost of the deviation since the beginning of the trip, and let $a_1 = 2I_1/t_{12}$. The formula for $f(K)$ does not have a closed form. Therefore, we approximate the sum $1 + 1/2 + 1/3 + \ldots 1/\sqrt{k/a_1}$ by $\ln\left(1/\sqrt{k/a_1}\right)$, since $\ln(n)$ is an approximation of the nth harmonic number. Thus, the approximation function of $f(K)$ is $g(K) = \left(C_1 + 0.5K + C_2 K \left(1 + \ln 1 / \sqrt{k/a_1}\right)\right) / \sqrt{k/a_1}$. The derivation of $g(K)$ is 0 when K is the solution of the equation $\ln(K) = d_1 / K - d_2$ with $d_1 = 2C_1 / C_2$ and $d_2 = 1/C_2 + 4 - \ln(a_1)$. By using the well-known Newton-Raphson method, we can find a numerical solution to this equation. The solution leads to the new threshold th_2, and m sets the uncertainty threshold `loc.uncertainty` to a fractionally decreasing value starting with th_2.

After t_2 time units, the deviation exceeds the current uncertainty threshold, which is equal to th_2 / t_2, and a location update containing th_3 is transmitted. The value th_3 is computed as previously but with a new slope a_2. I_2 is the deviation cost during the previous t_2 time units. This process, which continues until the end of the trip at each update instant, determines the next optimal threshold by incorporating the constants C_1 and C_2 and the slope a_i of the current deviation approximation function.

An interesting question now is which of the three discussed dead-reckoning location update policies causes the lowest information costs. This has been empirically investigated in a simulation test bed used to compare the information cost of the three policies on the assumption that the uncertainty threshold is arbitrary and fixed. The result of this comparison is that the *adr* policy is superior to the other policies and therefore has the lowest information cost. It may even have an information cost that is six times lower than that of the *sdr* policy.

11.5 THE UNCERTAINTY OF THE TRAJECTORY OF A MOVING OBJECT

We have seen that uncertainty is an inherent feature in databases storing information about the current and near-future locations of moving objects. Unless uncertainty is captured in the model and query language, the burden of coping with it and reflecting it in the answers to queries will inevitably, and at the same time hopelessly, be left to the user. In this section, we consider the issue of *uncertainty* of the *trajectory* of a moving object.

The concept of trajectory goes beyond the simple model of motion vectors treated so far in this chapter. A trajectory can be viewed as a motion plan for the future, but it can also be used to represent a history of movement. Nevertheless, we treat it in this chapter, since also bounded uncertainty is involved, which is related to the update policies discussed in the previous section.

11.5.1 A Model of a Trajectory

Usually, the trajectory of a moving object is modeled as a polyline in three-dimensional space. Two dimensions relate to space and the third dimension to time. If we in addition aim at capturing the uncertainty aspect, we can model the trajectory as a cylindrical volume in three-dimensional space. We can then ask for objects that are inside a particular region during a particular time interval. Due to the uncertainty aspect, we can go a step further and take into account the *temporal uncertainty* and *regional uncertainty* of objects. We can then query the objects that are inside the region *sometime* or *always* during the time interval (temporal uncertainty). Similarly, we may ask for the objects that are *possibly* or *definitely* inside the region. This allows us to pose queries such as:

- Retrieve the current location of the trucks that will *possibly* be inside a region *R sometime* between 1:00 P.M. and 1:10 P.M.
- Retrieve the number of planes that will *definitely* be inside the region *R sometime* between 4:30 P.M. and 4:45 P.M.
- Retrieve the police cars that will *possibly* be inside the region *R always* between 9:20 A.M. and 9:50 A.M.

We now characterize the spatiotemporal nature of a moving object by the following definition of a trajectory.

Definition. A trajectory of a moving object is a polyline in the three-dimensional space, where two dimensions refer to space and the third dimension refers to time. It is represented as a sequence of points $\langle (x_1, y_1, t_1), \ldots, (x_n, y_n, t_n) \rangle$ with $t_1 < \ldots < t_n$. For a given trajectory *tr*, its spatial projection on the *xy*-plane is called the route of *tr*.

The location of a moving object is here given as an implicit function of time. The object is at position (x_i, y_i) at time t_i, and during each period $[t_i, t_{i+1}]$, the object is assumed to move along a straight line from (x_i, y_i) to (x_{i+1}, y_{i+1}) at a constant speed.

Definition. For a given trajectory *tr*, the *expected location* of the moving object at a point in time *t* between t_i and t_{i+1} with $1 \leq i < n$ is obtained by linear interpolation between the positions (x_i, y_i) and (x_{i+1}, y_{i+1}).

The trajectory can be thought of as a set of points describing the future *motion plan* of the object. This set of points is visited and traversed by the object. Between two consecutive points we assume the object is moving along the shortest path (i.e., on a straight line, with constant speed).

11.5.2 Uncertainty Concepts for Trajectories

To express the uncertainty of a trajectory or motion plan, we associate an uncertainty threshold *th* with each line segment of the trajectory. In total, we thus obtain a three-dimensional, cylindrical "buffer zone" around the trajectory. For a given motion plan, the corresponding buffer zone has the following meaning for the moving object and the server: The moving object will update the server if its actual location deviates from its expected location by the distance *th* or more.

In practice, we can imagine that the on-board computer of the moving object is equipped with a GPS device, which receives an update every two seconds so that it knows its actual position. In addition, the moving object is aware of its motion plan and thus its trajectory so that, on the assumption of constant speed, it can interpolate its expected location at any instant. The deviation can then be simply computed as the distance between the actual and the expected location.

More formally, we can describe these uncertainty concepts for trajectories by the following definitions.

Definition. Let th be a positive real number and tr be a trajectory. The corresponding *uncertainty trajectory* is the pair (tr, th). The value th is called the *uncertainty threshold*.

Next, we give a definition for the buffer zone.

Definition. Let $tr = \langle (x_1, y_1, t_1), \ldots, (x_n, y_n, t_n) \rangle$ be a trajectory and th be the uncertainty threshold. For each point (x, y, t) along the time axis, its *th uncertainty area*, or *uncertainty area* for short, is given by a horizontal circle with radius th centered at (x, y, t), where (x, y) is the expected location at time $t \in [t_1, t_n]$.

An interesting issue now is which motion curves are allowed in the uncertainty area so that a location update does *not* have to be propagated to the database.

Definition. Let $tr = \langle (x_1, y_1, t_1), \ldots, (x_n, y_n, t_n) \rangle$ be a trajectory and th be the uncertainty threshold. A *possible motion curve* is the image of any function of the set $PMC_{tr,th} = \{f : [t_1, t_n] \to \mathbb{R}^2 \mid f \text{ is continuous} \wedge \text{for all } t \in [t_1, t_n], f(t) \text{ is located inside} \}$ the th uncertainty area of the expected location of tr at time $t\}$. Its two-dimensional, spatial projection is called *possible route*.

Consequently, a moving object does not have to update the database as long as it is on some possible motion curve of its uncertain trajectory. We are now able to define the buffer zone around a line segment of the trajectory.

Definition. For an uncertain trajectory (tr, th) and two end points (x_i, y_i, t_i) and $(x_{i+1}, y_{i+1}, t_{i+1})$ of tr, the *segment trajectory volume* of (tr, th) between t_i and t_{i+1} is the set of all points (x, y, t) such that (x, y, t) belongs to a possible motion curve of tr and $t_i \leq t \leq t_{i+1}$. The two-dimensional, spatial projection of the segment trajectory volume is called the *segment uncertainty zone*.

This definition can now be easily generalized to the whole trajectory.

Definition. For a trajectory $tr = \langle (x_1, y_1, t_1), \ldots, (x_n, y_n, t_n) \rangle$ and an uncertainty threshold th, the *trajectory volume* of (tr, th) is the set of all segment trajectory volumes between t_i and t_{i+1} for all $1 \leq i < n$. The two-dimensional, spatial projection of the trajectory volume is called the *uncertainty zone*.

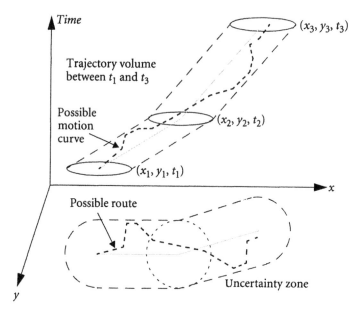

FIGURE 11.4

A possible motion curve, its possible route, and its trajectory volume.

The preceding definitions are illustrated in Figure 11.4. Each segment trajectory volume between t_i and t_{i+1} has a cylindrical body. Its axis is the vector from (x_i, y_i) to (x_{i+1}, y_{i+1}), which specifies the three-dimensional trajectory line segment, and its bases are the circles with radius tb in the planes at $t = t_i$ and $t = t_{i+1}$. This cylindrical body is different from a tilted cylinder. The intersection of a tilted cylinder with a horizontal xy-plane yields an ellipse, whereas the intersection of the cylindrical body, which we have obtained here, with such a plane yields a circle.

11.5.3 Querying Moving Objects with Uncertainty

The interesting issue now is: How can we query moving objects with uncertainty given by their trajectories, and what are the most essential operators for doing this? First, we can identify two operators that relate to a single trajectory. This leads us to *point* queries. Second, we present a collection of six operators specifying Boolean conditions that assess a qualitative description of the relative position of a moving object with respect to a given region within a given time interval. This leads us to a concept for *spatiotemporal predicates*. The application of each of these eight operators corresponds to a spatiotemporal *range* query.

The two operators for point queries are named whereAt and whenAt with the following signatures:

```
whereAt:    trajectory × time → point
whenAt:     trajectory × point → instants
```

The operator `whereat(tr, t)` returns the expected location (i.e., a two-dimensional point) on the route of *tr* at time *t*. The operator `whenAt(tr, l)` returns the times at which an object moving along trajectory *tr* is at an expected location *l*. Here, the answer may be a set of times captured by a value of a type `instants`, in case the moving point passes through a certain location more than once. If the route of *tr* does not traverse *l*, we determine the set *C* of all those points on this route that are closest to *l*. The operator then returns the set of times at which the moving object is expected to be at each point in *C*.

Next, we consider six Boolean predicates, which all share the property that they are satisfied if a moving object is inside a given region *R* during a given time interval $[t_1, t_2]$. This means we can use them for spatiotemporal range queries. Their differences result from existential and all quantifications with respect to three aspects. First, we can temporally quantify the validity of a predicate and ask whether the moving object satisfies the condition *sometime* or *always* within $[t_1, t_2]$. Second, we can spatially quantify the validity of a predicate and ask whether the object satisfies the condition *somewhere* or *everywhere* within the region *R*. Third, we can quantify the validity of a predicate with respect to uncertainty and ask whether the object satisfies the condition *possibly* or *definitely*.

Since we have three kinds of quantification, there are 3! different orders (permutations) to arrange them. For each fixed order, we have 2^3 possibilities to combine the three quantification aspects. This results in $2^3 \times 3! = 48$ possible operators. Since it is not reasonable to require that a point object is *everywhere* in *R*, we do not consider this quantification in the following. This means that the spatial quantifier *somewhere* is the default. Therefore, we only obtain $2^2 \times 2! = 8$ possible operators. These eight predicates π_i all have the signature:

π_i: `uncertainTrajectory × region × time × time → bool`

and are now defined.

Definition. Let *r* be a *simple* query region (i.e., a region whose interior is connected and that does not have holes). Let *ut* = (*tr*, *th*) be an uncertain trajectory. We can then define the following *spatiotemporal predicates*:

1. The predicate `PossiblySometimeInside`(*ut*, *r*, t_1, t_2) is *true* if there is a possible motion curve *c* of *ut* and there is a time $t \in [t_1, t_2]$ such that *c* is inside *r* at *t*.
2. The predicate `SometimePossiblyInside`(*ut*, *r*, t_1, t_2) is *true* if predicate `PossiblySometimeInside`(*ut*, *r*, t_1, t_2) is *true*.
3. The predicate `PossiblyAlwaysInside`(*ut*, *r*, t_1, t_2) is *true* if there is a possible motion curve of *ut* that is inside *r* for every $t \in [t_1, t_2]$.
4. The predicate `AlwaysPossiblyInside`(*ut*, *r*, t_1, t_2) is *true* if for every instant $t \in [t_1, t_2]$ a possible motion curve of *ut* exists that will intersect *r* at time *t*.
5. The predicate `AlwaysDefinitelyInside`(*ut*, *r*, t_1, t_2) is *true* if at every time $t \in [t_1, t_2]$ every possible motion curve of *ut* is in *r*.

6. The predicate `DefinitelyAlwaysInside`(*ut, r, t₁, t₂*) is *true* if predicate `Always-DefinitelyInside`(*ut, r, t₁, t₂*) is *true*.
7. The predicate `DefinitelySometimeInside`(*ut, r, t₁, t₂*) is *true* if for every possible motion curve of *ut* a time *t* ∈ [*t₁, t₂*] exists in which this motion curve is inside *r*.
8. The predicate `SometimeDefinitelyInside`(*ut, r, t₁, t₂*) is *true* if an instant *t* ∈ [*t₁, t₂*] exists at which every possible motion route of *ut* is inside *r*.

Intuitively, the validity of the predicate in item 1 implies that the moving object may take a possible route within its uncertainty zone, such that this route will intersect *r* between t_1 and t_2. In item 3, the predicate is satisfied if the motion of the object follows at least one particular two-dimensional possible route, which is completely contained within *r* during the whole query time interval. Item 4 requires for the validity of the defined predicate that for each instant of the query time interval a possible motion curve can be found that intersects *r* at that instant. In item 5, the validity of the predicate is given if, for whatever possible motion curve the object chooses, it is guaranteed to be located within the query region *r* throughout the entire query time interval. Item 7 expresses that no matter which possible motion curve within the uncertainty zone the moving object takes, it will intersect the query region at some instant of the query time interval and thus fulfill the predicate. However, the time of intersection may be different for different possible motion curves. Satisfaction of the predicate in item 8 means that, for whatever possible motion curve the moving object takes, at the particular instant *t* the object will be inside the query region.

Due to the semantic equivalence of the predicates `PossiblySometimeInside` and `SometimePossiblyInside` (items 1 and 2), as well as the semantic equivalence of the predicates `AlwaysDefinitelyInside` and `DefinitelyAlwaysInside` (items 5 and 6), we can reduce the number of spatiotemporal predicates from eight to six. These two semantic equivalences could also have been formulated in two lemmas, whose proofs are then based on the two logical rules $\exists x \exists y \, P(x, y) \Leftrightarrow \exists y \exists x \, P(x, y)$ and $\forall x \forall y \, P(x, y) \Leftrightarrow \forall y \forall x \, P(x, y)$, respectively. Figure 11.5 illustrates two-dimensional, spatial projections of the six predicates. Dashed lines show the possible motion curve(s) to which the predicates are satisfied. Solid lines indicate the routes and the boundaries of the uncertainty zone.

The predicates `PossiblyAlwaysInside` and `AlwaysPossiblyInside` (i.e., items 3 and 4), as well as the `SometimeDefinitelyInside` and `Definitely-SometimeInside` predicates (i.e., items 7 and 8), are not equivalent. Instead, only `PossiblyAlwaysInside`(*ut, r, t₁, t₂*) ⇒ `AlwaysPossiblyInside`(*ut, r, t₁, t₂*), and `SometimeDefinitelyInside`(*ut, r, t₁, t₂*) ⇒ `DefinitelySometimeInside`(*ut, r, t₁, t₂*) hold. The proofs rest on the logical rule that $\exists x \forall y \, P(x, y) \Rightarrow \forall y \exists x \, P(x, y)$.

Thus, that on the left side of the implication symbol is stronger than that on the right side. If *r* denotes a *convex* simple region, the special case can be proved that `PossiblyAlwaysInside`(*ut, r, t₁, t₂*) ⇔ `AlwaysPossiblyInside`(*ut, r, t₁, t₂*). Figure 11.5(b) and (c) illustrate that the `AlwaysPossiblyInside` predicate

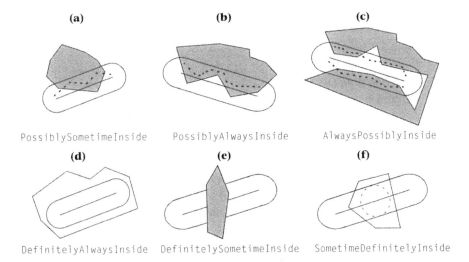

FIGURE 11.5

Examples (of the spatial projections) of the spatiotemporal predicates.

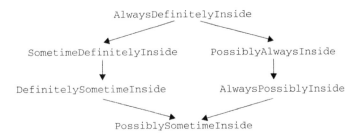

FIGURE 11.6

Relationships among the spatiotemporal predicates.

may be satisfied by two or more possible motion curves together, none of which satisfies PossiblyAlwaysInside by itself. Similarly, in Figure 11.5(b) the query region fulfills DefinitelySometimeInside, but since it does not contain the uncertainty zone for any time point, it does not satisfy the predicate SometimeDefinitelyInside.

The relationship between the six predicates is depicted in Figure 11.6, where an arrow denotes an implication. More complex query conditions can be formulated by composition of the operators. For instance, the query "Retrieve all the objects that are possibly within a region r, always between the times the object A arrives at the locations l_1 and l_2" can then be formulated as:

PossiblyAlwaysInside(*ut, r,* whenAt(*ut$_A$, l$_1$*), whenAt(*ut$_A$, l$_2$*))

11.5.4 Algorithms for Spatiotemporal Operations and Predicates

The algorithms for implementing the two operators for point queries are straightforward. The `whereAt` operator applied to a trajectory with n line segments can be implemented in time $O(\log n)$. This time includes a binary search to determine the line segment between (x_i, y_i) and (x_{i+1}, y_{i+1}) for some $1 \leq i < n$ such that $t_i \leq t \leq t_{i+1}$ and a linear interpolation in constant time to compute the location at time t. The `whenAt` operator is implemented in $O(n)$. Each line segment is examined in constant time for a time t when tr is at location l.

Next, we present algorithms for the six spatiotemporal predicates. These algorithms follow straightforward applications of computational geometry techniques with well-known run-time complexities. The essential idea is to reduce three-dimensional geometric problems to the two-dimensional case, where they can be solved in a much easier way. For reasons of simplicity, we here restrict query polygons to *convex* polygons. Optimizations of part of the described algorithms and a generalization to concave query regions can be found in the literature (see Section 11.7).

Let t_1 and t_2 be two instants. Two-dimensional spatial objects moving over time can be considered as three-dimensional objects with time as the third dimension. A query polygon r with the query time interval $[t_1, t_2]$ can then be represented as a prism $p(r) = \{(x, y, t) \mid (x, y) \in r \wedge t_1 \leq t \leq t_2\}$, which is called *query prism*. Further, each segment trajectory volume between times t_i and t_{i+1} is approximated by a *minimum bounding volume* (MBV), whose faces are all parallel to the three possible planes. These MBVs serve as filters and as a three-dimensional indexing scheme for accelerating query processing. During the *filtering* step, those line segments of trajectories are retrieved whose MBV intersects with $p(r)$. These form the *candidate set* we have to deal with. In the *refinement* step, the line segments of the candidate set are investigated by an exact algorithm. The algorithms in the following will assume the existence of a candidate set and restrict themselves to a description of the refinement step. Let $v(ut)$ denote the trajectory volume of a given uncertain trajectory $ut = (tr, th)$ between t_1 and t_2, and let $v(ut, r) = v(ut) \cap p(r)$ be the intersection of the trajectory volume and the query prism. Finally, let $\pi(tr)$ denote the spatial projection of tr on the xy-plane (i.e., its route).

For the algorithms we also need the concept of the *Minkowski sum*, denoted by the symbol $\oplus$. This operation takes a polygon q and a disk $d(c)$ with radius c as operands and computes $q \oplus d(c)$ comprising all points in the plane that are either elements of the boundary of q, elements of the interior of q, or elements of the "sweep" of $d(c)$ when its center moves along the edges of q. Therefore, for a convex polygon, the boundary of $q \oplus d(c)$ consists of straight-line segments between vertices of q and of arcs at the vertices of q (Figure 11.7). If q has n edges, we know from computational geometry that the run-time complexity to compute $q \oplus d(c)$ is $O(n)$.

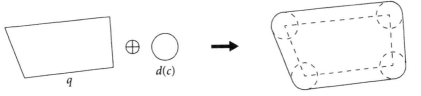

FIGURE 11.7

Minkowski sum of a convex polygon with a disk.

The predicate *PossiblySometimeInside* is obviously true if, and only if, the intersection of the trajectory volume and the query prism is nonempty (i.e., if $v(ut, r) \neq \emptyset$). This leads us to the following algorithm.

ALGORITHM. *PossiblySometimeInside (ut, r, t_1, t_2)*

    construct $r \oplus d(th)$;
    if $\pi(tr) \cap (r \oplus d(th)) = \emptyset$ **then return** *false*, **else return** *true* **endif**
end.

In other words, $v(ut, r)$ is nonempty if, and only if, $\pi(tr)$ intersects the expanded polygon $r \oplus d(th)$. The complexity of the algorithm is O(kn), where k is the number of line segments of *tr* between t_1 and t_2, and n is the number of edges of *r*.

For the predicate *PossiblyAlwaysInside*, we can prove that it yields true if, and only if, $v(ut, r)$ contains a possible motion curve between t_1 and t_2. The algorithm is then as follows.

ALGORITHM. *PossiblyAlwaysInside (ut, r, t_1, t_2)*

    construct $r \oplus d(th)$;
    if $\pi(tr)$ lies completely inside $r \oplus d(th)$ **then return** *true* **else return** *false* **endif**
end.

Again, the complexity is O(kn). Since we have confined ourselves to convex polygons, we can apply this algorithm also for the predicate *AlwaysPossiblyInside*.

For the predicate *DefinitelyAlwaysInside*, we can prove that it yields true if, and only if, $v(ut, r) = v(ut)$. As an algorithm we obtain the following.

ALGORITHM. *DefinitelyAlwaysInside (ut, r, t_1, t_2)*

    for each straight-line segment of *tr* **do**
        if the uncertainty zone of the segment is not inside *r* **then return** *false* **endif**
    endfor;
    return *true*
end.

The algorithmic step to find out if the uncertainty zone of a segment of *tr* is not contained in *r* can be processed by checking if the route segment has a distance from some edge of *r* that is less than *th*. This requires O(kn) time.

For the predicate *SometimeDefinitelyInside*, we can prove that it yields true if, and only if, $v(ut, r)$ contains an entire horizontal disk. This holds for concave polygons as well. The algorithm can be formulated as follows.

ALGORITHM. *SometimeDefinitelyInside (ut, r, t₁, t₂)*

    for each straight-line segment s of tr with $\pi(s) \cap r \neq \varnothing$ **do**
      if r contains a circle with radius th centered at some point on s **then**
        return *true*
      endif
    endfor;
    return *false*
end.

The run-time complexity of this algorithm is again $O(kn)$.

For the last predicate, we need to define the property of connectivity. This property usually requires the existence of some *path* between any two points in a given set, which in our case is a subset of $\mathbb{R}^3$. Given any two points a and b in $\mathbb{R}^3$, a path from a to b is any continuous function $f : [0, 1] \to \mathbb{R}^3$ such that $f(0) = a$ and $f(1) = b$. For two instants t_1 and t_2, a set $S \subseteq \mathbb{R}^3$ is called *connected between* t_1 and t_2, if two points $(x_1, y_1, t_1), (x_2, y_2, t_2) \in S$ exist that are connected by a path in S. We can now prove that the predicate `DefinitelySometimeInside` yields true if, and only if, $v(ut) \backslash p(r)$ is not connected between t_1 and t_2. Otherwise, a possible motion curve exists between t_1 and t_2 that is completely in $v(ut) \backslash p(r)$ so that the predicate is not fulfilled.

Let $uz(ut)$ be the uncertainty zone of the trajectory volume of ut, and let $uz'(ut)$ be equal to $uz(ut)$ without the uncertainty areas at t_1 and t_2, which are two circles c_1 and c_2. Let B be the boundary of $uz'(ut)$. B consists of (at most) $2k$ straight-line segments and $k + 1$ arcs (at most one around the vertices of each segment). Let $B' = B \backslash (c_1 \cup c_2)$. Thus, B' consists of two disjoint lines l_1 and l_2 on the left and right sides of the route of tr. Figure 11.8 demonstrates some of the introduced concepts. The line l_2 has an arc at the end of the first route segment. The dashed semicircles belong to the boundaries of the uncertainty areas at t_1 and t_2. They are removed when evaluating the predicate. For the query region r, two paths can be found that make the predicate true—namely, the path from u to v and the path from w to z.

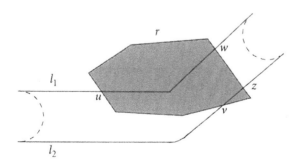

FIGURE 11.8

Processing of the `DefinitelySometimeInside` predicate.

ALGORITHM. *DefinitelySometimeInside (ut, r, t₁, t₂)*

> **if** there exists a path P between a point on l_1 and a point on l_2 that consists
>   completely of (parts of) edges of r **and** P is completely in $uz'(ut)$ **then**
>   **return** *true*
>   **else**
>   **return** *false*
>   **endif**
> **end.**

This algorithm requires $O(kn^2)$ time.

11.6 PRACTICE

FTL Query Language

In this task we consider some aspects of the FTL query evaluation. Evaluate the query:

```
RETRIEVE f.id, g.id FROM flights f, g
WHERE (dist(f, g) > 16 AND dist(f, g) < 30)
  until_after_1 (dist(f, g) < 10)
```

The relation `flights` has three tuples with the following values:

Motion (units/minute)	ID
$(0, 0) + (2, 1) a \cdot t$	LT
$(5, 0) + (-1, 2) b \cdot t$	IB
$(10, 2) + (-2, 1) c \cdot t$	AA

To make the calculation as easy as possible, three assumptions are made: the planes are nearly at the same altitude and the same velocity, so the third dimension was left out and $a = b = c = 1$; the current time corresponds to $t = 0$; and the `dist` function is defined as follows:

$$\text{dist}(f, g) = < \text{f.motion}(t) - \text{g.motion}(t), \text{f.motion}(t) - \text{g.motion}(t) >$$

with $<\cdot,\cdot>$ denoting the Euclidean scalar product.

> *Note:* The motion function is given in units per minute; since we can scale the units with an arbitrary length, every speed can be modeled. For example, if a unit stands for 7 kilometers, the planes will have a velocity of approximately 900 kilometers/hour.

Choosing an Optimal Threshold

Section 11.4.3 shows how to choose the uncertainty threshold K in order to minimize the average information cost per time unit. In that section, it is assumed that the future deviation is given by a linear function $a(t - t_1)$, where a is a positive constant and t_1 is the time at which the new threshold must be chosen. Now, we examine a slightly different scenario. We assume that the estimated future deviation is given by a quadratic function $a(t - t_1)^2$ between t_1 and t_2. This new deviation function yields a new formula for information cost. Find the new optimal value for K that minimizes the average information cost per time unit (i.e., perform an analysis analogous to the analysis in Section 11.4.3 but with the different deviation function).

Adaptive Dead-Reckoning Policy

This exercise asks you to apply the adaptive dead-reckoning policy to a simple example. We assume that the update cost is $C_1 = 50$, and the uncertainty unit cost is $C_2 = 1$. The threshold K is initially set to 12. At each location update, the moving object transmits its current speed and its current direction to the database. The moving object moves linearly from $(0, 0)$ to $(10, 0)$ within the time interval $[0, 20]$ (i.e., the location as a function of time is defined as $(t/2, 0)$). Subsequently, the moving object moves linearly from $(10, 0)$ to $(0, 0)$ within the time interval $[20, 30]$. In this scenario, answer the following questions:

1. When are location updates sent?
2. What is the value of the threshold K at time 30?
3. What is the information cost of this trip?

Remember that the moving object sends a location update at time 0. The deviation at time t is the Euclidean distance between the moving object's actual location and its location according to the database. The deviation cost (needed for computing the new threshold, Section 11.4.3) of a time interval is the integral of the deviation function over that time interval. You should not confuse this (observed) deviation with the deviation estimation by a linear function in Section 11.4.3. The deviation estimation by a linear function is a mathematical assumption used for deriving a formula for the optimal value of K. If that formula is applied to a real situation, we insert the observed deviation into that formula, not the estimated deviation.

Spatiotemporal Predicates

Let r be a simple query region and $ut = (tr, tb)$ be an uncertain trajectory. Show that the following implications don't hold:

1. $\text{PossiblySometimeInside}(ut, r, t_1, t_2)$
   $\Rightarrow \text{DefinitelySometimeInside}(ut, r, t_1, t_2)$

2. $\text{PossiblySometimeInside}(ut, r, t_1, t_2)$
   $\Rightarrow \text{AlwaysPossiblyInside}(ut, r, t_1, t_2)$

3. SometimeDefinitelyInside(*ut, r, t₁, t₂*)
   ⟹ AlwaysDefinitelyInside(*ut, r, t₁, t₂*)
4. PossiblyAlwaysInside(*ut, r, t₁, t₂*)
   ⟹ AlwaysDefinitelyInside(*ut, r, t₁, t₂*)

11.7 LITERATURE NOTES

The presentation in this chapter is based on Sistla et al. (1997, 1998) and Wolfson et al. (1998a, 1999a, 1998b). These publications introduce a concept that focuses on capturing the *current* motion of moving points and their anticipated locations in the *near future*. The concept of dynamic attributes (Section 11.1), the MOST data model (Section 11.2), and the query language FTL, as well as the evaluation of FTL queries (Section 11.3), are described in Sistla et al. (1997, 1998). The basic framework of the FTL language was introduced in an earlier article by Sistla and Wolfson (1995), which provided some additional details, for example, about bounded temporal operators. Sistla et al. (1998) also treat a more general case than what has been presented here, where object positions may have an associated uncertainty (e.g., by providing a lower and upper bound on the speed).

The problem of balancing location update costs and imprecision (Section 11.4) is discussed in Wolfson et al. (1998a, 1999a, 1998b). Civilis et al. (2004) have a related article discussing update policies.

The problem of inherent uncertainty associated with the location of moving points (Section 11.5) is addressed in Trajcevski et al. (2002). An extension and more detailed discussion of the uncertainty aspect can be found in Trajcevski et al. (2004). Related works on uncertain trajectories include Pfoser and Jensen (1999) and Mokhtar and Su (2004). Pfoser and Jensen (1999) discuss the relationship between the sampling rate of GPS observations and the known precision of the trajectory. Mokhtar and Su (2004) offer a probabilistic model of uncertain trajectories. A trajectory is viewed as a vector of uniform stochastic processes. They describe the evaluation of a class of queries called "universal range queries": The result is a set of pairs (<*o, p*>), where *o* is an object and *p* the probability that *o* has been in the range all the time. Probabilistic query evaluation for uncertain object locations is also discussed in Cheng et al. (2004); they consider range queries and nearest-neighbor queries.

The model described in this chapter has been realized in a prototype called DOMINO, which has been presented in several stages of implementation at various conferences (Wolfson et al., 1999b, 2000, 2002).

Index

A

Abstract classes, 117
Abstraction
    entity clustering, 160-163
    view integration, 154-157
ACID properties, 284
Acquisition of locks, 238
Active subsets, 242
Activity diagrams, 86-87
Acyclic graphs, 115
Adaptive dead-reckoning (adr) policy,
        321-323, 334
Additional column requirements, 186
addOnly attributes, 127
Administration issues, 279-280
Affinity diagrams, 274
Aggregation
    types, 139
    UML, 121-126
Air reservation databases, 32-36
ALL qualifier, 238
Analyzers, design, 83
Anomalies
    bad database design, 39-41
    decompositions for, 65-71
    first normal form, 211
AquaLogic tools, 273, 275
Armstrong's Axioms, 46-50
Assignment quantifiers, 308
Associations, in UML, 91-97
    derived, 122
    ORM to UML mapping, 134-135
    overview, 97-105
    redefinition, 130
    types, 121
    whole, 105
Assumptions, in MOST data model, 301-302
Asterisks (*) for derived types, 122
Atomic queries, in FTL, 309
Attached attributes, 18, 144
Attributes, 2, 83
    attached, 18, 144

cardinality, 29-30
changeability, 127-129
characteristics, 15-16
classifying, 143-144
closure, 51-53
column definition, 181-184
complex, 183-184
derivable, 182-183
dynamic, 300, 302
indexes, 231-233
multivalued, 15, 94-97, 144, 184-185
optional, 176
in ORM to UML mapping, 134-135
prime, 76
sets, 44, 51-53
transforming to relations, 16-17
UML, 91-97
in views, 249
Augmentation Rule, 47
Availability requirements, 227

B

B-tree indexes, 233-234
Bachman, Charles, 7
Bad database design, anomalies from,
        39-41
Balanced tree indexes, 233-234
Barker notation, 100, 128, 270
Base views, 248
Behavior diagrams, 86-87
BI environment, 272, 274-275
Binarization process, in UMLmap,
        132-133
Binary associations, 97-98, 100
Binary relationships, 147
    entities, 18-20
    transforming to relations, 25-28
Bit-mapped indexes, 234
Block level locks, 238
Blocks
    clustering, 235
    physical database design, 229

Booch, Grady, 7, 86
Bottom-up design approach, 141
Bounded temporal operators, 313
Bounds for UML attributes, 94
Boyce-Codd normal form (BCNF), 36,
72–76, 206, 216–217
Braces ({}), in UML, 92, 115, 125
Brackets ([]), in UML, 125
Buffers
moving objects trajectory, 324
physical database design, 236–237
Business metadata infrastructure,
269
administration issues, 279–280
challenges, 281
delivery considerations, 273–275
integration, 275–278
preexisting repositories, 281–282
repository build vs. buy decisions,
280–281
types, 269–271
warehouse, 271–273

C

C/C++ languages, 294
Candidate keys, 12, 15
Candidate sets in spatiotemporal
operations, 330
Cardinality
attributes, 29–30
entity participation in relationships,
21–25
Cartesian products, 221–223
CASE. *See* Computer-aided software
engineering tools
Case study for ER approach, 32–36
Category attribute implementation,
181–182
Changeability of attributes,
127–129
Chen, Peter, 8
Chen notation, 9
Class diagrams, 86–90
Class instance populations, 94
Classes
association, 103
entity, 173
UML, 90–91, 117

Classification
entities and attributes, 143–144
entity classes, 173
CLOB, 286, 289, 294
Closure
sets of attributes, 51–53
sets of functional dependencies, 50–51
Clustering blocks, 235
Clustering, in ER models, 160–165
Clustering indexes, 232
COBOL language, 294
Collaboration diagrams, 86–87
Column definition, 181
additional columns, 186
attribute implementation, 181
category attributes, 181–182
complex attributes, 183–184
data types, 186–187
derivable attributes, 182–183
multivalued attributes, 184–185
nullability, 187
relationship attributes, 183
Columns, 2
names, 200–201
specifications, 171
Compact derivational notation, 52–53
Company personnel example, 148–152
Complete axioms, 48
Complex attributes, 183–184
Component diagrams, 86–87
Component-integral aggregation, 121
Composite aggregation, 121–126
Composite attributes, 15
Compression, 236
Computer-aided software engineering
(CASE) tools, 82
Conceptual data modeling, 3–4, 141–142
classifying entities and attributes,
143–144
company personnel and project
database example, 148–152
defining relationships, 145–147
ER entity clustering, 160–165
identifying generalization hierarchies,
144–145
overview, 7–9
view integration, 152–160
Concrete classes, 117

Conflicts
    metadata, 277-278
    schema, 154
Conjunctive formulas, 312
"Connected between" sets, 332
Connectivity for ternary relationships, 147
ConQuer language, 97
Constants, in FTL, 308-310
Constraints, 11
   associations, 99-105
   attributes, 92-93
   entity clustering, 163
   integrity, 13
   join, 120
   ORM to UML mapping, 135-136
   ring, 119
   set-comparison, 105-113
   tables, 40
   value, 118-119
Constructors, 183
Continuous queries, 300, 304-305
Convex polygons, 330
Coreferencing, 104-105
Corrupting data, 39
Costs for location updates, 317-323
Cover
   FD sets, 51
   minimal, 53-57
Create Table statement, 7, 13, 27, 80
CRUD (create, read, update, delete)
   matrices, 277
   in physical database design, 227
Curly brackets ({}), in UML, 92, 115, 125
Current movement, 299
   FTL. *See* FTL query language
   location management, 299-301
   location updates, 317-323
   MOST model, 301-306
   trajectory. *See* Trajectory of moving
      objects

D

Data and database management, 1-2
Data description language (DDL), 7,
    202-203
Data Flux tool, 271
Data independence, 2
Data integrity with denormalization, 259

Data items, 1
Data manipulation language (DML), 7,
    230-231
Data modeling
   conceptual. *See* Conceptual data
     modeling
   MOST, 301-306
   notations, 201-203
   UML. *See* UML (Unified Modeling
     Language)
Data profiling metadata, 271
Data redundancy, 6, 39, 258. *See also*
    Normalization and normal forms
Data storage, in physical database design,
    235-236
Data types
   column definition, 186-187
   UML, 91
Data values, in UML, 90
Database administrators (DBAs), 11-12
Database designer options, 228-229
Database management systems (DBMSs),
    2, 228, 284
Database modeling and design, 11-12
   logical. *See* Logical database design
   physical. *See* Physical database design
Databases, 2
   design tools, 82-83
   life cycle, 2-7
   location updates, 317
   MOST data model, 303-304
   persistence, 284-287
   schemas. *See* Schemas, database
Date, Chris, 187
Dates
   integer storage, 247
   ranges, 187-188
DBAs. *See* Database administrators
DBMSs. *See* Database management systems
DDL. *See* Data description language
Dead-reckoning policies for location
    updates, 317, 320-323
Decompositions
   for anomalies, 65-71
   lossless, 37, 57-64, 68
Decreasing fractionally in location updates,
    321
Default values, in UML, 125, 127

Defining relationships, 145–147
Degrees of relationships, 18
Delete anomalies
  first normal form, 211
  overview, 40–41
Delivery considerations, 273
  BI environments, 274
  graphical affinity, 274
  legacy environment, 273–274
  mashups, 274–275
Denormalization, 7, 80, 251
  example, 260–266
  logical design, 261–263
  logical schema decisions, 242–243
  normalization basics, 251–255
  requirements specification, 260–261
  schema refinement, 263–266
  strategy, 259–260
  tips and insights, 266–267
  two entities in one-to-many relation-
    ships, 256–259
  two entities in one-to-one relationships,
    255–256
  and views, 249–250
Dependencies, 12
  functional. *See* Functional dependencies
  multivalued, 217–218
  schema conflicts, 154
  transitive, 77, 214–215
  trivial, 45–46
Dependency line, in UML, 131
Deployment diagrams, 86–87
Derivable attributes, 182–183
Derivable relationships
  foreign keys specification, 193–194
  many-to-many, 173–174
Derivation rules, 118–132
Derived associations, 122
Derived attributes, 249
Derived data, 130
Descriptive attributes, 15
Descriptors, 15
Design, database, 11–12
  logical. *See* Logical database design
  physical. *See* Physical database design
Design analyzers, 83
Design tools for databases, 82–83
Determinants, 212, 216

Deviation, location, 301, 317–318
Diagrams
  affinity, 274
  ER, 14–17, 152, 201–203, 205–206,
    261–262
  UML, 86–87
Diamonds for aggregation, 121
Directed acyclic graphs, 115
"Directly contains" relationships, 124
Disconnection detection dead-reckoning
  (dtdr) policy, 322
Discriminator labels, 117
Disjoint subtypes, 116
Disk space limitations, in physical database
  design, 228
DISTINCT keyword, 237
Distribution issues, in physical database
  design, 236
DML. *See* Data manipulation language
Document Object Model (DOM), 287
Documents, in XML, 290
Dominance grouping, in entity clustering,
  163
Drive usage, in physical database design,
  236
Duplication, in logical schema decisions,
  241–242
Dynamic attributes, 300, 302

E

Editors, design, 82
Employee information example, 37–39
Entities
  cardinality, 21–25
  characteristics, 13–15
  classifying, 143–144
  contents, 143–144
  instances, 14–15
  keys, 142
  logical database design, 173
  ORM, 89
  relationships among, 18–20
  transforming to relations, 16–17
  weak, 30–31
Entity clustering, 160
  concepts, 160–162
  grouping operations, 162–165
  technique, 163–166

Entity integrity rule, 27
Entity-relationship (ER) approach, 7–9
  attributes, 15–16
  cardinality of attributes, 29–30
  cardinality of entity participation in
      relationships, 21–25
  case study, 32–36
  database design tools, 82–83
  diagrams, 14–17, 205–206, 261–262
  entities, 13–15
  functional dependencies. *See* Functional
      dependencies
  generalization hierarchies, 31–32
  global schema, 151–152
  lossless decompositions, 57–64
  miscellaneous design considerations,
      80–82
  normalization. *See* Normalization and
      normal forms
  overview, 11–13
  relationship types, 25
  relationships among entities, 18–20
  transforming binary relationships to
      relations, 25–28
  transforming entities and attributes to
      relations, 16–17
  views based on requirements, 148–151
  weak entities, 30–31
Enumerations, 118
Equality constraints, 111
Equi-joins, 219–221
ER diagrams, 14–16
  denormalization, 261–262
  entities, 16–17
  translating into relations, 205–206
Escalated locks, 238
ETL tools, 272–274
Evaluation of FTL queries, 312–317
Exclusive-OR constraints, 111–113
EXISTS keyword, 237
External identifier attributes, 31

F

Factoring tables, 57–64
FDs. *See* Functional dependencies (FDs)
Federated metadata, 278
Fifth normal form (5NF), 207
Files, 1

Filled diamonds for aggregation, 121
Filtering step in spatiotemporal operations,
      330
First normal form (1NF), 36, 207
  problems with, 210–212
  repeating groups, 207–210
Flexibility with foreign keys, 198
Flights case study, 32–36
Foreign keys, 20, 27, 189
  derivable relationships, 193–194
  normal forms, 80
  one-to-many relationships, 190–192
  one-to-one relationships, 192–193
  optional relationships, 194–197
  overlapping, 197–198
  specification, 171–172
  split, 198–200
Form entity clusters, 165
Formal subtype definitions, 118
Fourth normal form (4NF), 206, 217–218
Free space issues, in physical database
      design, 235–236
Freshness requirements, in physical
      database design, 227
FTL (Future Temporal Logic) query
      language, 299–300, 306
  for current movement, 333–335
  query evaluation, 312–317
  query examples, 306–308
  semantics, 310–312
  syntax, 308–310
Function applications, in FTL queries, 312
Function symbols, in FTL, 308, 310
Functional dependencies (FDs), 6, 38,
      41–45
  Armstrong's Axioms, 46–50
  closure of attribute sets, 51–53
  closure of FD sets, 50–51
  denormalization, 261
  logical implications among, 45–46
  minimal cover, 53–57
  normal forms, 71–72, 254–255
  preserved, 73
  second normal form, 212–214
  set cover, 51
Functionality requirements, in
      administration, 279
Functions, mathematical, 42

Future database history, in MOST, 304
Future Temporal Logic. *See* FTL (Future Temporal Logic) query language

G

Generalization hierarchies, 31-32
 identifying, 144-145
 supertypes, 114
Generic hierarchies, 244-245
Global positioning system (GPS) for location updates, 318
Global schema, 2-3, 151-152
Graphical affinity, 274
Graphs, directed acyclic, 115
GROUP BY keyword, 237
Grouping operations, in entity clustering, 162-165
Groups, repeating, 207-210

H

Harris, John, 139
Hash tables, 234
Hay, Dave, 85
Heap tables, 234-235
Heat maps, 274
Hierarchies
 generalization, 31-32, 114, 144-145
 logical schema decisions, 244-247
 optional foreign keys in, 195-196
Higher arity associations, 98
Higher-level entity clusters, 165
Histories
 metadata objects, 280-281
 MOST model, 303-304
Hollow diamonds for aggregation, 121
Homonyms, 154
Horizontal table splitting, 239-240

I

Identifiers
 entity, 15
 external, 31
 UML, 89
Identifying generalization hierarchies, 144-145
IDS Visualization tools, 274
Illegal statements, 13
Implementation, database, 7

Implementation diagrams, in UML, 86-87
Imprecision in location updates, 317-323
Inclusion Rule, 45
Indexed sequential access method (ISAM), 234
Indexes, 229-230
 balanced tree, 233-234
 bit-mapped, 234
 and hash tables, 234
 and heap tables, 234-235
 ISAM, 234
 performance advantages, 231-232
 properties, 231-233
 query usage, 230-231
Inessential functional dependencies, 53
Information cost of trips, 318-320
Information Engineering approach, 100
Inheritance
 attributes, 176
 subtypes, 114-115
 type, 32
Initial values, in UML, 125-126
Inner joins, 195, 221
Input/output buffers, 236-237
Inputs, in physical database design, 226-228
Insert anomalies
 first normal form, 211
 overview, 40-41
Instance populations, 94
Instances
 entity, 14-15
 ORM, 89
 relationship, 18
Instantaneous queries, 304
Integer storage of dates and times, 247
Integration of business and technical metadata
 business and technical metadata, 275-277
 conflict resolution, 277-278
 technologies, 278
Integration of views, 4, 6, 152-153
Integrity
 constraints, 13
 entity integrity rule, 27
 referential, 27, 80, 180
Interaction diagrams, 86-87

International Standards Organization
    (ISO), 86
"Is-a" relationships, 31
"Is associated with" for metadata, 270
"Is part of" associations, 123
ISAM. *See* Indexed sequential access
    method

J

Java language, 294-295
JAXP specification, 295
JDBC API, 294-295
Joins
    constraints, 120
    equi-joins, 219-221
    and foreign keys, 195
    inner joins, 195, 221
    lossless, 254

K

Keys
    candidate, 12, 15
    entity, 142
    foreign. *See* Foreign keys
    lossless decompositions, 61
    normal forms, 80
    primary. *See* Primary keys
    schema conflicts, 154
    specifications, 171-172

L

Leaves, in subtype graphs, 116
Legacy environment, delivery in,
    273-274
Levels of generalization
    multiple, 177-178
    single, 176-177
Life cycle, database, 2-7
Links, in UML, 91
List notation, 202
Location updates in current movement,
    317-318
    dead-reckoning policies, 320-323
    information cost of trips, 318-320
    location updates, 317
    overview, 299-301
Locks, in physical database design,
    238

Logical database design, 2-4, 11
    column definition. *See* Column
        definition
    denormalization, 261-263
    foreign key specification. *See* Foreign
        keys
    notations, 201-203
    overview, 169-170
    primary key specification, 187-189
    table and column names, 200-201
    table specification. *See* Table
        specification
    transformation requirements, 170-172
Logical implications among functional
    dependencies, 45-46
Logical models. *See* Conceptual data
    modeling
Logical schema, 226, 238
    additional tables, 247
    alternative relationships, 238-239
    denormalization, 242-243
    duplication, 241-242
    hierarchies, 244-247
    integer storage of dates and times, 247
    ranges, 243-244
    table merging, 240-241
    table splitting, 239-240
Lossless decomposition, 37, 57-64, 68
Lossless joins, 58, 254
Lossy-join decomposition, 59

M

Mandatory attributes, in UML, 91
Mandatory participation in relationships,
    28
Many-to-many relationships, 22, 25,
    173-175
Many-to-one relationships, 22-23, 25
Mapping ORM to UML, 132-136
Mashups, 274-275
Master data management (MDM) projects,
    277
Material-object aggregation, 121
Mathematical Cartesian products, 221-223
Mathematical functions, 42
Maximal chains in FTL queries, 315
Maximum cardinality, 21-22
MBV. *See* Minimum bounding volume

MDM. *See* Master data management
    projects
Media, persistent, 288–289
Member-bunch aggregation, 121
Member-partnership aggregation, 121
Memory issues, in physical database
    design, 236–237
Merged table views, 250
Merging
    schemas, 155
    tables, 240–241
Message queuing systems, 283–284
Metadata. *See* Business metadata
    infrastructure
Metadata warehouses, 271–273
Methods, overriding, 114
Minimal cover, 53–57
Minimal FD sets, 51
Minimum bounding volume (MBV), 330
Minimum cardinality, 21–22
Minkowski sum, 330–331
Mixtures, 119
Modeling
    conceptual. *See* Conceptual data
        modeling
    MOST, 301–306
    notations, 201–203
    UML. *See* UML
Modification, 7, 39–40, 211
Monitoring, 7
MOST (moving objects spatiotemporal)
    model, 299, 301
    basic assumptions, 301–302
    database histories, 303–304
    dynamic attributes, 302
    object position representation,
        302–303
    query types, 304–306
Motion function, 333
Motion plans, 324
Movement modeling. *See* Current
    movement
Multilevel data objects in entity clustering,
    163
Multiple levels of generalization of
    subtypes, 177–178
Multiple tables, lossless join decomposition
    with, 64

Multiplicity constraints
    associations, 99–103, 106
    UML attributes, 92
Multivalued attributes, 15
    column definition, 184–185
    conceptual data modeling, 144
    UML, 94–97
Multivalued dependencies, 80, 217–218
Multivalued relationship participation, 25

N

N-1 relationships, 27–28
n-ary relationships, 19
N-ary symbols, in FTL, 308
N-N relationships, 26
Nama. *See* Not Another Modeling
    Approach!
Names
    association, 97
    schema conflicts, 154
    subsets, 108
    tables and columns, 200–201
Native XML databases, 287–288
Natural equi-joins, 219–221
Nested object types, in ORM, 103
Newton-Raphson method, 323
Nicknames, in UML, 95
Nominalization, 103
Nonpersistent XML data, 295–297
Nonstructural data requirements, in
    physical database design, 227
Normalization and normal forms, 5–6,
    12, 65, 205–207
    for anomalies, 39–41, 65–71
    basics, 251–255
    Boyce-Codd normal form, 72–76,
        216–217
    decompositions in, 65–71
    denormalization. *See* Denormalization
    employee information example, 37–39
    equi-joins, 219–221
    FDs in, 71–72
    fifth normal form, 207
    first normal form, 207–212
    fourth normal form, 217–218
    guidelines, 224
    overview, 36–37
    prime attributes, 76

review, 79–80
    second normal form, 78, 212–214
    third normal form, 76–79, 214–215
Not Another Modeling Approach! (nama), 85
Not null unique columns, 13
Notes, in UML, 92
Null values, in UML, 94, 125
Nullability, column, 187
Nullable foreign key columns, 195–197

O

Object Constraint Language (OCL), 86
Object Data Management Group (ODMG), 287
Object diagrams, in UML, 86–87, 94
Object Management Group (OMG), 86
Object Modeling Technique (OMT), 86
Object-oriented (OO) code, 88–91
Object-oriented database management systems (OODBMS), 286–287
Object-Oriented Software Engineering (OOSE), 86
Object Query Language (OQL), 97
Object-relational database management systems (ORDBMS), 287–288
Object Role Modeling (ORM), 87–90
    associations, 97–105
    attributes, 92–97
    derivation rules, 118–132
    mapping to URL, 132–136
    nested object types, 103
    object orientation, 88–91
    set-comparison constraints, 105–113
    subtyping, 113–118
Objectified associations, 103–104
Objects
    moving. *See* Current movement
    ORM, 89
Occurrences
    entity, 14–15
    relationship, 18
OCL. *See* Object Constraint Language
ODMG. *See* Object Data Management Group
OLAP. *See* Online analytical processing
OLTP. *See* Online transaction processing
OMG. *See* Object Management Group

OMT. *See* Object Modeling Technique
One-to-many relationships
    foreign keys specifications, 190–192
    two entities in, 256–259
One-to-one relationships, 22, 25
    foreign keys specifications, 192–193
    two entities in, 255–256
Online analytical processing (OLAP), 7, 251
Online transaction processing (OLTP), 251
OO. *See* Object-oriented code
OODBMS. *See* Object-oriented database management systems
OOSE. *See* Object-Oriented Software Engineering
Optimal threshold in current movement, 334
Optional attributes, 92, 176
Optional foreign keys, 195–196
Optional relationships, 28, 176, 194–197
OQL. *See* Object Query Language
ORDBMS. *See* Object-relational database management systems
ORDER BY keyword, 237
Ordinary associations, 121
ORM. *See* Object Role Modeling (ORM)
Overflow situations, in physical database design, 235
Overlapping foreign keys, 197–198
Overlapping subtypes, 116
Overnormalization, 80
Overriding methods, 114
Ozone database system, 287

P

Partitions
    table, 236
    in UML, 117
Passengers system case study, 32–36
Past database history, in MOST model, 304
Performance
    indexes for, 231–232
    in physical database design, 228
Persistence, 284
    databases, 284–287
    media, 288–289
    native XML databases, 287–288
    shredding data, 289–293
    XML data, 294–295

Persistent queries, 304–306
Personnel example, 148–152
Physical database design, 5–7, 225–226
   data storage, 235–236
   database designers, 228–229
   indexes, 229–235
   inputs, 226–228
   locking, 238
   logical schema. *See* Logical schema
   memory usage, 236–237
   query optimization, 237–238
   views, 247–250
Physical models, 6
Physical schema, 226
Place-area aggregation, 121
Point objects, 301–302
Point queries, 326
Poly-morphism, 114
Polygon objects, 301, 330
Populations, in UML, 94–95
Portion-object aggregation, 121
Predicates, 221–222
   FTL symbols, 308, 310
   spatiotemporal, 326–329, 334–335
Preexisting repositories, 281–282
Preserved FDs, 73
Primary identifiers, 15
Primary keys, 12
   first normal form, 211
   logical database design, 187–189
   specification, 171–172
   for tables, 171
Prime attributes, 76
Privileges, in UML, 139
Process design, 181
Process/entity matrices, 227
Process models, 227
Product operations, 221–223
Programming errors, 40
Project database, 148–152
Proper subsets, 72
Proper subtypes, 114
Properties. *See* Attributes
Pure-XML database systems, 288

Q

Qualified associations, 104–105
Qualifiers, 104

Queries
   current movement. *See* Current
     movement
   indexes in, 230–231
   optimization, 237–238
Query prisms, 330

R

Ranges, 118
   current movement queries, 326–327
   date, 187–188
   logical schema decisions, 243–244
Rational Rose, 201–203
Rational Unified Process (RUP), 87
RDBMSs. *See* Relational database
     management systems
readOnly attributes, 127, 129
Records, 1–2
Recursive relationships, 18
Redefinition, association, 130
Redundancy, 6, 39. *See also* Normaliza-
     tion and normal forms
   denormalization with, 258
   relationships, 145–146, 155
Referential cycles, 107
Referential integrity, 27
   normal forms, 80
   supertype, 180
Refinement step in spatiotemporal
     operations, 330
Regional uncertainty with moving objects,
     324
Relational algebra operations, 219
Relational database management systems
     (RDBMSs), 285
Relational databases, 285–286
Relational notation, 202
Relational tables, 11
Relationships, 17
   alternative implementations, 238–239
   cardinality of entity participation in,
     21–25
   defining, 145–147
   and entities, 16–20
   in entity clustering, 163
   generalization, 31–32
   many-to-many, 22, 25, 173–175
   many-to-one, 22–23, 25

with more than two entity classes, 175
one-to-many, 190–192, 256–259
one-to-one, 22, 25, 192–193, 255–256
optional, 28, 176, 194–197
transformation rule, 25–28
translating ER diagrams into, 205–206
whole–part, 121
Release, lock, 238
removeOnly attributes, 127
Repeating groups
  characteristics, 207–208
  handling, 208–210
Replication issues, in physical database design, 236
Repository
  build vs. buy decisions, 280–281
  preexisting, 281–282
  tools, 276–277
Requirements analysis, 2–4, 141–142
  denormalization, 260–261
  overview, 142–143
Restrict operations, 221, 223
Restructuring schemas, 155
Retention requirements, in physical database design, 227
Reverse engineering, 6, 190
Ring constraints, 119
Rings, 18
Roles
  relationships, 24
  UML attributes, 96
Root entity clusters, 160, 163
Root subtypes, 116
Rose, Jordan, 274
Row data type facility, 183
Row level locks, 238
Rows, 2
Rumbaugh, James, 7
RUP. *See* Rational Unified Process

S

Schemas, database, 60
  comparison, 154
  conformation, 154–155
  with denormalization, 263–266
  global, 2–3
  logical. *See* Logical schema

merging and restructuring, 155
physical, 226
in view integration, 152–155
Sdr. *See* Speed dead-reckoning policy
Second normal form (2NF), 36, 78
  FDs, 212–214
  problems with, 214
Security issues, in physical database design, 228
Seepower tools, 274
select command, 7
Semantic modeling, 83
Semantics of FTL, 310–312
Sequence diagrams, 86–87
Services, business metadata as, 278
Set-comparison constraints, 105–113
Sets
  attributes, 44, 50–53
  closure, 51–53
  cover, 51
  entities, 14
  FDs, 44, 50–51
  minimal cover, 53–57
Shared aggregation, 121
Shredding, 286, 289–293
Simple aggregation, 121
Single-level of generalization of subtypes, 176–177
Single-valued attributes, 91
Single-valued relationship participation, 25
Skilled programming issues, in physical database design, 228
Slashes (/) for derived associations, 122
Sorting indexes, 232
Spatial object classes, 301
Spatiotemporal operations and predicates
  algorithms, 330–333
  exercise, 334–335
  moving object queries, 326–329
Specialization of subtypes, 114
Speed dead-reckoning (sdr) policy, 321, 323
Split foreign keys, 198–200
Split table views, 250
Splitting tables, 239–240
SQL/XML type, 293–294

SQL99 Set Type Constructor feature
   alternative relationships, 238-239
   many-to-many relationships, 175
   multivalued attributes, 185
   one-to-many relationships, 191
Square brackets ([]), in UML, 125
Stability, associations for, 96
Standard transformations
   column definition, 181
   table specification, 172-173
Statechart diagrams, 86-87
States, database, 303
Static attributes, 302
Static structure case diagrams, 86-87
Storage
   dates and times, 247
   in physical database design, 235-236
   XML. *See* XML data
Streaming, 283
Strong aggregation, 121
Structural schema conflicts, 154
Subattributes for point objects, 302
Subclasses
   in ORM to UML mapping, 134-136
   UML, 114, 116-117
Subsets
   constraints, 107-110
   proper, 72
Subsets property, 107-108
Subtypes
   in generalization hierarchy, 31-32
   implementation, 175-181
   UML, 113-118
   views, 180, 248
Superclasses, 114
Supertypes
   in generalization hierarchy, 31-32
   implementation, 175-181
   views, 180, 248
Synonyms, 154
Syntax, 83
   diagrammatic, 152
   FTL, 308-310
   UML diagrams, 87-90

T

Table spaces
   locks, 238
   usage, 235

Table specification, 170-172
   entity class classification, 173
   entity class exclusions, 173
   many-to-many relationships, 173-175
   relationships involving more than two
      entity classes, 175
   standard transformations, 172-173
   supertypes/subtypes, 175-181
Tables, 2
   locks, 238
   merging, 240-241
   names, 200-201
   partitioning, 236
   splitting, 239-240
Target DBMS, in physical database design,
      228
Technical integration, 275-278
Temporal operators, in FTL, 312-313
Temporal uncertainty in object trajectory,
      324
Ternary associations, 98, 102
Ternary relationships, 19-20, 145, 147
Textual constraints, 92
Textual notations, 201-203
Third normal form (3NF), 36-37, 76-77,
      206, 214-215
   well-behaved, 78-79
Thresholds for moving objects, 317, 325,
      334
Time object, 302
Times, integer storage of, 247
Top-down design approach, 141
Total information costs for location
      updates, 320
Trajectory of moving objects, 323
   model, 323-324
   queries, 326-329
   spatiotemporal algorithms, 330-333
   uncertainty concepts, 324-326
Transferable one-to-one relationships, 192
Transformations
   binary relationships to relations, 25-28
   column definition, 181
   conceptual data models to SQL tables, 6
   entities and attributes to relations, 16-17
   in logical database design, 170-172
   table specification, 172-173
Transformers for database design, 82-83
Transitive dependencies, 77, 214-215

Translating ER diagrams into relations, 205-206
Trivial dependency, 45-46
Tuples, 2
Two entities in one-to-one relationships, 255-256
Types
   entity, 14
   inheritance, 32
   schema conflicts, 154

U

UML (Unified Modeling Language), 7, 85-87
   associations, 96-105
   attributes, 91-97
   constraints and derivation rules, 118-132
   diagrams, 86-87
   many-to-many relationships, 174
   mapping ORM to, 132-136
   object orientation, 88-91
   set-comparison constraints, 105-113
   subtyping, 113-118
UMLmap procedure, 132-136
Uncertainty cost function, 319
Uncertainty in current movement
   cost-based optimization, 320-321
   location updates, 317-319, 321-323
   trajectory models, 323-333
Uncertainty subattributes, 303
Unicode character set, 285
Unified Modeling Language. *See* UML
Uniform deviation cost function, 318
UNION operator, 244
   optimizing queries, 238
   subtype views, 248
Unique attribute values, 61-62
Unique indexes, 231
Uniqueness constraints, 92
Universal tables, 36
Unrestricted attributes, 127
Updates
   anomalies, 39-40, 211
   current movement location, 317-323
Upper bounds, of UML attributes, 94
Use case diagrams, 86-87

V

Validating cluster diagrams, 165
Value constraints, 118-119
Values
   default, 125, 127
   initial, 125-126
   ORM, 89
Variables, in FTL, 308, 310
Vertical table splitting, 240
View integration, 4, 6, 152-153
   example, 155-160
   preintegration analysis, 153-154
   schema comparison, 154
   schema conformation, 154-155
   schema merging and restructuring, 155
Views, 247-248
   and denormalization, 249-250
   derived attributes in, 249
   ER modeling, 148-151
   split and merged tables, 250
   supertypes and subtypes, 180, 248
Virtual tables, 248
Visibility markers, 125
VisuaLinks tools, 274
Volume requirements, in physical database design, 227

W

Warehouses, metadata, 271-273
Weak entities, 30-31
Web 2.0 technology, 274-275
Well-behaved 3NF decomposition, 78-79
WHERE clauses, 248
Whole associations, 105
Whole-part relationships, 121
World Wide Web (WWW), 290

X

XML data, 283-284
   accessing, 294-295
   nonpersistent data, 295-297
   persistence. *See* Persistence
   SQL/XML type, 293-294
XPath, 286
XQJ specification, 295
XQuery, 286, 295

Y

Yet Another Modeling Approach! (*yama*), 85

Printed and bound by CPI Group (UK) Ltd, Croydon, CR0 4YY

03/10/2024

01040314-0007